Retention of Title in and out of Insolvency

Consulting Editor **Marcel Willems**
on behalf of the International Bar Association

Consulting editor
Marcel Willems
On behalf of the International Bar Association

Managing director
Sian O'Neill

Retention of Title in and out of Insolvency
is published by
Globe Law and Business Ltd
3 Mylor Close
Horsell
Woking
Surrey GU21 4DD
Tel: +44 20 3745 4770
www.globelawandbusiness.com

Print and bound by CPI Antony Rowe

Retention of Title in and out of Insolvency
ISBN 9781909416796

Table of contents

Australia

Ian Walker
Minter Ellison

1. General remarks about retention of title

1.1 Transfer of ownership

Australia's state and territory laws relating to the sale of goods are substantially uniform,[1] based on the English legislation on that subject passed at the end of the 19th century.[2] A contract of sale of goods is a contract through which the seller transfers the property in the goods to the purchaser for the price.[3] Where the transfer of the property in the goods is to take place at a future time, or subject to a condition still to be fulfilled, that is called an agreement to sell.[4] The agreement to sell will become a sale when the time elapses or the conditions are satisfied subject to which the property in the goods is transferred.[5]

The general statutory rule that governs when property passes in specific or ascertained goods is that the property passes when the parties to the contract intend it to be transferred.[6] In order to determine the intention of the parties the terms of the contract, the conduct of the parties and the circumstances will be relevant.[7]

Australian sale of goods legislation contains a number of rules that are used to ascertain the intention of the parties as to when the property in the goods is to pass to the buyer on the basis that the parties have no expressed intention or not recorded it.[8] The rules vary depending on the nature and state of the goods and the terms of the contract.

For example, in an unconditional contract for the sale of specific goods that are in a deliverable state, the property in goods passes to the buyer when the contract is made, regardless of whether the time of payment or delivery are postponed.[9] In a contract for the sale of specific goods where the seller still has something to do to the goods to put them into a deliverable state, property in the goods does not pass until that is done and the buyer is notified.[10] If other actions have to be taken by the seller

1 (ACT) Sale of Goods Act 1954; (NT) Sale of Goods Act 1972; (NSW) Sale of Goods Act 1923; (Qld) Sale of Goods Act 1896; (SA) Sale of Goods Act 1815; (Tas) Sale of Goods Act 1896; (Vic) Goods Act 1958; (WA) Sale of Goods Act 1895.
2 Sale of Goods Act 1893, now the Sale of Goods Act 1979.
3 Goods Act 1958 (Vic), Section 6(1).
4 Goods Act 1958 (Vic), Section 6(3).
5 Goods Act 1958 (Vic), Section 6(3) and (4).
6 Goods Act 1958 (Vic), Section 22(1).
7 Goods Act 1958 (Vic), Section 22(2).
8 Goods Act 1958 (Vic), Section 23, Rules 1 to 5.
9 Goods Act 1958 (Vic), Section 23, Rule 1.
10 Goods Act 1958 (Vic), Section 23, Rule 2.

in respect of specific goods, such as weighing, measuring or testing for the purpose of ascertaining the price, property in the goods does not pass until that has been done.[11] If the contract is for the sale of unascertained or future goods by description and goods of the description in a deliverable state are unconditionally appropriated to the contract by the buyer or the seller with the assent of the other party, then property in the goods passes to the buyer.[12]

1.2 Title and ownership

(a) Retention of title

Australian sale of goods legislation allows the seller of specific or subsequently appropriated goods to retain the property in goods subject to certain conditions being satisfied.[13] Property in the goods generally denotes the rights of ownership capable of being asserted against the world at large. While title is designed to be a reference to the rights passing between the seller and the buyer.[14]

(b) Statutory basis of retention of title – as a security interest under the PPSA

Under Section 24(1) of the Goods Act 1958 (Vic) a contract for the sale of specific or subsequently appropriated goods can reserve for the seller the right of disposal of the goods until certain conditions are complied with. The right of disposal covers both the retention of ownership and the reservation of power to resell.[15] It seems that reservation of the right of disposal is synonymous with the reservation of property in the goods[16] and in that respect Section 24(1) of the Goods Act 1958 (Vic) can be viewed as a legislative basis for a reservation of title clause.[17] Section 24(1) provides:

> *Where there is a contract for the sale of specific goods or where goods are subsequently appropriated to the contract the seller may by the terms of the contract or appropriation reserve the right of disposal of the goods until certain conditions are fulfilled.*

The right of disposal is not defined in the Goods Act, but it is said by some commentators to cover the position where the ownership is retained as reservation of the power to resell the goods.[18] Others consider Section 22 of the Goods Act governs the retention of title provision.[19] Section 22 (1) provides:

> *Where there is a contract for the sale of specific or ascertained goods the property in them is transferred to the buyer at such time as the parties to the contract intend it to be transferred.*

So it seems a clause in a contract that reserves title to the purchaser until payment will work as a retention of title, as also will a clause that reserves the right

11 Goods Act 1958 (Vic), Section 23, Rule 3.
12 Goods Act 1958 (Vic), Section 23, Rule 5(1).
13 Goods Act 1958 (Vic), Section 24(1).
14 Gerard McCormack, *Reservation of Title*, 2nd edition (Sweet & Maxwell, 1995), p 8.
15 *Ibid.*, p 16; KCT Sutton, *Sales & Consumer Law*, 4th edition (LBC Information Services, 1985), para 14.46.
16 Sutton, *Sales & Consumer Law*, para 14.46.
17 McCormack, *Reservation of Title*, p 1.
18 McCormack, *Reservation of Title*, p 16.
19 Berna Collier, *Romalpa Clauses: Reservation of Title in Sale of Goods Transactions* (Law Book Company Ltd, 1989), pp 48-54.

to dispose of goods until certain conditions are fulfilled when property in the goods will only pass upon fulfilment of the conditions.

The concept of a retention of title clause, which is a mechanism for the seller to retain ownership of the goods in possession of the buyer, was enhanced in Australia by the Court of Appeal decision in *Aluminium Industrie Vaassen BV v Romalpa Aluminium Limited.*[20] Following that decision retention of title clauses came to be called Romalpa clauses in Australia.

Prior to January 30 2012, the right to use a Romalpa clause or retention of title clause was based on the Goods Act provisions that entitled a seller to reserve the right of disposal of goods or specifically intended when property in the goods would pass. Statute law did not strongly govern retention of title provisions in contracts. The retention of title clause always had to be considered by a court in the context of the totality of the contractual arrangements between the seller and the purchaser,[21] as well as the terms and effect of the retention of title clause itself.

On January 30 2012 the federal Personal Property Security Act 2009 (Cth) (PPSA) entered into effect. This act has had a dramatic impact on retention of title clauses in Australia, as from that date a retention of title clause could become a security interest under the PPSA.[22] The PPSA does not alter the general contract rules dealing with matters such as the formation, validity and interpretation of contracts.[23] It is modelled on similar laws in New Zealand, Canada and Article 9 of the United States' Uniform Commercial Code,[24] although in Australia, unlike in Canada and the US, there is only the one PPSA and one personal property securities register with no separate state or territory laws covering the same issues.

Under the PPSA, a conditional sale agreement that includes an agreement to sell subject to retention of title is a security interest where the transaction's substance secures the payment or performance of an obligation.[25] When a security interest such as a retention of title is taken in collateral to secure all or part of the purchase price then it is defined as a purchase money security interest.[26] Collateral is defined as meaning personal property to which a security interest is attached. In this chapter a reference to a purchase money security interest is a reference to a retention of title clause.

However the rule that heavily governs ownership in common law – that you cannot pass title in something that you do not own – does not apply under the PPSA. For example, someone who is not the owner of goods, but who is in possession of the goods where title has been reserved by the vendor/owner, can actually give a security interest over the goods not only to the vendor but also to a third party.[27] The PPSA also provides protection for the proceeds of the sale of goods that are subject of a

---

20 [1976] 1 WLR 676.

21 *Dwyer & Ors (as joint and several liquidators of Harris Scarf Limited) (Rec and Mgrs Apptd) (In Liq) v Chicago Boot Co Pty Ltd*, 82 ACSR 193, 217; [2011] SASC 27.

22 Personal Property Securities Act 2009 (PPSA), Section 12(2)(d).

23 Personal Property Securities Bill 2009, Replacement Explanatory Memorandum, para 7.59.

24 Personal Property Securities Bill 2009, Replacement Explanatory Memorandum, p 11.

25 PPSA, Section 12(2).

26 PPSA, Section 14(1)(a).

27 PPSA, Section 19(2)(a) and (5) and Section 14(1)(a).

retention of title, without the need for any fiduciary relationship or a requirement for a formal trust to apply in respect of the proceeds. In addition, common law doctrines such as specification confusion and mixtures are now dealt with in PPSA provisions that deal with security interests that go into commingled and processed goods.

Sale of goods legislation remains applicable, and the PPSA specifically provides that it is not intended to exclude or limit the operation of a state or territory law, or the general law to the extent that it is capable of operating concurrently with the PPSA.[28] There is some overlap between the PPSA and the sale of goods legislation in a number of respects. For example there are rules in the sale of goods legislation that govern transfer of title in goods by non-owners, while the PPSA also permits such transfers.

1.3 Foreign and international law

Under the PPSA a retention of title claim is a security interest, and the PPSA, which is a Commonwealth law, applies to the security interest in goods or even financial property if the location of the goods or property is in Australia or the grantor is an Australian entity, even if the grantor and the secured party are located in different states.[29] Location of a company is based on its place of incorporation.[30] There are also conflict of law provisions in Part 7.2 of the PPSA entitled "Australian Laws and Those of Other Jurisdictions".

The validity of a security interest in goods is governed by the law of the jurisdiction (other than the law relating to the conflict of laws) in which the goods are located when the security interest attaches to the goods under that law.[31] Validity in this context is whether the security interest is effective and enforceable between the parties, and not whether the security agreement itself is valid as a contract.[32] The PPSA provides that the perfection and the effect of perfection or non-perfection of a security interest[33] in goods is governed by the law of the jurisdiction in which the goods are located at that time.[34] This does not include the law in the jurisdiction relating to the conflict of laws.[35] In other words, the PPSA excludes the doctrine whereby the conflict of laws provisions of a foreign jurisdiction may be applied, so that the only relevant choice of law is the law of contract and security interests of the jurisdiction where the goods are located, not the conflict of law provisions of that jurisdiction.[36]

If an Australian proceeding were commenced, the law of the relevant jurisdiction specified by Part 7.2 of the PPSA in relation to security interests governs the validity, perfection and the effect of perfection or non-perfection.[37] However, Part 7.2 of the PPSA does not affect the law that governs the contractual obligations that exist

---

28 PPSA, Section 254(1).
29 PPSA, Section 6(1).
30 PPSA, Section 235(3).
31 PPSA, Section 238(1).
32 Duggan and Brown, *Australian Personal Property Securities Law*, para 7.7.
33 PPSA, Section 238(1A).
34 PPSA, Section 238(1A).
35 PPSA, Section 238(1A).
36 Duggan and Brown, *Australian Personal Property Securities Law*, para 14.17.
37 PPSA, Section 234(1).

between the parties; meaning that the law as chosen by the parties and evidenced by the terms of the contract will apply.[38] The parties will be entitled to agree that Australian law applies even if one of the parties is incorporated outside Australia.[39]

Goods relocated to Australia from a foreign jurisdiction are considered as continuously perfected in the foreign jurisdiction prior to their move to Australia if the security agreement was effective and enforceable against third parties.[40] The continuous perfection starts if the law of the foreign jurisdiction provides for perfection and registration whenever the security interest was perfected or registered under the law of the foreign jurisdiction.[41] This is an automatic perfection provision. Even if there is no requirement for perfection or registration of the security interest in the foreign jurisdiction, then there is still a perfection period that is deemed to start when the retention of title becomes enforceable against third parties under the foreign law. That perfection period comes to an end when the property becomes located in Australia.[42] To protect the foreign security interest, it should be registered and perfected in Australia before it is located there. However, if the collateral comprises goods that are located outside Australia, but the grantor is an Australian entity, then the PPSA applies[43] even if the goods are located outside Australia.[44]

1.4 Retention of title in insolvency

If the buyer of goods subject to a retention of title clause that is a purchase money security interest granted by the grantor/buyer under the PPSA goes into insolvency, then issues may arise as to the status of the security interest granted by the grantor/buyer to the seller of the goods. If the grantor is a company, the security interest must be perfected before it goes into any form of insolvent administration, whether a voluntary winding-up, a court ordered winding-up or administration under Part 5.3A, or before a deed of company arrangement is executed by the company. If the grantor is a natural person, the security interest must be perfected before a sequestration order is made against the person under the Bankruptcy Act.

If the security interest is unperfected due to a failure to register by the 'critical time' when the insolvency is deemed to begin,[45] the security interest held by a secured party is treated as vesting in the company that granted the security immediately before the insolvency administration commences.[46] The effect of the vesting is that there is no longer a security interest for the vendor.[47]

In addition, even if a security interest is properly perfected, registered or enforceable against third parties under Australian law, if the registration did not occur at least six months before the commencement of the insolvency or was not

---

38 Personal Property Securities Bill 2009, Replacement Explanatory Memorandum, para 7.8.
39 PPSA, Section 237.
40 PPSA, Section 39(1).
41 PPSA, Section 39(2).
42 PPSA, Section 39(2)(a) and (b).
43 PPSA, Section 6(1)(b).
44 PPSA, Section 152.
45 Defined under Section 588FL(7) of the Corporations Act as the dates prescribed by Sections 513A, 513B and 513C of that act.
46 PPSA, section 267.
47 *Albarran v Queensland Excavation Services Pty Ltd* [2013] NSWC 852.

registered within 20 business days of the security agreement coming into force, it can still be voidable by the insolvency practitioner appointed to the company due to the registration, as it will vest in the company.[48] In respect to a security agreement that gives rise to security interest under a foreign law, Australian registration of the security interest must occur when it is first enforceable against third parties under the law of Australia, and that registration must occur more than six months prior to the commencement of the insolvency, or it must be registered within 56 days of it becoming so enforceable in Australia.[49] Failure to register the security interest in those timeframes will lead to it vesting in the company.[50]

Where goods are sold subject to a retention of title and the seller becomes insolvent before the price for the goods is paid, then it would be expected that the security interest in the goods – an asset of the insolvent seller – would be enforceable by the liquidator or administrator of the seller as long as the purchase money security interest was perfected. If it was not perfected and there was a competing perfected security interest granted by the buyer over all its property, including the goods in its possession, that could have priority over the seller's unperfected security interest.[51] That perfected security interest would also apply to the proceeds of sale of the goods that are the subject of the unperfected purchase money security interest, and would give priority over the proceeds to the competing security interest, provided it is perfected.[52]

2. Retention of title

2.1 Validity and formal requirements

In Australia, since the commencement into effect of the PPSA on January 30 2012, it is necessary to comply with the provisions of the PPSA in respect of retention of title clauses that are treated as a security interest under that act.[53] On the other hand, there are aspects of the common law that used to be used to overcome issues with regard to the use of goods subject to a retention of title that are now no longer required: for example, setting up a fiduciary relationship in order to trace the proceeds, or contractual provisions known as aggregation clauses designed to deal with commingling or mixing goods into a single product.

(a) Operation of the PPSA in respect of retention of title security interests

Under the PPSA, for a security interest to be enforceable against the grantor in respect of particular collateral, the security interest must be attached to the collateral. In order for the security interest to attach to the collateral there must be a valid security agreement, the grantor must have rights in the collateral, and the secured party must give value for the security interest.[54]

---

48 Corporations Act, Section 588FL(2)(b)(i), (ii) and (4).
49 Corporations Act, Section 588FL(2)(b)(iii).
50 Corporations Act, Section 588FL(4).
51 PPSA, Section 55(3).
52 PPSA, Sections 62(1) and 32(1).
53 PPSA, Section 12.
54 PPSA, Section 19(1) and (2).

As noted, a security interest is only effective if it has attached to collateral. This only occurs when the security provider (known as the 'grantor') has rights in the collateral or the power to transfer rights in the collateral to the secured party, and either value is given for the security interest or the grantor performs an act by which the security interest arises.[55] The grantor has sufficient rights in collateral to permit the grantor to create a security interest in the context of a retention of title agreement when the grantor obtains possession of the goods.[56] Under the PPSA, even where the grantor or buyer does not own the goods it is still able to provide the seller with a security interest.

(b) The importance of perfection in the context of priority

'Perfection' is an important expression under the PPSA, as a security interest is perfected when it has attached to the collateral and the secured party registers a financing statement on the Personal Property Securities Register or takes possession or control of the collateral. The financing statement is only a summary of the details of the transaction. It does not involve actually lodging the security agreement on the register.

In order to ensure the purchase money security interest is enforceable against a third party claiming a competing security interest in respect of the same collateral, the purchase money security interest must be attached to the collateral and the security agreement that provides for the purchase money security interest must be evidenced in writing signed by the grantor, or adopted or accepted by the grantor by an act or omission that reasonably appears to be done with the intention of adopting or accepting the writing.[57] The requirement that the grantor adopt or accept the security agreement other than by signing it was included to accommodate what often occurs in relation to retention of title agreements.[58] For example, if the security interest is contained in the terms and conditions of supply, or the invoice, then notice of these to the grantor before or at the time when the contract is made will be enough for the grantor to be treated as accepting them if they know that the provisions govern the delivery of the goods.[59]

2.2 Scope of retention of title

As well as governing the security interest in the collateral that has been sold, the PPSA also extends the security interest to the proceeds for the benefit of the secured party. It is no longer necessary for parties to include express proceeds provisions in the contract to the effect that the buyer will hold the proceeds of sale on trust or in a separate account, or to establish a fiduciary relationship as the basis for a claim on the proceeds.[60] There is no longer a need for formal characterisation of the claim, which was often a major element in the pre-PPSA case law, where there were arguments about the consequences of the nature of the trust over the proceeds.

---

55 PPSA, Section 17.

56 PPSA, Section19(5).

57 PPSA, Section 20(1) and (2).

58 Duggan and Brown, *Australian Personal Property Securities Law*, para 4.29.

59 McCormack, *Reservation of Title*, p 64.

60 Duggan and Brown, *Australian Personal Property Securities Law*, para 11.7.

(a) *Sale of goods delivered under retention of title*

Under the PPSA, if goods subject to purchase money security interest in the form of a retention of title are sold, giving rise to proceeds in the hands of the grantor, the security interest continues in the goods sold unless the secured party with that interest expressly or impliedly authorised the disposal that gave rise to the proceeds. If the disposal was authorised by the seller then the security interest would be extinguished and the security interest will not continue in the goods in the hands of the third party.

However where there is no consent or authority for the sale, the security interest will attach automatically to the proceeds of sale of the goods unless the security agreement provides otherwise.[61]

Proceeds of sale of collateral subject to a perfected security interest are traceable whether or not there is a fiduciary relationship between the person that has the security interest in the proceeds under Section 32 and the person that has rights in or has dealt with the proceeds.[62] Accordingly it is no longer necessary for there to be express provisions in the security agreement that either require the proceeds of collateral sold to be held in trust by the grantor for the security holder or for there to be a fiduciary relationship.

(b) *Combining/mixing/commingling goods delivered under retention of title*

Under the PPSA there is scope for the seller of goods subject to a security interest in the form of a retention of title that become part of a new product to continue to make and enforce a claim as a secured creditor. The PPSA contains specific provisions in relation to commingling and processing of goods containing the subject of security interests, in contrast to the pre-PPSA common law where the doctrines of specification and confusion potentially applied when goods subject to a retention of title were used in a production process.[63]

The PPSA deals with processed or commingled goods and with security interests in goods that have become an unidentifiable part of a larger product or mass.[64] A security interest in the original goods that subsequently becomes part of the product or mass continues in the product or mass, if the goods are so manufactured, processed, assembled or commingled, that their identity is lost in the product or mass.[65]

The consequence of the security interest attaching to the commingled goods means that the security interest continues. If there is another security interest over the goods then the security interest in the product or the mass is limited to the value of the goods on the day on which they become part of the product or mass.[66]

On the basis that the security interest in the goods processed or commingled is a perfected purchase money security interest based on the retention of title, that interest has priority over any non-purchase security interest in the goods that

---

61 PPSA, Section 32(1)(b).
62 PPSA, Section 31(2).
63 RCC Cumming, C Walsh and R Wood, *Personal Property Security Law*, 2nd edition (2012), p 606.
64 PPSA, Part 3.4: Processed or commingled goods.
65 PPSA, Section 99(1).
66 PPSA, Section 101.

continues in the product or mass and any other non-purchase money security interest in the product or mass given by the grantor.[67]

(c) *Impact of accessions*

Under the common law accessions doctrine, accessions essentially become the property of the owner of the goods to which the accessions were attached.[68] Under the PPSA, security interests in accessions will need to be attached to protect the accession. Under the PPSA, 'accessions' to other goods means goods that are installed in or affixed to other goods unless both the accession and the other goods are required or permitted by regulation to be described by a serial number.[69]

Under the provisions on accessions in Part 3.3 of the PPSA, it is clear that the security interest in goods that become an accession to other goods continues in the accession.[70] The default priority rule is that if there is a security interest in goods that is attached to them before they become an accession to other goods, the security interest in the accession has priority over a claim to the goods as an accession made by a person with an interest in the goods as a whole.[71]

For example, if a secured party (A) has a security interest in the grantor's motor vehicle and another secured party (B) provides the grantor with tyres, supplied subject to a reservation of title that gives rise to a security interest for B, which attaches to the tyres before they become affixed to the car, that would give B first claim to the tyres as an accession to the vehicle over A. However, in a situation where tyres are supplied to the grantor subject to a retention of title that is a purchase money security interest and the grantor installs them on a vehicle and then sells the vehicle to a third party, if the security interest in respect of the tyres was not perfected, then the third party will take the vehicle free of the security interest relating to the tyres.[72]

In contrast to the above example, if the accession security interest in the tyres does not attach until after the tyres become an accession, then A takes priority and B's security interest in the tyres is subordinated to A's security.[73]

There are other priority rules that provide that the security interest in goods that become an accession can be subordinated to other security interests. A person who acquires for value an interest in the whole of the goods after the other goods became an accession, but before the security interest in the accession was perfected takes priority over the accession.[74]

There are a series of controls in the PPSA over a secured party who wants to remove an accession. Before removing it, the secured party is required to give notice of intention to remove the accession to the grantor and to any secured party that has higher priority.[75]

---

67 PPSA, Section 103.
68 McCormack, *Reservation of Title*, p 51.
69 PPSA, Section 10.
70 PPSA, Section 88.
71 PPSA, Section 89.
72 Duggan and Brown, *Australian Personal Property Securities Law*, para 9.10.
73 PPSA, Section 91.
74 PPSA, Section 90(a).
75 PPSA, Section 95.

(d) Processing of goods delivered under retention of title

Section 99 of the PPSA provides in effect that in the case of a retention of title that is a security interest being held in goods that subsequently become part of a product or mass, the security interest continues in the product or mass if the goods are so manufactured, processed, assembled or commingled that their identity is lost in the product or mass.[76] The identity of the goods is treated as lost in the product or mass under the PPSA if it is not commercially practical to restore the goods to their original state.[77]

One example where the security interest continues in the product produced is where a supplier provides resin subject to a retention of title clause to a chipboard manufacturer. Provided the supplier registers a financing statement and perfects the security interest, and the chipboard manufacturer uses the resin to make chipboard, then the perfected security interest continues in the chipboard.[78]

The survival of the security interest after commingling or processing depends on it continuing in the product created. However if the manufacturing process simply consumes the product, then the security interest in the goods consumed will not benefit from Section 99. As an example, a security interest in food that is fed to an animal does not result in a continuation of the security interest in the animal. Nor would a security interest over fuel that is used to power the machinery that produces the goods continue.[79] Once stock subject to a retention of title security interest is sold, then it is necessary for the owner to rely on proceeds tracing provisions in respect of the debts payable to the seller of the product.[80]

(e) Extension of retention of title

Effectively a security interest in the form a retention of title is constrained as to what it can secure, due to the provisions in the PPSA that cover the meaning of 'purchase money security interest'. The purchase money security interest will obviously cover the purchase price and the provision of funding by a third party to enable the grantor to acquire rights in the collateral;[81] these are what are described as purchase money obligations.[82]

However if the security interest in the collateral secures not just the purchase money obligations but other obligations, the security interest is a purchase money security interest only to the extent that it secures purchase money obligations.[83] If the security interest is granted in personal property (purchase money collateral) that secures a purchase money obligation together with other collateral: the security interest is only a purchase money security interest to the extent that it is granted in the purchase money collateral, but it does not lose its purchase money security interest status because other collateral also secures the purchase money obligation.[84]

---

76 PPSA, Section 99(1).
77 PPSA, Section 99(2).
78 Duggan and Brown, *Australian Personal Property Securities Law*, para 9.22.
79 *First National Bank of Brush v Bostron*, 564 P 2d 964 (Colo App 1977); *In Re McDougall* 60 BR 635 (1986); Cumming, Walsh and Wood, *Personal Property Security Law*, p 606.
80 *New Zealand Associated Refrigerated Food Distributors Limited v Simpson*, CIV-2007-485-1563 [25].
81 PPSA, Section 14(1).
82 PPSA, Section 14(3).
83 PPSA, Section 14(3).
84 PPSA, Section 14(4); Duggan and Brown, *Australian Personal Property Securities Law*, para 8.16.

2.3 Legal effect of retention of title

(a) *Effect towards third parties*

There are a number of ways that a third party can buy goods subject to a retention of title (as a purchase money security interest) and obtain clear title to the goods. The first opportunity arises where the security interest is not perfected and the buyer of the property provided value for the property, in which case the buyer will get clear title.[85] However, this will not apply if the buyer was a party to the security agreement under which the unperfected security interest was created.[86]

The main rule governing the sale of personal property subject to a purchase money security interest is that if it is sold in the ordinary course of the seller's business of selling personal property, that will provide the buyer with the personal property free of the security interest.[87] However that does not apply if the buyer who acquires the goods holds the goods as inventory, or as an agent for a party that holds the goods as inventory, and it must be described by serial number under the regulations.[88]

If, due to a sale in the ordinary course of business, a buyer has taken the goods free of the purchase money security interest and the grantor rescinds the contract or repossesses the goods, then the original security interest reattaches to the goods and the security interest is treated as if the goods had never been sold.[89]

Super priority for retention of title: A purchase money security interest in the form of a retention of title granted over the collateral and its proceeds will have priority over a non-purchase money secured interest in favour of another creditor in respect of the same collateral. For that to occur the purchase money security interest holder's security interest must be perfected by registration and the financing statement must record that the security interest is a purchase money security interest.[90]

If the grantor sold the goods subject to a retention of title as a purchase money security interest in the ordinary course of business and is indebted to the Australian Tax Office (ATO), then the ATO may give a garnishee notice to a purchaser who purchased goods from the grantor on credit, which would require the debt to be paid to the ATO by the purchaser rather than to the vendor/grantor who the ATO is looking to collect tax from.[91] Giving a garnishee notice may be the only way for the ATO effectively to claim priority over the holder of the purchase money security interest in respect of the proceeds of the collateral.

The service of the garnishee notice creates a statutory charge on the debt owed to the grantor by the debtor when the notice is served. The garnishee charge is not a security interest covered by the PPSA, as it is a charge that arises under a law of the

85 PPSA, Section 43(1).
86 PPSA, Section 43(2).
87 PPSA, Section 46(1).
88 PPSA, Section 46(2)(a).
89 PPSA, Section 37(1).
90 PPSA, Section 62(1).
91 Taxation Administration Act 1953 (Cth), Schedule 1, Section 260-5.
92 *Macquarie Health Corp Ltd v Commissioner of Taxation* (1999) 96 FCR 238; [1999] FCA 1819 at [80]; *Re Octaviar* [2009] QSC 202.

Commonwealth.[92] If future debts are payable to the grantor they will be subject to the security interest given to the holder of the purchase money security interest in the grantor's present and after-acquired property. However, attachment in relation to the future debts may not arise until the grantor has rights in the debts, such as when the goods have been sold and an invoice is issued to the third party creating an account that is subject to the purchase money security interest in favour of the secured party.[93] Given that the ATO garnishee charge has effect immediately on service, it should prevail over the security interest in future debts if that has not attached when the garnishee notice is served.[94]

(b) Effect in case of seizure of goods delivered under retention of title

If the debtor is in default under a purchase money security interest in the form of a retention of title, the secured party is entitled to seize the collateral that is the subject of the security interest by any method permitted by law.[95] The default provisions in the security agreement contained in Chapter 4 of the PPSA will generally govern what occurs. Any rights, duties and obligations that arise under Chapter 4 regarding enforcement have to be exercised or discharged honestly and in a commercially reasonable manner.[96]

However the PPSA does not limit the rights and remedies the parties have in respect of enforcement under the security agreement in relation to a default by the debtor. The provisions contained in Chapter 4 of the PPSA in relation to enforcement do not apply to a grantor company[97] while there is a receiver, or a receiver and manager, in control of the property. The agreement can provide additional remedies to those in the PPSA.[98] Generally speaking this will involve ensuring the seizure process does not involve a trespass or a breach of the peace.

However, if the goods that are the subject of the retention of title have been sold, and debts owing by third parties remain payable to the grantor in respect of the sale of the goods, then the secured party is entitled to give a written notice equivalent to a garnishee notice to one or more of the persons who owe an amount to the grantor in respect of the collateral, requiring them to pay the debt to the secured party. The debtors are then obliged to pay to the secured party the amount they owe to the grantor within five business days after the notice is received or after the day the amount becomes due and payable.[99]

It is possible for competing purchase money security interests to exist in relation to the same collateral. A seller's purchase money security interest in the form of a retention of title will, as long as it is perfected, have priority over a lender's purchase money security interest.[100] If neither interest holder is a seller, then the super priority

---

93 PPSA, Section 19(2).
94 James O'Donovan, *Company Receivers and Administrators* (Law Book Company), vol 2, APX 4.870.
95 PPSA, Section 123(1).
96 PPSA, Section 111.
97 PPSA, Section 116.
98 Duggan and Brown, *Australian Personal Property Securities Law,* para 12.15.
99 PPSA, Section 120.
100 PPSA, Section 63; Duggan and Brown *Australian Personal Property Securities Law,* paras 8.38-8.39.
101 PPSA, Section 62.

provision does not apply,[101] and the ordinary default priority rules that provide priority to the first registered security interest apply.[102]

Once the secured party enforces his interest by seizing the collateral and proposing to dispose of it, the secured party must give notice to the grantor and also any secured party with a security interest in the same collateral that has higher priority.[103] It is also possible for the secured party that has seized the collateral to retain it. During passage of the bill that became the PPSA, this was said to correspond to a creditor's existing right to seize and retain collateral under a retention of title arrangement.[104] The right to retain is not available where the grantor uses the collateral predominantly for personal domestic or household purposes.[105] The secured party's right to retain the collateral if it has seized the collateral is also said to be equivalent to a mortgagee's equitable right of foreclosure.[106]

In order to retain the collateral it has seized, the secured party is required to give notice to the grantor at least 10 business days before retaining the collateral. If the retention of title is a purchase money security interest then notice must also be given to any secured party over whom the holder of the purchase money security interest has priority but who has a security registration that describes the collateral.[107] The notice must include details of the amount to be paid to avoid the secured party retaining the collateral.[108] Persons to whom these notices are given may object to the purchase or retention[109] and the foreclosure cannot be completed. If an objection notice is served on a secured party that wants to retain the collateral then there has to be a disposal of the collateral by private or public sale,[110] which must be done with reasonable care by the secured party who disposes of it to obtain market value or the best price available at the time of disposal.[111] The secured party has the right to purchase the collateral providing it goes through the proper sale process.[112]

However if a purchase money security interest in the form of a retention of title has priority over the security interest of a third party who has seized and sold the collateral, any sale by the third party security holder will not extinguish the higher ranking security interest of the purchase money security interest. A buyer could take the collateral still subject to the purchase money security interest as a priority security interest.[113]

(c) Effect in case of security right established over goods delivered under retention of title

In Australia if the purchase money security interest in the form of retention of title

102 PPSA, Section 55.
103 PPSA, Section 130(1).
104 Personal Property Securities Bill 2009, Replacement Explanatory Memorandum, para 4.80.
105 PPSA, Section 109(5)(e).
106 Duggan and Brown *Australian Personal Property Securities Law*, para 12.58.
107 PPSA, Section 135(1).
108 PPSA, Section 135(3).
109 PPSA, Section 137.
110 PPSA, Section 128(2).
111 PPSA, Section 131.
112 PPSA, Section 129.
113 PPSA, Section 133.

is over inventory or its proceeds then the purchase money security interest will have priority over a non-purchase money security interest provided the purchase money security interest is perfected by registration when the grantor obtains possession of the goods that are the inventory and the perfected registration declares that the security interest is a purchase money security interest.[114]

If the property is not inventory but personal property or its proceeds, then the purchase money security interest has priority if it is perfected by registration before the end of 15 business days after the day the grantor obtains possession of the goods.[115]

It is theoretically possible for a third party to be given a security interest over both fixed and circulating assets of the grantor, including inventory. However, provided the priority rules contained in Section 62 operate, the purchase money security interest will have priority over the general security agreement given as a security interest over the same collateral, as the circulating security interest is not a purchase money security interest.[116]

(d) *Effect in case of insolvency*

Insolvency of corporations is governed by the Corporations Act and, apart from the vesting provisions in the context of unperfected security interests and the priority in provisions in the PPSA, the Corporations Act will govern what happens with the security interest and its proceeds.

The Corporations Act has been amended by introducing two classes of retention of title property. The first is a new concept known as 'PPSA retention of title property' which is defined as personal property that is used or occupied by, or is in the possession of, the corporation, which does not have title to it, and which has a PPSA security interest attached to it and the corporation is the grantor of the PPSA security interest.[117] The second type of retention of title property is property subject to a retention of title clause under a contract for the sale of property that contains a provision whereby the seller retains title in the property until the purchase price or other amount has been paid in full. The contract must not give rise to a PPSA security interest in the property. This definition is said possibly to include retention of title property that is not personal property within the meaning of the PPSA where the retention of title clause does not secure payment or performance of an obligation, or the relevant interest is excluded as security interest under the PPSA.[118]

There are some limitations in the Corporations Act on the property affected. For example sub-section 51F(2) provides that a reference in the Corporations Act: "to the property of a corporation does not include a reference to any PPSA retention of title property unless provided for expressly or by implication."

If a security interest has vested in the grantor company in liquidation then the

---

114 PPSA, Section 62(1)(a)-(c).
115 PPSA, Section 62(3).
116 PPSA, Section 62.
117 Corporations Act, Section 51F(1).
118 Personal Property Securities (Corporations and other Amendments) Bill 2010, Explanatory Memorandum, para 5.5.

Corporations Act provisions will apply to PPSA retention of title property that has vested in the grantor company. Section 465 of the Corporations Act provides that property of a company in a winding-up, in insolvency or by the court, includes retention of title property where the security interest has vested in the company because of the operation of Section 267(A) of the PPSA or Section 588FL of the Corporations Act.

The effect of the different definitions is in the interests of a creditor with a purchase money security interest in PPSA retention of title property, as that property is excluded from the property of the company in the context where the property of the company is insufficient to meet the payment of unsecured creditors so that employee entitlements have priority over circulating security interests. If PPSA retention of title property were included as company property it would be subordinated to employee priorities and PPSA retention of title property holders would lose their priority. Accordingly property of company used in the Corporations Act to reflect the priority of employee claims over circulating security interests excludes PPSA retention of title property in this context.[119]

When a company is being wound up, the liquidator is required to take custody of the property to which the company is entitled, which includes any PPSA retention of title property that has vested in the company due to non-perfection of the security interest.[120] The liquidator has the power to sell or otherwise dispose of all or any part of the property of the company, and to do all things necessary for winding up the affairs of the company and distributing its property, this includes PPSA retention of title property.[121]

In insolvent administration or a deed of company arrangement, property that is subject to a security interest such as a purchase money security interest in the form of a retention of title which falls within the definition in the Corporations Act of PPSA retention of title property must not be disposed of by the administrator.[122] However this does not prevent a disposal in the ordinary course of the company's business, or with the consent of the secured party or leave of the court.[123] However if the property is PPSA retention of title property, or is subject to a retention of title clause, and the owner demands the return of the property, then a disposal of the property that occurs after the demand is made does not mean the disposal is in the ordinary course of the company's business.[124]

Where exercising a power of sale of property that is subject to a security interest under Part 5.3A of the Corporations Act, the administrator must act reasonably in exercise of that power.[125] If the administrator disposes of PPSA retention of title property of the company by sale, the administrator is required to apply the proceeds

119 Personal Property Securities (Corporations and other Amendments) Bill 2010, Explanatory Memorandum, para 5.14.
120 Corporations Act, Sections 474 and 465.
121 Personal Property Securities (Corporations and other Amendments) Bill 2010, Explanatory Memorandum, paras 5.18 and 5.20.
122 Corporations Act, Section 442C(1)(a).
123 Corporations Act, Section 442C(2).
124 Corporations Act, Section 442C(8).
125 Corporations Act, Section 442CB.

of sale in the same way that a secured party is required under Section 140 of the PPSA to dispose of the proceeds received as a result of enforcing a security interest in the property by its sale. Section 140 of the PPSA provides an order of application[126] of the proceeds that requires the proceeds to be applied:

- first, to obligations to persons holding interests in the collateral that are not security interests covered by the PPSA, such as common law liens or pledges;
- secondly, to cover reasonable expenses incurred in relation to the enforcement of the security interests, to the extent that they are secured by the security interests;
- thirdly, to persons holding security interests that have a higher priority than the interest of the secured party;
- fourthly, to obligations to the secured party secured by the security interest in the collateral;
- fifthly, to persons holding interests or security interests in the collateral that have a lower priority than the secured party; and
- sixthly, to the grantor, where the proceeds are part of the pool of assets from which creditors' claims may be paid.[127]

If there is retention of title property (not PPSA retention of title property) that is sold for a price that equals or exceeds the original purchase price, or so much of the purchase price under the original contract as remains unpaid, and there are other debts secured over the property, then the administrator is required to set aside and pay so much of the net proceeds as equals the purchase price and other debts secured over the property. But if the proceeds fall short and not enough is available to pay all debts in full, then the proceeds are to be applied proportionately.[128]

If collateral cannot be readily removed from a grantor's premises, or the secured party has no adequate storage facilities readily available, the secured party can effectively seize the collateral by taking what is called 'apparent possession' of the collateral. The secured party is then entitled to sell it despite it being on the grantor's premises under the disposal regime set out in Section 128 of the PPSA, which entitles a secured party to dispose of collateral that it has seized in exercise of the right of enforcement.

(e) Effect in case of partial payment of the purchase price

The option for the seller to recover possession of goods subject to a purchase money security interest from a buyer who has only paid part of the debt secured by the goods will depend on there being an event of default in the security agreement that entitles the seller to seize the goods.[129] There is a requirement for notice to be given to the grantor.[130] Once the seizure occurs then there is an obligation on the secured party either to dispose of the collateral or to take action to retain it.

126 Corporations Act, Section 442CC(1A).
127 PPSA, Section 140(2).
128 Corporations Act, Section 442CC(2).
129 PPSA, Section 123(1).
130 PPSA, Section123(2).

However following seizure, if there is another secured party with higher priority than the enforcing party that is also entitled to seize the collateral, then that higher priority party may give a notice to the enforcing party requiring possession of the seized collateral.[131] Once possession is provided to the higher priority party then it must pay the enforcing party's reasonable expenses incurred in relation to the enforcement that occurred before the hand-over of possession.[132]

Disposal of the collateral requires a notice to be given to the grantor or any other secured party with a higher priority security interest in the collateral. The notice must contain a description of the collateral and warn that it is to be disposed of unless an amount is paid to satisfy the obligation secured by the security interest by a date which must be at least 10 business days after the day the notice is given.[133]

3. Enforcement of retention of title

There is no specific organisation that needs to be authorised or involved to repossess goods subject to a retention of title.

There is no definition of default in the enforcement provisions of Chapter 4 of the PPSA, but default probably means a breach of the security agreement, such as a failure to pay an amount due or otherwise to perform an obligation secured, or, if the security agreement contains a trigger event for the realisation of the enforcement rights, when that event occurs.[134] The National Credit Code applies where the debtor is a natural person and the credit is provided for personal, domestic or household purposes, or to purchase, renovate or improve a residential property for investment purposes.[135] If the credit is covered by the National Credit Code then the default notice requirements under the code must be complied with.[136]

Enforcement of a purchase money security interest is governed by Chapter 4 of the PPSA, although it is possible for the parties to have contracted out of number of provisions of Chapter 4 where the security interest relates to collateral that is not used for personal, domestic or household purposes. However, it is not possible to contract out of the obligation on the secured party to exercise all rights honestly and in a commercially reasonable manner.[137] If the debtor is in default under the security agreement and the secured party proposes to enforce its rights under the security agreement, it is entitled to seize the collateral by any method permitted by law.[138] General law covers such things as trespass and other actions associated with the enforcement process. For instance, if the property subject to the purchase money security interest is on premises that the secured party does not have permission to enter, or the retention of title provisions do not cover all debt owed by the grantor, this can lead to a trespass.[139] Normally one would expect the written security

131 PPSA, Section 127(2) and (3).
132 PPSA, Section 127(6).
133 PPSA, Section 130(1) and (2).
134 Duggan and Brown, *Australian Personal Property Securities Law*, para 12.29.
135 National Consumer Credit Protection Act 2009, Schedule 1, National Credit Code, Section 5.
136 National Credit Code, Section 88.
137 PPSA, Section 111(1).
138 PPSA, Section 123(1).
139 *Hardie Finance Corporation Pty Ltd v Ahern [No 3]* [2010] WASC 404.

agreement would contain a licence that permits the secured party to gain access to the premises where the goods are located.

For enforcement purposes at a practical level, the nature of the purchase money security interest will prompt the secured party to recover physical possession of what effectively is its own property when the grantor defaults. The first issues will be whether the secured party or its agent who is authorised to collect the secured property will be entitled to enter the premises where the property is located. Entry on to the premises will require the debtor's consent. This is something that is generally incorporated in the security agreement. If the debtor refuses access to the premises then entry without consent can be a trespass and there can be no unlawful force used to gain access.[140] At this point a court order for possession is the only option. If the debtor company is in liquidation or administration then there is a stay on enforcement without the consent of the insolvency practitioner or leave of the court.[141]

Having seized the goods on default then the secured party can dispose of the collateral by private or public sale, including by auction or closed tender.[142] There is a requirement that a secured party who proposes to dispose of the collateral following the debtor's default must give notice to the grantor and to any other secured party with an interest in the collateral that has a higher priority.[143] However notice is not required every time: if, for example the debtor cannot be found, or the grantor waives the notice requirement, or a court is satisfied that notice is not required.[144]

The notice to be given must contain a description of the collateral and provide that the collateral will be disposed of unless an amount is paid within 10 business days after the notice is given, or an obligation observed within that time.[145]

Once the secured party has seized the collateral subject to the purchase money security interest, that secured party has to secure, store and value the collateral and work out how to deal with it. The period for this to be done is meant to be reasonable, subject to the provisions of the security agreement.[146] When exercising the power to dispose of the goods, the secured party has a duty to the grantor and to any other person who has a security interest in the goods to exercise reasonable care to obtain the market price, where one exists, or otherwise the best price obtainable in the circumstances.[147]

---

140 Duggan and Brown, *Australian Personal Property Securities Law*, para 12.34.
141 Corporations Act, Sections 471B and 440B.
142 PPSA, Section 128.
143 PPSA, Section 130.
144 PPSA, Section 144.
145 PPSA, Section 130(2).
146 PPSA, Section 125(2).
147 PPSA, Section 131.

Austria

Arno Brauneis
Maria Vertesich
Brauneis Klauser Prändl

1. Acquisition of ownership

Under Austrian law, ownership may be acquired as original or derivative rights. The acquisition of ownership is derivative if the ownership is transferred from one person to another. In this case, the acquiring party derives its position from the previous owner (Section 423 of the Austrian Civil Code). The acquisition of ownership is original if the legal position is not derived from anyone, but the ownership rights originate with the acquiring party. Original acquisition of ownership is not discussed further in this chapter.

The prerequisite conditions for a derivative acquisition of ownership are title, procedure and the prior holder's right to transfer ownership.

1.1 Title

The title for derivative acquisition of ownership can be a contract, a testamentary disposition, a judicial decree or a statutory order (Section 424 of the Civil Code). Contracts governed by the Civil Code include in particular sales contracts, barter agreements, gifts, mandates and settlements. But other grounds for acquisition (such as leases, mining contracts or contracts for delivery) can also be title for the transfer of ownership.[1] However, transfer of ownership is not effected by the conclusion of the title contract (eg, the sales contract), but only upon handover of the subject of the contract from the seller to the buyer (Section 1053 of the Civil Code).

1.2 Procedure

The necessary procedure consists of handover and acceptance (Section 425 of the Civil Code). As a rule movable physical objects can only be transferred by physical handover from one person to another (Section 426 of the Civil Code) but transfer by signs (Section 427 of the Civil Code) or by declaration (Section 428 of the Civil Code) is also possible. The physical transfer and acceptance has the effect that the transferring party loses his exclusive power of disposition and the acquiring party obtains the exclusive power of disposition. Transfer by signs is only possible for physical objects if a physical handover is not possible or feasible. According to case law of the Austrian Supreme Court, the impossibility of physical transfer must be justified by the nature of the object to be transferred. However, this does not mean that physical transfer must be absolutely impossible, but rather that a physical

1 Klicka and Reidinger in Schwimann and Kodek, *ABGB Praxiskommentar* 24 § 424 Rz 1.

transfer must be infeasible due to the nature of the object. In this sense, the physical transfer of a machine is infeasible according to case law if it weighs about 2.5 tons.[2] The purpose of allowing transfer by declaration is the prevention of unnecessary moving back and forth of the object. One can distinguish three types of transfer by declaration: conveyance of possession; constructive possession of chattels based on agreement; and third-party possession orders.

Furthermore, the Civil Code governs sales shipments. In this case, the subject is transferred by shipment (Section 429). A special feature of transfer of ownership by shipment is that if an obligation to send is agreed on between transferor and transferee, the transferee acquires ownership upon the handover of the subject to the carrier. An obligation to send is agreed on if the transferee determines the mode of shipment or agrees to it.[3] The Austrian Consumer Protection Act provides an exception for transactions with consumers. The consumer only acquires ownership upon delivery of the object by the carrier, so the risk of loss or damage during transportation is not borne by the consumer (Section 7b of the Consumer Protection Act).

1.3 Entitlement of the previous holder

The necessary right of the previous holder to transfer ownership is present if the previous holder was either owner himself or held a power of disposal from the owner.

1.4 Transfer of ownership

In principle, ownership in movable items passes upon the handing over of the object.[4] The transfer of ownership in respect of immovable property is not a subject for this chapter.

With regard to sales contracts, the Civil Code stipulates that ownership does not pass immediately upon conclusion of the title transaction (the sales contract) but only upon the handing over of the object from the seller to the buyer (Section 1053 of the Civil Code). The Civil Code thus establishes a system of contemporaneous performance for sales contracts, whereby the primary obligation of the seller is to keep safe the object until the transfer and to hand it over to the buyer (Section 1061 of the Civil Code); while the primary obligation of the buyer is to take over the object immediately or at the agreed time, and, concurrently, to pay the purchase price (Section 1062 of the Civil Code). However, the Civil Code also governs the common case of so-called 'credit purchases', which sets out a departure from the principle of concurrent settlement of sales contracts. In this situation the object is handed over to the buyer before the payment of the purchase price, and ownership is transferred to the buyer at the same time (Section 1063 of the Civil Code). Under this provision, the position of the seller, in particular in the event of the buyer's insolvency, is weak, because he gives up his ownership by the sale, but in the event of an insolvency could only seek payment by filing a claim against the insolvency estate.

---

2 6 Ob 246/65.
3 Klicka and Reidinger in Schwimann and Kodek, *ABGB Praxiskommentar* 24 § 429 Rz 2.
4 Verschraegen in Kletečka and Schauer, *ABGB-ON* 1.01 § 1063 Rz 6.

The provisions outlined above are dispositive (as opposed to mandatory). This means that contractual parties can agree on a point in time for the transfer of ownership that deviates from what is set out in the statutory provisions, or can attach conditions to the acquisition of ownership. In the course of trade, contracting parties regularly agree otherwise, providing for retention of title.

2. Retention of title

2.1 Retention of title as dispositive law

Retention of title is not regulated by statutory law. In Section 224 of the Austrian Insolvency Act, the legislator only refers to retention of title by governing how retention of title is treated in the course of insolvency proceedings if the object of the retention of title is located in another country than the country in which insolvency proceedings have been initiated. Apart from that, the legislator only refers to retention of title in Section 86(2) of the Austrian Marriage Act by determining that, in the division of marital assets, the court can only order the transfer of rights and obligations in respect of an asset with the owner's approval. Accordingly, retention of title is not governed by statutory law, but is still recognised as a matter of customary law, so that the legislator took it into consideration in the provisions noted here.

A number of court rulings have dealt with the possibility of an agreement on retention of title and its form. In particular questions regarding the prerequisites for a valid agreement of retention of title have repeatedly come before the Supreme Court; including the question of whether retention of title can be declared unilaterally[5] (which is discussed in more detail at point 2.2(b) below). The courts and Austrian legal doctrine differentiate between various types of retention of title, namely: ordinary retention of title, extended retention of title[6] and prolonged retention of title.[7]

2.2 Validity and formal requirements

(a) Time of transfer of ownership and retention of title

At the time of the handover of goods to the buyer, ownership in the goods is in principle transferred to the buyer. This weakens the position of the seller if payment as agreed on is not immediately obtained in exchange, but is postponed.

By retention of title, the acquisition of ownership by the buyer is made subject to the condition of payment of the purchase price. Retention of title has the effect that despite the procedure being carried out, ownership of the purchased goods does not pass to the buyer at the time of the handover, but only upon full payment of the purchase price. The seller's position is improved by the retention of title: the seller remains owner of the goods until the purchase price is paid by the buyer in full. In

---

5 5 Ob 18/97a.
6 Verschraegen in Kletečka and Schauer, *ABGB-ON* 1.01 § 1063 Rz 16.
7 Binder and Spitzer in Schwimann and Kodek, *ABGB Praxiskommentar* 44 § 1063 Rz 62.

the case of insolvency, the buyer can claim his ownership. This issue will be dealt with in more detail below (see section 2.2(b) below).

(b) *Agreement on retention of title*

The validity of retention of title requires an agreement between the parties to the agreement, namely seller and buyer. According to consistent case law, the unilateral declaration of retention of title is ineffective in terms of property law. A unilaterally declared retention of title cannot prevent the transfer of ownership to the buyer upon handover of the goods.[8] Even if the agreement of a retention of title is customary in commercial practice, retention of title is not valid on the grounds of general custom or commercial practice. In commercial practice, retention of title must be separately agreed on between seller and buyer.

The agreement on retention of title may be entered into by seller and buyer expressly or implicitly (=tacitly). According to case law, the implicit agreement on retention of title is already assumed if in the course of a longer business relationship invoices, delivery notes etc repeatedly contain such a note and the buyer accepts this without objection.[9] However, if after an oral conclusion of a contract, general terms and conditions containing a retention of title clause are sent together with an order confirmation, retention of title is not implicitly agreed.[10] Nor is retention of title implicitly agreed if it is stated only by a note on the invoice, the delivery note or in another manner by the seller. An implicit agreement cannot be effected in this case, because the will to consent by the buyer cannot be assumed, because a retention of title is only a disadvantage for him.[11]

(c) *Form of the agreement on retention of title*

An agreement on retention of title does not require any particular form to be effective. In particular, it does not need to be in a written form.

Nor does the valid conclusion of an agreement on retention of title require registration in a public registry or confirmation by a notary public under Austrian law.

(d) *Retention of title in general terms and conditions*

If a retention of title-clause is contained in general terms and conditions, special provisions apply. According to consistent case law, general terms and conditions require incorporation in the contract and only apply if they have been included in the content of the agreement by an appropriate indication to that effect in the body of the contract, or have at least been included implicitly. In assessing whether general terms and conditions have been made part of the contract, strict standards apply. However, it has repeatedly been stated that tacit submission to general terms and conditions imposed by the other contracting party will be assumed if the first contracting party can clearly recognise that the other contracting party only wishes

---

8 ÖBA 2010, 215.
9 6 Ob 73/01f.
10 1 Ob 673/79.
11 See note 10 above.

to conclude the agreement subject to its general terms and conditions. General terms and conditions can also implicitly become part of the contract by the contracting parties' indicating the applicability of those general terms and conditions in the course of their commercial relationship, and such indication has remained unobjected.

One issue discussed in case law is the so-called 'battle of forms', where a retention of title is provided in the seller's general terms and conditions, but its applicability is excluded in the buyer's terms and conditions.[12] In this case, due to the conflicting terms, no agreement is reached on retention of title, and the statutory provisions apply under which ownership is transferred with the handing over of the goods to the buyer.[13] What is relevant here is the hypothetical will of the parties.[14] If retention of title is provided for in the general terms and conditions, its validity requires that the general terms and conditions were properly agreed on between seller and buyer.

(e) Handover

The validity of a retention of title clause generally requires the handing over of the goods to the buyer. After the handover, the seller remains owner of the goods. The buyer only acquires ownership upon full payment of the purchase price.

2.3 Scope of right of retention

(a) Resale of goods sold subject to retention of title by the buyer

Retention of title has the effect that the buyer has an expectant right to ownership of the goods concerned pending payment of the purchase price. The buyer can transfer this expectant right without limitations. If the buyer sells not only the expectant right, but the goods as well, he is in breach of his contract with the seller unless the seller has authorised resale of the goods. In this case, the final buyer acquires derivative ownership of the goods. Whether the seller has granted the authority to resell the goods is a matter of construction of the purchase agreement. Such a power of disposal may be granted expressly or implicitly. In cases of doubt, an implicit power of disposal is limited to resale in the ordinary course of business operations.[15] According to court rulings, this means that the question whether the seller's consent to resale is given or not depends on whether the buyer is reselling the goods within the ordinary course of his business in order to enable payment of the purchase price to the seller.[16] If the resale is not effected in the ordinary course of business, and in cases of doubt, no authority for resale is deemed to have been given by the seller.

Statutory law provides for no formal requirements for the authorisation of resale to be granted by the seller. An agreement to that effect is therefore sufficient.

---

12 RS0013952.

13 A lack of consensus in conflicting general terms and conditions does not hinder the coming into effect of the contract if the parties' will is to make the contract.

14 Binder and Spitzer in Schwimann and Kodek, *ABGB Praxiskommentar* 44 § 1063 Rz 30.

15 Verschraegen in Kletečka and Schauer *ABGB-ON* 1.01 § 1063 Rz 22.

16 5 Ob 642/89.

In the case of authorised resale of the goods by the buyer before payment of the purchase price, the final purchaser generally pays the purchase price to the buyer (under a purchase agreement) and the buyer pays the purchase price to the seller. However, there are no statutory provisions preventing an agreement between the final purchaser and the buyer under which the final purchaser pays the purchase price directly to the original seller.

Whether the final purchaser acquires ownership at the time of the handover or only upon payment of the purchase price depends on the agreement. In particular, the buyer can resell the goods subject to retention of title (secondary retention of title). If the resale has been effected where authorisation for the resale was granted by the original seller, the final purchaser acquires ownership derivatively. If the resale was effected without such authorisation, the final purchaser can only acquire ownership if he acted in good faith. In both cases, the final purchaser acquires ownership upon payment of the purchase price to the buyer. The original seller then loses his ownership.[17] If no retention of title was agreed on for the resale, the final purchaser acquires ownership in accordance with the relevant statutory provisions. If the buyer was authorised to make the resale, the buyer acquires ownership derivatively at the time of the handing over of the goods. If the buyer was not authorised to make the resale, the final purchaser only acquires ownership derivatively at the time of the handover if he is acting in good faith.

(b) *Retention of title in drop shipment*

In business transactions it is often the case that a seller does not deliver the goods to his buyer, but directly to the final purchaser. This process is referred to as 'drop shipment'. The special feature of the so-called drop shipment is that while there is a chain of two purchase agreements, the handover is only effected between the final purchaser and the seller. Loss of the seller's ownership only occurs if either the seller validly authorised the buyer to resell the goods without reservation, or if the final purchaser acquired ownership in good faith. An unauthorised resale by the seller constitutes a breach of contract, and in this case the final purchaser can acquire ownership only if he is acting in good faith. If, however, the final purchaser acquires the goods in knowledge of the fact that they were acquired by the reseller subject to retention of title, he does not acquire ownership in good faith. A final purchaser acting in bad faith only acquires ownership once the retention of title by the original seller is extinguished by payment of the purchase price.

The original seller's retention of title remains valid if the final purchaser has not acquired ownership in the goods in one of the manners described above. The seller has a claim to surrender (of the goods) against third-party possessors. This claim can be enforced in particular by way of a claim by the owner for return of his property (known as *rei vindicatio*) under Section 366 of the Civil Code.

(c) *Mingling or confusion of goods subject to retention of title*

By mingling or confusing goods subject to retention of title, retention of title is in

17 Binder and Spitzer in Schwimann and Kodek, *ABGB Praxiskommentar* 44 § 1063 Rz 66.

principle not extinguished, but in cases of doubt, joint ownership in proportion to each owner's respective share in the value is established (Sections 415 and following of the Civil Code). Confusion of the goods acquired subject to retention of title with goods of the same type in one warehouse results in joint ownership if the goods are not marked and therefore no longer identifiable.

In the case of a mingling of movable goods acquired subject to retention of title with other movable goods, the decisive question is whether a separation of the goods is possible. If the mingling of parts with the main object is so close that they could no longer be separated or only by commercially unreasonable measures, the components are considered dependent. If separation of the goods is no longer possible, joint ownership in proportion to the value of the goods is established. Retention of title no longer exists. According to court rulings, for instance, the motor is regarded as an ancillary object to the motor vehicle, for which reason the owner of the motor vehicle can acquire ownership in a motor belonging to another party by its installation in his motor vehicle.[18] If, however, the value of the object in which goods are incorporated is significantly higher, sole ownership on the part of the person carrying out the combination is established. If separation is still possible, retention of title is maintained.[19]

If retention of title is extinguished by mingling or confusion, the seller only has contractual claims against the buyer. Return of the goods can no longer be claimed in this case. If retention of title is maintained with regard to goods that are still separable, the principle that the buyer only acquires ownership upon full payment continues to apply.

(d) *Processing of goods subject to retention of title*

The processing of goods acquired subject to retention of title does not cause the retention of title to cease to exist, but in cases of doubt, the seller will have joint ownership of the processed goods in proportion to the respective shares of the value of his goods at the time of the processing.[20]

What needs to be taken into consideration in the case of processing is the value of the work performed in relation to the goods acquired subject to retention of title. If the value of the work is considerably lower than the value of the goods, the seller remains sole owner. The contracting parties may also agree that the retention of title ceases to exist upon processing, and sole ownership in the goods is transferred to the buyer. The parties to the contract may not, however, agree that a share in the processed goods accrues to the ownership of the seller, because this would be equivalent to a chattel mortgage and such an agreement requires an act of publicity.[21]

(e) *Extended retention of title*

Retention of title principally applies exclusively to the object of the purchase agreement containing the retention of title clause. In the literature, a retention of

---

18 RS0012015.
19 Aicher in Rummel, *ABGB* I3 § 1063 Rz 95.
20 RS0011061.
21 Binder and Spitzer in Schwimann and Kodek, *ABGB Praxiskommentar* 44 § 1063 Rz 66.

title requiring the fulfilment of additional requirements in addition to payment of the purchase price is referred to as an 'extended retention of title'.[22] Such an agreement is invalid under Austrian law. Prevailing legal doctrine takes the view that under Austrian law, the extension of a security interest to other claims would constitute circumvention of the publicity requirements for liens, and would therefore be invalid in terms of property law.[23]

2.4 Legal effect of retention of title

(a) *General effect*

Retention of title offers the seller protection in the sense that he can claim the surrender of the goods if the buyer fails to pay the purchase price. To this end, the seller must withdraw from the contract and demand the surrender of the goods. The seller may also take back the goods while maintaining the contract, if a 'return clause' has been agreed on between the parties to the contract.

The seller can also demand the return of the goods before the buyer defaults on payment, by way of a preliminary injunction securing his claim. The seller must demonstrate that there is a danger that the buyer could take measures that violate their contract and that would jeopardise retention of title by the seller; for instance a resale contrary to the contract.[24]

If third parties take possession of the goods acquired subject to retention of title at the buyer's premises, the seller has the right to reclaim his property under Section 37 of the Austrian Execution Act. If the third party, however, pays the seller the outstanding purchase price, the seller loses his right to reclaim the goods, and the third party can levy execution on the goods that are subject to retention of title.[25]

(b) *Effect in case of resale by the buyer/acquisition in good faith*

If a third party acquires goods subject to retention of title in good faith, the buyer acquires ownership in the goods. Good faith is assumed, and is present if the buyer believes that he is acquiring the goods from the owner, or if the third party knows that the buyer is not the owner, but the third party trusts that the buyer is authorised to resell the goods. According to consistent case law, the third party is obligated to undertake further inquiry if he is acquiring goods that are generally sold under retention of title. The third party must investigate the buyer's power of disposal by inspection of invoices and payment receipts. A failure to do so constitutes gross negligence.[26] The third party is not obligated to undertake further investigations if he acquires the goods from an entrepreneur in the ordinary course of business operations.[27]

If the buyer sells the goods subject to retention of title to a third party and the third party acquires ownership in good faith, the agreement regarding retention of

---

22 Binder and Spitzer in Schwimann and Kodek, *ABGB Praxiskommentar* 44 § 1063 Rz 16.
23 Aicher in Rummel, *ABGB* I3 § 1063 Rz 108.
24 Binder and Spitzer in Schwimann and Kodek, *ABGB Praxiskommentar* 44 § 1063 Rz 40.
25 3 Ob 91/38.
26 5 Ob 523/84.
27 1 Ob 614/87.

title by the seller is breached. However, the buyer is not obligated to surrender the advantage obtained from the transaction with the third party. The buyer is obligated only to compensate the seller for the replacement costs if the goods can be replaced on the market without difficulty.[28]

(c) Effect of pledge by the buyer

The buyer is not authorised to pledge goods acquired subject to retention of title. The buyer's pledgee, like a third-party buyer, is obligated to investigate whether retention of title has been established with regard to the goods to be pledged if such goods are generally sold subject to retention of title. In the event of bad faith, the pledgee becomes liable for damages. If the pledgee has acted in good faith, however, he must render account to the conditional seller after the disposal of the goods, and surrender the profit from the sale to the seller.[29]

(d) Effect of retention of title in cases of insolvency of buyer

If bankruptcy proceedings are initiated over the assets of the buyer, the seller who sold subject to retention of title has a claim to separation of assets in respect of the goods sold, under Section 44 of the Austrian Insolvency Act, as long as the purchase price has not yet been paid in full and the retention of title is therefore still effective. Furthermore, retention of title entitles the seller to rescind the contract in the event of default with regard to payment, without this right having to be granted separately. The seller claims his ownership rights, reserved pending full payment of the purchase price, by rescinding the contract and demanding the surrender of the goods by separation of assets.

As long as the seller has not paid the purchase price, the sales contract qualifies as a mutually uncompleted contract for the purposes of Section 21 of the Insolvency Act. Section 21 grants the administrator of the buyer's estate the right either to enter into the mutually uncompleted contract and to fulfil the contract – by paying the purchase price in full – or to rescind the contract. If the seller declared the rescission of the contract, the insolvency administrator no longer has the option to fulfil the contract. In the case of rescission of the contract by the administrator, the seller may have a claim to separation of assets in respect of the goods sold subject to retention of title, but must surrender any part of the purchase price he has already received.

(e) Effect of retention of title in cases of insolvency of seller

In the event of insolvency proceedings in respect of the seller who sold goods subject to retention of title, and in the event of incomplete fulfilment of the contract, through the buyer defaulting on payment, the seller's insolvency administrator principally has the choice to rescind the sales contract and demand return of the goods, or to demand payment of the purchase price from the buyer. However, this is controversial in legal doctrine. The literature states the opinion that the seller has no choice, since his performance has already been rendered and therefore no more performance is to be rendered.

---

28 1 Ob 173/75.

29 Binder and Spitzer in Schwimann and Kodek, *ABGB Praxiskommentar* 44 § 1063 Rz 15.

Section 224(2) of the Insolvency Act provides that the initiation of insolvency proceedings over the assets of the seller of goods after their delivery does not justify the rescission or termination of the sales contract, and does not rule out the acquisition of ownership by the buyer if, at the time of the initiation of proceedings, the goods are located in the territory of another country than that of the initiation of proceedings. If the subject of the retention of title is not located within the territory of the country in which the proceedings were initiated, rescission or termination of the sales contract is therefore excluded.

(f) ***Effect of retention of title in cases of insolvency proceedings abroad***

In the event of insolvency proceedings over the assets of the conditional purchaser being initiated in another country, the provisions of EU Directive 1346/2000 on insolvency proceedings are particularly relevant from an Austrian point of view. Article 3(2) of EU Directive 1346/2000 on insolvency proceedings provides that the courts of the member state having jurisdiction for the initiation of insolvency proceedings are those in whose territory the debtor has his principal centre of interest. For corporations and legal entities, it is assumed that the principal centre of interests lies at the location of the corporate seat until the contrary is proven. Articles 4(1) and (2)(b) of the same directive further provide that the insolvency law of the member state in which the proceedings are initiated applies to the insolvency proceedings and its effects, unless the directive provides otherwise. The law of that member state governs the conditions under which the insolvency proceedings are initiated, how they are carried out and how they are terminated. In particular, it governs which assets are included in the estate and how assets acquired by the debtor after the initiation of proceedings shall be treated.

EU Directive 1346/2000 contains a provision on retention of title. Article 7(1) provides that the initiation of insolvency proceedings against the buyer of an asset leaves the seller's rights on the basis of retention of title unaffected if this asset is located within the territory of another member state at the time of the initiation of the proceedings.

Within the scope of application of EU Directive 1346/2000, the effects of the initiation of insolvency proceedings by a foreign state are determined by the legal system of that state. If, however, the asset in respect of which retention of title has been established is not located within the territory of the country in which proceedings were initiated, the initiation of insolvency proceedings shall have no effect on the retention of title.

International insolvency law applies to insolvency proceedings initiated in non-EU-member states. The Austrian Insolvency Act provides that the laws of the state in which the proceedings are initiated apply to the prerequisites and effects of insolvency proceedings, so long as Sections 222 to 235 of the Insolvency Act do not provide otherwise (Section 221(1) of the Insolvency Act). In principle, the Austrian legal system thus acknowledges proceedings abroad as well as the requisite provisions. The effect of insolvency proceedings initiated in Austria basically also extends to assets located abroad, unless the debtor's principal centre of interests lies abroad, or insolvency proceedings have already been initiated and the foreign assets have been included in such insolvency proceedings (Section 237 of the Insolvency Act). The Austrian Insolvency Act likewise acknowledges the effects of insolvency proceedings initiated abroad as well as the decisions rendered in such proceedings, if the debtor's principal centre of interests is in that other country and the insolvency proceedings are essentially comparable to Austrian insolvency proceedings (Section 240 of the Insolvency Act). Proceedings are not acknowledged if insolvency proceedings have been initiated in Austria or if they infringe the doctrine of public policy.

Sections 222 to 235 of the Insolvency Act govern certain exceptions to the general principles of Section 221 of the Insolvency Act. Section 224(1) of that act, in conformity with Article 7(1) of EU Directive 1346/2000 on insolvency proceedings, provides that the initiation of insolvency proceedings over the assets of the buyer of an object leaves the seller's rights on the grounds of a retention of title unaffected if the object was located in the territory of another country than that in which proceedings were initiated at the time of the initiation of proceedings.

(g) *Effect of retention of title in cases of partial payment*

As long as the purchase price has not been fully paid by the buyer, the seller retains ownership in the goods. Seller and buyer may agree on partial payment or payment in instalments, but this has no effect on the time at which the ownership passes upon full payment of the purchase price. If the seller rescinds the contract and demands surrender of the goods, the seller shall repay any payments already made to the buyer. The seller must repay not just the part of the purchase price or the purchase price instalments received, but also statutory (or any higher agreed) interest, because the seller should not make money out of the rescission of the contract.[30]

3. Enforcement of retention of title

In order to enforce his retention of title, the seller must rescind the contract in the event of the buyer defaulting on payment and demand the surrender of the goods by the buyer. Only if the buyer and seller have concluded a separate agreement in the sales contract may the seller also demand surrender of the goods while maintaining the sales contract.[31]

Rescission of the contract has the effect that both the seller and the buyer are obligated to return to the other party what they have obtained. The seller may demand surrender of the goods by the buyer by way of an action of claim of ownership and title (Section 366 of the Civil Code). This action achieves the surrender of the goods in their current condition. The seller can also demand the surrender of the goods in the event of the insolvency of the buyer, but not by way of an action of claim of ownership and title; the seller only has a claim to separation of assets (Section 44 of the Insolvency Act).

What is not governed by statutory law is any agreement between seller and buyer

30 Binder and Spitzer, in Schwimann and Kodek, *ABGB Praxiskommentar* 44 §1063 Rz 86.
31 Binder and Spitzer, in Schwimann and Kodek, *ABGB Praxiskommentar* 44 §1063 Rz 88.

under which the seller can collect the goods sold subject to retention of title from the buyer's premises in the event of the buyer defaulting on payment. Whether such an agreement between seller and buyer is in principle permissible has not yet been the subject of any ruling by the Austrian courts. If the seller and the buyer have entered into such an agreement, there are sound reasons for saying that the enforcement of such an agreement would have to be made by court order should the buyer refuse to grant the seller access. For instance, in connection with a leasing agreement, the Austrian Supreme Court has declared impermissible a clause by which the lessor was to be allowed to collect the leased asset from the lessee's premises.[32]

There are good reasons for assuming the invalidity of an otherwise valid agreement that provides in its general terms and conditions that the seller can enter the buyer's premises without further ado in case of the buyer defaulting on payment. Under Austrian law, general terms and conditions are subject to special requirements in order to protect against unfairness. General terms and conditions are subject to a review of their validity (Section 864a of the Civil Code) and a review of their contents (Section 879(3) of the Civil Code). For general terms and conditions to be valid they must have become part of the contract on the one hand (review of validity) and on the other hand, they must not constitute a gross disadvantage (review of contents). If the review of contents establishes that clauses in the terms constitute a gross disadvantage, those clauses are invalid. If the buyer to whom the terms are intended to apply is a consumer, the Austrian Consumer Protection Act must also be taken into consideration, under which certain clauses are automatically invalid. In view of these special requirements for general terms and conditions, there are sound reasons for taking the view that an agreement allowing the seller to enter the premises of the buyer and to collect goods sold subject to retention of title in the event of the buyer defaulting on payment will be found to be grossly disadvantageous, and that such a clause could therefore not be validly agreed on in general terms and conditions.

If the goods have already been destroyed, an action of claim of ownership and title would no longer be promising, and damages would have to be claimed.

An action for claim of ownership and title (*rei vindicatio*) can be brought against anyone who currently possesses the goods, therefore including a person other than the buyer. However, if the third party can demonstrate that he acquired ownership of the goods in good faith, he is not required to surrender the goods to the seller.

If execution is being levied against the buyer by a creditor of the buyer, the seller may demand surrender of the goods by the creditor through an action reclaiming property being executed. By payment of the purchase price to the seller, the creditor can secure the goods, so that they no longer need to be surrendered to the seller.

4. Retention of title and conflict of laws

Austrian private international law is based on the Austrian Act on International Private Law, international treaties and EU regulations. The Act on International

32 1 Ob 81/09g.

Private Law entered into force in 1979, and by its structural nature it is an overall codification of the conflict of laws provisions.

Neither the Act on International Private Law nor the 'Rome I' Regulation (EU Regulation 593/2008 on the law applicable to contractual obligations) contain substantive law provisions, but only determine which national laws apply to which factual situations. Accordingly, neither the Act on International Private Law nor the Rome I Regulation contains provisions on conditions for retention of title.

Under Section 31(1) of the Act on International Private Law, the acquisition of property rights over physical assets (such as a lien or collateral ownership), and therefore also retention of title, is governed by the laws of the state in which the asset is located following completion of the factual situation forming the basis for the acquisition. Section 31(1) of the Act on International Private Law also applies to the assessment of retention of title. Since, under Austrian law, an agreement between the parties is in itself sufficient for a valid retention of title, retention of title is also effective under Austrian law even if under foreign law registration or other requirements would be necessary. If, under Section 31(1) of the Act on International Private Law, a foreign legal system applies, the Austrian court must apply the foreign legal system, even if it leads to other results than those arising under Austrian substantive law.

For matters falling within its scope of application, the Rome I Regulation determines the law applicable to contractual obligations. Under Article 3(1) of the Rome I Regulation, a contract is governed by the legal system chosen by the parties. The choice of law must be made expressly or clearly demonstrated from the provisions of the contract or the circumstances of the case. If the parties have made no choice of law, the applicable law is determined by the regulation itself. The intention of the Rome I Regulation is that in the absence of a choice of law, the laws of the country to which the contract is most closely connected shall apply (Articles 4(3) and (4) of the Rome I Regulation).

Belgium

Yves Lenders
Tom Reingraber
Lydian

1. General remarks about retention of title

1.1 Title, and transfer of ownership

Transfer of ownership takes place when parties reach an agreement on the essential and substantial elements of the purchase agreement – ie, the goods and the price. The mere consent to the agreement suffices. For its validity, no formalities or written documents are required. Indeed, transfer of ownership does not even require the goods to be delivered and/or the purchase price to be paid, as confirmed in Article 1583 of the Belgian Civil Code.

These principles, as laid down in the Civil Code, are merely 'supplementary' law. Parties are allowed to derogate from these principles and to contractually modulate the transfer of ownership. Parties can link the transfer of ownership to the fulfilment of future but certain conditions, such as the delivery of the goods or the payment of the purchase price. In other words, Belgian law allows for the parties to agree upon a retention of title.

A retention of title is a modality of transfer of ownership. The retention of title does not affect the constitution of the sale and purchase agreement. A sale and purchase agreement, subject to a retention of title, is therefore an effective sale and purchase agreement, and not merely a conditional sale.

Under Belgian law, the transfer of ownership implies the simultaneous transfer of risk relating to loss of or damages to the sold goods. If the transfer of ownership is delayed as a result of the retention of title, in principle this also implies a deferred transfer of risk. However, parties are allowed to (and should) contractually derogate from this principle, and stipulate that the risk is transferred to the buyer when concluding the sale and purchase agreement or upon delivery of the goods, regardless of the pending retention of title.

1.2 Retention of title in insolvency

Retention of title currently has no specific statutory basis in Belgium; its conditions are mainly based on case law. Only Belgium's Bankruptcy Act of 1997 provides for specific rules, and these relate to the retention of title and its effectiveness in the event of the bankruptcy of the buyer.

Article 101 of the Bankruptcy Act states that the owner of the goods that are located with its debtor in bankruptcy can successfully rely on his retention of title if:

- The retention of title was agreed in writing, at the latest when the goods were delivered;

- The goods still have to be located *in natura* with the buyer/debtor;
- The goods must be identifiable as property of the unpaid seller – ie, they may not have become immovable due to incorporation, or been combined or 'mixed' with goods of other owners; and
- The owner of the goods has invoked its retention of title before the bankruptcy trustee has filed its first report concerning the verification of claims, which is usually done within one month following the start of the bankruptcy proceedings. The timing thereof is published and can be consulted by the creditors.

Parties can contractually stipulate that the buyer has to inform the seller of any bankruptcy proceedings, to ensure that the seller can invoke his retention of title in a timely manner – ie, before the filing of the first report concerning the verification of claims.

Certain legal scholars maintain that the conditions for enforcement, as set out in Article 101 of the Bankruptcy Act, should also apply in other cases of *concursus creditorum*, such as a seizure or a liquidation. The retention of title will be enforceable if:

- it has been agreed in writing prior to the delivery of the goods;
- the goods are still located *in natura* with the debtor/buyer; and
- the goods are still identifiable – ie, they have not become immovable due to incorporation, nor have they been combined or mixed with other goods.

The foregoing requirements as set forth in Article 101 of the Bankruptcy Act will almost entirely be overruled by the Act of July 11 2013 regarding securities on movable assets (hereinafter the Securities Act), which will enter into force on January 1 2017. The Securities Act only requires for a retention of title agreed upon in writing, at the latest when the goods were delivered.

The Securities Act confirms the general opposability of retention of title, regardless of the type of *concursus creditorum*. From a strict point of view, the Securities Act is more lenient than the Bankruptcy Act because it only requires the retention of title to be agreed upon at the latest when the goods are delivered. However, for the retention of title to be effective, the goods still have to be present *in natura* with the buyer and have to be identifiable, which is also explicitly required in the Bankruptcy Act. In other words, the Securities Act does not alter the rule of opposability of the retention of title, as defined in the Bankruptcy Act (with the exception of the requirements regarding the timing of invocation before the first report concerning the verification of claim), but provides a general legal basis for it, regardless of the type of *concursus creditorum*.

1.3 Foreign and international law

As indicated above, the Belgian legal provisions on retention of title are not considered to be of public order, save for Article 101 of the Bankruptcy Act. As a result, Belgian parties are free to determine that foreign laws apply to the retention of title clause.

In accordance with Belgian law, agreements on the international sale of goods are governed by the United Nations Convention on Contracts for the International Sale of Goods (known as the Vienna Sales Convention) since Belgium is a party to this convention. However, Article 4(b) of the Vienna Sales Convention clearly states that it does not govern the effect that the contract may have on the property in the goods sold.

As a result, the Belgian rules of international private law come into play. In this regard, Article 98(1) of the Belgian Code on International Private Law implies that a retention of title clause included in an international sale of goods is governed by Regulation (EC) 593/2008 of June 17 2008 on the law applicable to contractual obligations (the Rome I Regulation). In turn, Article 4.1(a) of that regulation states that a contract for the sale of goods, including a retention of title clause, is governed by the country where the seller has its habitual residence.

The possibility of acquiring rights *in rem* over goods that are subject to a retention of title is governed by the law of the state where the goods are located at the moment of enforcement of such rights (*lex rei sitae*). The *lex rei sitae* will determine the existence of the securities, as well as their rank and opposability in relation to third parties. That law will also govern the retention of title where the buyer becomes subject to insolvency proceedings. However, the insolvency proceedings as such will be governed by Regulation (EC) 1346/2000 of May 29 2000 on insolvency proceedings (the Insolvency Regulation).

1.4 Retention of goods

As well as retention of title, Belgian law also acknowledges the principle of the retention of goods. The retention of goods allows a party to hold on to goods which are owned by another party in case the latter does not comply with its contractual obligations. The retention of goods is based on a general principle of Belgian contract law (*exceptio non adempleti contractus*, or ENAC), allowing for a party to suspend its contractual obligations if and for as long as the other party does not perform its own contractual obligations. For example, the leasing company of a storage unit can hold on to stored goods owned by the lessee if, and for as long as, the latter does not pay the rental charges.

The practicalities surrounding the retention of goods have mainly been developed through case law, based on the above-mentioned general principle of contract law. However, some Belgian legislation explicitly provides for a right of retention of goods, such as for a shipping agent in Belgium's Act on the Commercial Pledge and Commission of May 5 1872.

2. Retention of title

2.1 Validity and formal requirements

Belgian contract law is based on the contractual freedom of parties. In principle, Belgian law does not require the fulfilment of any specific formalities in order for the retention of title clause to be valid. A retention of title clause does not have to be agreed upon in writing. However, in order to avoid any issues regarding the proof of consent and to ensure opposability in relation to third parties, retention of title clauses are generally agreed in writing.

Such clauses are also commonly included in general terms and conditions. Parties are thereby free to determine the scope of the retention of title. No specific wording or other formalities are required.

To ensure that opposability is provided in the general terms and conditions, including a retention of title clause, it is necessary that the other contracting party has not only been duly informed of the terms and conditions (or at least had the opportunity of consulting them) but also accepted those terms and conditions. Acceptance can be in writing or implied – eg, by executing the agreement and by not contesting the terms and conditions printed on the back of invoices.

Article 101 of the Bankruptcy Act explicitly requires a retention of title to be agreed upon in writing, at the latest by the time of the delivery of the goods, as one of the conditions for the retention of title to be opposable to the other creditors (see section 1.2 above). However, the Securities Act, which will enter into force on January 1 2017, will require all retention of title clauses to be agreed upon in writing, at the latest by the time of the delivery of the goods. Any retention of title clause following the delivery of the goods (for example, a retention of title clause included in an invoice) will not then be enforceable.

If one of the contracting parties is a consumer, the Securities Act states that the consumer's consent to the written retention of title also needs to be shown in writing – eg, by signing the contract that includes the retention of title clause.

It is not required that the goods are delivered directly to the purchaser for the retention of title clause to be valid. The goods may also be delivered to a third party.

2.2 Scope of retention of title

Retention of title implies that the ownership of the goods remains with the seller until the buyer has paid the full purchase price. As a result, the buyer has no ownership over the goods until the purchase price has been paid in full. Since the buyer does not own the goods pending the retention of title, he is not entitled to sell the goods until the purchase price has been paid. However, if the buyer were nonetheless to sell the unpaid goods, the subsequent buyer will be considered as the (new) lawful owner of the goods if he acted in good faith (see section 2.3 below).

The retention of title only relates to goods that are identifiable. For instance, if the goods concern car tyres which are attached to a car, the retention of title will remain valid as the car tyres are still identifiable based on their brand, type etc and the seller can still repossess them.

If the goods are no longer identifiable after being combined/mixed with other goods, the retention of title will become unenforceable. For example, if the goods concern clay that is mingled with other clay of the same type and colour to make pottery, the clay delivered by the seller will no longer be identifiable. As a result, the seller can no longer invoke its retention of title, since it is no longer possible to identify the specific clay that it delivered. The retention of title also becomes unenforceable when the unpaid goods have been incorporated in newly assembled goods and the unpaid goods cannot be removed without damaging the newly assembled goods.

The outcome will be different if (in our example) the clay had been put in a warehouse (filled with other clay) upon delivery, but had not yet been combined with other clay. If the volume of clay that is subject to the retention of title is still identifiable through, for instance, a storage lot number or recognisable packaging of the seller, the retention of title is still in play.

In such circumstances it is up to the seller to demonstrate that the goods are indeed his property. To ensure the enforceability of the retention of title, parties can stipulate that the buyer has to properly store the goods, separately from other stored goods, in such a way that they remain identifiable.

To avoid these issues where the combining or processing of the goods might occur, the parties can explicitly stipulate that the combining or processing of the unpaid goods is not allowed until the purchase price has been paid in full. However, if the buyer were nonetheless to process or combine the unpaid goods, this could render the goods unidentifiable and the retention of title would become unenforceable, so that the unpaid seller would only be able to claim damages for breach of contract. The value of the delivered goods, the value of the combined goods, the fact that the other parts of the combined goods (eg, other clay or car parts) are delivered by a party other than the seller and/or whether the other parts have been paid for are all irrelevant in this regard.

To overcome the issues with an individual repossession, Belgian legal scholars allow for a collective repossession of goods. If a buyer uses several individual goods from different suppliers which are subject to a retention of title – eg, car parts from different suppliers to assemble a car – the car will be considered to be co-owned by the different suppliers. If the different suppliers remain unpaid, they can formulate a claim relating to the newly processed product (ie, the car) equal to its share in the new product. In other words, they can repossess the car and divide the profit from the sale in accordance with the respective value of the parts they delivered.

The new Securities Act, which will enter into force on January 1 2017, has now confirmed the aforementioned practice of collective repossession where retention of title applies, and provides it with a legal basis. Nevertheless, an unpaid seller still has to demonstrate both its ownership and the fact that the goods are still present and to what extent.

In addition, the new Securities Act has provided for specific rules where mixing or combining the unpaid goods occurs when retention of title applies. If the buyer is contractually allowed to process the unpaid goods, the retention of title will apply to the newly assembled product. If the buyer is not allowed to process the goods, the retention of title will apply to the newly assembled product but the unpaid seller will have to reimburse the buyer for the labour costs related to processing the goods in a case where he decides to enforce its retention of title.

The retention of title of the unpaid seller will apply to the processed goods, regardless of the fact that the processed goods might also include goods from third parties. If it is impossible to separate the unpaid goods from the newly assembled product without damaging the new product, the retention of title will only stand up if these goods have the largest value within the newly assembled product. For example, if an unpaid seller delivered an engine that has subsequently been installed in a car, the seller can still enforce its retention of title and repossess the car; the third party that owns other parts of the car, such as the tyres, steering wheel etc, can then formulate a claim towards the unpaid seller for the value of those parts.

It must be pointed out that retention of title is indivisible. Retention of title implies that the seller remains the sole owner of the sold goods as long as the purchase price has not been paid in full.

In relation to the scope of retention of title, the question remains whether the retention of title is limited to the goods that have been sold, or whether the retention of title can also extend to, and be used to secure, any other claims the seller might have towards the buyer that are not related to the purchase agreement. Belgian legal scholars accept that the parties can validly provide such an 'extended' retention of title in their contract. Thus, in our foregoing example the seller can invoke its retention of title, which is assumed to be included in a sales contract for a car, in order to ensure the claim it has towards the buyer regarding the sale of the car.

2.3 Legal effect of retention of title

Regarding the opposability of the retention of title, a difference is made among the following (each of which is described in greater detail below):

- opposability towards a subsequent buyer acting in good faith;
- opposability towards other creditors of the buyer;
- opposability in the case of insolvency proceedings of the buyer; and
- opposability towards creditors of the unpaid seller.

(a) Opposability towards a subsequent buyer acting in good faith

If the first buyer of the goods sells the goods to a third party pending the retention of title, the retention of title is not opposable to the subsequent buyer acting in good faith. A buyer is considered to act in good faith if he was not aware of the retention of title or could not reasonably have been aware thereof given the circumstances. The subsequent buyer is the rightful owner of the goods.

The retention of title will nevertheless be extended to the claim of the first buyer towards the subsequent buyer, in order to cover the unpaid purchase price.

An example can be helpful to clarify things. A seller sells a car to the first buyer for €1000 under a retention of title, and an amount of €500 remains unpaid. If the first buyer sells the car to a subsequent buyer for €750, the unpaid seller can collect €500 from the subsequent buyer, as he is subrogated in the rights of the first buyer in accordance with the (extended) retention of title.

However, as explained in section 1.2 and elsewhere above, retention of title only applies to identifiable goods. If in our example the subsequent buyer has already paid the first buyer what is owed, the monies received by the first buyer for the car will no longer be identifiable within his assets and, as a result, the retention of title of the first buyer will no longer be effective or enforceable. To ensure the enforceability of the subrogated retention of title, the unpaid seller can seize the claim for the purchase price of the first buyer towards the subsequent buyer. In doing so, the unpaid seller prevents the first buyer from collecting the claim from the subsequent buyer and in addition prevents the retention of title from becoming unenforceable.

If the retention of title becomes ineffective, the unpaid seller can claim full indemnities from the first buyer due to breach of contract – ie, selling a car that had not been paid for.

(b) *Opposability towards other creditors of the buyer*

If another creditor of the buyer would seize the goods pending the retention of title, legal scholars accept that the seller can invoke his retention of title towards the other creditor. As is standard, retention of title will be opposable if it has been agreed in writing prior to the delivery of the goods, the goods are still located *in natura* with the debtor/buyer, and the goods are still identifiable – ie, they have not become immovable due to incorporation or having been combined or mixed with other goods.

The retention of title will also be opposable to another creditor of the buyer if he tries to establish any securities on the unpaid goods. According to Belgian law, only a right of pledge can be established over movable assets. If the seller were to be confronted with a pledge granted on the unpaid goods, the retention of title supersedes the creditor's right of pledge if the retention of title was agreed upon by the time of delivery of the goods and prior to the vesting of the pledge.

In this regard, it is irrelevant whether the pledgee was aware of the retention of title – ie, whether he acted in good faith. To ensure that the creditors of the buyer are aware of the retention of title and to avoid any discussions in this regard, the unpaid seller should clearly mark the unpaid goods with its company name/logo and, if possible, with a clear statement that the goods remain its property while unpaid.

The same goes for creditors of the buyer who have privileges on certain assets of the buyer that include the unpaid goods. For example, a leasing company that leases the offices of a buyer has a privilege on all movable assets that are located at the offices and belong to the buyer/lessee, in order to ensure the payment of the lease. A similar situation arises with a creditor that has established a pledge on business assets.

(c) *Opposability in the case of insolvency proceedings of the buyer*

Retention of title will be opposable to other creditors in a case of bankruptcy, in accordance with the conditions as set forth in Article 101 of the Bankruptcy Act (see section 1.2 above).

If the buyer is subject to a judicial reorganisation, a difference is made between a seller that has not yet delivered the goods and a seller that has delivered the goods. If the seller has not yet delivered the goods, the seller can exercise its right of retention on the unpaid goods, notwithstanding the insolvency proceedings. If the unpaid seller has already delivered the goods, its contractual rights are temporarily suspended. In other words, the unpaid seller will not be able to enforce its retention of title, nor will it be able to claim the dissolution of the sale and purchase agreement during the judicial reorganisation proceedings. However, the judicial reorganisation will not affect the unpaid seller's retention of title. The judicial reorganisation proceedings, whether they fail or whether they would be successful, will not affect the amount of the claim of the unpaid seller.

(d) Opposability towards creditors of the unpaid seller

Since the sold goods are still owned by the unpaid seller pending the retention of title, the creditors of the seller can also execute their claims on the goods at hand. However, the creditors of the unpaid seller can only do so if the goods are still owned by the unpaid seller. In other words, the retention of title still has to be effective and enforceable. If the goods at hand are no longer identifiable, the retention of title becomes ineffective and the creditors of the seller are not able to execute their claim on these goods.

If the buyer has paid the purchase price in full prior to execution by the seller's creditors, the ownership will be transferred to the buyer and the goods will no longer be owned by the (paid) seller. As a result, the creditors of the seller will also no longer be able to execute their claim on these goods.

Should the creditors nonetheless execute their claim (eg, through seizure), the buyer can object to the seizure if it can demonstrate that it indeed paid the purchase price and thus became owner of the goods prior to the seizure. If, however, the buyer has not paid the purchase price prior to execution by the seller's creditors, the seller's creditors will be able to enforce their claim because the goods are still owned by the unpaid seller, pending the retention of title.

In other words, the buyer can only oppose enforcement measures if he can demonstrate that he owned the goods – ie, that he paid the purchase price in full – at the time of execution by the seller's creditors. The payment of the purchase price in full after execution by the seller's creditors (eg, seizure) will thus be irrelevant in this regard.

3. Enforcement of retention of title

If a seller wants to invoke its retention of title, it has to request the buyer to fulfil its contractual obligations, emphasising that the goods remain the seller's property until the contractual obligations (eg, full payment of the purchase price) have been fulfilled, in accordance with the retention of title clause.

The buyer can decide to either pay (the remainder of) the purchase price and keep the goods, or to not pay the purchase price and to hand over the goods to the seller in accordance with its retention of title.

If the buyer does not react to the notice of default, or contests the validity or the applicability of the retention of title, the buyer has two options. First, the buyer can initiate summary proceedings in order to have the goods seized or stored with a custodian, pending discussion with the buyer; secondly, the buyer can start proceedings on the merits of the case. These two options are discussed next.

3.1 Enforcement through summary proceedings

Summary proceedings can only be used in a case of urgency and are used to obtain urgent provisional measures within a short period of time. Summary proceedings will not consider the merits of the case and will only render a judgment *prima facie*. Summary proceedings are mostly used when the seller has reason to believe that the goods might perish in the near future, either because of their nature (eg, fruit) or because the goods are expected to be unrightfully sold by the buyer. The buyer can request the goods be handed over, or be stored with a custodian.

In order to ensure that the buyer complies with any injunction granted, the buyer can specifically request that the execution of the injunction by the buyer is linked to the payment of penalties where the buyer does not comply in a timely manner. For example, a seller can request the injunction in order to force the buyer to place the goods with a custodian within three calendar days following the granting of the injunction, under penalty of a payment of a fixed amount for each day that the buyer does not comply.

3.2 Enforcement through proceedings on the merits of the case

Alternatively, the seller can initiate proceedings on the merits of the case, concerning the validity and applicability of the retention of title.

During these proceedings, the seller can also request a preliminary injunction to have the goods placed with a custodian if the same fears about the goods have arisen. However, it usually takes longer to obtain a preliminary injunction during proceedings on the merits of the case. So if the situation is urgent (eg, in the case of perishable goods), the seller will usually first obtain an injunction through summary proceedings, followed by proceedings on the merits of the case. The judge dealing with the merits of the case, involving by its nature a discussion relating to the ownership of the goods, will not be bound by the decision rendered during the (*prima facie*) summary proceedings.

Similarly to the summary proceedings, the seller can also request a judgment, in combination with the payment of penalties, should the buyer not comply in a timely manner with the injunction to hand over the goods in accordance with the retention of title.

Repossessing the goods will take place through a bailiff, based on the court judgment. Should the buyer not comply with the court judgment to hand over the goods (directly to the buyer or to a custodian), the buyer can contact a bailiff to enforce and execute the court judgment.

Although there are no formal requirements for identifying the goods subject to the retention of title, it is recommended that the goods should be clearly marked using serial numbers and the owner's logo, name and address etc. This facilitates the execution and enforcement of the retention of title.

3.3 Enforcement in a case of insolvency of the buyer

If the buyer is subject to bankruptcy proceedings, the seller will have to contact the bankruptcy trustee, and not the buyer directly, to execute the retention of title. However, retention of title during bankruptcy proceedings is subject to the conditions set out in section 1.2 above.

The trustee can decide to either pay (the remainder of) the purchase price and keep the goods, or to not pay the purchase price and to hand over the goods to the seller in accordance with its retention of title.

If the trustee contests the validity or the applicability of the retention of title clause, the seller can initiate proceedings against the trustee, as described in section 3.2 above.

If the buyer is subject to judicial reorganisation proceedings, the unpaid seller will in principle still be able to enforce its retention of title, provided that the unpaid goods still remain with the buyer and are still identifiable (see section 2.3(c) above).

3.4 Enforcement when the goods are stored with a third party

If the goods are located on the premises of a third party, the seller needs to demonstrate the existence and validity of the retention of title towards the third party.

If the third party does not agree to hand over the goods, the seller can initiate proceedings towards both the buyer and the third party. Although the seller has no contractual relationship with the third party in this context, it is in the interest of the seller to include the third party in the proceedings for the judgment to be opposable towards the third party and to avoid any discussions in this regard.

The retention of title clause can stipulate that the buyer will grant the seller access to its premises to recollect the goods, in a case of default of the purchaser. However, such clauses will only be effective if the buyer agrees to cooperate. If the seller were to come to collect back the goods and the buyer refuses access to its premises, for instance because the buyer contests the validity and/or applicability of the retention of title clause, the buyer will need a court judgment in order to enforce its retention of title.

3.5 Enforcement in a case of the retention of goods by another creditor

Enforcement of the retention of title can be hindered by a creditor of the buyer which exercises its right of retention on the unpaid goods. An example may clarify things.

A buyer purchases a car and has it delivered to a storage unit owned by a leasing company (making it a third party to the arrangement). The purchase agreement concerning the car provides for a retention of title clause in favour of the car manufacturer. However, the buyer is behind on his rental payments to the leasing company. As a result, the leasing company can exercise its right of retention of goods (ie, the car) until the buyer/lessee has cleared its debt. The fact that the car is still owned by the car manufacturer, because of the retention of title clause, is irrelevant in this regard.

Canada

Kelby Carter
Jennifer Stam
Gowling Lafleur Henderson LLP

1. General remarks about retention of title

Under a contract, certain clauses may exist which either transfer title of an asset from a buyer to a seller, or create a creditor-debtor relationship between two parties whereby the debtor becomes indebted to the creditor to some extent. With respect to the first scenario, two parties will, presumably, enter into a contract whereby the intention of both parties is to transfer an asset to the other, without any future obligations. Once all conditions, as set out in the contract between the parties, have been met, title to the asset will transfer. With respect to the second scenario, however, title does not necessarily pass at the conclusion of the contract. When the contract creates an interest in personal property that secures payment or performance of an obligation between two parties, this security interest (and the title that goes along with it) will fall under the Personal Property Security Act.[1] The first scenario, where title passes under the contract from one party to another, where securing payment or performance of an obligation is not at issue, will fall under the Sale of Goods Act.[2]

Determining whether the Personal Property Security Act applies to a retention of title clause within a sales contract is the first fundamental point in ascertaining a vendor's rights, generally and especially in a bankruptcy scenario. Generally speaking, the test for whether the Personal Property Security Act applies to a contract is whether the retention of title within the contract, in substance, creates a security interest.[3] Leading case law such as *Adelaide Capital Corp v Integrated Transportation Finance Inc*[4] and *356447 British Columbia Ltd v Canadian Imperial Bank of Commerce*[5] demonstrate that it is not enough for the contract explicitly to say that the transaction does or does not create a security interest, nor is it enough to call the contract a security agreement. What is imperative is that the agreement, *in substance*, sets out a transaction whereby one party retains an interest in order to secure payment of performance of an action. If it does, then the contract will be considered, at least in part, a 'security agreement' and the Personal Property Security Act, including the requirements to perfect a security interest (discussed below) apply. If the retention of title is a true hold back of title, then the Personal Property Security Act does not apply and the Sale of Goods Act will govern.

---

1 Personal Property Security Act, RSO 1990, c P. 10.
2 Sale of Goods Act, RSO 1990, c S.1, Section 18(1).
3 Personal Property Security Act, Section 2.
4 *Adelaide Capital Corp v Integrated Transportation Finance Inc* (1994), 16 OR (3d) 289; 111 DLR (4th) 493 (Ont Ct J (Gen Div).
5 *356447 British Columbia Ltd v Canadian Imperial Bank of Commerce* (1988), 48 BCLR (3d) 1; 157 DLR (4th) 682 (BC CA).

1.1 Transfer of ownership

As noted above, in Canada, the primary pieces of legislation governing retention of title are the Sale of Goods Act and the Personal Property Security Act. Where the transfer of ownership of assets is at issue, the Sale of Goods Act will govern. The Sale of Goods Act is provincial legislation that varies slightly from province to province. For the purpose of this chapter, the Ontario Sale of Goods Act will be the focus.

Under the Sale of Goods Act, a party may become the owner of an asset upon the making and signing of a contract. If the parties to the contract do not express any contrary intention to the passing of ownership, ownership will pass on execution of the contract, unless conditions precedent to the transfer are express or implied. The transfer of an asset does not necessarily depend on payment of the purchase price or delivery of the asset to the transferee. The terms of the transfer are determined by the language of the contract between the parties.[6]

1.2 Retention of title

Although title can be transferred on execution of a contract where there are no specific conditions precedent, the parties are able to set specific conditions if they so desire. Section 20 of the Sale of Goods Act states:

> *The seller may reserve the right of disposal of the goods until certain conditions are fulfilled; in such a case despite delivery of the goods to the buyer the property does not pass to the buyer until conditions imposed by the seller have been fulfilled.*[7]

In Canada, retention of title has both a statutory and a common law basis. In terms of its statutory basis, retention of title is primarily governed by:

- the Sale of Goods Act;
- the Personal Property Security Act, which, like the Sale of Goods Act, is provincial legislation (this chapter will focus on the Ontario Personal Property Security Act); and
- the Bankruptcy and Insolvency Act,[8] which is federal legislation.

Under Section 2(2) of the Sale of Goods Act, it is stated that a contract of sale may be absolute or conditional, so long as the intent is to transfer title outright from one party to another. In the event that a party opts to retain title after a sale to secure the payment or performance of an obligation, the Personal Property Security Act applies. This is by virtue of Section 1(1) of the Personal Property Security Act which defines, and includes within the scope of the act's application, a 'purchase money security interest'. Retention of title in a conditional sales agreement (whereby the seller retains title while the buyer takes possession of the goods) leads to a creditor having a purchase money security interest over the goods bought on credit, under the Personal Property Security Act.[9]

In order to hold a purchase money security interest and to gain special protection

---

6 Sale of Goods Act, Section 18(1).
7 Sale of Goods Act, Section 20.
8 Bankruptcy and Insolvency Act, RSC 1985, c B-3.
9 Bruce MacDougall, *Canadian Personal Property and Security Law*, (Markham: Lexis Nexis Canada Inc, 2014), at 118.

under the Personal Property Security Act, a creditor must take specific steps, as outlined in the act, to perfect its security interest, generally by way of registration. A more detailed discussion of perfection under the Personal Property Security Act can be found below in the subsection entitled "Validity and formal requirements of retention of title". Once properly perfected, the holder of a purchase money security interest under the Personal Property Security Act can take advantage of preferential priority rules to obtain a better priority position over other secured creditors than it would otherwise have. This type of priority is called a 'superpriority'.[10]

Under the common law and the Sale of Goods Act, the retention of title by the seller allows the seller to regain actual legal possession of the goods in the event that the buyer fails to pay.[11]

A contract for the sale of goods whereby the seller retains title in the goods until the buyer has finished making payments is commonly referred to, under the common law, as a conditional sales contract.

1.3 Foreign and international law

In the event that an agreement to transfer title, or a specific clause regarding the transfer of title in an agreement, is governed by a law other than the laws of Ontario, a court will have the ability to decide which jurisdiction has the closest substantial connection to the transaction in question, in order to determine which jurisdiction is to apply.[12] The court may consider whether the agreement expressly chooses the governing law, whether that choice was genuine, whether there is a policy reason to not give weight to the contractual choice, or whether the law of the jurisdiction where the contract was largely performed would deem the contract to be illegal, notwithstanding the choice of law.[13]

In addition to the common law approach, the Personal Property Security Act contains rules to sort out jurisdictional conflicts. Subject to a number of exceptions set out in the act, the validity, perfection and effect of perfection or non-perfection of a security interest in the collateral is governed by the law of the jurisdiction where the collateral is located at the time the security interest attaches to the collateral.[14] The validity, perfection and effect of perfection or non-perfection and the priority of a security interest in intangibles or goods that are of a type that are normally used in more than one jurisdiction, where goods are classified as 'equipment' or 'inventory' under the Personal Property Security Act, shall be governed by the law of the jurisdiction where the debtor is located at the time the security interest attaches to the collateral.[15]

The Personal Property Security Act also states that in the event that a security interest is perfected outside of Ontario, the interest will continue to be perfected in Ontario if the financing statement is registered in Ontario before the goods are

---

10 MacDougall, *Canadian Personal Property and Security Law*, at 119.
11 *Pickles Tents & Awnings Ltd v Joseph Group of Cos* [1981] 10 Man R (2d) 19, 127 DLR (3d) 176 (Man CA).
12 MacDougall, *Canadian Personal Property and Security Law*, at 467.
13 *Cardel Leasing Ltd v Maxmenko* (1991), 30 ACWS (3d) 502, 2 PPSAC (2d) 302 (Ont Gen Div).
14 Personal Property Security Act, Section 5(1).
15 Personal Property Security Act, Section 7(1).

brought into Ontario or the security interest is perfected in Ontario within certain timeframes (as outlined in the act).[16]

While the conflict of law rules set out in the Personal Property Security Act are helpful, they do not establish a complete code. As such, general common law principles pertaining to conflicts of law will apply in some cases.

Understanding conflicts of law in the context of title may be crucial, with the result potentially having serious consequences for a secured party. For example, in a scenario where a seller in one jurisdiction has reserved title, a future sale by the buyer in a new jurisdiction under that new jurisdiction's law will depend upon whether the new jurisdiction recognises the reservation of title in the original seller's jurisdiction. If the new jurisdiction does not recognise the reservation of title in the original jurisdiction, the seller's title may be effectively destroyed and title would pass to the third-party buyer. Determining the result may depend on whether the court of the forum gives extra-territorial effect to the law of the original location of the goods, in regard to the reservation of the original seller's title, or gives paramount effect to its own law. The same considerations apply if the reservation is ineffective by the law of the original transaction but could be effective by the law of the subsequent dealing. If the forum gives full effect to the first law, the subsequent title will be invalid.[17]

2. Retention of title

2.1 Validity and formal requirements of retention of title

(a) Writing requirements

Where the Sale of Goods Act is to govern the transaction, there is no requirement under that act that the contract be in any specific form or in writing, meaning that the parties may enter into an oral or written contract. Such matters are largely governed by general contract law.[18]

Where the Personal Property Security Act is to govern the transaction, however, and there is only an oral contract, the creditor will have an enforceable right against the debtor, pursuant to general contractual principles, but this right will not prevail against third parties.[19] In order for a creditor to have an enforceable right over a debtor's collateral against third parties under the Personal Property Security Act, the creditor must have possession of the debtor's collateral or have met formal writing requirements as set out in the act.[20]

(b) Substantive content requirements

There are no substantive content requirements under the Personal Property Security Act as such; however, the substance of the security interest may determine how one's

16 Personal Property Security Act, Section 5(2).
17 GHL Fridman, *Sale of Goods in Canada* (Scarborough: Thomson Reuters Canada, 2013), at 400.
18 MacDougall, *Canadian Personal Property and Security Law*, at 105.
19 MacDougall, *Canadian Personal Property and Security Law*, at 107.
20 MacDougall, *Canadian Personal Property and Security Law*, at 106; Personal Property Security Act, Section 11(2).

retained title is protected or the interest is advanced. Before the act, the protection afforded to a secured party and its ability to retain (or gain) title depended in large part on the nature of the security agreement. However, the Personal Property Security Act sought to eliminate the idiosyncrasies of the various categories of security agreement and bring them all under the same umbrella.[21] As a result, the nature of the security agreement that creates the security interest is not supposed to matter (whether it is a chattel mortgage, floating charge, pledge, assignment of book debts, conditional sale, etc) as long as there can be said to be a transaction that in substance creates a security interest.[22] Therefore, it is not a question of the nature of the security agreement, but whether or not the security interest arises from a transaction – it is crucial that the interest in the property be granted to secure performance or an obligation. Because of this definitional requirement, an interest or right to recover payment that arises from a court order would not create a security interest under the Personal Property Security Act regime because there is no transaction involved.[23] This does not mean that a proprietary interest and a right to retain title cannot arise where there is no transaction, rather, it means that such an interest or title will not be subject to the rules of title that are advanced by the Personal Property Security Act. Instead, when a party retains (or gains) title through means other than through a transaction, the rules of common law and equity will be considered. Subject to the rules of common law and equity, a court will determine priority between multiple claims of title in the same property, and any such title may run the risk of being defeasible to title held by another party.[24]

It is possible for the parties to agree upon a retention of title clause in general terms because the Personal Property Security Act, while it eliminates idiosyncrasies of each type of transaction once it is brought under the umbrella of the act, does not eliminate the different forms of transaction themselves. Such transactions still have weight under the common law.[25] For example, once parties enter into a true conditional sales contract, by the nature of the arrangement, the seller will retain title in the property until the buyer has fully paid the purchase price, or subject to any other terms and conditions that the parties determine as between themselves.[26] This is true notwithstanding the fact that the purchaser will likely have taken possession of the property.[27] However, regardless of the terms of the contract as between the parties, if the retention of title is not protected through perfection and registration under the Personal Property Security Act or some other relevant statute, but is merely set out in an agreement between the transacting parties, that title may also be defeasible to a competing interest or title held by a third party. For greater clarity, the terms of a security agreement that is unperfected will only be effective

21 Personal Property Security Act, Section 2.
22 Personal Property Security Act, Section 2(a).
23 MacDougall, *Canadian Personal Property and Security Law*, at 116.
24 *iTrade Finance Inc v Bank of Montreal*, 2011 SCC 26; [2011] 2 SCR 360.
25 MacDougall, *Canadian Personal Property and Security Law*, at 115.
26 As noted above, under "Retention of title", Section 20 of the Sale of Goods Act permits parties to determine when title passes and to set those terms and conditions in a contract. Section 9 of the Personal Property Security Act also allows parties to set the terms of their security agreement as they choose, subject to any statutory limits.
27 MacDougall, *Canadian Personal Property and Security Law*, at 118-119.

asbetween the signatories, but not against third parties with greater rights as a result of relevant legislation, particularly the Personal Property Security Act.

It is also possible for two secured parties to agree amongst themselves who should prevail in priority with respect to title, notwithstanding the priority imposed by the Personal Property Security Act, through the use of subordination or priority agreements.

However, with respect to the ability of parties to dictate the terms of retention of title as between them, it is important to note that the Personal Property Security Act expressly provides for the parties' ability to govern the terms of their security agreement. However, that ability may be limited by express provisions of the Personal Property Security Act or other relevant legislation to the contrary.[28]

(c) ***Requirements of perfection***

In order for a security interest under the Personal Property Security Act to have any valuable priority in competition with the security interests of third parties, the security interest must be in writing and perfected. This is the best possible position for the creditor to attain under the Personal Property Security Act.[29] If the creditor requires security but does not have possession of the collateral, the creditor must have a fully executed security agreement with debtor and register a financing statement with the personal property security registrar.[30]

The description of the collateral in the security agreement must describe the collateral sufficiently to enable it to be identified. The debtor, or the authorised agent or representative of the debtor, must sign the written agreement.[31]

(d) ***Requirements for a purchase money security interest***

A purchase money security interest is a type of security interest under the Personal Property Security Act that receives superpriority ahead of all other security interests.[32] However, in order for a creditor to benefit from this superpriority, certain requirements must be met.

First, the transaction must meet the definition of a purchase money security interest under the Personal Property Security Act:

- the seller must take or reserve title in the collateral;
- giving value to the purchaser for the purpose of enabling the purchaser to acquire rights in the property; and
- the purchaser must then take that value and actually use it to obtain rights in the collateral.[33]

In simpler terms, a purchase money security interest usually applies in the

---

28 Personal Property Security Act, Section 9(1).

29 MacDougall, *Canadian Personal Property and Security Law*, at 243.

30 MacDougall, *Canadian Personal Property and Security Law*, at 112. Without the debtor's signature, the courts have held that attachment cannot occur: *Astral Communications Inc v 825536 Ontario Inc (Trustee Of)* (2000), 46 OR (3d) 477; 183 DLR (4th) 455 (Ont CA).

31 Personal Property Security Act, Section 11(2); see *Access Advertising Management Inc v Servex Computers* (1993), 15 OR (3d) 635; 21 CBD (3d) 304 (Ont Gen Div).

32 Personal Property Security Act, Section 20(3).

33 Personal Property Security Act, Section 1(1).

context of a true conditional sale, whereby the seller gives the purchaser rights to use and possess the goods without them having paid the full purchase price, but retains the title to the goods until the full purchase price is received. It will also be deemed to apply where the goods are leased for a term over one year.

Secondly, the seller must meet the perfection requirements under the Personal Property Security Act.

Where the relevant goods are inventory and its proceeds, before the debtor takes possession of the goods, the seller must give notice of its intent to take a purchase money security interest over every other party who has already registered an interest against that debtor under the Personal Property Security Act, if the registered financing statement indicates that the party has an interest in collateral that includes inventory or accounts.[34] The purchase money security interest must be perfected at the time that the debtor takes possession of the goods.[35]

If the relevant goods are not inventory and its proceeds, the seller's interest must be perfected within 15 days of the purchaser receiving rights over the goods. In this case, the seller is not obligated to put any other potential creditors on notice.[36]

If the above requirements are not met, then the seller will not receive the superpriority or special protection with respect to the goods. Instead, priority will be determined on the same basis as every other interest under the purview of the Personal Property Security Act (see heading "Effect towards third parties" below, for further information).

2.2 Scope of retention of title

(a) Sale of goods delivered under retention of title

The general rule that is advanced by the Sale of Goods Act is that one cannot sell what one does not have.[37] Where the Sale of Goods Act is applicable, only the party that retains the title is permitted to dispose of it. However, this principle is subject to numerous exceptions. For one, if the party that has title to the goods acts in a way that would otherwise preclude them from later claiming rights to the goods (such as by abandoning the goods), then someone else may take up the goods and be permitted to dispose of them as if they had title.[38]

The Sale of Goods Act also provides that, in the event of a validly agreed upon retention of title between buyer and seller, the buyer is entitled to sell the goods to a third party before the buyer has paid the purchase price to the seller and before the buyer even possesses title. For this to work, the buyer must have possession of the goods by consent of the seller, and the ultimate buyer will have to effect the purchase of title in good faith and without any notice or knowledge of any lien or right of the original seller.[39] Where the ultimate purchaser is aware that title is not held by the

34 Personal Property Security Act, Section 33(1)(b).
35 Personal Property Security Act, Section 33(1)(a).
36 Personal Property Security Act, Section 33(2).
37 Sale of Goods Act, Section 22.
38 Sale of Goods Act.
39 Sale of Goods Act, Section 25(2).

party selling to them, the Sale of Goods Act stipulates that any contract that purports to sell goods that are not yet owned by the seller will be treated as an agreement to sell, and title in those goods will not pass to the ultimate buyer until the first buyer meets the conditions of the first sale and title is able to pass to him or her.[40]

Similarly, the Personal Property Security Act provides some latitude for a party to sell goods that it possesses but to which that party does not have title. Even where the goods are subject to a retention of title by the original seller, the buyer of those goods may pass good title onto a third party so long as the seller sells the goods in the ordinary course of his or her business.[41] This is true even if the creditor's security interest is perfected under the Personal Property Security Act and the ultimate purchaser is aware of the encumbrance on the goods, so long as the ultimate purchaser did not know that the purchase was in contravention of the security agreement as between the original seller and purchaser.[42]

Where a party's security interest is unperfected under the Personal Property Security Act, a party with possession of the goods but without clear title may also pass clear title to a third-party purchaser so long as that third party:

- gives value;
- takes delivery of the goods; and
- had no knowledge of the retention of title agreement.[43]

This does not apply with respect to goods subject to a retention of title that is in the form of a purchase money security interest, however.

Further to these conditions, the third-party buyer will only be protected to the extent that the goods purchased are identified in the contract of sale or lease. Identification of such goods can be accomplished if the goods are identified and agreed upon by the parties at the time the contract is made, marked or designated in the contract by the original buyer, or by the third-party buyer with the original buyer's consent.[44]

(b) Combining/mixing/mingling and processing goods delivered under retention of title

In the event that the relevant goods are combined, mixed or commingled, a perfected security interest under the Personal Property Security Act in the goods that subsequently become part of a product or mass will continue in the product or mass. If the goods are so manufactured, processed, assembled or commingled that their identity is lost in the product or mass, and if more than one security interest attaches to the product or mass, the security interests will rank equally according to the ratio that the cost of the goods to which each interest originally attached bears to the cost of the total product or mass.[45]

40 Sale of Goods Act, Sections 6(3) and 2.
41 Personal Property Security Act, Section 28(1).
42 Personal Property Security Act.
43 Personal Property Security Act, Section 20(1)(c).
44 Personal Property Security Act, Section 28(1.2) and (1.3).
45 Personal Property Security Act, Section 37.

(c) Extension of retention of title

Depending on the agreement, the secured party can include or tack on amounts related to taxes, registration fees, insurance, maintenance costs and so on. Clauses in security agreements dealing with tacking on future advances will be interpreted narrowly if there is doubt as to their meaning. Tacking on is largely treated as a freedom of contract issue as it relates contracts both governed by the Sale of Goods Act and the Personal Property Security Act.[46]

Under the Sale of Goods Act, a seller is permitted to incorporate conditions into the contract that delay the transfer of title until such conditions are met.

Section 20 of the Sale of Goods Act states:

(1) *Where there is a contract for the sale of specific goods or where goods are subsequently appropriated to the contract, the seller may,* by the terms of the contract or appropriation, *reserve the right of disposal of the goods until certain conditions are fulfilled, and in such case, despite the delivery of the goods to the buyer or to a carrier or other bailee for the purpose of transmission to the buyer, the property in the goods does not pass to the buyer until the conditions imposed by the seller have been fulfilled.*

(2) *Where goods are shipped and by the bill of lading the goods are deliverable to the order of the seller or the seller's agent, the seller in the absence of evidence to the contrary reserves the right of disposal.*

The right of disposal under the Sale of Goods Act is commonly understood as retaining title, including the right to regain possession (if buyer took possession) and the right of resale on default.[47]

There is no specific language in the Sale of Goods Act that requires these conditions to be limited to receipt of the purchase price in full, nor is there any case law (at the date of writing) that restricts these conditions. The parties are free to contract in any way they choose, and may incorporate any conditions to extend a retention of title in their discretion, subject to general contractual principles (illegality, considerations for public policy, etc).

2.3 Legal effect of retention of title

(a) Effect towards third parties

The terms of the Sale of Goods Act that relate to retention of title are automatic in effect: a party who wants to validly retain title to goods is not required to record its rights on paper, nor is the party required to register its interest. Should another party with possession of the goods seek to sell them without consent of the owner, good title will, as a general rule, not pass to the purchaser.[48] If a party has retained title according to the Sale of Goods Act's provisions and its interest is challenged by a third party or is otherwise in conflict with another's interest, the party is entitled to bring an action to enforce its interest.[49]

---

46 MacDougall, *Canadian Personal Property and Security Law*, at 99.

47 *Barclays Business Credit Inc v Fletcher Challenge Canada Ltd* (1993), 13 OR (3d) 118 at para 19-21; 39 ACWS (3d) 1056 (Ont Sup Ct).

48 Sale of Goods Act, Section 22.

49 Sale of Goods Act, Section 55.

That is not to say that a party's rights under the Sale of Goods Act are immutable. A third party may usurp greater title to the same goods if a sale was effected by a purchaser who had not yet obtained proper title because of an unsatisfied condition, but who had possession by consent of the owner, and the second purchaser transacted with the first "in good faith and without notice of any lien or other right of the original seller."[50] The owner's rights will be trumped if this happens.

The practical difficulty in this is that, unlike under the Personal Property Security Act, there is no registry that a third party can review in order to ensure that the goods that they are acquiring are being transferred with good title. It is, therefore, more improbable that a purchaser will be able to discover the original party's rights. As a matter of public policy, it would be unfair to penalise a party who had no way to discover that the title to the goods was encumbered when they entered into an otherwise valid arrangement. It seems then that title held under the Sale of Goods Act is less secure from third-party intervention as it relies on the good faith and honesty of the party in possession to alert any prospective purchaser that the goods are encumbered.[51]

In the context of the Personal Property Security Act, a creditor's security interest must be perfected in order to prevent third parties from intervening.[52] Registration puts into effect a system of notice, whereby any prospective purchaser is expected to know, or at least to inquire into the status of the title to the goods before taking them or before placing a further encumbrance on the goods. However, even with the additional protection afforded by registration and putting the public on notice, the creditor's interest in retaining the title is still not absolute. For example, under the Personal Property Security Act, a third-party buyer in good faith will be able to retain title to an asset where the sale happened in the ordinary course of business and the third-party buyer did not have knowledge of the relationship between the original seller and buyer. Consequently, where a seller and a buyer have not completed the transfer of title (because conditions precedent to transfer have not been satisfied) and the buyer then sells the asset and title to the asset to a third party, the third party will take the asset and title free and clear if the sale happens in the ordinary course of business and where the third party did not have knowledge of the outstanding conditions precedent between the original seller and buyer.

It is also important to note that a retention of title is only as good as the priority it is afforded under the Personal Property Security Act. Generally, the rules of priority are as follows:

- If there are two agreements that afford retention of title in the same goods and both are registered under the Personal Property Security Act, then the first to register that agreement will have priority in enforcement;
- If there are two agreements that afford retention of title in the same goods and one is registered under the Personal Property Security Act and the other is not, then the registered agreement will have priority over the unregistered agreement in enforcement;

---

50 Sale of Goods Act, Section 25(2).
51 Douglas G Baird, "Notice Filing and the Problem of Ostensible Ownership" (1983), 12 J Leg Stud 53 at 59.
52 Personal Property Security Act, Section 20(1).

- If there are two agreements that afford retention of title in the same goods and both are otherwise perfected under the Personal Property Security Act, then the first to perfect the agreement will have priority in enforcement; and
- If there are two agreements that afford retention of title in the same goods and both are unperfected under the Personal Property Security Act, then the first security interest to attach will have priority in enforcement.[53]

If one or neither of the security interests are captured under the scope of the Personal Property Security Act, priority will be determined on the basis of common law and equity.[54]

Notwithstanding the above, if a party's retention of title was established through a purchase money security interest (a true conditional sales contract, duly registered under the Personal Property Security Act), that party can take advantage of preferential priority rules to receive a superpriority.[55]

In the case of collateral other than inventory and intangibles, where the purchase money security interest in collateral or its proceeds is perfected not later than 15 days after the purchaser obtains possession of the collateral, the interest will have priority over any other security interest in the same collateral.[56] This means that the interest would take priority even if it was not the subject of the first filing.

Where the collateral is inventory, the superpriority will apply if the interest was perfected at the time the debtor obtained possession, or at the time when a third party, at the debtor's request, obtained possession, whichever is earlier.[57] The secured party must also give notice of this inventory purchase money security interest in writing to every other secured party who has, before the date of registration by the secured party, registered a financing statement.[58]

The parties in competition must be secured parties of the same debtor for the superpriority rules to apply.[59] Thus, if the third party is a secured party of the seller and not of the purchaser, the seller will not be able to benefit from his superpriority.

If the purchase money security interest priority rule applies, a superpriority is given not just in respect of the original collateral but also to/in respect of any proceeds from that collateral.[60]

(b) Effect in case of seizure of goods delivered under retention of title

Where the Personal Property Security Act is applicable, goods may be seized and sold where the debtor defaults on the loan given by the creditor, provided that the creditor is entitled to such seizure.[61] As previously noted, there are two types of creditor under the Personal Property Security Act: secured and unsecured. Secured

53 Personal Property Security Act, Section 30(1).
54 *iTrade*, cited above.
55 MacDougall, *Canadian Personal Property and Security Law*, at 382.
56 Personal Property Security Act, Section 33.
57 Personal Property Security Act, Section 33(1)(a).
58 Personal Property Security Act, Section 33(1)(b).
59 Personal Property Security Act, Section 33(1) and (2): "in the same collateral given by the same debtor."
60 Personal Property Security Act, Section 33(1): "or its proceeds."
61 See below, under heading 3 "Enforcement of retention of title".

creditors, meaning the creditor has a perfected security interest, rank in priority to unsecured creditors.[62] When a debtor defaults on a loan, the secured creditors get priority on what they are owed (determined by the priority ranking under the Personal Property Security Act[63]) and the unsecured creditors are left with the remainder of the debtor's assets (if anything).

In a situation where a third party seizes the goods and that third party is not a creditor, the secured creditors are entitled to the proceeds of the goods, so long as the proceeds are traceable (a concept which is outlined under the Personal Property Security Act). The same is true if the third party is a creditor ranking subordinate to other secured creditors.[64]

(c) Effect in case of a security right established over goods delivered under retention of title

Many transactions that are governed by the Personal Property Security Act do not require the creditor to maintain possession of the goods in order to perfect the security interest. The only requirement is that a creditor is taking security over assets to secure the payment or performance of an obligation. It is common that the creditor will not possess the goods. Where the creditor does not maintain possession of the goods, there is a security agreement between the parties and the creditor registers a financing statement with the personal property security registrar. This creates an obligation to pay a debt and security over future or existing property (depending on what is contained in the security agreement and financing statement), to ensure that the obligation of the debtor is paid to the creditor.

A secured possessory interest under the Personal Property Security Act can be created through a pledge, whereby a debtor transfers property (the assets) to the creditor. Any asset that is capable of being possessed can be pledged. While the assets are in the possession of the debtor, the debtor is responsible for those assets.[65] When the debt has been repaid in full by the debtor, the creditor may return the assets to the debtor.

The debtor may also enter into a contract to pledge goods to provide security to a creditor (the pledgee). A pledge can only be created where the pledged goods are delivered to or remain in the possession of the pledgee. Accordingly, a special property interest in the pledged goods passes to the pledgee in possession. This interest grants the pledgee the right to sell or otherwise dispose of the goods on default and after notice to the debtor. Where a debtor pledges goods to which he or she does not have title (for example, where there is a retention of title clause), the pledgee is permitted, if necessary, to deliver the goods to the true owner.[66]

(d) Effect in case of bankruptcy

In the case of bankruptcy, the assets of the debtor/bankrupt party are frozen upon the filing of bankruptcy. Under the Bankruptcy and Insolvency Act, a trustee is

---

62 Personal Property Security Act, Section 20(1).
63 See above, under heading 2.3(a) "Effect towards third parties".
64 Personal Property Security Act, Section 25(1).
65 MacDougall, *Canadian Personal Property and Security Law*, at 37-38.
66 CED (online), "Pledges", "Third Parties: Where Pledgor Having No Title" (III.2) at §81-84 (WestLawNext Canada).

appointed to maintain and distribute the debtor's assets among creditors that have previously secured themselves under the Personal Property Security Act. Once a trustee is appointed, the debtor ceases to have capacity to dispose of or otherwise deal with its property, as the property vests in the appointed trustee.[67]

Upon filing for bankruptcy, the trustee will obtain the same rights and title as the debtor had in the property; it will not obtain greater or lesser title.[68] The trustee, however, is only present to distribute the assets appropriately to creditors. The way by which the assets are distributed is governed by the Bankruptcy and Insolvency Act. Creditors who have perfected their security interest under the Personal Property Security Act will receive priority over the bankrupt's assets, in the order of their priority ranking as determined under the Personal Property Security Act.[69] For example, where a creditor can prove it has perfected a security interest, such as a purchase money security interest, under the Personal Property Security Act, that creditor will receive priority over all other creditors in the event of a bankruptcy (see discussion on priorities under heading 2.3(a) "Effect towards third parties" above).

Conversely, unsecured creditors will receive what is left (if anything) on an equal footing and in an equal ratio in comparison to the other interests, after the secured creditors have realised their claims on the assets. In circumstances where the Personal Property Security Act is applicable, retaining title to goods under the Sale of Goods Act does not provide creditors with any protection that would put their interest ahead of another creditor in a bankruptcy situation.

As stated above, in the event of a bankruptcy, only the property of the bankrupt party vests with the trustee. Where the Sale of Goods Act is applicable, property will not vest with the trustee if the bankrupt party does not hold title to that property. For example, if a party retained title to an asset, but that asset happened to be in possession of the bankrupt party at the time of bankruptcy, title to that asset would not vest with the trustee. The owner (the party who retained title to the asset) would have the ability to collect that asset, as title was never transferred. In the event of bankruptcy, however, the trustee will take possession of the assets in possession of the bankrupt party, meaning that the owner (the party that holds title) would be required to file a proof of claim pursuant to Section 81(1) of the Bankruptcy and Insolvency Act. The proof of claim must contain information which enables the asset to be identified by the trustee. Once filed, the trustee must, within 15 days of filing or within 15 days of the first meeting of creditors (whichever is the later), either admit the claim and return the asset to the owner, or provide the owner with notice that the claim is disputed.

In a situation where a buyer goes bankrupt in the course of a transaction, the Sale of Goods Act provides that the unpaid seller who has parted with possession of the goods has the right to stop delivery of goods while they are in the course of transit, if and when the seller becomes aware of the buyer's bankruptcy (or inability to pay debts as they come due).[70]

---

67 Bankruptcy and Insolvency Act, Section 71.

68 *Halsbury's Laws of Canada* (online), "Bankruptcy and Insolvency", "Bankruptcy Trustee: Functions/Role of Bankruptcy Trustee" at HBC-462 "Property of the Bankrupt" (LexisNexis).

69 Personal Property Security Act, Section 20(1)(b).

70 Sale of Goods Act, Section 42.

The process of dividing assets to pay out existing creditors in a scenario covered by the Personal Property Security Act excludes property that the bankrupt party is holding in trust for another, or that is otherwise exempt from seizure under the Bankruptcy and Insolvency Act. No other parties may enter into arrangements with a bankrupt party regarding property that is not exempt. Accordingly, a bankrupt party could not, either through the purchase or sale of goods, or transfer of assets, enter into an agreement that allows another to retain title of property that that party owned at the time of bankruptcy.

If a party enters into a transaction that takes security over property held by a bankrupt party between the date of the first bankruptcy event[71] and the date of bankruptcy, the security will be valid only if that party entered into the transaction in good faith.

Similarly, courts have noted that, with respect to property that is acquired after the date of bankruptcy, a third party may enter into a transaction with a bankrupt party so long as the third party is acting in good faith, value is exchanged from both parties, and the transaction is completed before the intervention of the trustee in bankruptcy. Despite the requirement that the third party act in good faith, it is still permissible for the third party to have knowledge of the bankruptcy, and this knowledge will not, by itself, mitigate against the validity of the transaction.[72] Whether the party is acting in good faith is fact-specific and there have been instances where the third party's knowledge of the bankrupt's "dire financial difficulties" and otherwise bankrupt status was held to negate good faith requirement based on the particulars of the transaction that was struck.[73]

Any property that is held or owned by a bankrupt that is exempt from bankruptcy proceedings may be used in any transaction with a third party without restriction. However, if a bankrupt party uses exempt property to acquire title to non-exempt property, that non-exempt property is subject to distribution to existing creditors.

(e) Effect in case of partial payment of purchase price

With respect to a bankrupt party, if the purchaser has not fully paid for the goods, an unpaid supplier may have access to, and repossess, the goods. However, where the goods have been partly paid for, the supplier's right to repossess the goods shall be a right either to repossess a portion of the goods proportional to the unpaid amount, or to repossess all of the goods on paying the purchaser, trustee, or receiver an amount equal to the partial payment previously made to the supplier.[74]

A secured party under the Personal Property Security Act can have resort to the collateral through its security interest only to satisfy the payment of that amount owing – not later amounts that have not yet become due. If those subsequent

71 The "date of first bankruptcy event" is defined as the earliest of the date of filing or making of: an assignment; a proposal; a notice of intention to make a proposal; an application for a bankruptcy order; or proceedings under the Companies' Creditors Arrangement Act.

72 See LW Houlden & Geoffrey B Morawetz, *Bankruptcy and Insolvency Law of Canada*, 4th edition, (Scarborough, Ont: Carswell, 2009) at F§240; *Cohen v Mitchell* (1890), 25 QBD 262 (CA).

73 See *Re Haley* [1944] 2 DLR 765; 25 CBR 170 (Ont SC).

74 Bankruptcy and Insolvency Act, Section 81.1(1) and (2).

payments are also unpaid as they arise, then the secured party will keep having to take further steps to realise its claim on the collateral.[75]

For the most part, the Personal Property Security Act and the Sale of Goods Act do not provide for alternative requirements where a defaulting debtor has paid part of the purchase price. The only exception to this is with respect to 'consumer goods' (as defined in the Personal Property Security Act).

Section 65 of the Personal Property Security Act provides that where the debtor has paid 60% or more of the purchase price of the consumer goods, upon default, the creditor is required to dispose of the goods properly, according to the guidelines in Section 63, and must account for any surplus back to the debtor. If the creditor fails to do so, the debtor has recourse under Section 67(2) of the act to have a judgment against the creditor to recover the greater of $500 or the actual loss or damages suffered.

In any case, the creditor always has the option of disposing of the property in a commercially reasonable manner, and is required to distribute the surplus to any other parties who have an interest in the property and to the debtor, if any surplus remains after debts are satisfied.[76] However, the creditor also retains the right in all cases, other than with respect to consumer goods where the debtor has paid more or equal to 60% of the debt, to retain title to the property in full satisfaction of the debt.[77]

Where the debtor believes that the creditor's disposition rights or rights of retention have prejudiced its rights, the debtor is always entitled to make an application to the court under Section 67 of the Personal Property Security Act for relief. This section provides that the Superior Court of Justice may give directions and grant a range of orders regarding the exercise of the secured party's rights and the discharge of the debtor's obligations under Part V of the act.

3. Enforcement of retention of title

Under the Sale of Goods Act, if a seller has not received the full purchase price for goods sold but the title to the goods has passed to the buyer, the seller still has, so long as it remains in possession of the goods or the goods are still in transit to the buyer, by implication of law, four main rights:

- The seller can take a lien over the goods, or partial goods, so long as the seller is in possession of the goods and remains in possession of the goods until payment is made;[78]
- The seller has a right to stop the delivery of goods, or delivery of partial goods, while they are in transit and retains this right until the goods are in possession of the buyer (after which the right is extinguished);[79]
- Generally, the seller has a right to resell the goods, notwithstanding that the goods have already been sold;[80] and
- The seller has any other contractual remedies provided for in the sales contract.

---

75 MacDougall, *Canadian Personal Property and Security Law*, at 102.
76 Personal Property Security Act, Sections 63 and 64.
77 Personal Property Security Act, Section 65(2).
78 Sale of Goods Act, Sections 38(1)(a), 39 and 40.
79 Sale of Goods Act, Sections 38(1)(b) and 40.
80 Sale of Goods Act, Section 38(1)(b).

Under the Sale of Goods Act, if a seller has not received the full purchase price, whether or not the seller retains title and/or retains possession, the seller may bring an action against the buyer for the full contract price.[81]

There is nothing under the Sale of Goods Act, however, that automatically permits the seller to, upon breach of contract, seize the goods from the buyer. Such an enforcement mechanism would need to be set out in the contract as between the parties and enforced in court, if necessary. In addition to the above stipulated enforcement mechanisms, the seller may apply to the court for the enforcement of any "right, duty or liability" that the Sale of Goods Act creates.[82]

In the case of enforcement, a secured party is entitled to follow the rules as set out under the Personal Property Security Act. The law is silent as to whether there is a specific organisation that is solely authorised or needs to be involved in the repossession of goods for the owner, but it is assumed that the secured party is entitled to involve a bailiff or agency to realise its right of enforcement, if it chooses.

However, in the event that the debtor has filed for bankruptcy, in order to realise its security, a creditor with retention of title must provide the debtor with a notice of intention in accordance with Section 244 of the Bankruptcy and Insolvency Act not less than 10 days prior to the date on which it intends to enforce.[83]

In terms of the mechanics of realising on its security interest, a creditor only has a right to take possession of the collateral[84] if:

- the debtor has failed to pay its debt when due;
- the debtor otherwise failed to perform an obligation when required; or
- there is an event that the terms of the security agreement deems to be a default.[85]

If the collateral is the right to collect on an account or on chattel paper, the secured party has a right to notify any person obligated under the account or chattel paper that they will henceforth be obligated to it, instead.[86] In the case of conversion (an action or act which is inconsistent with the owner or possessor's rights), a creditor can take control of any proceeds to which it is entitled, so long as the proceeds of the collateral are traceable.[87] The property, however, must be seized by peaceful means, without provoking a breach of the peace, and without trespass.[88]

There is no statutory rule under the Personal Property Security Act that requires a secured party to give notice to the debtor when deciding to enforce its interest upon default, however, the common law requires the secured party both to give notice of default and the demand for payment to the debtor,[89] and to give the debtor sufficient time to remedy the default, prior to it proceeding against collateral.[90] It has

81 Sale of Goods Act, Section 47.
82 Sale of Goods Act, Section 55.
83 Bankruptcy and Insolvency Act, Section 244(2).
84 Personal Property Security Act, Section 62(1)(a).
85 Personal Property Security Act, Section 1(1).
86 Personal Property Security Act, Section 61.
87 Personal Property Security Act, Sections 61(1)(b), and 25(1).
88 Personal Property Security Act, Section 62(10(a); *Regina v Doucette*, [1960] OR 407 (Ont CA).
89 *RE Lister Ltd v Dunlop Canada Ltd*, [1982] 1 SCR 726; 42 NR 181.
90 *Waldron v Royal Bank* (1991), 53 BCLR (2d) 294; 78 DLR (4th) 1.

been suggested in certain jurisdictions that parties may be able to contract out of this common law notice period in the security agreement itself, however to date, this has not been found to be valid.[91]

With respect to the length of the common law notice period, there is no prescribed length of time. Instead, notice periods are determinable on a case-by-case basis with consideration owed to the amount of the loan, the risk to the creditor of losing its money, the length of the relationship between the parties, the character and reputation of the debtor, the potential ability of the debtor to raise the money required in a short period, and the circumstances surrounding the demand for payment.[92]

Repossession requires actual physical possession of the collateral by the creditor. However, if the collateral is equipment and is on the debtor's premises and it is not reasonable to remove it in order to take possession, the creditor is able to merely render the equipment unusable by the debtor in order to be deemed to have taken possession.[93]

A secured party is also able to appoint a receiver or receiver and manager if the security agreement provides for that, or have any one of those appointed by a court, if necessary.[94]

Once the secured party has repossessed the property, it may choose (in most cases) to retain the property in full satisfaction of the debt,[95] or to dispose of the property and apply the proceeds to its debt.[96] In either case, the secured party must give 15 days' notice in writing to the debtor who owes the payment, every party that is known by the creditor to be an owner of the collateral, and every party that has a security interest in the collateral.[97]

The notice of disposal must have a number of features, including a description of the collateral, the amount needed to satisfy the obligation, and a statement that unless the amounts due are paid, the collateral will be disposed of and the debtor may be liable for any deficiency.[98]

Notice of disposal is not required in a number of different circumstances, including where the collateral is perishable, where the collateral will decline speedily in value, and where the cost of care and storage of the collateral is disproportionately large relative to its value.[99]

If the property is disposed of and the proceeds applied to the debt, any surplus achieved from the sale is required to be distributed, in order, to any other party with a subordinate, perfected security interest in the collateral, any other party with an interest in the surplus who has delivered written notice, and then all that remains shall go to the debtor or any other party who had an ownership interest in the

---

91 MacDougall, *Canadian Personal Property and Security Law*, at 428-429.

92 *Kavcar Investments v Aetna Financial Services Ltd* (1989), 70 OR (2d) 225; 62 DLR (4th) 277 (Ont CA); MacDougall, *Canadian Personal Property and Security Law*, at 429.

93 Personal Property Security Act, Section 62(1).

94 Personal Property Security Act, Section 60.

95 Personal Property Security Act, Section 65(2).

96 Personal Property Security Act, Section 64.

97 Personal Property Security Act, Section 63(4).

98 Personal Property Security Act, Section 63(5).

99 Personal Property Security Act, Section 63(7).

collateral.[100] Where there is a deficiency, the secured party is still entitled to collect the remainder of the debt from the debtor, subject to contrary terms in the Personal Property Security Act or unless otherwise agreed in the security agreement.[101]

The collateral must be sufficiently identifiable in order for a creditor or third party to seize the collateral of the debtor.

If the property that is subject to retention of title has been disposed of by the buyer to a third party or otherwise, and it is no longer recoverable, the secured party may have tracing rights with respect to the proceeds of the disposition.[102]

Other than property that is disposed of, there is no specific additional or alternative protocol that must be followed in the event that the property subject to the retention of title is in the possession of a third party. The same protocol would apply whether the property is in the debtor's possession or in the possession of a third party.

The authors would like to thank Jessica George and F Jeremy Hourigan (summer student and student-at-law, respectively, at Gowling Lafleur Henderson LLP) for their contributions to this chapter.

100 Personal Property Security Act, Section 64(1).
101 Personal Property Security Act, Section 64(3).
102 Personal Property Security Act, Section 25(1).

China

Kelly Bai
Rogier van Bijnen
R&P China Lawyers

1. General remarks about retention of title

Although the concept of private property has been recognised in China for many years, both in practice and in the law,[1] it was not codified in China's Constitution until 2004.[2] It took China even until 2007 to enact its first ever Property Law. In that sense it is remarkable that retention of title had already been codified since 1999 in Article 134 of the Contract Law:[3]

> *The parties to a sales contract may agree that the ownership shall belong to the seller if the buyer fails to pay the price or perform other obligations.*

Even though China is considered a civil law jurisdiction, it does not have a civil code. Instead, it has enacted several separate laws, each of which deals with its own specific topic. The result is a set of laws that is by no means complete, and there is no all-encompassing system of civil law with well-established legal doctrines. Furthermore, case law is not considered a binding precedent for future cases, although it can help one understand how Chinese judges generally apply the law.

Key legislation for issues related to retention of title includes:

- the Contract Law (1999);
- the Property Law (2007);
- the Security Law (1995), regulating security rights together with the Property Law;
- the Bankruptcy Law (2007);
- the Civil Procedure Law (1991, last amended 2012) regulating enforcement; and
- the Law on the Application of Laws for Foreign-related Civil Relationships (2010) (referred to below as 'the Conflicts Law'), containing China's main body of international private law.

In addition, the Supreme People's Court has issued certain so-called

1 See for example Article 71 of the General Principles of Civil Law of the People's Republic of China (1986), which describes property ownership as "the owner's rights to lawfully possess, utilise, profit from and dispose of his property."

2 The Constitution of the People's Republic of China was first adopted in 1982; since its fourth amendment in 2004, Article 13 states: "The state protects the rights of citizens to own lawfully earned income, savings, houses and other lawful property."

3 According to certain scholars retention of title had an implicit legal basis before under Article 72 of the General Principles of Civil Law (1986), and Article 84 of Interpretations of the Supreme People's Court on Certain Issues Concerning the Implementation of the General Principles of the Civil Law of the People's Republic of China (1988) (referred to below as the 'SPC Civil Law Interpretations').

interpretations of the above laws, providing further guidance. Unlike case law, Supreme People's Court interpretations do bind lower Chinese courts, and therefore in practice have the effect of law. The following three Supreme People's Court interpretations contain specific provisions on retention of title:

- Interpretations on Issues Concerning the Application of the Law for the Trial of Cases of Disputes over Sales Contracts (2012) (referred to below as the 'SPC Sales Contract Interpretations');
- Second Interpretations on Various Issues in Relation to the Application of the Bankruptcy Law (2013) (referred to below as the 'SPC Bankruptcy Interpretations'); and
- Interpretations of the Authority for People's Courts to Seal up, Seize and Freeze Property in Civil Enforcement (2004, amended 2008) (referred to below as the 'SPC Enforcement Interpretations').

Given the recent history of ownership and other relevant legal concepts, it should not surprise that the legal framework for retention of title in China has not yet been fully developed and certain questions remain. Retention of title is, however, generally recognised and routinely enforced by Chinese courts, while there are few formalities for establishing a valid retention of title. It is therefore a proven and cost-effective method for sellers to protect their interests.

2. Transfer of ownership

Articles 6 and 23 of the Property Law provide that ownership of movable property transfers at the time of delivery, unless otherwise provided by law. Article 133 of the Contract Law, which applies to sales contracts, provides the same, but adds that contracting parties are free to agree on any other moment of transfer. The same follows from Article 72 of the General Principles of Civil Law, while Article 84 of the SPC Civil Law Interpretations adds that if property has been delivered, transfer of ownership may still be subject to conditions.[4] This includes the possibility to agree on retention of title, as has explicitly been confirmed by Article 134 of the Contract Law, quoted above. Besides the time of transfer, parties are also free to determine the time, location and method of delivery.[5]

Other means of transfer and delivery of movable property that have explicitly been recognised under Chinese law (subject to contractual arrangements otherwise) are:

- in the case of property that is already in the possession of the transferee, delivery occurs and title transfers upon execution of the contract;
- in the case of property that is in the possession of a third party, delivery (and thereby transfer of title) may also occur by transferring the right to require delivery from such third party;
- in the case of property that is and remains in the possession of the transferor, title transfers upon execution of the contract; and

4 SPC Civil Law Interpretations (see note 3 above).
5 Articles 61, 62 and 138 to 141 of the Contract Law.

- in the case of property that needs carriage, delivery (and thereby transfer of title) occurs when the seller hands over the goods to the first carrier.[6]

The ownership of immovable property transfers upon completion of the registration thereof with the relevant authorities.[7] Retention of title with respect to an immovable property is, however, explicitly prohibited in China,[8] so in this chapter we will only focus on movable goods.

Article 106 of the Property Law is a key provision when it comes to retention of title. The first part of this article provides the legal basis for retention of title having legal effect against third parties (see further below):[9]

Where immovable or movable property is transferred to a transferee by a person without the authority to do so, the rightful owner shall have the right to recover such property.

As in many jurisdictions, third parties acting in good faith are also protected in China. Article 106 of the Property Law therefore further provides that, despite an unauthorised transfer, a third party shall nevertheless acquire ownership if three conditions can be satisfied:

unless otherwise provided by law, the transferee shall obtain ownership of such immovable or movable property if:

(i) the transferee acquired the property in good faith;

(ii) the property was transferred at a reasonable price; and

(iii) the transferred property has been duly registered in accordance with the law if so required, or has been delivered to the transferee if no registration is required.

In addition, when it comes to movables for which registration of transfer is required (such as vessels, aircraft and motor vehicles), Article 24 of the Property Law provides that the transfer of ownership cannot be held against a third party acting in good faith before such registration has been completed (thereby effectively removing reasonable price as an independent condition). The result is that sellers of such movable property which requires registration enjoy quite strong protection under Chinese law if they sell the goods subject to retention of title (provided the registration remains unchanged).[10]

This is of course quite different for sellers of goods that do not require any registration, which is the majority of movables. Since third parties are unable to verify the existence of any retention of title, it is these third parties who enjoy most protection (provided they can satisfy all the criteria mentioned above). Article 106 of

6 Articles 25 to 27 of the Property Law; Articles 140 and 141 of the Contract Law.

7 Articles 6 and 9 of the Property Law.

8 Article 34 of the SPC Sales Contract Interpretations; see also further below under "Scope of retention of title".

9 See also Article 34 of the PRC Property Law, which provides the more general rule that if someone takes possession of property without the right thereto, the person entitled to possession may request the return of such property.

10 Even if the registration has changed, seller may still be protected: in *Shanghai Jiuhe Boat Import/Export Co, Ltd vs Zhoushan Fushen Boat Mortgage Co.* (2014 浙海终字第17号) the ownership registration was changed to buyer, but seller withheld the title certificate, upon which the court found the mortgagee to have been acting in bad faith, since as a professional mortgage company it should have understood that, despite the change in registration, there was a seller with retention of title rights now buyer could not produce the title certificate.

the Property Law confirms that where a third party has acquired ownership, all that is left for the original seller would be a claim for damages:

Where the transferee has obtained the ownership in respect of immovable or movable property in accordance with the preceding paragraph, the original owner of the right shall have the right to claim damages from the party that had no right of disposal.

The last part of Article 106 of the Property Law confirms that the protection of third parties acting in good faith also applies to other property rights (such as security rights, see further below):

Where the parties concerned have obtained other property rights in good faith, the preceding two paragraphs shall apply mutatis mutandis.

3. Establishing a valid retention of title provision

Retention of title is explicitly allowed in China and codified in Article 134 of the PRC Contract Law:

The parties to a sales contract may agree that the ownership shall belong to the seller if the buyer fails to pay the price or perform other obligations.

There are no further formalities required and parties are free to agree on a retention of title provision in their contract as they deem fit. This means that retention of title can be agreed upon both orally and in writing.[11] There is no need for any notarisation or registration, and there are no requirements as to the wording of the retention of title clause (as long as the parties' intention to establish retention of title is apparent).

Rules of evidence in China are very strict, however, so it is advisable to obtain an original written agreement from the counterparty with its official company chop affixed to it.[12] Otherwise, a seller could find itself in great difficulty proving the existence of the retention of title. If this is not practicable, one should at least obtain an email or fax from the other side (preferably from someone with authority) wherein the contract terms (including the retention of title) are confirmed, but this method is obviously not 100% waterproof.[13]

It is permissible to agree on retention of title in general terms and conditions, and Chinese courts have enforced such retention of title provisions.[14] General terms, however, need to be explicitly confirmed by affixing the counterparty's company chop thereto. Simply referring to general terms on letterhead or in the main contract will usually be without effect (even if the other side has been provided with a copy of the terms). The party drafting general terms should abide by the principle of fairness (which may affect certain far-reaching forms of retention of title), and the rule that the construction to be adopted will be that least favourable to the person seeking to rely on the document applies when it comes to interpreting terms and conditions.[15]

---

11 Article 10 of the Contract Law.

12 Affixing the official company chop constitutes a legally binding agreement under Chinese law. As to signatures, only the signature of the so-called legal representative of a Chinese company will bind that company (unless there is a power of attorney, but this requires the company chop or the legal representative's signature).

13 According to Article 1 of the SPC Sales Contracts Interpretations, if there is no written contract, but there are "delivery notes, goods received notes, settlement statements and invoices", Chinese courts may conclude that there is a contract on the basis of "the transaction methods and customary business practices between the parties as well as other relevant evidence".

14 See, eg, *Wuxi Lude Technology Co v Shanghai BaozhenXin Trading Co* (2006).

Chinese law does not require goods to be delivered directly to the purchaser, in order for retention of title to be effective. As mentioned above, parties are free to determine their own place of delivery. The ownership of goods will therefore also remain with the seller under a retention of title provision if the parties have, for example, agreed on delivery at a warehouse.[16]

4. Scope of retention of title

Besides Article 134 of the Contract Law, quoted above, there are no other Chinese laws explicitly dealing with retention of title. In 2012, the Supreme Court therefore provided further guidance in the SPC Sales Contract Interpretations. Below we discuss Articles 34 to 37 of these interpretations which determine the scope of retention of title in China.

Article 34 of the SPC Sales Contract Interpretations makes clear that retention of title is not allowed when selling immovable property:

Where a party to a sales contract claims that the provisions on the retention of ownership of the subject matter in Article 134 of the Contract Law apply to immovable property, the people's court shall not support such claims.

The first paragraph of Article 35 of the SPC Sales Contract Interpretations provides that a seller may reclaim its property under a retention of title provision if the purchase price has not been paid when due, other specific conditions in the contract have not been met, or the buyer disposes of or pledges the goods (regardless of whether this occurs in the ordinary course of business):

If the parties agree on the retention of ownership, and prior to the transfer of ownership of the subject matter, the buyer meets any of the following conditions and causes damage to the seller, and the seller claims recovery of the subject matter, the people's court shall support such claims:

(1) fails to make payment as agreed;

(2) fails to fulfil specific conditions as agreed; or

(3) sells, pledges or conducts any other improper disposal of the subject matter.

The last condition in the third indent confirms that the basic rule of Article 106 of the Property Law, allowing an owner to recover its property from third parties if it is transferred to them without authorisation (see above), also applies to retention of title. This means that a buyer receiving goods subject to retention of title is in principle not allowed to transfer these goods, and if he does, the retention of title provision has automatic effect against third parties.

The above is subject to any contractual arrangement to the contrary. If parties, for example, agree that buyer is allowed to sell or encumber the goods in its ordinary course of business, such agreement shall prevail.[17] Parties may also agree that any purchase price received from a third party shall automatically be transferred to the seller, but such an agreement has no effect against third parties (this could be different in an enforcement situation, see below).

15 Articles 39 and 41 of the Contract Law.

16 See, eg, *Zhang v Hebei Geological Mining Construction Group* (2013).

17 According to Article 51 of the Contract Law any unauthorised transfer may also be ratified after the fact.

The phrase "fails to fulfil the specific conditions as agreed" in the second indent set out above,[18] suggests the scope of retention of title may be widened to become an 'all monies' retention of title provision. Under such an arrangement, title only transfers upon the buyer satisfying all its outstanding debts with seller, including debts related to other contracts. There are, however, examples of Chinese courts rejecting such a broad interpretation.[19] In any event, the 75% rule, discussed below, will most likely block an all monies retention of title provision in practice.

The second paragraph of Article 35 of the SPC Sales Contract Interpretations holds the buyer responsible for any diminution in value of the goods recovered by seller under a retention of title provision:

If the value of the recovered subject matter is substantially reduced, and the seller demands that the buyer compensates him for losses, the people's court shall support such demands.

The first paragraph of Article 36 of the SPC Sales Contract Interpretations introduces the 75% rule, which denies seller the right of recovery if buyer has paid at least 75% of the purchase price:

If the buyer has paid 75% or more of the total price of the subject matter, and the seller claims recovery of the subject matter, the people's court shall not support such claims.

Even though in theory it may be permissible to make the transfer of title subject to other conditions than payment of the purchase price (see above), such conditions will probably fail in practice due to this 75% rule. In general, this rule, which seems to be strictly enforced by the Chinese courts,[20] poses an important limitation on the seller's protection under a retention of title provision (although in a bankruptcy situation the seller would have priority over common creditors, see below). This is especially true since it is not uncommon for Chinese buyers to delay or withhold the last payment once goods have been delivered. Note that if the buyer has paid 80% or less and the agreement qualifies as an instalment contract (which it usually will), Article 167 of the Contract Law may be an alternative. Under this article the seller may terminate an instalment contract (and claim a usage fee for the period until termination) if the buyer's overdue payments amount to at least 20% of the total purchase price, which also applies if the goods are sold subject to retention of title.[21]

We referred above to the basic rule of Article 106 of the Property Law, which implies that a retention of title provision has automatic effect against third parties. However, Article 106 also protects third parties acting in good faith, who paid a reasonable price, where the transfer has been registered (if required) or the property has been delivered (if no registration is required). The second paragraph of Article 36 of the SPC Sales Contract Interpretations explicitly confirms that such protection also applies if the relevant property is subject to retention of title (although the seller enjoys priority over common creditors in a bankruptcy setting, see below):

Under the circumstances as prescribed in Item (3) of Paragraph 1 of Article 35 of these

---

18 Note that this is very similar to "fails to … perform other obligations" as stated in the key provision on retention of title in Article 134 of the Contract Law (see above).

19 See, eg, *Zhanjiang Potou Co v Li Changfu* (2004).

20 See, eg, *Handan Jinshi Cotton Machine Co Ltd v Agricultural Bank of China* (2014); *Lu Wandu v Henan Jinfu Leiwo Engineering Machinery Co* (2013).

21 See, eg, *Ningxia Weicheng Engineering Machinery Co v Ma Lizhong* (2013).

Interpretations, if a third party has acquired ownership of the subject matter or other property rights in good faith according to Article 106 of the Property Law, and the seller claims recovery of the subject matter, the people's court shall not support such claims.

The phrase "other property rights" mainly includes security rights. Below we discuss that good-faith holders of certain security enjoy similar protection as third-party transferees, and may have priority over a seller with retention of title. Besides a third party obtaining ownership or security rights in good faith, there are no other special mechanisms under Chinese law protecting creditors of the buyer or governmental bodies (such as tax authorities) against claims from sellers under retention of title provisions.

Finally, Article 37 of the SPC Sales Contract Interpretations deals with the aftermath of when a seller has successfully recovered goods subject to retention of title. The first paragraph states that the seller must grant the buyer a grace period to pay the purchase price, and if the buyer pays within that period, the buyer may redeem the goods:[22]

After the subject matter is recovered by the seller, if the buyer eliminates the grounds for recovery of the subject matter by the seller within the redemption period agreed upon by both parties or as designated by the seller, and the buyer claims redemption of the subject matter, the people's court shall support such claim.

The last part of Article 37 of the SPC Sales Contract Interpretations sets the rules applicable in the event that the buyer still does not pay within the grace period. If the seller decides to sell the goods, it may set off all its damages against the proceeds of the sale and return the rest to the buyer (which will largely depend on how much of the original purchase price the buyer has already paid to the seller). If the price received is insufficient to cover the seller's damages, the buyer shall be liable for the remainder, unless the seller sold the goods below market value:

If the buyer fails to redeem the subject matter within the redemption period, the seller may sell the subject matter. If the seller sells the subject matter and there is a remainder of the proceeds derived from the sale after the expenses regarding the return, custody, resale, interest, and unliquidated price have been deducted, the remainder shall be returned to the original buyer; if the proceeds derived from the sale are insufficient, if the seller demands that the original buyer pays off the outstanding amount, the people's court shall support such request, except where the original buyer has evidence to prove that the seller's selling price was clearly below the market price.

5. Combining, mixing and processing of property

Chinese law provides little guidance as to what will happen with ownership rights if property is combined or mixed with other property, or when it is processed. The Property Law does recognise in various provisions that property rights can be extinguished, but is silent on the specific conditions therefor.[23] Article 115 of the

22 In practice, the buyer will often also have a grace period prior to recovery, since the seller usually needs to initiate legal proceedings in order to recover its property if buyer is not cooperative (see further below in discussion of enforcement).

23 For example, Articles 6, 9, 14, 15, 24, 28 and 30 of the Property Law; note that property rights of an immovable property can only be extinguished upon registration thereof (Articles 6 and 9).

Property Law states that accessory property shall be transferred together with its principal property (unless the parties have provided otherwise), but it is not fully clear whether this also applies if such accessories are owned by a third party.

In practice, if a person's property is combined with, or attached to, someone else's immovable property (but is still identifiable), Chinese courts have often relied on Article 86 of the SPC Civil Law Interpretations.[24] This article provides that an owner may require its attached property to be dismantled if possible (unless the parties have agreed otherwise), but it is not fully clear whether this also applies when movables are being attached to other movables (such as a motor in a car):

Where any party other than a property owner adds appurtenance to any other person's property that he/she uses, if the property owner agrees to such an addition and an agreement on how to deal with the appurtenance is made, such agreement shall apply; where there is neither such agreement nor any agreement reached through consultation, if the appurtenance can be dismantled, that party may be ordered to dismantle it; if the appurtenance cannot be dismantled, that party may convert it into money and pay the money to the property owner, and shall be liable for compensation in the event of any loss caused to the property owner.

The result is that sellers with ownership rights under retention of title do not necessarily lose ownership if their property is attached to other property, since they may be allowed to have it dismantled if possible. There are, however, no clear criteria to decide whether dismantling is still possible.[25] In one particular case a court ruled, for example, that the seller, who sold gas pipes subject to retention of title, was still the owner thereof, despite the pipes having been connected to the municipal gas network. Nevertheless, the seller had no right of recovery, since the court attached more weight to the public interest.[26]

It becomes of course more difficult when a property owner is no longer able to identify its property, because it has been mixed (commingled) with other property, or processed into something else. There are no clear rules on how to deal with such situations under Chinese law, and the main hurdle for a property owner seems to be that he will no longer be able to prove his ownership.[27]

When clarifying several issues with respect to the Security Law, the Supreme People's Court has recognised in its interpretations, in the context of mortgaged goods, that ownership may pass to a third party due to attachment, mixture or processing with other property:[28]

---

24 See note 3; see, eg, *Beijing Xin Heng Xin Chang Information Consulting Co v Beijing Jing Men Liang Shi State Owned Property Management Co* (2005); *Xiamen Haicang District Longxiangsheng Construction Machinery Co v Xiamen Chongfa Machinery Co* (2011); *Wang Wende v Zhang Liang* (2012).

25 Some have argued that Article 110 of the Contract Law should apply by analogy, which provides that a creditor of a non-monetary debt may not require specific performance if this would be factually impossible, not allowed by law, unsuitable or excessively expensive; but this view has not (yet) been confirmed.

26 *Henan Province Natural Gas Group Guo Long Co v Shanxi Dongshen Plastic Pipes Co* (2014).

27 Sometimes courts help a seller facing such difficulty; in *Zhejiang Chenggong Plastic Co v Ningbo Zhenhai Haizhu Chemicals* (2013) the seller had trouble identifying certain gas it sold subject to retention of title, upon which the court shifted the burden of proof, and required the buyer to prove it had actually sold this gas to a third party.

28 Article 62 of the SPC Interpretations of Several Issues Concerning the Application of PRC Security Law (2000) (referred to below as the "SPC Security Law Interpretations").

If ownership of the mortgaged property passes to a third party due to attachment to or mixture with other property or through processing, the effect of the mortgage extends to the consideration paid for the foregoing.

When delivering goods subject to retention of title that are of such a nature that it is likely the buyer will mix or process them, there is a clear risk under Chinese law that ownership passes and the retention of title will be without effect. Contractual provisions prohibiting a buyer from mixing or processing goods will have little effect if the buyer breaches such provisions. Only factual measures, such as marking goods or storing them separately, may possibly prevent this.

The SPC interpretations quoted above suggest that a mortgage provides a seller with rights superior to retention of title in the event of attachment, mixture or processing of property. In such a case the mortgage would extend to the consideration received by the buyer for the attached, mixed or processed goods. This suggests that the mortgagee enjoys priority over ordinary creditors regarding such funds.

6. Retention of title and security rights

Mortgage and pledge are the two types of security that are relevant in the context of retention of title. A mortgage is non-possessory security (possession is not transferred to the mortgagee), while a pledge is possessory security (possession is transferred to the pledgee).[29] Note that there is no transfer of title to the security holder under either mortgage or pledge (unlike with mortgages in common law jurisdictions, where there is usually a transfer of title).

There are some restrictions as to what property may be mortgaged or pledged, but generally speaking all goods that in practice could be made subject to retention of title could at the same time also serve as collateral under a Chinese-law governed mortgage or pledge (such as vessels, aircraft, motor vehicles, production equipment, raw materials, half-products and products).[30] It is not permissible to agree that the mortgagee or pledgee may retain the goods if the debtor defaults; so in such circumstances the goods need to be sold or auctioned, after which the proceeds will be used to satisfy the debt.[31]

It is also possible to create a floating mortgage over existing and future property (similar to the common law floating charge). Property that can be made subject to a floating mortgage is limited to production equipment, raw materials, half-products and products.[32] Unlike an ordinary mortgage where each transfer requires the mortgagee's approval, the mortgagor under a floating mortgage may sell the encumbered assets to third parties who purchase them against a reasonable price in their ordinary course of business.[33]

---

29 Articles 33 and 63 of the Security Law; note that Article 223 of the Property Law also allows for a pledge on rights (eg, shares, bills of lading, accounts receivable), but this type of pledge falls outside the scope of this chapter.

30 Articles 180, 184 and 209 of the Property Law; certain specific types of property may not be mortgaged, while in principle all movables may be pledged, provided possession can be legally transferred to the pledgee.

31 Articles 186 and 211 of the Property Law; Articles 40 and 66 of the Security Law; note that such agreement is allowed *after* the debtor has defaulted.

32 Article 181 of the Property Law; institutions, social organisations and natural persons not engaged in production activities may, however, not encumber their assets under a floating mortgage.

33 Articles 189 and 191 of the Property Law.

Both a mortgage and a pledge require a written contract.[34] A mortgage comes into effect upon registration thereof (in the case of immovable property) or upon the conclusion of the mortgage contract (in the case of movables), while a pledge becomes effective upon delivery of the movable to the pledgee.[35] A mortgage on a movable has, however, no effect against third parties acting in good faith until registration of the mortgage has been completed.[36]

A party possessing certain property may only mortgage or pledge this if he has ownership rights or any other rights of disposal.[37] The buyer of property subject to retention of title is therefore not allowed to mortgage or pledge this without approval of the seller. In the event of an unauthorised pledge, Chinese law is clear that the seller may recover its property, since Article 35 of the SPC Sales Contract Interpretations explicitly allows for recovery if the buyer "sells, pledges or conducts any other improper disposal of the subject matter".

There is, however, no "disposal of the subject matter" when creating a mortgage.[38] This only occurs when the mortgagee enforces the mortgage, by which time it is usually too late from the seller's perspective. Under Chinese law it is unclear whether the seller could recover its property subject to retention of title upon the creation of an unauthorised mortgage.[39] It is therefore advisable for a seller to add the provision that the buyer is not allowed to encumber the goods subject to retention of title, and that the seller is entitled to immediate recovery in case of any breach of that provision.

Even though the buyer of goods subject to retention of title is not allowed to encumber them, a third party taking security in good faith may, however, enjoy protection under the basic rule of Article 106 of the Property Law (see above). This article applies (with the necessary changes) to security rights (see above), which results in the following conditions:

- the security holder must have acted in good faith;
- the encumbered property must have been valued at a reasonable price;[40] and
- a mortgage must have been registered, while pledged property must have been delivered to the security holder.

---

34 Articles 185 and 210 of the Property Law; Articles 38 and 64 of the Security Law.

35 Articles 187, 188 and 212 of the Property Law; Articles 41, 43 and 64 of the Security Law; if the pledged good is in the possession of a third party, the delivery of the good to the pledgee may be effected by sending the possessor written notice thereof, see Article 88 of the SPC Security Law Interpretations.

36 Articles 188 and 189 of the Property Law; note that there is no centralised register for mortgages in China. Most movables should be registered at the local administration of industry and commerce where the property is located (Article 42(5) of the Security Law), while a floating mortgage should be registered at the administration of industry and commerce of the mortgagor's place of incorporation (Article 189 of the Property Law). Certain movables (such as cars, ships or planes) are subject to special regulations (Vehicle Registration Regulations 2012, the Maritime Law or the Civil Aviation Law) and require registration elsewhere.

37 Articles 180 and 209 of the Property Law; Article 34 of the Security Law; Article 84 of the SPC Security Law Interpretations.

38 In such a case there is also no unauthorised possession, which would entitle an owner to recover its property under Article 34 of the Property Law, nor any unauthorised transfer, which would result in a right of recovery under Article 106 of the Property Law.

39 Under Article 35 of the Property Law the seller may be able to require the buyer to relinquish the mortgage.

40 See above; this condition does not apply for movables that require registration of ownership (such as cars, planes or vessels).

Although there are plenty of cases involving bad faith, the key question in practice is usually whether the mortgage has been properly registered or the pledged assets have actually been delivered.

Whether a floating mortgage captures any goods subsequently delivered subject to retention of title will largely depend on the wording of the underlying mortgage agreement and the description of the mortgaged property in the register. Is the security limited to certain types of asset owned by the mortgagor, or does it simply refer to all assets in the possession of the mortgagor or all assets located at certain premises?

Where a good-faith security holder is protected in accordance with the above, the security will be validly established. A seller can in such a case only recover its property subject to retention of title with the approval of the security holder.[41] Such approval is of course unlikely if the buyer does not clear its debts, in which case the seller will only be left with a claim for damages against the buyer for unauthorised infringement of the seller's property rights (although the seller will enjoy priority over common creditors if buyer goes into bankruptcy; see below).[42]

Given the strong protection for mortgage holders under Chinese law, a seller could also consider establishing a mortgage instead of a retention of title, provided the value of the goods is such that it is worth going to the trouble of entering into a separate mortgage agreement and registering the mortgage. Assuming there is no existing floating mortgage already capturing the property, the risk of third parties obtaining superior rights is minimal if the mortgage is properly registered, since it will take priority over mortgages that have been registered at a later date and also over pledges (only the holder of a lien has superior rights; see below).[43] Note that even though restrictions for foreign security holders have recently been relaxed, they may still require government approval for establishing valid security on domestic assets.[44]

There is no retention of title in China by operation of law. A lien has, however, similar characteristics. A creditor who is in the lawful possession of a debtor's movable property may retain such property where the debtor defaults (a lien should therefore not affect a seller's rights to retention of title, since it only captures the debtor's property).[45] This is mainly relevant for construction, warehousing, repair, transportation and processing contracts. A lien is automatically established by operation of law, although parties are free to agree otherwise or to modify the terms under which the lien operates.[46] The lien is a rather strong security right, since it gives a creditor priority, not only over common creditors, but also over holders of a mortgage or pledge.[47]

41 Article 191 of the Property Law requires approval for a transfer in case of a mortgage, while in case of a pledge it follows from Article 219 of the Property Law that the pledgee only needs to return the pledged assets when the debtor has repaid its debts.
42 Article 106 of the Property Law; Article 84 of the SPC Security Law Interpretations.
43 Article 199 of the Property Law; Article 79 of the SPC Security Law Interpretations.
44 Provisions on the Administration of Foreign Exchange for Cross-Border Security (2014) issued by the State Administration for Foreign Exchange; Article 6 of the SPC Security Law Interpretations.
45 Article 230 of the Property Law. For instance, if a buyer instructs a warehouse operator to hold goods that are still subject to retention of title, the lien will only come into existence once the retention of title has terminated and the ownership has transferred to the buyer.
46 Articles 230 and 232 of the Property Law.
47 Articles 230 and 239 of the Property Law.

7. Retention of title in bankruptcy

Article 38 of the Bankruptcy Law lays out the key principle with respect to retention of title in the event that the buyer goes into bankruptcy: property in the possession of a debtor subject to bankruptcy proceedings, but not owned by the debtor, may be recovered by its rightful owners through the administrator. In the event that the seller goes into bankruptcy, Article 17 of the Bankruptcy Law sets out the key principle regarding the seller's property subject to retention of title: any person holding property of the party subject to bankruptcy proceedings should deliver such property to the administrator.

Another key principle relevant for retention of title is set out in Article 18 of the Bankruptcy Law: once bankruptcy proceedings have commenced, the administrator may, in its discretion, elect either to terminate or to continue any unfulfilled contract. In the event of continuance, the counterparty is obliged to perform the contract, but is entitled to request the administrator to provide security for the debtor's performance.

The Bankruptcy Law does not contain any provisions specifically addressing retention of title, but in 2013 the Supreme People's Court provided extensive guidance in the SPC Bankruptcy Interpretations. Article 34 of the SPC Bankruptcy Interpretations explicitly confirms that the administrator may also elect either to terminate or to continue the contract if it contains a retention of title provision:

If the parties to a sale and purchase contract specify in the contract that ownership of the subject matter is retained and one of the parties goes into bankruptcy before ownership of the subject matter passes to the buyer in accordance with the law, and performance of the sale and purchase contract has not been completed by either party, the administrator shall have the right, pursuant to Article 18 of the Bankruptcy Law, to decide either to terminate or to continue performing the contract.

In the remainder of this section we will discuss the four scenarios that may arise in a bankruptcy concerning retention of title: where the buyer goes into bankruptcy and the administrator decides to continue or to terminate the contract; and where the seller goes into bankruptcy and the administrator decides to continue or terminate the contract. In order to get a better grasp of these four scenarios, we summarise the key rules in the matrix on the opposite page.

7.1 Bankruptcy of buyer

In the following paragraphs we focus on the situation where the buyer of property subject to retention of title has gone into bankruptcy proceedings. Article 2 of the SPC Bankruptcy Interpretations first of all confirms that any property subject to retention of title shall not be deemed property of the bankrupt debtor:

The following property shall not be considered property of a debtor: ... property in a retained ownership transaction, whereby the debtor has yet to secure ownership.

(a) Contract continued

If the buyer of property subject to retention of title goes into bankruptcy, and its administrator decides to continue performance of the contract, the first paragraph of Article 37 of the SPC Bankruptcy Interpretations provides that the buyer's obligations shall be accelerated and become immediately due:

Bankruptcy of:	Contract continued	Contract terminated
Buyer	• Goods are not buyer's property • Buyer's obligations accelerated, purchase price immediately payable • If buyer fails to perform, seller may recover goods, unless more than 75% paid or property rights held by third party in good faith • If seller is unable to recover, priority claim for damages over common creditors	• Goods are not buyer's property • Seller may recover its goods • Seller to refund price already received, but may set off damages with priority • If price already paid by buyer is insufficient to cover seller's damages, seller has priority claim over common creditors
Seller	• Buyer to perform in accordance with the contract (no acceleration) • If buyer fails to perform, seller may recover goods, unless more than 75% paid or property rights held by third party in good faith • If seller is unable to recover, buyer shall be liable	• Buyer to return goods, even if buyer did not breach the contract • If buyer did not breach the contract, but already paid part of the price, buyer enjoys priority over common creditors when claiming refund of that payment

If the buyer goes into bankruptcy and its administrator decides to continue to perform the retained ownership sale and purchase contract, the due date specified in the original sale and purchase contract for the payment of the price or performance of other obligations by the buyer shall be deemed to have expired at the time of the acceptance of the bankruptcy petition, and the buyer's administrator shall pay the price to seller or perform the other obligations in a timely manner.

The second paragraph of Article 37 of the SPC Bankruptcy Interpretations confirms that if the buyer's administrator elects to continue the contract, the normal rules for recovery of property subject to retention of title (see above) continue to apply, as do the exceptions thereto (the 75% rule and protection of third parties acting in good faith, both discussed above).

If the buyer's administrator fails to pay the price or complete performance of other obligations in a timely manner without a legitimate reason, or if the buyer's administrator sells, pledges or otherwise improperly disposes of the subject matter, causing damage to the seller, and the seller requests recovery of the subject matter pursuant to Article 134 of the Contract Law, the people's court shall uphold such request, unless the buyer has already paid at least 75% of the total price for the subject matter or a third party has secured ownership of, or other property rights in, the subject matter in good faith.

This does not mean that the seller is left empty-handed if he is unable to recover his property where the buyer already has paid at least 75% or third parties have obtained superior rights. The last paragraph of Article 37 of the SPC Bankruptcy Interpretations provides that the seller will have a claim of 'common interest' in such a case. This means that seller enjoys priority, since debts of common interest are settled prior to all other claims from creditors, save for bankruptcy expenses and claims over secured property:[48]

If the subject matter cannot be recovered as specified in the second paragraph of this article and the seller requests in accordance with the law that the buyer continues to pay the price or completes performance of its other obligations and bear the attendant liability for compensation, the people's court shall uphold such request. If the seller requests that the debt arising from the damage incurred as a result of the failure by the buyer to pay the price or complete performance of the other obligations, or the buyer's administrator selling, pledging or otherwise improperly disposing of the subject matter be discharged as a debt of common interest, the people's court shall uphold such request.

(b) *Contract terminated*

Article 38 of the SPC Bankruptcy Interpretations deals with the opposite situation, whereby buyer's administrator terminates the contract. The first paragraph confirms that in such a case the seller will be entitled to recover its property under Article 38 of the Bankruptcy Law:

If the buyer goes into bankruptcy and the administrator decides to terminate the retained ownership sale and purchase contract, and the seller requests recovery of the subject matter of the transaction pursuant to Article 38 of the Bankruptcy Law, the people's court shall uphold such request.

In contrast to the rules for when an administrator continues the contract, in the event of the administrator terminating the contract, there is no mention of the customary exceptions to the seller's right to recover its property subject to retention of title (ie, the 75% rule and third parties obtaining property rights in good faith). The most logical interpretation is therefore that these exceptions do not apply if the buyer's administrator terminates the contract (but it cannot be ruled out that the courts will adopt another interpretation).[49] As a result, it is likely that a buyer's

48 Articles 43, 109 and 113 of the Bankruptcy Law. See also Article 42(1) of the Bankruptcy Law, which determines that debts incurred by the bankrupt debtor in performing contracts that are continued shall all be deemed to be of common interest.

49 Article 83 of the Law of Legislation (2000) provides that a specific law takes priority over a general law, and it can be argued that since the SPC Bankruptcy Interpretations provide for a more specific situation than the SPC Sales Contract Interpretations, the former prevails (but note that the Law of Legislation does not refer to SPC interpretations). See further note 51 below.

50 Article 106 of the Property Law, which protects third parties who acquire property rights in good faith (see above), of course continues to apply in respect of such third parties, so if the buyer's administrator elects to terminate the contract he would find himself in the unfavourable situation where he has to return the goods subject to retention of title to the seller, but at the same time would be unable to do so due to the third parties' rights.

administrator will elect to continue the contract if one of these exceptions applies, so that he can avoid returning the goods to the seller.[50]

The remainder of Article 38 of the SPC Bankruptcy Interpretations deals with the refund of the purchase price already paid by the buyer and with damages due to the seller, where the administrator has terminated the contract and returned the property to the seller. The key features are that the seller enjoys priority when setting off its damages against the purchase price it needs to refund, and that if the purchase price already paid by buyer is insufficient to cover the seller's damages as a result of the decreased value of the returned property, the remaining claim by the seller shall be a debt of common interest (which gives the seller priority; see above):

If the buyer's administrator requests that the seller refunds the price paid after recovery of the subject matter of the transaction, the people's court shall uphold such request. If the value of the recovered subject matter has been substantially reduced, causing the seller to incur a loss, the seller may, after deducting the amount of such loss from the price paid by the buyer on a priority basis, refund the remainder to the buyer; if the seller requests that the claim arising from the loss incurred as a result of the price paid by the buyer being insufficient to cover the decrease in value of the subject matter be discharged as a debt of common interest, the people's court shall uphold such request.

The last part provides a seller with retention of title rights a rather unusually strong position: not only is the seller entitled to recover its property, but it also enjoys priority over ordinary creditors when recovering certain damages. Since the paragraph starts with the condition that the administrator has claimed a refund, it seems, however, that the seller will only enjoy such priority if there is an actual claim for such a refund (although other interpretations cannot be ruled out). The administrator will of course not require a refund if no purchase price has been paid at all, or if he anticipates that the seller's damages exceed the purchase price that may be refunded.

7.2 Bankruptcy of seller

(a) Contract continued

We will now focus on the situation of bankruptcy of the seller. Article 35 of the SPC Bankruptcy Interpretations applies in the event that the seller's administrator requires continuance of the contract. The rules are basically the same as with bankruptcy of the buyer (see above), with the key difference that the buyer's obligation to pay the purchase price will not accelerate if the administrator demands performance. Instead, the buyer should simply continue to perform its obligations in accordance with the contract:

If the seller goes into bankruptcy and its administrator decides to continue performing the retained ownership sale and purchase contract, the buyer shall pay the price or perform other obligations in accordance with the original sale and purchase contract.

If the seller's administrator requires continuance, but the buyer fails to perform in accordance with the contract, the last part of Article 35 of the SPC Bankruptcy Interpretations confirms that the ordinary rules for recovery of property subject to retention of title apply, as do the usual exceptions (the 75% rule, or third parties obtaining property rights in good faith). If the property cannot be recovered, the buyer shall be liable therefor:

If the buyer fails to pay the price or complete its performance of other obligations as agreed, or sells, pledges or otherwise improperly disposes of the subject matter, causing damage to the seller, and the seller's administrator requests in accordance with the law recovery of the subject matter, the people's court shall uphold such request, unless the buyer has already paid at least 75% of the total price for the subject matter or a third party has secured ownership of, or other property rights in, the subject matter in good faith.

If the subject matter cannot be recovered as specified in the second paragraph of this article and the seller's administrator requests in accordance with the law that the buyer continue to pay the price or complete performance of its other obligations and bear the attendant liability for compensation, the people's court shall uphold such request.

(b) Contract terminated

Article 36 of the SPC Bankruptcy Interpretations covers the opposite scenario whereby the seller's administrator decides to terminate the contract, and confirms that in such a case the basic principle of Article 17 of the Bankruptcy Law applies. This means that the buyer should return the property subject to retention of title to the seller's administrator, even if the buyer did not breach any of its obligations:

If the seller goes into bankruptcy and its administrator decides to terminate the retained ownership sale and purchase contract, and pursuant to Article 17 of the Bankruptcy Law, requests that the buyer delivers to it the subject matter of the transaction, the people's court shall uphold such request.

If the buyer argues in defence that it did not fail to pay the price or complete its performance of other obligations as agreed, or did not sell, pledge or otherwise improperly dispose of the subject matter, the people's court shall reject such argument.

It is of course quite harsh for a buyer who has already paid part of the purchase price to have to return the goods subject to retention of title to a bankrupt seller. The last paragraph of Article 36 of the SPC Bankruptcy Interpretations therefore determines that if the buyer did not breach the contract, his claim to get the part of the purchase price he already paid refunded shall be deemed a debt of common interest, for which the buyer enjoys priority over common creditors:

After the buyer performs its contractual obligations in accordance with the law and delivers the subject matter of the transaction to the seller's administrator pursuant to the first paragraph of this article, the buyer's claim arising from the loss incurred as a result of payment of the price shall be discharged as a debt of common interest. However, if the buyer breached the contract and the seller's administrator requests that the aforementioned claim be discharged as an ordinary bankruptcy claim, the people's court shall uphold such claim.

In contrast to the position where the seller's administrator continues the contract, the regular exceptions for recovery of property subject to retention of title are not explicitly mentioned if the administrator terminates the contract (which is similar to the case where the buyer's administrator terminates the contract, see above). This suggests that the buyer would need to return the property subject to retention of title even if he has already paid at least 75% (but he will get a priority claim in return). It will be more problematic for the buyer if he has already transferred ownership to, or encumbered the goods in favour of, a third party acting in good faith (which he was not allowed to, since ownership remained with seller, see above). Since these third parties enjoy protection,[51] the buyer may simply be unable to return the goods in such a case.

8. Enforcement

There are few specific rules for a seller to enforce its ownership rights in China regarding goods subject to retention of title. Buyers will, generally speaking, not be inclined to return the goods in an enforcement situation, and cooperation by third parties is often also unlikely (although a warehouse operator may, for example, choose to do nothing until it is clear who may take possession of the goods). Self-help (an owner retrieving its property by itself) is not uncommon in China, but usually not recommended for foreign parties.

The courts are the only organisations in China allowed to repossess goods on behalf of an owner if the party possessing them does not cooperate. Each court has its own enforcement department, which has broad powers to seal up, seize and freeze property; and if there is a lack of cooperation, its officers may even issue fines, detain persons and search premises.[52]

A court is only allowed to enforce on the basis of a legally effective judgment, ruling or arbitral award.[53] Unlike the enforcement of security rights,[54] there is no separate, simplified type of legal proceeding for the enforcement of ownership rights. This means that a seller of assets subject to retention of title needs to initiate a general civil proceeding (or arbitration, if so agreed) requesting the court to confirm its ownership rights and to issue a notice of enforcement for the repossession of its property.[55] Once such a judgment (or award) becomes legally effective,[56] if the person possessing the goods still refuses to comply, the seller may request the court of first instance or the court where the property is located to enforce the judgment.[57]

An agreement between a buyer and seller wherein the buyer grants the seller access to its premises to collect the property under certain circumstances will do very little for the seller. Even though there is nothing prohibiting such an agreement under Chinese law, the seller would in practice still need to go to court if the buyer in the end denies access to its premises.

There are no specific rules or formalities the seller needs to fulfil when reclaiming its property in court proceedings. The key challenge for the seller will be identifying

51 It is highly unlikely the SPC Bankruptcy Interpretations will be interpreted by a Chinese court to trump the protection for third parties acting in good faith set forth in the Property Law.

52 Chapter 21 of the Civil Procedure Law.

53 Articles 224, 236 and 237 of the Civil Procedure Law.

54 Articles 196 and 197 of the Civil Procedure Law.

55 The legal basis therefore is usually Articles 32 and 34 of the Property Law, entitling an owner whose property rights are being infringed to initiate litigation and request repossession of its property.

56 This occurs usually after the term for appeal has lapsed, or after the appeal judgment has been rendered (in China there is generally only one appeal possible, while a judicial review is possible once thereafter, but such a judicial review does not suspend the legal effect of the appeal judgment).

57 Article 224 of the Civil Procedure Law.

the relevant goods and proving he is actually the owner thereof. Note that Chinese rules of evidence tend to be very strict: original documents are usually required, which also need to be notarised and legalised if they originate from abroad.

It happens quite regularly that a creditor seizes a debtor's property through the court, while such property is still subject to a seller's retention of title. Article 227 of the Civil Procedure Law explicitly allows a third party to intervene in enforcement proceedings, which may result in the suspension of the enforcement. There are examples of a seller intervening as late as the goods already being auctioned, upon which the court still ruled that the goods should be returned to seller on the basis of its retention of title rights.[58]

Article 18 of the SPC Enforcement Interpretations provides specific guidance in the event that a creditor of the buyer applies for enforcement with respect to property subject to retention of title. The creditor will be allowed to enforce, provided it has paid the remaining part of the purchase price to the seller (note that the seller is referred to as a third party in this article), or if the seller has agreed to be paid, with priority, from the proceeds of the sale of the property subject to retention of title:

> *Where a person subject to enforcement purchases any property from a third party, has paid part of the purchase price and has taken actual possession of such property, but the third party has retained ownership pursuant to the contract, whereby the person applying for enforcement has paid the remaining purchase price to the third party or the third party has agreed in writing that such remaining price may be paid with priority from the proceeds of the property, the people's court is allowed to seal up, seize or freeze the property.*

The second paragraph of Article 18 of the SPC Enforcement Interpretations confirms the basic rule that if the seller is entitled to terminate the contract and repossess its property, the court should stop the ongoing enforcement initiated by the creditor and release the goods. In such a case the creditor may, however, enforce the buyer's rights to be refunded that part of the purchase price that the buyer has already paid to the seller:

> *If the third party terminates the contract in accordance with the law, the people's court shall grant permission, and the sealing, seizing or freezing measure shall be cancelled, provided that the people's court may, upon request by the person applying for enforcement, enforce the creditor's rights of the person subject to enforcement against the third party with respect to the purchase price already paid.*

Article 16 of the SPC Enforcement Interpretations applies to the opposite situation whereby a creditor of the seller applies to the court for seizure of the goods subject to retention of title, which are in the possession of the buyer (note that the buyer is referred to as a third party in this article). In such a case, seizure is allowed, but the buyer may request to perform the contract, whereby the property will be released again to the buyer once he has paid the remaining part of the purchase price to the court within a reasonable time:

> *Where a person subject to enforcement sells its property to a third party, and such third*

58 See, eg, *Dongguan Computer Technology Co v Dongguan Knitting Co* (2011); *Luo Shubang v Zhuhai Zhenjie Injection Molding Machine Co* (2014); *Shaoxing Jinlong Trading Co v Fujian Yongxin Numerical Control Technology Co* (2014).

party has paid part of the purchase price and has actually taken possession of such property, but the person subject to enforcement has retained ownership pursuant to the contract, the people's court is allowed to seal up, seize or freeze the property; if the third party requests continuance of the contract, the people's court shall rule on rescinding the sealing, seizure or freezing measure after the third party has paid the remaining price to the people's court within a reasonable time.

9. International aspects

In the preceding sections we assumed that all elements of the retention of title were solely governed by Chinese law. The Conflicts Law does however allow and recognise that laws of other jurisdictions may be applicable to civil relationships, and if so, Chinese courts are required to ascertain and apply such foreign laws.[59]

A key concept in Chinese private international law is the 'foreign-related civil relationship'. Foreign laws can only apply if there is a foreign element to the relationship. A foreign element can be:

- a foreign party;
- the facts establishing, amending or terminating the relationship occurring outside China; or
- the subject matter being located outside China.[60]

If there is no foreign element to a civil relationship, Chinese law is mandatory.[61] If there is a foreign element, the key principle is, in absence of a choice by the parties involved (if such choice is allowed), that: "the laws that have the closest connection to the relevant foreign-related civil relationship shall govern."[62]

Parties to a foreign-related contract are free to choose the applicable law for their contract, but they must do so explicitly.[63] There is no need for such law to be connected to the foreign-related relationship between the parties.[64] If the parties do not make a choice:

the laws of the place where the party whose performance of its obligations manifests the character of the contract is normally resident, or other laws that have the closest connection with the contract in question, shall govern.[65]

---

59 Article 2 of the Conflicts Law; there is however a public policy exception (Article 5 of the Conflicts Law); *renvoi* (applying the conflict of laws rules of the foreign jurisdiction as well as its substantive rules) has been explicitly excluded (Article 9 of the Conflicts Law); if PRC law contains mandatory provisions on the subject matter, such provisions shall prevail (Article 4 of the Conflicts Law); and if the foreign law cannot be ascertained or is silent on the subject matter, Chinese law shall apply (Article 10 of the Conflicts Law); see further Articles 17 and 18 of the PRC Supreme Court Interpretations of the PRC Conflicts Law (2012) (referred to below as the "SPC Conflicts Law Interpretations") on how Chinese courts should ascertain the substance of foreign law.

60 Article 1 of the SPC Conflicts Law Interpretations. Note that the list is not exhaustive, since the last category is: "Other circumstances that may be determined as a foreign-related civil relationship."

61 In addition, Chinese law can also be mandatory for contracts where there is a foreign element (such as contracts between Chinese and foreign investors for joint ventures incorporated in China, and equity subscriptions or transfers by foreign investors with respect to companies incorporated in China).

62 Article 2 of the Conflicts Law.

63 Articles 3 and 41 of the Conflicts Law; Article 126 of the Contract Law; see notes 59 and 61 above on the limits of parties' freedom to select applicable law.

64 Article 7 of the SPC Conflicts Law Interpretations.

65 Article 41 of the Conflicts Law.

It is unclear how a Chinese court should decide if these two principles should conflict with each other.

Note that so called foreign-invested entities (companies incorporated in China with one or more foreign shareholders) are nevertheless considered domestic parties. Chinese law is therefore mandatory for a contract between such a foreign-invested entity and a purely Chinese company (assuming no other foreign element exists). An easy work-around is, however, to include the foreign parent company as a party, thereby establishing the required foreign element. Do make sure there is a sound business rationale for including such foreign party, however, because if the structure is clearly designed to circumvent Chinese law, the choice of law would be deemed invalid.[66]

If we assume that a contract containing a retention of title provision is governed by a foreign law, Chinese courts will have to decide on the validity, interpretation and scope of such that provision on the basis of that foreign law. We discussed above that establishing retention of title under Chinese law requires few formalities, but if a foreign law applies instead, the conditions of that foreign law for a valid retention of title provision would need to be fulfilled. The capacity of a Chinese counterparty will, however, still be governed by Chinese law.[67]

We mainly dealt above with the scope of retention of title as prescribed by the SPC Sales Contract Interpretations. If a foreign law governs a sales contract, this body of Chinese contract law regulations will no longer apply. Everything we have mentioned concerning the conditions for the seller to recover its property subject to retention of title, compensation and the 75% rule will not apply, unless a Chinese court should, for example, accept a public policy exception (which we cannot rule out with respect to the 75% rule). The parts of the SPC Sales Contract Interpretations that mainly clarify Article 106 of the PRC Property Law would, however, most likely continue to apply, since these provisions relate to property rights (unless the relevant property is also to be governed by a foreign law; see below).

Chinese law is quite liberal in the sense that parties to a foreign-related civil relationship are free to choose the applicable law with respect to their movable property.[68] As with contracts, this has to be done explicitly, but there is no requirement that the selected law needs to have a connection with the parties or the subject matter. This means that property rights over movables located in China could be governed by a foreign law. If the parties have not made an explicit choice, the law of the jurisdiction where the movable property is located would govern, unless the goods are, or have been, in transit, in which case the law of their destination would govern.[69]

If a foreign law governs the ownership of goods subject to retention of title, the transfer of ownership rules and the rules on combining, mixing and processing of property discussed above shall in principle not apply between the buyer and seller.

---

66 Article 11 of the SPC Conflicts Law Interpretations.

67 Article 14 of the Conflicts Law.

68 Article 37 of the Conflicts Law; there is no such freedom regarding immovable property, which needs to be governed by the law where it is located, under Article 36 of the Conflicts Law.

69 Articles 37 and 38 of the Conflicts Law.

These Chinese laws will of course continue to apply in any relationship between the buyer or seller on the one hand and a third party on the other hand (provided the relevant movables are in, or in transit to, China and the third party has not agreed to another applicable law). This means that a third party acting in good faith will still enjoy protection under Chinese law when acquiring ownership or taking security. A third party may also still obtain additional ownership rights under Chinese law if its property is combined or mixed with the property of the seller.

With respect to cross-border bankruptcy there is still little guidance in China. Article 5 of the Bankruptcy Law determines that Chinese bankruptcy proceedings shall also have effect regarding the debtor's property outside China. This means that if a seller based in China goes into bankruptcy, and that seller has property subject to retention of title outside China, the Chinese court will handle this in accordance with the rules set out in the section on bankruptcy above. Whether a Chinese court will respect any ownership or security rights from third parties (acting in good faith) established under the laws of the jurisdiction where the goods are located remains to be seen. As a matter of practice, such third parties will, however, usually be able to enforce their rights directly under the laws of such foreign jurisdiction where the goods are located.

Article 5 of the Bankruptcy Law is also relevant to the situation where a foreign seller goes into bankruptcy, and that seller has property subject to retention of title within China. It provides that foreign bankruptcy rulings regarding property located within China shall be recognised on the basis of applicable treaties or the principle of reciprocity, provided such ruling does not violate the basic principles of Chinese law, jeopardise the sovereignty, security or public interest of China, or undermine the legitimate rights and interest of creditors within China.

We believe it is highly unlikely that any foreign judgment that does not respect third-party rights validly established (in good faith) under Chinese law, or otherwise leaves Chinese creditors (disproportionally) unpaid will be recognised. In general, even though Chinese law allows for reciprocity, in practice Chinese courts simply refuse to enforce foreign judgments in commercial cases, unless there is a treaty.[70] To date, we have only seen an Italian and a French bankruptcy judgment, which have both been recognised on the basis of a treaty for judicial assistance.[71]

In general, the same is true for foreign judgments outside bankruptcy (such as a foreign court allowing a seller to recover its goods subject to retention of title from a Chinese buyer).[72] Recognition of such judgments is highly unlikely, unless there is an applicable treaty. China is, however, a signatory to the New York Convention, so foreign arbitral awards made in other contracting states should be recognised, unless one of the exceptions in the convention applies (such as if the award is contrary to public policy, or there was no proper notice).[73] In order to curb local protectionism,

70 China has entered into treaties for judicial assistance in civil matters with a few dozen countries, but with some exceptions (eg, France, Italy, Spain, Russia, Korea and Brazil), this does not include many of the world's largest economies.

71 *B&T Ceramic Group* (Guangdong Foshan Intermediate People's Court, 2002); *Antoine Montier v Pellis Corium* (2005).

72 Articles 265 and 266 of the Civil Procedure Law.

73 Article 267 of the Civil Procedure Law.

Chinese courts who refuse enforcement of a foreign arbitral award require approval from the Supreme People's Court. In practice we, however, sometimes see that foreign parties have difficulties in getting their application for recognition accepted, or their case is delayed almost indefinitely.

10. Conclusion

There are few formalities for establishing a valid retention of title provision under Chinese law, making retention of title a cost-effective method for sellers to protect their interests, which is also routinely enforced by Chinese courts. Retention of title has legal effect against third parties and in the event of an unauthorised transfer by the buyer, the seller may in principle recover its property.

Third parties are, however, protected if they acted in good faith, paid a reasonable price and either the transfer has been registered (if required) or the property has been delivered to the third party (if no registration is required). Similar protection applies for third parties who obtained security rights in good faith. Another important limitation under Chinese law is that a seller may no longer recover its property if the buyer has paid at least 75% of the purchase price.

In the event of the bankruptcy of the buyer, the seller may usually recover its property unless certain exceptions apply, but in such a case the seller will have a priority claim over common creditors. If the seller goes into bankruptcy and the administrator terminates the contract, the buyer needs to return the goods subject to retention of title even if he did not breach the contract. The buyer does, however, have a priority claim over common creditors to get the amount of the purchase price it has already paid refunded.

Enforcement in China is the exclusive domain of the Chinese courts. The courts may only enforce on the basis of a legally effective judgment or arbitral award, which means that a seller desiring to recover its property would always need to initiate legal proceedings or arbitration first if the buyer does not cooperate. Chinese law is mandatory if there are no foreign elements to a contract, otherwise parties are free to choose the law governing both their contract and movable property (even if such property is within China).

Czech Republic

Ernst Giese
Veronika Strizova
Giese & Partner

1. General remarks about retention of title

As an effective yet feasible method of securing a counterparty's payment obligation arising from a purchase transaction, retention of title is a popular instrument of Czech contract law. Despite the fact that Czech civil law has been completely restructured by a new legislative framework – Act 89/2012 Coll, the Civil Code – which entered into force as of January 1 2014, retention of title has preserved its place within civil doctrine and will doubtless feature in purchase deals to come. The Civil Code imposed a new legal framework both for the general provisions relating to purchase contracts and for the subsidiary provisions relating to the purchase contracts. By far the most commonly used subsidiary provision within purchase contracts is retention of title.

1.1 Transfer of ownership

As a rule, ownership of movable assets (hereinafter also referred to as 'the goods') is transferred from one party to the other simply by the handing over of such assets upon the conclusion of a purchase agreement (whether executed in a written or verbal form). When these two requirements are fulfilled, the buyer attains the ownership title. In other words, it is not obligatory for the purchase price to pass from the buyer to the seller in order for the buyer to become the owner of the goods.

The transfer of ownership may be subject to alternative arrangements of the contractual parties. The most widespread among these so-called subsidiary provisions is retention of title. Under a retention of title clause, the seller and the buyer typically agree to postpone the buyer's acquisition of ownership until the payment of the purchase price is made in full. Thus, the transfer of title is directly linked to the payment of the purchase price and is postponed until the payment is performed.

1.2 Retention of title

The most significant advantage of reservation of title is that it allows the purchaser to possess the purchased asset prior to the payment and at the same time secures the seller's ownership of the asset until the purchase price is fully paid. By retaining title until payment the seller is more likely to engage in a contractual relationship with a buyer who would otherwise not have the capacity to enter into such a transaction due to the lack of financial means. Since the buyer's monetary obligation is secured, the seller does not bear the risk of losing ownership before receiving payment and is therefore willing to trade under such conditions. The benefits the retention of title brings to the buyer are even more obvious, as under a retention of title provision he can gain the asset without the necessity of taking a loan elsewhere. The buyer is also permitted to (under certain requirements) use the acquired goods to generate a profit and so subsequently pay the price to the seller.

Prior to the recodification of Czech civil law the legal provision governing retention of title was set out in Section 601 of Act 40/1964 Coll, the Civil Code (hereinafter referred to as 'the former Civil Code'). Since January 1 2014 retention of title is regulated by Section 2132 and following of the (new) Civil Code. Section 2132 states:

If a seller reserves the right of ownership of an asset, the buyer is presumed to become the owner only upon the full payment of the purchase price. However, the risk of damage to the asset passes to the buyer as early as upon its takeover.

Under Czech civil law, a retention of title clause is not merely limited to postponing the ownership until payment of the full price. In line with the principle of contractual freedom, the parties to the contract are free to decide on the terms of the contract in accordance with their best interests and may therefore modify the retention of title clause in order to suit their needs. Apart from payment of the purchase price, other conditions may also be set as prerequisite for the transfer of title. Various arrangements may result in the transfer of title being postponed until they are fulfilled. However, a common aspect relating to them all is that they alter the time of transfer of the title.

1.3 Foreign and international law

Where an international element exists within the contractual relationship of the parties, it may be the case that the whole transaction, including the retention of title clause, will be governed by a foreign legal system. Since different jurisdictions may have great disparities in the prerequisites for concluding a valid retention of title clause, it may be the case that by fulfilling the conditions for validity in one jurisdiction it is not necessary to fulfil the requirements of another.

This was especially the case prior to 2014 in the Czech Republic, when the law applicable was determined by the location of the asset. Since the law of the state in which the asset was located at the time of concluding the purchase agreement (containing the retention of title clause) could impose different prerequisites than the law of the state where the asset was delivered or handed over, the retention of title could easily lapse. As of January 1 2014 this has changed. Under Section 70(2) of Act 91/2012 Coll, the Act on Private International Law, the law applicable to the transfer of ownership under a contract will be the law which governs the contract itself. This provision provides legal certainty for the reservation of title clause as now it is clear that, in the absence of a choice of law by the parties, the issue of retention of title will be governed by the same law as the purchase agreement itself.[1] With respect to the rank and rights of secured creditors within an insolvency or distraint proceeding taking place in the Czech Republic, Czech law will apply and govern these issues.

1 Monika Pauknerová, *Zákon o mezinárodním právu soukromém: komentá* , 1st edn (Prague, Wolters Kluwer, 2013).

Foreign retention of title clauses are acknowledged by Czech law. A retention of title agreed under a foreign legal system remains valid and is respected by Czech law.

1.4 Retention of title in insolvency

A retention of title clause is of key importance when one of the contractual parties goes bankrupt. If there is a reasonable concern prior to the conclusion of the purchase agreement that the purchaser could go bankrupt before paying the purchase price, it is highly advisable to insert a retention of title clause into the contract. The retention of title clause will safeguard the seller's property from the consequences of the purchaser becoming insolvent. The major risk associated with such a situation is that the appointed insolvency administrator could easily include the property in the estate of the debtor.

The effects of retention of title in insolvency proceedings are governed by Section 260 of Act 182/2006 Coll, the Insolvency Act, which states:

(1) If the debtor sold an item with retention of title before the declaration of bankruptcy order and handed it to the buyer, the buyer may return the item or insist on the agreement.

(2) If the debtor bought and accepted an item with retention of title before the declaration of the bankruptcy order without acquiring the ownership rights to it, the seller may not claim the return of the item if the insolvency administrator fulfils the obligation under the agreement without undue delay after they were called upon to such action by the seller.

Depending on which of the two contractual parties is declared bankrupt, the following scenarios may occur under Czech law:

- If the seller is declared bankrupt after handing the asset over to the purchaser, the purchaser is left with two options. The purchaser can hand the property over to the insolvency administrator, as the title has not yet passed from the seller to the purchaser and the goods are therefore still the property of the seller and form part of the insolvency estate which will be distributed for the benefit of the seller's creditors. Alternatively, the purchaser may demand the completion of the original transaction and therefore pay the purchase price to the insolvency administrator (as he is now the person in possession of the insolvency estate and is in charge of all the claims). The purchaser will consequently become the owner of the property as originally planned.[2]
- If the purchaser is declared bankrupt right after acquiring the asset – that is to say having already obtained possession of the goods but not ownership of them – then the seller needs to communicate details of the transaction to the insolvency administrator. The seller is obliged first to request completion of the transaction, by contacting the insolvency administrator and asking for payment. The insolvency administrator may either pay the price to the seller, in which case the asset becomes a rightful part of the insolvency estate, or he may refuse to pay, in which case the seller still holds the ownership title and

2 Jolana Maršíková, *Insolvenční zákon: s poznámkami, judikaturou, nařízením Rady ES 1346/2000 a prováděcími předpisy, ve znění zákonů č. 69/2011 Sb. a č. 73/2011 Sb.* (Prague, Leges, 2011).

may therefore request that the property be returned to him at once. The seller may only demand the release of the asset following a prior call to the insolvency administrator to perform payment.

It may be the case that the insolvency administrator appropriates the asset subject to retention of title and collects it as part of the insolvency estate. If the asset appears on the list of the insolvency estate, the legitimate owner needs to claim his rights by means of a legal action. In order to protect the seller's ownership rights, an action for the exemption of the property from the insolvency estate in accordance with Section 159 and following of the Insolvency Act must be filed with the insolvency court.

Should the buyer or the seller be subject to an insolvency proceeding outside Czech jurisdiction, the competency of Czech insolvency courts will be determined by Section 111 and following of the Act on International Private Law, in combination with the respective provisions of the European Insolvency Regulation.[3]

2. Retention of title

2.1 Validity and formal requirements

Since a retention of title clause is usually contained within a purchase agreement (whether in a written or a verbal form), its validity is directly linked to the validity of the purchase agreement itself. If the retention of title clause is contained in a purchase agreement, it can only be performed if the agreement is valid and effective. If a purchase contract becomes invalid, the retention of title clause cannot be executed as it would have no legal grounds for its performance and therefore the ownership remains with the initial owner.

The actual form of the retention of title clause within a purchase contract (for the sale of goods) is left completely up to the parties. The law does not impose an obligation to conclude the contract (including any retention of title clause) in a written form. As for the wording of the clause, no special formal requirements apply. A simple phrase containing the basic principle that the ownership of the goods is reserved until payment of the full purchase price will suffice. Nonetheless, it is, of course, advisable to conclude the agreement in a written form in order to avoid future misinterpretations of the terms.

However, a retention of title clause in verbal form has no effect in respect of third parties. In order for retention of title to apply to third parties it needs to be executed and concluded in a written form, and the signatures of the undersigning parties need to be authenticated by a notary public in accordance with Section 2134 of the Civil Code.

The retention of title clause does not necessarily need to be included as a provision of a written purchase agreement. It may also be agreed upon in the form of a separate annex to the purchase agreement. In order to avoid future disputes, it is however advisable expressly to specify the retention of title clause within the purchase agreement itself, as this is a more practical approach in terms of gathering evidence for potential future disputes. As a purchase is executed by, first, the

3 Council Regulation (EC) 1346/2000 of May 29 2000 on insolvency proceedings.

conclusion (signing) of the agreement and, secondly, the handing over of the goods, an amendment containing a retention of title clause would only be valid if it was concluded before the goods were handed over.

Under Czech law it is also possible to insert a retention of title clause into the general terms and conditions. The contents of the general terms and conditions must be acknowledged by both parties, so they must either be already obvious to the parties or they must form a part of (be attached to) the agreement itself.[4] If the general terms and conditions are not attached to the agreement, then the retention of title clause contained therein is not valid and has no legal effect whatsoever. The new civil legislation aims to provide the consumers with significant protection against the misuse of general terms and conditions (unclear wording, inappropriately small letter size and so on). As a result of these protective intentions it is possible to claim ineffectiveness of so-called 'unexpected clauses' within the general terms and conditions.[5] Currently a retention of title clause contained in the general terms and conditions may therefore be subject to disputes over the invalidity of such an arrangement. Section 1753 of the Civil Code states:

> *A provision of the standard commercial terms which the other party could not have reasonably expected is ineffective, unless expressly accepted by that party; any stipulation to the contrary is disregarded. Whether or not a provision is of such a nature is not assessed with regard to its content as well as to the manner in which it is expressed.*

As a result, one party can always claim that the retention of title clause was hidden in the general terms and conditions and could therefore not have been reasonably expected. This may eventually cause the retention of title clause to be ineffective.

As for the requirement of delivery of the goods to the purchaser, this condition may be modified by the contractual parties. In line with the principle of contractual freedom, the parties are able to arrange an alternative place of delivery, such as delivery of the goods to a warehouse or to a carrier. It may be agreed that the seller delivers the subject of the sale to the buyer through a third party. This type of delivery however, needs to be arranged in advance. There are no limits to the arrangements that may be made by the parties as long as the place of delivery is specified clearly and sufficiently.[6]

2.2 Scope of retention of title

Provided a retention of title clause is concluded in accordance with the relevant legal provisions and is therefore beyond doubt valid, the parties to the purchase agreement are bound by the following obligations and are granted the following rights.

---

4 Ernst Giese, *Zajištění závazků v České republice*, 2nd edn (Prague, CH Beck, 2003).

5 Martin Hout, *"Překvapivé klauzule v obchodních podmínkách aneb Kam kráčíš, ochrano spotřebitele?"* (2014), available at www.epravo.cz/top/clanky/prekvapive-klauzule-v-obchodnich-podminkach-aneb-kam-kracis-ochrano-spotrebitele-93410.html.

6 Josef Bejček, Karel Eliáš and Přemysl Raban, *Kurs obchodního práva: obchodní závazky*, 3rd edn (Prague, CH Beck, 2003).

The primary obligations forming the contractual relationship are the obligation of the seller to hand over the property to the buyer and the obligation of the buyer to pay the purchase price. Under a retention of title clause the purchaser gains possession over the goods, that is to say has physical control over it but does not yet hold the legal title to it. As such the possessor is obliged to treat the property as if it belongs to someone else (as it does). This however, is not an absolute rule. The possessor is allowed to use the property, as well as the proceeds from the property, and even to dispose of the property as long as such behaviour is in line with the purpose of the purchase agreement, or in line with the purpose it obviously serves. As an example, one can imagine an entrepreneur doing business in a technical field who buys a special machine. If it is obvious from the purchase agreement that he is buying this special machine in order to finalise or run a project within his course of business, he may use the machine prior to the transfer of title, as such behaviour would be in line with the retention of title clause so long as he uses the money earned thereby for payment of the purchase price. If the purchase price is not paid and the machine is returned to its owner, the owner may claim damages or unjustified enrichment against the purchaser.

(a) Sale of goods delivered under retention of title

As already mentioned above, the buyer has the right validly to transfer the goods to another person. Surprisingly enough, Czech case law concerning the possibility of the buyer disposing of the property before gaining the title to it was established by an important decision of a criminal court. The Supreme Court of the Czech Republic presented its opinion concerning this matter in a criminal case where the buyer was accused of the crime of embezzlement for selling goods to another buyer before acquiring the legal title to them. Both the court of first instance and the appellate court ruled that since the defendant was not the legitimate owner of the goods he was not yet allowed to resell them, and had therefore committed embezzlement. The reasoning behind these decisions was that the defendant appropriated goods which were (only) entrusted to him and by doing so he had caused damage to another person's property. The Supreme Court, however, did not find such reasoning compliant with the law. The Supreme Court ruled that given the nature of the goods (multiple chunks of pork meat), the intention of the purchaser to resell was obvious and was absolutely in compliance with the purpose of the purchase agreement. The obvious intent of the purchaser was to sell these chunks of meat for further manufacturing and to earn money (to repay the purchase price) by doing so. The Supreme Court ruled that since the seller should only be concerned with receiving the purchase price, and given the fact that the purchase agreement did not explicitly forbid the transfer to another person, no damage had been done. According to the Supreme Court the defendant was wrongfully accused of embezzlement of goods (not money) even though he acted in line with the terms of the purchase agreement by disposing of the goods. Of course should the defendant not transfer the money gained by the resale to the seller, such behaviour could qualify as embezzlement (of money), but this was not the case.

On the basis of this criminal case, civil legislation states that the resale of the goods by the possessor who has gained them under a purchase agreement containing a retention of title clause is not considered a breach of the purchase agreement as long as the resale is in line with the purpose of the purchase agreement. The parties may also prolong the retention of title and assign any future claim against the second purchaser in favour of the original seller. Such an arrangement protects the claim of the original seller where the goods are sold on before payment of the purchase price by the original buyer.

(b) Combining/mixing/mingling and processing of goods delivered under retention of title

In general, a retention of title is terminated by the combining, mixing or processing of the goods (unless agreed otherwise).[7] In accordance with Section 1078 of the Civil Code:

(1) If movable things of several owners become mixed in such a way that the restoration of the previous state is impossible but the whole may be divided into parts without interfering with the essence, each person will be at liberty to choose whether to separate for himself a proportion of what has been created by mixing, or whether to require compensation for what he has lost. If the person who has mixed things did not act in good faith, the owner has the right to relinquish his share in the mixed thing to him in exchange for a full compensation.

(2) Section 1075(2) applies by analogy.

The consequences of mixing, combining or processing of goods as described by the above legal provisions may be regulated by the contractual parties. In order to reduce the seller's risk of losing its title, a special type of a retention of title clause may be concluded to overcome the obstacles linked to the combining or processing of goods. As Section 2132 and following of the Civil Code only serve as a legal framework for retention of title arrangements, the legal provisions can be deliberately modified by the contracting parties. Typically, the parties may arrange that when a new product is assembled by the act of combining or mixing several assets the seller will gain ownership, or perhaps co-ownership, of the new product (contrary to what is presumed by law, which is that the person who created the new product becomes its owner).

According to Section 1074 of the Civil Code:

(1) A new thing created by processing movable things of several owners in such a way that the processed things cannot be restored to the previous state at all, or only at a significant cost or with a substantial loss, is owned by the person whose material or work made the largest contribution to the resulting value.

(2) The owner of the new thing shall pay the person who has lost the right of ownership the value of the processed thing and remunerate the person having contributed with work for the work performed.

The question in hand here is the economic value of the asset produced. Based on the value added by the act of processing, the retention of title either lapses or

---

7 Luboš Tichý, *Kupní smlouva v novém ob anském zákoníku: komentá : [§ 2079-2183]*, 1st edn (Prague, CH Beck, 2014).

persists. In order for it to lapse the value of the newly produced asset cannot be substantially lower than the value of the material used. For the estimation of the value of the newly produced asset, the critical measure is the value added by the processing, not the initial value plus the costs of the processing. However, the legal provisions may be avoided by a so-called prolonged retention of title.

An example of a prolonged retention of title clause may sound like this:

The transfer of ownership of the goods from the seller to the buyer is reserved until the purchase price is paid in full. Any processing or re-assembling of the goods is performed to the benefit of the seller, as the processor. The ownership or co-ownership of the new goods of the buyer is automatically transferred to the seller in the amount of its respective share on the new goods. The buyer performs its duty of care over the goods free of charge. The buyer is entitled to process or dispose of the goods in the ordinary course of business, unless in payment default. Establishing a pledge over the goods is prohibited.

(c) Extension of retention of title

Another useful means of extending retention of title is the use of a so-called 'all sums due' or 'all monies' clause, which is especially practical due to its ability to secure all claims the seller has against the purchaser. It offers additional securitisation of existing claims which are not directly linked to the current purchase agreement. The all sums due clause therefore offers an easy type of security as ownership of title is reserved not just until the goods sold under the current purchase agreement are paid for, but until all invoices for all goods delivered are paid for. It is also possible to extend such an obligation to non-contractual claims such as damages. Such an extended retention of title is not a very commonly used instrument, but it may be employed under Czech law.[8]

2.3 Legal effect of retention of title

(a) Effect towards third parties

According to Section 2134 of the Civil Code:

Reservation of the right of ownership is effective with respect to the buyer's creditors only if the stipulation was made in the form of a public document, or if it was made in writing and the signatures of the parties were authenticated, but in this case it is effective only from the date of the authentication of signatures. However, if the reservation of the right of ownership has been stipulated in respect of a thing registered in a public register, it has effect against third persons only if it has been registered in that register.

The retention of title clause is therefore not effective towards all third parties automatically. In order to safeguard the seller's position as owner of the goods with priority over creditors of the purchaser (including governmental bodies such as tax authorities), it is necessary for the retention of title (either the agreement as a whole

---

8 Luboš Tichý, *Kupní smlouva v novém ob anském zákoníku: komentá : [§ 2079-2183]*, 1st edn (Prague, CH Beck, 2014).

or a separate clause to the agreement) to be concluded in a written form with signatures verified by a notary public, or in the form of a public document, that is to say a notarial deed. Should these requirements not be met, the retention of title has no effect towards these third parties – the purchaser's creditors – and as such may not serve its intended purpose to protect the seller's right to ownership. In this regard it is important to note that, in the case of assets that are by operation of law registered in a public register, the retention of title clause has an automatic effect not only towards creditors of the purchaser but also towards any other third parties as of the date of publishing such an entry; in other words, as of the date the record becomes public and therefore accessible to all.

If the purchaser sells the asset to a third party before he pays the purchase price – before he becomes the legitimate owner of the asset – that transfer is only valid if the third party acquired the assets in a good faith belief that it was buying the asset from an authorised owner. If the acquisition of ownership by a third party is executed in good faith, then the original seller is only left with the option of claiming damages against the original purchaser (as the retention of title clause ceases to exist).

Proof of the contrary can however rebut the presumption of good faith. If the legitimate owner – the original seller – proves that the subsequent buyer must have had a reasonable suspicion that the seller (the original purchaser) was not the legitimate owner (for instance, due to an unreasonably low purchase price), then the (proven) lack of good faith causes the invalidity of such a transaction and the retention of title endures. Good faith cannot be attributed to a purchaser if the respective asset is subject to mandatory registration in a public register, as such information is accessible and can therefore not be neglected. In addition, the Supreme Court has ruled that: "a certain level of caution, such as a reasonable person should on average have, is required from the buyer".[9]

(b) Effect in case of seizure of goods delivered under retention of title

If third parties – the purchaser's creditors – seize goods delivered under retention of title, that retention of title continues and is effective towards these third parties only if it was executed in the form of a public document (a notary deed or a written agreement the signatures to which were authenticated by a notary public). This is to avoid the possibility that the buyer and seller could use the retention of title simply to 'hide' the asset from the creditors. The creditors of the purchaser may seize the asset up until the moment of the verification of signatures on the relevant purchase agreement, as until this moment the retention of title has no effect towards them. Towards all other third parties the retention of title is therefore effective as of the date of the handing over of the goods upon the signing of the purchase contract (with the exception of assets registered in a public register, as mentioned before). As for the proceeds, these come to the possessor – as the original buyer – at no cost, as it is presumed that the payment of the proceeds has already been included in the purchase price, unless other arrangements have been made by the parties. The

9 Decision of the Supreme Court of the Czech Republic dated January 26 2011(NS 22 Cdo 877/2009).

possessor is also obliged to safeguard the property from damage, destruction or loss until the title is transferred.[10] The corresponding rights to the above-mentioned obligations are the right of the purchaser to acquire ownership and the right of the seller to the purchase price.

(c) ***Effect in case of a security right established over goods delivered under retention of title***

According to Section 1343 of the Civil Code:

(1) A contracting pledger may pledge a thing of another only with the consent of the owner.

(2) Where the contracting pledger pledges a movable thing of another without the consent of the owner, the pledge is created if the thing is delivered to the pledgee and the pledgee receives the thing in good faith that the contracting pledger is entitled to pledge the thing.

(3) If a person has a right in rem *to the thing being pledged which is incompatible with the pledge, Subsections (1) and (2) apply by analogy.*

In line with what has been discussed above, the law enables a possessory security right to be established over an asset without the consent of its owner if the asset is movable and if it is physically handed over to the pledgee who accepts it in good faith (that he is obtaining it from its owner). In contrast the security right cannot be established over an asset under these conditions if the pledge is subject to being registered in a special register.[11]

The actual hand-over of the asset itself is an essential prerequisite as it justifies the good faith of the pledgee that the pledger, as the person physically holding the asset, is its legitimate owner.[12] There is a tendency to grant greater legal protection to the pledgee rather than the rightful owner where the pledgee has acted in good faith that the pledger possesses a legitimate title to the goods and is therefore authorised to establish a pledge over it (whether by identifying himself as the owner or by providing an owner's consent with the pledge).

In accordance with Section 1310(2) of the Civil Code it is possible to establish a security right over an asset which is yet to be acquired by the debtor in the future. Regardless of the fact that the purchaser under retention of title is not the owner of the asset and shall only become the pledger (and legitimate owner) in the future, a security right may be established over the asset. The security right may be established as a 'future pledge' but is perfected and effective only after the transfer of ownership.

(d) ***Effect in case of partial payment of the purchase price***

Generally speaking, a party may withdraw from a contract if the other party to the contract fundamentally breaches the contract in terms of delay. According to Section 1977 of the Civil Code: "If, by its default, a party fundamentally breaches its

---

10 Luboš Tichý, *Kupní smlouva v novém občanském zákoníku: komentá : [§ 2079-2183]*, 1st edn (Prague, CH Beck, 2014).

11 Lukáš Vymazal, *Zástavní právo v novém občanském zákoníku: (zákon . 89/2012 Sb)* (Prague, Linde, 2014), monograph.

12 *Ibid.*

contractual duty, the other party may withdraw from the contract if it notifies the party in default accordingly without undue delay after learning of the default."

In relation to the retention of title, the contracting parties may agree that the purchase price shall be paid in instalments and that the ownership is reserved until the payment of the last instalment. According to Section 2133 of the Civil Code:

If the acquisition of the right of ownership by the buyer is subject to the payment of the purchase price in instalments, the buyer's default of instalments not exceeding one tenth of the purchase price does not in itself entitle the seller to withdraw from the contract and demand the return of the thing, provided the buyer pays the instalment no later than when the next instalment becomes due together with the instalment which is due.

The above provisions specify that if the purchaser is past due with one instalment this cannot qualify as a fundamental breach of the contract, unless this instalment is greater than 10% of the total amount (of the purchase price). If this one instalment past due is of a greater value than 10% of the purchase price, then this is considered a fundamental breach of the contract and withdrawal may take place. Upon withdrawal the seller may request the goods to be returned to him. The seller is entitled to withdraw from the contract and claim the goods back only after the payment date is past due. If no such arrangement (concerning partial payments) has been agreed between the parties and the purchaser has only paid a partial amount of the full price, then the seller has the right (upon prior notice) to withdraw from the contract and take back the goods. If the purchaser has paid a partial amount of the purchase price already, the seller is obliged to return this amount to the purchaser, but is entitled to the reimbursement of all related necessary expenses. Should either the money or the goods not be transferred to the respective party, provisions on unjust enrichment should be applied for enforcement of the obligation.

3. Enforcement of retention of title

Enforcement of the retention of title may be imposed either by the court or by a distraint officer appointed by the court. If a buyer who is in default refuses to return the goods to the seller even after he has withdrawn from the contract and is demanding the goods at once, the person entitled to collect the goods for the seller is a distraint officer (bailiff), or more specifically the employees of his office. It is advisable always to label goods sold subject to a retention of title adequately as this improves the ability of the seller to identify his goods when collecting it from the purchaser's premises. Specific packaging may also protect the goods in this manner. However, in order to enforce the retention of title and gain the goods, a motion to open a distraint proceeding has to be filed. Along with filing the motion it is mandatory to provide the distraint office with a so-called distraint title. Presuming the seller only holds the purchase agreement including the retention of title clause, it needs to file an action with the court in order to obtain a judicial decision which serves as a distraint title for the enforcement of the ownership rights. The action claims protection of ownership and the retrieval of the asset. This action is governed by the procedural provisions of Section 79 and following of Act 99/1963 Coll, the Civil Procedure Code. If the purchase agreement altogether with the retention of title clause is executed in the form of a notarial deed containing a direct enforceability clause, such agreement itself is sufficient as a distraint title. Irrespective of the location where the goods are stored, either the purchaser provides access to the seller, who is entitled to collect his goods after his withdrawal from the agreement, or if the purchaser refuses to do so, the goods shall be collected by force within the formal distraint procedure.

Given that obtaining a judicial decision through a formal judicial proceeding might take some time and the seller needs to safeguard his assets – which are physically controlled by the purchaser – from damage or further transfer, a preliminary injunction may serve to protect the owner until the court reaches a decision. Under a preliminary injunction granted in accordance with Section 74 and following of the Civil Procedure Code, the possessor may be ordered by the court not to dispose of the goods until the court comes to a decision on the substance of the claim. The preliminary injunction may also require that the goods are to be stored in the custody of the court until a decision is reached.

Where the buyer is subject to insolvency proceedings, the seller should address the insolvency administrator as the person in possession of the insolvency estate. If the purchaser did not pay for the goods prior to becoming bankrupt, the seller must first request that the conditions of the contract be fulfilled and therefore must notify the insolvency administrator that the purchase price is yet to be paid. Only after such a request for payment may the seller demand that the goods are actually returned to him as the legitimate owner. Should a dispute arise over the ownership of the goods and the insolvency administrator has already listed the goods as part of the estate, the seller needs to invoke his ownership rights by means of a special type of action on the exclusion of the asset from the estate, which needs to be filed with the insolvency court under Section 159 and following of the Insolvency Act.

Denmark

Carsten Ceutz
Bech-Bruun

---

1. General remarks about retention of title

1.1 Transfer of ownership

Acquisition of title to property, which takes place by way of the transfer of the right from a previous owner, is in Danish law referred to as derivative acquisition, which will typically be in the form of a purchase.

The time of the passing of title depends on whether the sale of specific goods or generic goods is involved.

For specific goods, meaning an individualised asset, title to such asset will be considered as having passed and is consequently protected against the seller's other assignees and creditors upon conclusion of the agreement.

For generic goods, meaning an asset of a specific type, title to the object will be considered as having passed and is consequently protected against the seller's other assignees upon conclusion of the agreement but only when the object being transferred has been specified to a sufficient extent. However, the transfer will not be valid as regards the seller's creditors until the object has been individualised with binding effect, meaning that the buyer and seller have agreed on the object and it has been separated, that the object has been shipped from the seller to the buyer at the buyer's expense and risk, or that the seller has notified the buyer that the separation has taken place.

Therefore, the general rule is that registration of the transfer of the asset is not required in a public register or the like. In connection with transfer of real estate, however, such transfer must be registered in the land register in order to obtain property protection, see the below.

The parties may agree that the transfer of ownership will take place later than the conclusion of the agreement.

1.2 Retention of title

In situations where the object sold is handed over from the seller to the buyer and payment does not take place at the same time, the seller may under Danish law invoke retention of title to the object. The legal effect of a valid retention of title is that the seller, despite the surrender of the object sold to the buyer, may demand that the buyer returns the object in the event of the buyer's breach of its payment obligation.

In Danish legal literature, there are discussions as to whether the buyer is the owner of the object sold subject to a retention of title, or whether title remains with the seller until payment is made.

In a non-published judgment rendered by the Court of Holstebro on December 12 2014, the court stated that "... a retention of title does not mean that ownership is upheld, but it is merely security in the goods meaning that where payment is not made, the goods may be taken back by the seller."

Valid retention of title is therefore considered as conditional title for the buyer and constitutes a form of charge for the seller providing security for the seller for payment of the purchase price.

Agreement on a retention of title under Danish law follows from Section 28(2), third limb, of the Sale of Goods Act. The standard requirements of validity of a retention of title are described in legal literature and are based on the standard legal doctrines in property law and case law.

The Sale of Goods Act does not cover real estate and therefore it is not possible to agree on a retention of title when the object is real property. In addition to the general requirements of validity, the following follows from Sections 34-48 of the Credit Agreements Act:

- that the retention of title must have been agreed at the latest by the surrender of the object sold to the buyer;
- that the total amount to be paid, including the down-payment made, must exceed DKK2,000 (around €270); and
- that the purchase on credit must not have taken place in accordance with an agreement on credit with variable loan amounts.

In consumer transactions, an additional requirement applies, namely that the seller upon surrender of the object sold must have received at least 20% of the cash purchase price.

Under Section 50(2) of the Credit Agreements Act, a number of the additional requirements of validity set out in Sections 34-48 of the Credit Agreements Act do not apply outside consumer transactions. This, among other things, means that:

- a requirement for a minimum down-payment does not apply in transactions between traders;
- consumer protection rules on recovery do not apply; and
- the restrictions on the seller's right to levy execution do not apply.

1.3 Foreign and international law

In a situation where the retention of title or the agreement in which the retention of title has been made is subject to a legal basis other than Danish law, as a consequence of a choice of law provision, for instance, this provision will apply to the relationship between the parties, whereas the choice of law for the assessment of the retention of title issue will be determined by the principle which according to case law is referred to as 'the law of the importing country'.

If the asset covered by the retention of title is located in Denmark, Danish law will apply with respect to any property law conflict, irrespective of the fact that the agreement is governed by the law of another country. If, as part of the agreement creating the retention of title, the asset is sold to a party in another country where the asset is meant to stay, the principle of the law of the importing country will lead to application of the rules of that country.

According to Danish private international law, the individual aspects in an agreement on retention of title are to be assessed separately.

The actual sales agreement containing the retention of title is governed according to any agreement as to choice of law made between the parties. Where the parties have not agreed on any choice of law, the country in which the seller resided when he received the order will be selected as the relevant jurisdiction on the basis of the rules governing choice of law.

Any property law aspect, including the question of compliance with special conditions for the validity of the retention of title as regards creditors, is to be assessed according to the principle of the law of the importing country.

Certain aspects which are naturally characteristic of a purchase subject to retention of title are nonetheless, according to case law, to be dealt with as part of the issues relating to the contract and not as issues of property law. This, for instance, applies to rules on a minimum down-payment on purchases subject to retention of title, as these rules do not aim at the protection of creditors' interests, but are merely a part of the contract between the parties.

1.4 Retention of title in insolvency

A valid retention of title is not affected by the debtor's bankruptcy, see Sections 82(1) and 58(3) of the Bankruptcy Act. The seller's right to recover property in the event of the buyer's breach of its payment obligations therefore also applies as regards the buyer's bankruptcy estate where the seller, in respect of its claim, is considered a secured creditor.

The bankruptcy estate of a buyer with whom a valid agreement on retention of title has been entered into, as a general rule under Section 55 of the Bankruptcy Act, is entitled to become a party to the bilateral agreements entered into by the debtor, including with a seller who has a retention of title. When becoming a party to such agreements, the buyer's bankruptcy estate becomes entitled and obligated in accordance with the terms of the agreement.

In the event that bankruptcy proceedings against a buyer are instituted outside Denmark, but the buyer has entered into a valid agreement on retention of title, the property law conflict will as a general rule be decided according to Danish property law to the extent the object is located in Denmark.

The situation is the same where the seller is subject to insolvency proceedings outside Denmark.

If, prior to the bankruptcy, the agreement has been fully performed by the seller and the seller subsequently becomes bankrupt, the contractual relationship is not covered by the rules on becoming a party to agreements according to Part 7 of the Bankruptcy Act. The claim against the buyer will be included in the assets of the bankruptcy estate, and the estate may demand payment of the outstanding claim without thereby being deemed to have become a party to the agreement.

2. Retention of title

2.1 Validity and formal requirements

The only requirement for the validity of a retention of title clause between the buyer and seller is that the parties have agreed on the retention of title before the object sold is handed over to the buyer.

According to Danish law, retention of title cannot be taken unilaterally by the seller, but must be based on a mutual agreement between the buyer and the seller. In addition, the retention of title may be made orally, in writing, be implied by way of the parties' behaviour, or as a standard term agreed between the parties.

In order for it to be possible to enforce the retention of title against the buyer's assignees and creditors, it is a requirement that a clear and express agreement exists. Whether an agreement on retention of title exists is determined according to the general contract law rules on conclusion, gap-filling, interpretation, adoption and so on. The standard of proof for the existence of retention of title is strict when the retention of title is based solely on an oral agreement. There are no statutory rules stipulating that the retention of title is to be worded in a specific way in order to be valid.

It should, however, be noted that the right to seek immediate satisfaction with the assistance of the court in enforcing the seller's title over the objects sold, requires that the retention of title has been agreed in writing, see Section 36(1) of the Credit Agreements Act, which in practice means that the retention of title should always be drafted in writing.

As a general rule, a retention of title clause is valid between the parties as from the time of conclusion of the agreement. This also applies even where the agreement has been entered into after the surrender of the goods to the buyer, unless the buyer is a consumer in which case the mandatory rules of the Credit Agreements Act stipulate that the retention of title must, in order to be valid, have been agreed, at the latest, at the time of the surrender to the consumer of the objects purchased (Section 34(1)(i) of the Credit Agreements Act).

In order for the retention of title to be valid as regards third parties, including the buyer's subsequent assignees and creditors, if any, the general requirements of validity must be met. Therefore the retention of title must:

- have been made by way of a clear and express agreement, at the latest at the time of surrender to the buyer of the object sold;
- concern individualised objects; and
- relate to the seller's claims under the sales agreement.

The seller's right to recover property therefore applies simply when meeting the general requirements of validity and without any need for an act of perfection. Retention of title in a motor vehicle must, however, be registered in the motor vehicles securities register in order to be valid against the buyer's subsequent assignees and creditors (Section 42d(1) of the Registration of Property Act).

There are no statutory requirements as to the form of the wording of a retention of title clause, but the retention of title must be made in a clear and express agreement. It has been held in case law that the wording that the sale was being made on "general purchase agreement terms" was not sufficient to establish retention of title, and a provision in the invoice reading "net cash upon receipt, as the goods remain our property until payment has taken place" was in another case also held to be insufficient.

To our knowledge it is not possible to have retention of title in place by operation of law.

Retention of title cannot be validly adopted merely by reference to standard practice in the industry or general trade usage between the buyer and the seller, but must meet the requirement for an express agreement, as discussed above with regard to the general conditions for validity. A standard term with a reference to the conclusion of retention of title may, however, be considered an express agreement, if the standard terms have been customary in other transactions between the parties.

It is stipulated in Section 28(2) of the Sale of Goods Act that the seller's right to terminate the purchase for cause ceases when the object has been surrendered to the buyer, unless he has made a valid retention of title. Other relevant legislation does not stipulate that the surrender must be made to the buyer himself. It must be assumed that surrender to a third party at the request of the buyer should also be considered as equivalent to surrender to the buyer. There is no case law requiring that surrender must take place directly to the buyer and not to a third party.

2.2 Scope of retention of title

Provided that it has been validly adopted, a retention of title, as a general rule, grants the seller the right to recover his property, whereby the seller, despite surrender of the object to the buyer, is entitled to take the object sold back if the buyer fails to meet its payment obligation. This right to recover property applies against the buyer and also good-faith assignees to whom the object has been surrendered or the buyer's creditors if they have sought satisfaction through the object.

It has been held in case law that a valid retention of title also grants the seller a right to recover property in situations where the object subject to retention of title has been resold to subsequent assignees acting in good faith (see, for instance, U 1952.69 H, where an object with a valid retention of title could be recovered from a subsequent assignee acting in good faith even though the object had been resold three times from the original buyer before the original seller invoked its retention of title).

Retention of title therefore places restrictions on the buyer as it prevents transactions involving the object sold unless it is taken subject to the retention of title.

A seller who has a valid retention of title must, however, be aware that assignees acting in good faith may extinguish the seller's right under the retention of title in line with general legal rules in this regard, such as where the seller has displayed inaction or carelessness.

According to a legal doctrine developed in case law it is a general rule that the seller runs the risk that subsequent assignees acting in good faith may extinguish the seller's right under the retention of title in a situation where the seller knew or ought to know that his buyer is a distributor of objects of the type to which the retention of title relates. In the relationship between a seller who knows about his buyer's standing as distributor and the subsequent buyer who buys from the distributor in good faith with respect to the retention of title, consideration for the good-faith buyer takes priority.

There may also be a situation where the object is stored with a third party who is a distributor of goods of the type in question and who, without being entitled to do so, sells the object to a customer. In this situation, the seller runs the risk that his right is extinguished with reference to the seller, by having displayed carelessness and inaction by letting the object be stored with the third party in question.

Retention of title may also lapse where the third party stores the object subject to retention of title together with other objects of the same type, as the object in such a case cannot be individualised to a sufficient extent.

If the buyer and seller want to enter into an agreement stating that the buyer is entitled to resell the goods to a third party before having paid the seller, the parties may enter into a consignment agreement. Consignment is not governed by statutory law, but is based on a contractual relationship. Consignment entails the buyer buying its goods on credit from the seller, with retention of title for the seller, but with permission to resell the goods to the buyer's customers and with an agreement on continuous payments from the buyer to the seller. In the event of default by the buyer, the seller may invoke the retention of title and demand the return of goods not yet sold. However, it is not possible to demand return of goods which have been sold by the buyer to a third party. The seller may, however, as a general rule invoke its retention of title with respect to the goods not sold as against the buyer's creditors.

Consignment agreements must be in accordance with the general requirements of validity applicable to an agreement on retention of title. In addition, certain additional requirements have arisen from case law, and are described in the legal literature as follows:

- The goods are to be kept separate from the distributor's other similar goods;
- The distributor must, on a continuous basis, pay the seller in line with any resales made to customers; and
- The seller must, on an ongoing basis, ensure that the distributor makes continuous payments as agreed and that the goods not sold are in the possession of the distributor and have therefore not been sold without payment being made.

Consignment agreements are not covered by the Credit Agreements Act (see Section 2, second sentence, of that act) and consequently do not need to comply with the requirements for validity under that act.

Debtor substitution in credit agreements – that is to say, the extent to which the buyer and a subsequent third-party purchaser can agree that the obligation to pay the seller is transferred to the third party, while the seller's retention of title is maintained against that third party – is governed by the general rules of the law of obligations, from which it follows that debtor substitution can, as a general rule, only take place when the creditor (the original seller) grants its consent. It furthermore follows from case law that the creditor does not lose its retention of title on debtor substitution (see U 1959.246 Ø). Where the seller and the new assignee under such a substitution agree on new conditions or changed terms for the credit agreement, this will be considered a new purchase on credit and not a substitution, with the consequence that the seller will lose its retention of title. In such a case it will be necessary to agree on a new retention of title which will be subject to the same requirements as regards validity.

(a) *Combining/mixing/mingling goods delivered under retention of title*

With regard to the consequences of the object being combined, mixed or mingled with other objects by the buyer, it is relevant to take note of the general requirement for the validity of retention of title according to which the seller must be able to identify the objects to which the retention of title relates at the buyer's premises.

As regards the inter-party relationship between the buyer and the seller, it is in principle sufficient for the validity of the retention of title merely that the retention of title was agreed. The specification requirement, however, serves as security against the buyer's other assignees and creditors and is therefore one of the requirements securing protection for the retention of title.

The specification requirement is in practice normally met through identification of the object(s) covered by the retention of title by, for instance, stating the make, type, year and serial number, or by marking the objects in a way which cannot easily be removed. With regard to retention of title in cars, special identification requirements apply in order for the right to be entered in the motor vehicles securities register.

If the object to which the retention of title relates is mixed with other objects of the same type without being labelled specifically such that the objects covered by the retention of title can be identified, the retention of title cannot be invoked. This has been determined in case law, such as in U 1979.430 V, a case where the retention of title could be upheld as the animals to which the retention of title related were not located in premises where there were other animals which could be mistaken for them, and as the parties did not disagree as to which animals were covered by the retention of title.

The same problem was at issue in U 1987.629 H, where it was held that the owner of a pork processing plant could not rely on a retention of title which the processing plant had on pigs which it had delivered to a farmer. The reason given was that the pigs were not marked in the way which had been agreed according to the contract between the parties. It did not matter that the farmer stated to the Supreme Court that he had kept the pigs separated from the other pigs he had on the farm and that he had put the pigs covered by the retention of title in specific boxes.

It is of no significance to compliance with the specification requirement that the object has been delivered by a party other than the seller; in which connection it is noted that the seller bears the risk that the object is not described sufficiently clearly. If the seller cannot prove the identity of the goods, retention of title cannot be invoked against the buyer, its assignees or its creditors. Lack of identification or specification does not affect the validity from a contract law perspective, but the seller will have to prove which objects are covered in order to be able to invoke the retention of title.

The relevant point in time at which the specification requirement has to be met is the time at which the seller seeks to take back the object. In practice, stricter requirements are made for specification when the validity of a retention of title is disputed by assignees or creditors of the buyer than when it is the buyer itself that is disputing which objects the seller can take back. The fact that the time of assessment of compliance with the specification requirement is the time at which the goods are to be taken back means in practice that the specification requirement may well have been met at the time when the agreement was entered into, but is not met at the relevant time, if the buyer subsequently mixes the objects with objects of the same type which are not covered by the retention of title.

An otherwise valid retention of title therefore does not lapse immediately upon the mixing of objects not covered by the retention of title, but the retention of title should be safeguarded by way of sufficient specification at the time the goods are to be taken back.

Danish law does not specifically cover whether an otherwise valid retention of title lapses when the object is meant to be combined, and actually is so combined, with other objects not covered by the retention of title. The legal position in this area has therefore been laid down by way of case law, which, however, is ambiguous.

One such case, U 1961.148 H, concerned a seller, which was a German factory, and a buyer, which was a Danish moped factory. According to the consignment agreement between the parties, the seller, subject to a specified retention of title, delivered motor casings to the buyer to be used for the buyer's manufacture of motors. The purchase price did not fall due for payment when the goods were used and not even when the finished motors were sold, but rather after the expiry of a fixed credit period of 90 days, and the seller did not conduct any control over when the goods were used for manufacturing the motors.

The Supreme Court stated that, following the buyer's bankruptcy, the retention of title could not be invoked against the buyer's creditors because the conditions for the consignment had not been met. The Supreme Court also stated that even if the conditions for the consignment had been met, the retention of title would still have lapsed with respect to the motor casings which had already been used for the manufacture of motors. The same legal position is illustrated in U 2001.2400 V.

Another case, U 1969.914 V, concerned the buyer of a truck purchased on credit from seller 1, who had retained title in the truck and a set of tyres purchased on credit from seller 2, who had also retained title in the tyres. The truck was subsequently resold. Upon the buyer's default as regards payment of seller 2 the issue arose as to whether the seller could recover the tyres despite the fact that they were fitted on the truck.

The High Court found for seller 2 and allowed the seller to recover the tyres despite the fact that they were fitted on the truck. In its grounds, the High Court placed priority on the fact that the tyres could be separated from the truck without any difficulties and without causing a significant reduction in the total values, as well as the fact that it must be in the interest of the party having sold a truck subject to retention of title that the buyer of the truck should be capable of supplying the truck with new tyres even if they had been bought on credit and subject to retention of title.

Among the most recent decisions is U 2003.1499 H, where a manufacturer had delivered ship propulsion gear units for the building of ships in a shipyard. The manufacturer and the shipyard agreed that three main gear units for three ships, which were under construction, were to be delivered, and that the manufacturer retained title to the three units until they had been paid for in full. In accordance with the usual conditions for delivery, payment was to be made in three instalments: 5% on confirmation of the order, 60% on approved delivery of the gear units and 35% on approved delivery of the ships.

Bankruptcy proceedings were subsequently commenced against the shipyard, and at the time the third main gear had not been unpacked at the shipyard. The manufacturer asserted its claim alleging that it had status as a secured creditor, but the estate rejected this view and installed the gear unit in the ship, which was subsequently sold. The manufacturer then asserted its claim as a pre-preferential claim.

The Supreme Court stated that the retention of title was valid as the third main gear unit was individually prepared with a view to being incorporated into the ship and had not yet been incorporated at the time of the bankruptcy.

On the basis of the existing case law, it does not seem that any general rule can be derived as to when incorporation will trigger the end of the retention of title. In U 1961.148 H, the Supreme Court placed priority on the fact that the object had been used for preparation and that the retention of title had therefore lapsed, where a balancing of considerations in U 1969.914 V, including that separation could take place without difficulties, meant that the retention of title could be upheld.

(b) Processing of goods delivered under retention of title

In connection with actual processing of the object sold subject to retention of title, it appears that there is as yet no case law on whether and under which circumstances the retention of title can still be upheld and when it lapses.

In construction law, a special rule applies regarding separate rights in construction materials brought on to a construction site. It follows from Section 10(3) of the General Conditions for the Provision of Works and Supplies within Building and Engineering (AB92) that when materials are brought to a construction site to be used for the building of a construction project, any independent rights in terms of retention of title will lapse upon the introduction of the materials to the site. This is a special rule of law only governing in those specific circumstances.

Consideration of the parties' need to have a pragmatic solution and other principles outlined in case law seem to be arguments in favour of the seller being able to recover its processed object where this is physically possible; but in such a case he would have to compensate the buyer for the additional value which the processing represents.

(c) Extension of retention of title

Section 38 of the Credit Agreements Act, which applies to both consumer transactions and transactions between commercial parties subject to retention of title (but not cases where a consignment agreement has been entered into, as consignment agreements are not covered by the provisions of the Credit Agreements Act, by virtue of Section 2 of the act), includes an exhaustive list of which claims the creditor is entitled to include in the statement of its receivables in connection with recovery proceedings.

According to Section 38, the creditor's receivables must be stated as the sum of the unpaid part of the claim, interest on the amounts due and necessary expenses incidental to the recovery (collection expenses).

Where a purchase with retention of title covers more than one object, each individual object generally serves as security for the entire debt under the contract (see U 1987 360 V).

2.3 Legal effect of retention of title

(a) Effect towards third parties

In order for the retention of title to be valid against the buyer's subsequent assignees and creditors, the general requirements for validity under Danish law apply.

The agreement on the retention of title must be clear and specific, the retention of title must be mutually agreed at the latest by the time the object sold is surrendered, the object sold must be identifiable, and the retention of title can only relate to the seller's claims under the specific purchase agreement and therefore cannot relate to older claims.

If the retention of title is in a motor vehicle, the retention of title must be registered in the motor vehicles securities register in order to obtain protection against extinction (see Section 42d of the Registration of Property Act).

In addition to these conditions, the Credit Agreements Act stipulates certain additional requirements for validity and repeats some of the general conditions in Section 34(1)(i) to (iv) of the act, according to which:

- the retention of title must be agreed before surrender of the object sold;
- the total amount to be paid must exceed DKK2,000;
- the purchase on credit cannot be under an agreement on credit with a varying loan amount; and
- the seller, upon surrender of the object sold, must receive consideration corresponding to at least 20% of the cash purchase price.

The requirement for a minimum down-payment does not, however, apply to purchases other than consumer transactions (see Section 50(2) of the Credit Agreements Act).

In addition, it follows from Section 34(3) of the Credit Agreements Act that retention of title cannot be agreed as security for the consumer meeting its obligations regarding another purchase or to secure payment of other amounts which the creditor cannot legitimately secure under Section 38.

In this connection, it should be noted that the conditions of the Credit Agreements Act do not apply to situations involving traders' purchases for resale or purchases of materials for the operation of a business (see Section 2(1) of the Credit Agreements Act).

When the seller and the buyer have entered into an agreement on a valid retention of title, the effect in property law is that, in the event of a material breach by the buyer, the seller may demand recovery of the object sold, even where the buyer's other creditors have subsequently acquired rights in the object. This was established in, among other cases, U 1952.978 H, in which a car had been sold subject to retention of title. The buyer had mortgaged the car to a mortgagee. When the buyer defaulted on his payment, the seller became entitled to recover the car under the retention of title and to sell it to a new buyer irrespective of the mortgagee's subsequently created right.

(b) Effect in case of seizure of goods or security right established over goods delivered under retention of title

It is generally assumed that the holder of a validly created retention of title is not affected by any security right created by the buyer in favour of subsequent assignees, or by an execution levied by the buyer's creditors. This is because any such security rights are created only over the buyer's conditional title to the object. In this connection, it must be pointed out that if the retention of title is in a motor vehicle, the retention of title must be registered in the motor vehicles securities register in order to obtain protection against extinction (see Section 42d of the Registration of Property Act).

An owner of a commercial undertaking may mortgage what the undertaking owns and will acquire in future – a situation referred to as a company charge. It follows from Section 47c(6) and (7) of the Registration of Property Act that a company charge must be subject to any retention of title in movable property which has been agreed at the latest concurrently with the surrender of the object, as well as to any retention of title in motor vehicles which has been agreed and registered in the motor vehicles securities register concurrently with the surrender at the latest.

According to the rules on mortgage rights over equipment, separate rights over material to be used in a building, such as wires, heating installations, household machines or the like incorporated into a building at the owner's expense and for use by the building's occupants, cannot be upheld. According to Section 38 of the Registration of Property Act this applies to rights to title or other rights, including retention of title. A registered mortgage on a property also covers such equipment without the need for any separate process.

It is assumed in the legal literature that the extinction of retention of title under Section 38 of the Registration of Property Act also applies if the object sold subject to retention of title is incorporated into an aircraft or a vessel.

(c) Effect in case of insolvency

In the event that the buyer of an object sold subject to retention of title is declared bankrupt after recovery proceedings have been commenced, recovery will be excluded if the bankruptcy estate exercises its mandatory right to become a party to the contract (see Section 55 of the Bankruptcy Act). This is subject to the bankruptcy estate, before the recovery proceedings have been finalised, paying the entire amount that was not paid in due time, as well as interest and costs.

The estate may become a party to the agreement, even where the other contracting party benefiting from the retention of title may, as a secured creditor, demand recovery of a service delivered by him. However, where the other contracting party is entitled, under Section 58 of the Bankruptcy Act, to terminate the agreement for cause, the estate will be precluded from becoming a party.

When the bankruptcy estate becomes a party to the agreement, the estate will enjoy the same rights and obligations as the buyer. Danish law does not grant any specific rights to the bankruptcy estate in this connection.

The estate is never under an obligation to become a party, but it may become a party either by way of express notification that it wishes to become a party or by way of its actions. The estate's consumption of, or participation in transactions involving, the objects in question will often be considered to indicate that the estate has become a party to the agreement.

If the bankruptcy estate does not become a party to the agreement, the seller may, as a secured creditor under Section 82 of the Bankruptcy Act, seek satisfaction independently from the bankruptcy proceedings (see Section 58 of the Bankruptcy Act).

(d) Effect in case of partial payment of purchase price

It makes no difference to the rights of the buyer's bankruptcy estate that the buyer has made partial payment in advance of the bankruptcy, if the bankruptcy estate chooses to become a party to the agreement and makes the payment.

In connection with recovery, the principle set out in Section 57 of the Sale of Goods Act applies, according to which a seller is entitled to claim payment of the outstanding amount if the value of the object is lower than the outstanding amount, and must likewise pay the excess amount back to the buyer or the bankruptcy estate if the object recovered has a value that is higher than the outstanding amount.

The outstanding amount is defined in Section 38 of the Credit Agreements Act and essentially constitutes the unpaid part of the claim, interest accrued on amounts having fallen due and expenses incidental to the recovery.

In consumer transactions, the creditor may, if the value of the object sold exceeds the amount owed to it, only recover the object sold if the excess amount is paid to the consumer simultaneously (see Section 40 of the Credit Agreements Act).

To the extent that the value of the item being repossessed is, at the time of the recovery proceedings, lower than the outstanding amount owed, the creditor is only entitled to payment of the amount in excess, after the object has been recovered, and may only levy execution for it in special circumstances, in particular if the consumer has been negligent in their use of the object or its storage, or they have impeded the recovery proceedings (see Section 41 of the Credit Agreements Act).

3. Enforcement of retention of title

In the event of the buyer's breach of its payment obligation under a credit agreement with a validly adopted retention of title, the seller is entitled, within a specific framework, to seek satisfaction of its claim by way of recovery proceedings according to the rules on summary enforcement proceedings. Recovery is subject to the breach being material.

In connection with a retention of title covered by the Credit Agreements Act (a purchase on credit subject to retention of title) Section 29 of the act applies, both in consumer transactions and in transactions between traders (see Section 49 of the Credit Agreements Act). According to Section 29, a material breach exists when the party making a purchase on credit fails to meet its payment obligation 30 days after the due date. The amount due must constitute either at least 10% of the total purchase price (including any down-payment), and if the due amount includes more than one instalment, at least 5% of the total purchase price (including any down-payment), or the entire residual amount owed.

The party holding the retention of title may seek satisfaction by way of recovery both in court and out of court.

In connection with in-court satisfaction, recovery takes place by way of summary enforcement proceedings, meaning that the enforcement court is involved.

Out-of-court satisfaction in purchases with retention of title may as a general rule only take place if an agreement in this respect has been entered into. If the parties have not agreed that recovery may take place, this will in most cases constitute illegal self-help. Consent to recovery can be by way of express agreement, or can be inferred from the buyer's behaviour.

It must be assumed that a refusal by the buyer to comply with such an agreement would be unlawful.

In the event that recovery is to take place from a buyer who has the objects in his possession, the creditor may, according to the circumstances, claim satisfaction either in court or out of court.

A creditor wanting to undertake recovery through the court must file a written application to this effect with the enforcement court, which must include information about the party from whom the recovery is to take place and a statement of the amount owed to the creditor, together with the original sales agreement or a copy thereof (see Section 45(1) and (2) of the Credit Agreements Act).

In consumer transactions, it follows from Section 35 of the Credit Agreements Act that the creditor must seek satisfaction of its claim by way of recovery of the object sold unless the object would be exempt from execution according to the rules relating to such exemptions or if the object is of personal sentimental value (see Section 36(3) of the Credit Agreements Act, containing references to the relevant rules in this respect of the Administration of Justice Act).

In one case, U 1985.453/1Ø, it was held that a fridge-freezer purchased subject to retention of title was exempt from the levy of execution according to the rules on exemption in the Administration of Justice Act, while in U 2014.2268 Ø it was held that an iPhone 5 was not exempt from execution according to those.

It is a requirement in connection with recovery that the agreement was signed and a copy of the agreement handed over to the buyer, and that it contains a provision on retention of title (see Section 36 of the Credit Agreements Act).

In the event that the object sold is not at the premises of the consumer when recovery is attempted, the creditor may levy execution for the amount owed.

Upon recovery of the object concerned, the value of the object at the time of recovery must be included in the statement of account between the parties to the benefit of the consumer (see Section 39(1) of the Credit Agreements Act). The value of the object must be taken to mean the amount which the seller may obtain when selling the object in an appropriate way, possibly following reasonable repair (see Section 39(2) of the Credit Agreements Act).

If the value of the object exceeds the amount owed to the creditor, the creditor may only recover the object if the excess amount is at the same time paid to the consumer (see Section 40 of the Credit Agreements Act).

To the extent that the value of the item, at the time of the recovery proceedings, is lower than the amount owed to the creditor, the creditor is only entitled to payment of the amount in excess after the object has been recovered and may only levy execution for it in special circumstances, in particular if the consumer has been negligent in use of the object or its storage, or has impeded the recovery proceedings (see Section 41 of the Credit Agreements Act).

In transactions between traders, the creditor is not under an obligation to seek satisfaction by way of recovery, but is entitled, as an alternative, to seek satisfaction through the buyer's other assets. If the value of the object sold subject to retention of title is lower than the amount owed to the creditor, then according to Section 38, the creditor is entitled to receive payment of the amount in excess.

If the objects that are subject to recovery proceedings are not located at the buyer's premises, the creditor is entitled to levy execution against the buyer for the amount owed.

In such circumstances, the holder of the retention of title may recover the object in the same manner, as if he were doing so directly from the buyer, to the extent that the third party does not have a right that extinguishes the seller's retention of title.

A third party may as a general rule not refuse to hand over an object subject to an otherwise valid right of retention. The general rule is, however, derogated from in certain cases where the right of retention results from work performed by him which was necessary to protect the object or where the work performed has increased the value of the object. A third party wanting to enforce such a right of retention must have been acting in good faith.

If the holder of the retention of title wants to enforce its claim to recovery, he must do so with the assistance of the enforcement court.

According to Danish law, retention of title may only be enforced by recovery if the object to be recovered is properly specified. As the specification requirement is only really relevant when it comes to the possibility of enforcing retention of title, requirements for specification of the objects sold subject to retention of title may in principle be met at the time of delivery, but not at a later point in time, such as if the buyer subsequently acquires further objects which may be confused with the original objects.

In practice, the requirements for specification are assessed in each case on the basis of the facts and circumstances of the particular case. The assessment is aimed at identifying the object sold subject to retention of title among any other objects which the buyer may have.

An object subject to retention of title will typically be sufficiently specified if the make, type, number, year, colour and material are indicated, or if the agreement includes a reference to a label affixed on the object that cannot easily be removed. In relation to motor vehicles, the identification requirement is defined by way of the formal requirements regarding registration in the motor vehicles securities register (see Section 42d of the Registration of Property Act).

In practice, there is a tendency for the specification requirement to be examined more strictly if the validity of the retention of title is disputed in court proceedings initiated by the creditors or subsequent assignees of the buyer, than if it is disputed by the buyer during recovery proceedings initiated by the seller.

In the event of the buyer's bankruptcy, the holder of the retention of title must prove its claim to status as a secured creditor, or as a pre-preferential claim in the event that the asset covered by the retention of title is sold.

Finland

Pekka Jaatinen
Elina Pesonen
Christer Svartström
Castrén & Snellman

1. General remarks about retention of title

1.1 Transfer of ownership

The transfer of ownership, or title, to an asset is primarily based on the contractual freedom of the parties. Parties may freely agree as to how the transfer of ownership to an asset shall be deemed to have taken place. In the absence of any contractual provisions, ownership regarding movable property is determined by the transfer of physical possession.

There are certain exceptions to the general rule. The transfer of ownership of real property requires that the deed concerning the transfer of ownership be made in a specified form. Ownership to certain assets that require special permission due to their nature may not be transferred until the assignee has obtained any necessary permits.

Title to certain movable assets, such as marine and air vessels, may be registered in official registers. Although a contract between parties concerning the transfer of title is valid between those parties, the registration of ownership validates the transfer of title in relation to third parties, and may provide a buyer protection against loss of title, as registers of assets are deemed to be public knowledge. Generally, however, possession of an asset is a strong indicator of title.

Apart from the exceptions mentioned above, parties may freely agree on how and when the transfer of ownership takes place. For example, the transfer of ownership may be immediate, delayed or subject to set preconditions.

1.2 Retention of title

Finnish national law allows a seller to retain ownership of an asset until certain conditions have been met. Retention of title is, thus, a valid real security under Finnish law if duly perfected. There is, however, a distinction between the validity of the retention of title as security between the parties to the agreement and in relation to third-party creditors. The enforceability of the retention of title in statutory insolvency proceedings requires that the retention of title be valid in relation to third-party creditors. This is also the case in execution proceedings outside statutory insolvency proceedings when the execution of other creditors' debts is involved.

Although retention of title is originally based on case law, legal principles and real arguments, the validity of retention of title in statutory insolvency proceedings has been codified in the Bankruptcy Act (120/2004 as amended). According to

Chapter 5, Section 7 of the Bankruptcy Act, in order for a retention of title to be considered valid, the following conditions must be fulfilled:

- the asset must be clearly separable from the other assets of the buyer;
- the retention of title must be agreed on before the transfer of possession of the asset to the buyer; and
- the buyer may not be entitled to pass on or otherwise dispose of the asset, combine, mix or mingle it with its other assets, or otherwise dispose of the asset as if the owner.

These requirements set out in the Bankruptcy Act are also applied in restructuring proceedings in accordance with the Restructuring of Enterprises Act (47/1993 as amended).

Hire purchase agreements concerning movable property, where the purchase price is paid in several instalments of which at least one falls due after possession of the goods has been transferred, are governed by the Hire Purchase Act (91/1966 as amended). The Hire Purchase Act does not include provisions concerning the validity of a retention of title, but provides requirements concerning other provisions included in such agreements, as well as the procedure for repossessing goods sold under the act. Such requirements are, for example, the form in which the hire purchase agreement must be, the information which has to be included in the agreement and the amount of payments in arrears required for repossession of the security asset.

The validity of retention of title under the Hire Purchase Act is determined in accordance with the general principles discussed later.

1.3 Foreign and international law

The validity of retention of title in an agreement governed by a law other than Finnish law is determined between the parties to the agreement by the applicable law. However, the validity of the retention of title in relation to third-party creditors is judged solely by Finnish law if the asset in question is located in Finland.

Furthermore, insolvency proceedings taking place within Finnish jurisdiction are governed only by Finnish insolvency legislation, regardless of the contractual arrangement between the parties. As the validity of any retention of title in Finnish insolvency proceedings is determined by its effectiveness against third parties, the retention of title must satisfy the requirements set forth in the Bankruptcy Act.

1.4 Retention of title in insolvency

The Finnish insolvency regime consists of two forms of insolvency proceedings: bankruptcy and restructuring. In bankruptcy proceedings, authority over the debtor's assets is transferred to the bankruptcy estate, for which an administrator is appointed by a competent court. The purpose of bankruptcy proceedings is the complete liquidation of the debtor's assets and the distribution of the proceeds to the creditors in accordance with the ranking of their claims.

Restructuring proceedings aim to restructure the business of an insolvent debtor and thus prevent bankruptcy. Restructuring proceedings are based on the principle of debtor in possession, whereby a debtor generally retains control of its assets. An administrator is appointed by a competent court to oversee the proceedings and to prepare a restructuring programme outlining restructuring measures to be applied to debts and measures to be taken by the debtor.

In order for a retention of title to be valid and enforceable in Finnish bankruptcy and restructuring proceedings, the retention of title clause needs to be effective in relation to other creditors of the debtor. Therefore, the clause needs to fulfil the requirements set out in the Bankruptcy Act, as described above.

The stringent requirements concerning the validity of a retention of title clause leads to claims based on such clauses often being dismissed in insolvency proceedings. Under Finnish law, retention of title is ineffective if a debtor may dispose of an asset as if it were the owner of the asset. Such disposition does not need to have taken place; the mere possibility is sufficient. Furthermore, the right to dispose of an asset is presumed, based on the nature of the asset. Retaining title to certain assets, such as current assets, is rarely possible.

As only the Bankruptcy Act includes provisions concerning the validity of retention of title, these provisions are applied only in insolvency proceedings under Finnish law. Should the buyer be subject to insolvency proceedings outside Finnish jurisdiction, the validity of the retention of title is determined according to the laws of the relevant jurisdiction.

The purpose of the provisions outlined above is the protection of other creditors of the debtor. The validity of a retention of title is therefore unaffected should the seller be subject to statutory insolvency proceedings. In restructuring proceedings, the seller retains the right to invoke its retention of title in the event of a default by the buyer. In bankruptcy proceedings, the right to invoke retention of title is transferred to the bankruptcy estate.

2. Retention of title

2.1 Validity and formal requirements

Retention of title may be freely agreed on by the parties in order to be binding between them. However, the Bankruptcy Act contains provisions concerning the validity of the retention of title in relation to third parties. As the effectiveness of the retention of title as real security is determined based on its effectiveness against third parties, the requirements concerning the retention of title will be discussed here as they are set out in the Bankruptcy Act.

The retention of title does not have to be agreed upon in writing to be legally valid, and the law does not prescribe any form for the clause. However, due to the requirements of the Bankruptcy Act for a valid and enforceable retention of title clause, proving the exact content of the clause and when it was agreed upon can become practically impossible if the retention of title is not in writing. In practice therefore, a retention of title will only be valid in writing.

The Bankruptcy Act requires that the retention of title must have been agreed upon prior to the transfer of possession of the relevant assets. Once the buyer has taken possession of an asset, retention of title to the asset may no longer be effectively agreed upon.[1] Furthermore, the Bankruptcy Act requires that both parties have specifically agreed on the retention of title, and a unilateral declaration by the seller notifying the buyer of the retention of title is not sufficient to retain title to an asset.[2] The common practice of notifying the buyer of the retention of title in invoices pertaining to sold goods is therefore considered invalid.

There are no formal requirements as to the wording of the retention of title clause. To ensure that the requirements set forth in the Bankruptcy Act concerning retention of title are adhered to, it is generally advisable to prohibit the buyer from assigning the goods, or from mingling or mixing the goods with its other assets. However, the validity of the retention of title is judged by an overall assessment of the relevant circumstances, and as such, there is no generally accepted form for a valid retention of title clause.

The same principle of an overall assessment applies to a reference to a retention of title clause in an agreement. The retention of title must generally be referred to explicitly and specifically in an agreement to be considered valid, and the buyer must actually become aware of the clause prior to committing to the agreement. A retention of title clause in general terms and conditions may be considered valid if sufficient reference to the respective general terms and conditions has been made in an agreement, and the buyer has actually had the opportunity to review them. However, in light of case law concerning retention of title in insolvency and enforcement proceedings, there remains a certain degree of uncertainty as to the validity of retention of title if solely included in general terms and conditions.[3]

Goods to which title is retained may be delivered directly to the buyer, or to a third party. The law requires that the goods must be clearly separable from the assets of the buyer. As possession generally creates the presumption of ownership, assets for which title has been retained may be more clearly separable if held by a third party. This reduces the risk of mingling with the assets of the buyer, and thus the invalidity of the retention of title. Certain consignment stock arrangements may also provide sufficient separability of goods for which title has been retained.

2.2 Scope of retention of title

(a) *Sale of goods delivered under retention of title*

Ownership of an asset entails the right freely to sell the asset to other parties. For a retention of title to be valid in relation to third parties, the buyer must not be entitled to dispose of the asset as if its owner. Retention of title is, therefore, invalid in relation to third parties if the buyer has the right to sell the asset.

(b) *Combining/mixing/mingling goods delivered under retention of title*

Under the provisions of the Bankruptcy Act, a retention of title is invalid in relation

---

1 For example decision KKO 1986 I 2 of the Supreme Court.
2 For example decision KKO 1994:113 of the Supreme Court.
3 Decision KKO 1993:45 of the Supreme Court, whereby the retention of title clause included in general terms and conditions was not considered effective in relation to third parties, as the buyer did not have the opportunity to review the general terms and conditions prior to entering into the agreement.

to third parties if the asset for which title has been retained is not clearly separable from the assets of the buyer. If mixing has taken place, the asset may no longer be individualised as a security object, and the retention of title is considered ineffective. Furthermore, should the intended purpose or typical usage of the asset necessitate mixing or combining the asset with the assets of the buyer, the buyer is presumed to be entitled to mix or combine the asset with its assets. Unless this is expressly prohibited by the agreement, title to such assets may not be effectively retained. Such is the case with current assets, for which the retention of title is generally not possible without a consignment stock or other comparable arrangement.

The provisions of the Bankruptcy Act require that the entire asset be separable from the assets of the buyer. Separation through quantitative means is not sufficient for title to be retained. For example, oil sold to a buyer is considered mixed and loses its separability if stored in a tank already containing a certain quantity of oil, regardless of how reliably the sold quantity can be determined. Sufficient separability may be achieved through, for example, completely differentiated storage and proper labelling.

The same principle holds for assets which are combined with and become part of assets of the buyer, such as tyres and spare parts. As the ordinary usage of such assets requires their combination with other assets, a buyer is presumed to be entitled to combine the goods to his assets, unless explicitly prohibited in the contract of sale. Thus, the mere possibility of combining the assets as required by the ordinary usage of those assets may invalidate any retention of title in relation to third parties.

(c) ***Processing of goods delivered under retention of title***

As with mixing and combining, the retention of title to goods which are sold for the purpose of processing them into finished or semi-finished products is invalid in relation to third parties insofar as the buyer is not prohibited from taking the goods into use prior to full payment for them. Due to the nature of such goods, a buyer is presumed to be entitled to take the goods into use unless explicitly prohibited by contract. Furthermore, the goods must be separable from the property of the buyer.

Contractual provisions according to which title is retained to the finished or semi-finished products (or any products into which the sold goods have been incorporated) are considered null and void, as they do not sufficiently individualise the security asset underlying the retention of title clause. The same holds for provisions according to which a seller is entitled to any proceeds received for selling the original goods, or the finished or semi-finished products.

(d) ***Extension of retention of title***

A negative stance towards the extension of a retention of title to other claims of the seller has been adopted in Finnish case law.[4] Title may, therefore, be retained as security only for receivables directly related to the sale of the specific asset to the buyer.

The Hire Purchase Act prohibits the extension of a retention of title to other

4 For example decisions KKO 1977 I 1 and KKO 1992:122 of the Supreme Court.

claims of the seller in agreements falling under the scope of the act, whereby such provisions are also considered invalid between the parties to the agreement. The Hire Purchase Act is applicable to agreements where payment of the purchase price is made in instalments, of which at least one falls due after possession of sales object has been transferred to the buyer.

There are no provisions concerning the extension of retention of title to other claims of the seller for agreements falling outside the scope of the Hire Purchase Act, and extending the retention of title may therefore be valid as between the parties in such agreements.

2.3 Legal effect of retention of title

(a) *Effect towards third parties*

Retention of title will not have an automatic effect towards third parties, and must be invoked by the seller.

Retention of title may be invoked against the buyer upon the termination of the agreement. Should the buyer refuse to return the security asset, the seller may take action in court in order to repossess the asset. Such action may be taken even if the retention of title clause would only be binding between the parties.

A particular form of action for repossession is applicable when the contract falls under the scope of the Hire Purchase Act. Under that act, repossession of the security asset may be requested from an execution officer. An execution officer is authorised to take possession of the asset on behalf of the seller. The execution officer values the asset in order to determine the outstanding debt of the buyer after the repossession. Should the value of the asset exceed that of the remaining debt, the buyer is entitled to pay the remaining instalments together with costs incurred as a lump sum to the seller and take ownership to the asset, or, alternatively, to receive compensation from the seller for the value of the asset less the remaining instalments according to the agreement and the costs incurred by the seller due to the repossession proceedings.

A good faith subsequent buyer receives protection against loss of title where the original buyer has disposed of the asset in breach of the agreement between the seller and the original buyer. In this case, the seller retains the right to redeem the asset for the same price as the subsequent buyer paid for the asset. The original buyer is liable for such costs towards the seller, and payment may be demanded by the seller.

These possibilities are available to the seller even if the retention of title is effective only between the parties to the agreement. Enforcement of the retention of title in statutory insolvency proceedings (bankruptcy and restructuring) and in enforcement proceedings, where other creditors' claims are also enforced, requires the retention of title to be effective against third parties. This requires that the retention of title satisfy the requirements of the Bankruptcy Act discussed above.

(b) *Effect in case of seizure of goods delivered under retention of title*

For the retention of title to be valid in the event that the buyer's assets are seized, the retention of title must be effective against third parties as provided for in the Bankruptcy Act. In the case of an effective retention of title, the seller may invoke the retention of title and demand separation of the seller's assets from the seized assets by taking action for repossession.

Executing any transfer of goods for which title has been effectively retained may lead to liability on the part of the executing party towards the seller, if the executing party is, or should have been, aware of the effective retention of title and the goods have been passed on to a subsequent buyer. The seller retains the right to redeem the asset for the same price as the subsequent buyer has paid for the asset. The executing party's liability covers reimbursement of the redemption price plus costs incurred by the seller. The seller's title is always protected against a party not acting in good faith, if the retention of title is effective against third parties.

(c) ***Effect in case of a security right established over goods delivered under retention of title***

As with selling goods, establishing a security right over an asset is considered a disposition reserved for the owner of an asset. Retention of title by the seller is not effective against third parties if the buyer is entitled to establish a security over the asset.

The secured party would retain the security in the event that the retention of title does not fulfil the requirements of the Bankruptcy Act regarding effective retention of title in relation to third parties. Similarly, the asset would be counted as an encumbered asset should a floating charge be established over the assets of the buyer.

Should an asset for which title has been effectively retained be pledged to a secured party acting in good faith, the secured party is protected from the seller of the asset. The seller is, however, entitled to redeem the asset from the secured party. The buyer is liable toward the seller for costs related to the redemption of the asset.

Establishing a non-possessory security right, such as a floating charge, over the asset is generally not possible if the retention of title is effective against third parties.

(d) ***Effect in case of insolvency***

A debtor's contracts are not automatically terminated upon the initiation of bankruptcy proceedings, and provisions whereby a party's bankruptcy entitles the counterparty to terminate an agreement are considered null and void. According to the Bankruptcy Act, a bankruptcy estate has a right of subrogation to the debtor's contracts, enabling the bankruptcy estate to become part of the contract. Should the bankruptcy estate choose not to use this right, the contract may be terminated and any retention of title invoked, if it is regarded as effective against third parties.

Property owned by third parties does not belong to a bankruptcy estate. As a valid retention of title enables the seller to retain ownership to an asset, the seller has the right, upon termination of the relevant agreement, to repossess the asset. A bankruptcy estate is required by the Bankruptcy Act to hand over all assets owned by third parties and in possession of the estate to their rightful owners.

As with bankruptcy proceedings, contracts are not automatically terminated in restructuring proceedings. In contrast to bankruptcy proceedings, restructuring proceedings under the Restructuring of Enterprises Act rely on the principle of the continuity of agreements, whereby the parties' and the restructuring administrator's rights to terminate agreements are limited. Therefore, an agreement containing a retention of title clause remains in effect, and a valid retention of title in force.

Any indebtedness incurred prior to filing for restructuring is considered restructuring debt, and may be subject to restructuring measures, including cutting of the remaining debt capital. The initiation of restructuring proceedings freezes all a debtor's restructuring debts, and the debtor is prohibited from repaying such debts. Similarly, creditors are prohibited from enforcing these debts.

However, the Restructuring of Enterprises Act separates unsecured restructuring debt from secured debt. Secured debt is protected from the cutting of the debt capital insofar as the value of the security asset covers the debt. Furthermore, a secured creditor is entitled to compensation for any depreciation of the security asset due to its use by the debtor in its business operations during the restructuring proceedings.

A seller who validly retains title to an asset is considered a secured creditor insofar as the value of the asset at the time of initiation of the restructuring proceedings covers the debt. Such a seller may be entitled to compensation for depreciation if the asset is used by the debtor, such as may be the case with vehicles. The seller is also protected against the cutting of the debt capital. Finally, the seller retains the right to terminate the contract and repossess the security asset should the debtor breach other aspects of the contract not relating to the repayment of the original debt.

(e) Effect in case of partial payment of the purchase price

Agreements under which the purchase price is paid in instalments are governed by the Hire Purchase Agreement. According to that act, if the purchase price already paid exceeds the original debt less the value of the goods at the time of repossession and costs incurred to the seller, the seller is required to refund this amount to the buyer. The seller is not entitled to repossess the goods until payment is made to the buyer or, where the repossession has been carried out by an enforcement officer, the funds have been entrusted to the enforcement officer.

The buyer is entitled to acquire title to the goods by paying to the seller any outstanding monies owed by the buyer to the seller in connection with the agreement as a lump sum.

Agreements which do not fall within the scope of the Hire Purchase Act are governed by general principles concerning contracts and legal acts. Unless agreed otherwise, the seller is not required to accept partial payment, and partial payment may therefore be regarded as defaulting on payment of the purchase price. Consequently, the seller may take action for repossession based on the buyer's default.

Based on general contractual principles regarding unjust enrichment, the seller may, in the case of repossession of the asset, be required to reimburse the buyer for the value of the asset that exceeds the amount outstanding under the agreement plus any costs incurred by the seller.

3. Enforcement of retention of title

The process for repossession of goods for which title has been retained depends on whether the sales agreement falls within the scope of the Hire Purchase Agreement.

Repossession under that act is procedurally lighter than in cases outside the act. The parties may make an agreement regarding repossession, whereby the buyer returns the asset to the seller, and the parties settle any disparities between the outstanding debt and the purchase price already paid. Alternatively, an execution officer of the governmental execution office may be requested to repossess the asset and prepare an account of the outstanding debt and purchase price already paid. The execution officer maintains control over the asset for the duration of the proceedings.

The seller is not entitled singlehandedly to repossess goods from the buyer. Should the buyer not be willing to return the asset, the seller may request assistance from an execution officer for the repossession of the asset. The seller is not, however, prohibited from utilising private services in order to locate the asset, and such services are often utilised by financial institutions.

If the agreement falls outside of the scope of the Hire Purchase Act, repossession may also be agreed upon between the seller and the buyer. Should the buyer be unwilling to pass over the asset, however, the seller is required to initiate an action for repossession by filing an application to a competent court. Should the seller obtain a declaratory judgement concerning the asset from the court, the seller may request an execution officer to enforce the judgement to regain control of the asset.

In agreements both under the Hire Purchase Act and outside it, the seller must be able to individualise the asset for which enforcement measures are sought, and to produce an agreement showing the obligation of the buyer to the seller.

Repossession of goods sold subject to retention of title does not generally differ in situations where the buyer is subject to statutory insolvency proceedings. The retention of title must, however, be considered effective against third parties as set out in the Bankruptcy Act in order to be enforced in insolvency proceedings. It should be noted, though, that payment default may not be invoked in restructuring proceedings for debts that are regarded as restructuring debts, or have arisen prior to filing for restructuring. Enforcing such debts is prohibited by the Restructuring of Enterprises Act. The prohibition does not prevent enforcement of the retention of title in the event of a breach of contract unrelated to payment default.

France

Amélie Dorst
Anja Droege Gagnier
BMH Avocats

1. General remarks about retention of title

1.1 Transfer of ownership

French law has adopted a system of abstract and immediate transfer of ownership, which is simply based on agreement to the sale and the price to be paid.

According to Article 1583 of the French Civil Code:

The ownership is acquired as of right by the buyer with regard to the seller as soon as they have agreed on the thing and on the price, although the thing has not yet been delivered nor the price paid.

However, the rule set out in the Civil Code is not mandatory and the parties are free to agree to an alternative mechanism. The transfer of ownership may be postponed by inserting a time period or a condition. For instance, the transfer of ownership may be subject to a future event that will occur at a moment that is not yet known.[1]

1.2 Retention of title

Through the concept of a retention of title clause, the seller is entitled to postpone the transfer of ownership until receipt of full payment for the goods. The transfer of ownership is not an automatic effect of the contract anymore, but is subject to the performance of the buyer's obligation: the full payment.

French law has recognised the concept of retention of title clause since the 1980s[2] but its effect on third parties was limited to insolvency proceedings. Recently, reservation of title has been introduced by the Ordinance of March 23 2006 reforming securities law as a general contractual mechanism applicable in the absence of any insolvency proceedings.[3]

Retention of title is now codified as security in the French Civil Code under Articles 2367 to 2372 and in the French Commercial Code under Articles L 624-9 to L 624-18.

Article 2367 of the French Civil Code states the following:

The ownership of a thing may be retained as a guarantee as a result of a clause of reservation of ownership that suspends the transferring effect of a contract until

1 Article 1185 of the Civil Code.
2 Law 802-335 of May 12 1980.
3 P Crocq, *"Clause de réserve de propriété"*, *Jurisclasseur Contrats – Distribution*, 2012, paragraph 22.

payment in full of the obligation which compensates for it. The ownership thus reserved is the accessory of the claim whose payment it guarantees.

1.3 Foreign and international law

According to the choice of law principle, the parties are free under French law to choose which law is most convenient to their contract. However, in French international private law, the transfer of ownership is governed by the law of the place where the goods are located. Therefore, if the goods are located in France, the retention of title clause must be recognised as such by the French jurisdiction. In this regard, extended retention of title,[4] known in some jurisdictions (such as Germany), is not acknowledged under French law.

According to French international private law, the law which is applicable for the retention of title clause depends on the relevant relationship of the parties:

- With regard to matters concerning the relationship between the parties themselves, the validity and effectiveness of a retention of title provision is subject to the law that governs their contractual relations;
- With regard to matters concerning the relationship between the parties to the agreement and third parties, the validity of the retention of title provision will be governed by the law of the contract, and the effectiveness of the retention of title would be governed by the law of the place where the goods are located. Therefore, if the contract contains a German style of retention of title provision with an extended scope of application and if the goods are located in France, the clause would not be effective, since such a clause[5] is not recognised in France.

1.4 Retention of title in insolvency

Insolvency law provisions are matters of public policy: following the opening judgment of insolvency proceedings, retention of title is governed by insolvency law provisions.

French insolvency law is detailed in Book VI of the French Commercial Code, as reformed and amended from time to time, including in 2005 (Law 2005-845 of July 26 2005), in 2008 (Order 2008-1345 of December 18 2008), in 2010 (Law 2010-1249 of October 22 2010) and more recently in March 2014 (Order 2014-326 of March 12 2014).

French insolvency proceedings are court-controlled procedures, comprising different tools used according to the situation and difficulties faced by the debtor:

- the safeguard procedure (*sauvegarde*)[6] and the accelerated safeguard procedure (*sauvegarde accélérée*), including the accelerated financial safeguard procedure (*sauvegarde financière accélérée*), to be opened when the debtor is still solvent; and

---

4 With an extended retention of title, the seller's title to the delivered goods reserves ownership even if they were combined, mixed or processed with the purchaser's products or even if the goods were sold to a third party.

5 Cass Com, 1 Civ, July 8 1969, Société DIAC.

6 We have chosen to classify the safeguard procedure under insolvency proceedings even though the debtor is not yet insolvent when such proceedings are started, but only in financial difficulties it might not overcome.

- the reorganisation (*redressement*) and judicial liquidation (*liquidation judiciaire*) procedures, to be opened once the debtor becomes insolvent.

If the purchaser or the initial seller are subject to insolvency proceedings in France, the provisions of French insolvency law will apply and trigger a general stay of legal actions for the benefit of the debtor in insolvency.

If the purchaser is subject to insolvency proceedings in France, and if the seller has not yet delivered the asset, the seller can refuse to do so until full payment of the purchase price.

If the seller is subject to insolvency proceedings in France, it will be necessary to know whether the contract has already been performed or not. If the asset has not yet been delivered, the judicial administrator will be entitled to decide whether to perform the contract or not.

2. Retention of title

2.1 Validity and formal requirements

According to Article 2368 of the French Civil Code and the second paragraph of Article L 624-16 of the French Commercial Code, a retention of title clause must "be agreed to in writing" in order to be legally valid and have effects against third parties. This requirement aims to protect third-party creditors by reducing the risk of fraud.[7] But the clause does not need to be registered in a public register or acknowledged by a notary.[8]

The clause can simply stipulate that "the goods remain the property of the seller unless and until their full payment is received by the buyer".[9] There are no formal requirements regarding the wording, except that the clause must be clear enough and unequivocal so as to avoid any dispute with respect to its existence.[10] Therefore, the clause should not be printed using a small or illegible typeface, or be hidden among other generic clauses.

However, the clause must be stipulated (and agreed upon in writing) at the time of delivery at the latest, as stated in the second paragraph of Article L 624-16 of the French Commercial Code, because of the consensual character of the retention of title clause. "It can also be done in a written document governing all the commercial transactions agreed upon between the parties."[11] The same written document including the reservation of title can cover several commercial operations, as long as this is agreed to between the parties. Most of the time, the retention of title is agreed to between parties in the general terms and conditions of the seller.

Proof of agreement by the buyer to the clause is essential to its enforceability. The

---

7 P Crocq, *"Clause de réserve de propriété", Jurisclasseur Contrats – Distribution*, 2012, paragraph 61.

8 Although no formality of publicity is required by French law for the validity of a retention of title provision, publication of the contract containing the retention of title clause by the seller is recommended (see below).

9 The use of a foreign language is allowed if the language is commonly used and is that of one of the contracting parties.

10 Cass Com, March 3 1992.

11 Article L 624-16, second paragraph, of the Commercial Code.

agreement may be either express or tacit. For example, agreement is qualified as express when a representative of the buying company acknowledges receipt of the goods on a form mentioning the clause or signs a delivery invoice mentioning the clause.

The clause can be tacitly agreed to through the unconditional execution of a document mentioning the retention of title, for instance when the buyer fulfils the contract with full knowledge of the retention of title clause, without any complaints or denial.[12]

For the retention of title to be valid, it is not essential that the goods be directly delivered to the purchaser, the goods may be delivered to a third party as well.

With regard to risk transfer, French law provides that risks are transferred with ownership. Therefore, where there is a retention of title clause, the risks would normally remain with the seller under the reservation of title until full payment of the purchase price. However, the parties may agree otherwise in their contract. Therefore the risks are usually transferred to the purchaser at the date of the delivery of the goods.

2.2 Scope of retention of title

(a) Sale of goods delivered under retention of title

The purchaser is not entitled to sell and transfer goods under retention of title to a third party before having paid the purchase price due to the seller. Moreover, the parties cannot stipulate a clause which entitles the purchaser to sell the goods and commits the third party to transfer the purchase price to the initial seller.

French law is very clear about double selling. Under Article 1599 of the French Civil Code, the sale of any asset belonging to another person is void. Nevertheless, regarding movables, this rule is superseded by the rules on good-faith acquisition. According to Article 2276 of the French Civil Code: "as far as movables are concerned, possession equals title". The rules on good-faith acquisition protect the sub-purchaser who did not know or could not have known that its acquisition was encumbered by the ownership rights of the initial seller. In this respect, possession by the purchaser serves as title with respect to the sub-purchaser, who does not need to make any verification regarding the rights of the purchaser.

Therefore, in a sale of goods delivered under retention of title, the initial seller will lose its ownership if the subsequent buyer acts in good faith (see below). But the initial seller can claim for restitution of the price against the subsequent purchaser under Article 2372 of the French Civil Code, if the latter has not yet paid its seller. The mechanism here is a personal action against the subsequent purchaser. If the subsequent buyer has already paid its direct seller, the initial seller can only try to claim compensation for loss suffered against its direct purchaser.

(b) Combining/mixing/mingling goods delivered under retention of title

Under French law, combining, mixing or mingling generally leads to loss of ownership for the initial seller. But the initial seller can still claim for restitution in

12 Cass Com, June 27 1989, 87-15.847; Cass Com January 3 1995, Bull Civ 3, p2.

kind of fungible assets, if they are of the same nature and quality as the ones delivered by it, and if these assets are held by the debtor or on its behalf.[13] In this case the initial seller does not lose its ownership completely, but it is transformed into a 'real right' on someone else's goods.[14]

French law considers that an asset incorporated into another asset still exists in kind if it can be separated without causing any damage.[15] A substantial alteration caused to the asset by a separation would present such damage, but a decrease in value of the attached asset would not be considered as such.[16] For instance, if the reserved goods are incorporated into a building, dismantling is not possible and the incorporation leads to a transfer of ownership. The owner of the building becomes the owner of the asset and restitution of the goods is therefore excluded.

The initial seller is entitled to claim for restitution only if the goods at issue may be removed from the rest without any damage. Such a claim eliminates the right of the seller to the value of the claimed asset. In the event that the asset has increased in value, the difference in value must be paid to the purchaser.[17]

(c) *Processing of goods delivered under retention of title*

The processing of goods makes the seller lose its right to claim restitution of the goods under Article L 624-16 of the Commercial Code if the asset no longer exists in kind[18] as a result of the process. This legal provision is imperative: a clause attributing ownership of the transformed asset to the initial seller will be considered null and void by the judge.[19] However, the processing must lead to a substantial alteration; a simple change of colour does not have any consequences.[20]

(d) *Extension of retention of title*

A clause which extends the retention of title to other claims is not recognised by French law. However, in the event of a secondary purchase, the initial seller benefits from a personal action against the subsequent purchaser and can claim for the payment of the purchase price, as long as the latter has not paid its own seller (see below).

2.3 Legal effect of retention of title

(a) *Effect towards third parties*

Subsequent purchaser: A retention of title has no effect towards a subsequent purchaser acting in good faith. The seller has transferred possession, which allows the subsequent purchaser to acquire the goods in good faith under Article 2276 of

---

13 Under Article 2369 of the French Civil Code.
14 In this respect, the burden of proof is on the initial seller.
15 Under Article 2370 of the French Civil Code; Article L 624-16, third paragraph, of the French Commercial Code.
16 Cass Com, October 28 2008, 07-16.899.
17 Article 2371 of the French Civil Code.
18 An asset does not lose its nature through a normal development phase (such as transformation from must into wine).
19 The situation is different in German law where such a clause is allowed.
20 Transformation from must into wine does not present a substantial alteration but a normal development phase (Cass Com, June 11 2014, 13-14.844).

the French Civil Code. Hence, the initial seller loses its claim to restitution of the goods.

The initial seller can only claim for restitution of the price from the subsequent purchaser, and only if the latter has not already paid its own seller.[21] Nevertheless, the initial seller can claim for restitution directly against the sub-purchaser if the latter is acting in bad faith.[22]

Under Article L 624-18 of the Commercial Code, the initial seller has a special right in respect of any payment made after the opening of insolvency proceedings against the subsequent purchaser. But the initial seller must first make a claim for restitution of the goods within three months[23] after the publication of the opening judgment of insolvency proceedings in the *Bulletin officiel des annonces civiles et commerciales* (BODACC).[24]

In the event of double selling, if the subsequent purchaser pays the initial purchaser after the opening of the proceedings, the judicial administrator, or the representative of the initial purchaser if no judicial administrator has been appointed, has to reserve the purchase price for the payment of the initial seller; otherwise he could be held liable by the initial seller.[25]

Other creditors: The owner has an exclusive right on the asset sold under retention of title. Hence, he does not compete with other creditors of the purchaser.

Governmental bodies: Before the opening of insolvency proceedings, governmental bodies are not treated as privileged creditors. They have the same status as every other creditor. Therefore, an initial seller who is in possession of an exclusive right under a retention of title clause does not have to compete with any governmental bodies.[26]

(b) Effect in case of a security right established over goods delivered under retention of title

Under French law, a seller who has delivered goods under retention of title is not allowed, in the meantime, to establish a pledge over the same goods. The seller has to choose either the retention of title or a pledge in order to secure the goods.

However, the buyer is authorised to establish a security right over the asset delivered under retention of title.

Possessory security right: As with a third-party purchaser acting in good faith, the beneficiary of a possessory right[27] who acts in good faith will obtain a valid right over the goods. The beneficiary of a possessory right has no obligation to check if the asset

21 The initial seller benefits here from a personal action against the sub-purchaser.
22 The subsequent buyer is in bad faith if he knows or should have known that the asset is subject to a retention of title.
23 Article L 624-9 of the Commercial Code. There is no time extension for creditors located abroad (see below).
24 The French official bulletin for civil and commercial announcements.
25 CA Rouen, November 5 1998; Cass com, January 4 2000, Bull civ IV, 5.
26 Outside collective insolvency proceedings.
27 For example a pledge (Article 2237 of the Civil Code).

has been delivered under retention of title.[28] Its rights will therefore supersede those of the seller with a retention of title clause.[29]

Under French law, floating charges as such do not exist. Nevertheless, French law has recognised for many years the validity of the concept of a turning pledge with substitution of goods (*gage tournant avec substitution de marchandise*).[30]

In the case of competition between a turning pledge with substitution of goods and a retention of title, the pledgee will supersede the initial seller and obtain a right over the reserved goods as long as the turning pledge has been agreed on between the pledgee and the initial purchaser before the delivery of the reserved goods.[31] Therefore, the initial seller's claim in restitution will not be successful.

Non-possessory security right: If the beneficiary of a security right is not in possession of the asset, the initial seller with retention of title has priority in claiming the goods. But one exception is the landlord's right of distress: the landlord's right of distress is automatically established over all goods that are located in a rented flat, even if they belong to a third person. In this case, the landlord does not have to check the ownership of the assets which were carried in by the tenant and displaces the initial seller.[32]

Where the initial purchaser has sold the asset under retention of title to a subsequent purchaser who has not yet paid him, he is in possession of the purchase price claim. He can then assign this claim to a third party.[33] But under Article 2372 of the Civil Code the initial seller is substituted for the purchaser at the time of the secondary purchase and before the claim assignment. This means that he prevails over the third party and can claim the payment directly from the subsequent buyer. If the latter has already paid the third party, the initial seller can claim the payment directly from the third party[34] if the payment was made after the opening of the insolvency proceedings. On the other hand, restitution is impossible if the payment was made before the opening of the insolvency proceedings.[35]

(c) Effect in case of insolvency

Under Article L 624-9 of the Commercial Code, the initial seller has to claim for the return of the goods within three months after the publication of the opening judgment of insolvency proceedings in BODACC.[36] The claim must be lodged with the judicial administrator.

In the event of reorganisation or liquidation proceedings, a secondary purchase

---

28 Cass Com, September 11 2012, 11-22.240.

29 To be enforceable against third parties, the secured asset must be transferred to the pledgee or a third party to hold the asset on the pledgee's behalf. The possessory right must be real, obvious, apparent, continued and unequivocal. If the transferred assets have not been clearly identified, the pledge cannot be enforced against third parties (Cass Com, April 8 2015, 14-13.787).

30 The pledge agreement provides for a replacement by the pledger of the particular assets by equivalent assets.

31 Cass Com, May 26 2010, 09-65.812.

32 Cass Civ, June 24 2009, 08-14.357.

33 For example in a case of factoring.

34 Le Corre, *Droit et Pratique des procédures collectives* (2015), 816.47.

35 Le Corre, *Droit et Pratique des procédures collectives* (2015), 816.47.

36 Article L 624-9 of the Commercial Code. The opening of a new proceeding after the failure of a safeguard plan or a reorganisation plan may trigger a new three-month period.

of the goods that are subject to retention of title in the framework of a planned sale of assets is still possible without the title getting lost if the owner duly lodged a claim for the return of his goods. According to Article L 624-18 of the Commercial Code, the initial seller then has an exclusive right to the payment to be made by the subsequent purchaser.[37] The judicial administrator could be held liable if the estate is not able to pay the purchase price to the initial seller.

If, after a valid claim for the return of the goods has been lodged by the initial seller, the judicial administrator is of the opinion that the debtor's business needs the goods, he will have no other choice than to pay the purchase price. In principle, the payment is to be made immediately, unless the creditor consents to different payment terms.[38] The judicial administrator is personally liable for the payment of the purchase price; he must ascertain that the debtor has enough means to pay.[39]

In the event that the judicial administrator is unable to return the goods,[40] because the goods have been already sold to another purchaser or the goods have been already consumed, the claim arising from the non-payment of the purchase price would have to be declared to the insolvency estate[41] for the attention of the creditors' representative.[42] Such claims are privileged if they arose after the opening of insolvency proceedings.[43]

(d) Effect in case of partial payment of purchase price

If the goods have been delivered to the purchaser and if the latter has only paid a part of the purchase price, the retention of title clause continues to benefit the seller. Therefore if the purchaser does not pay the full price as previously agreed, the seller can enforce the retention of title; the seller is still owner of the goods.

The purchaser could parry this action by paying the total amount of the purchase price in cash or by way of set-off. If the purchaser does not pay, the initial seller can claim for restitution of the goods delivered under retention of title.[44] Should the initial seller repossess all the goods delivered, he will have to refund that part of the purchase price that he has received. However, the seller does not have to refund the total amount paid by the purchaser if the value of the repossessed goods is less than the claim which remains unpaid.

3. Enforcement of retention of title

3.1 Right of seizure

The enforcement of retention of title rights through repossession of the goods is

37 Provided the purchase price was neither paid nor settled in negotiable instruments, nor set off between the debtor and the purchaser.
38 Article L 624-16 of the Commercial Code; the agreement of the insolvency judge is required.
39 Such claims are privileged.
40 If no insolvency administrator is appointed, the representative of the debtor is personally liable.
41 See below.
42 At the opening of insolvency proceedings, the court appoints a creditors' representative entrusted with the listing of creditors' claims and with communication with them.
43 Article L 622-17 of the Commercial Code; basically, they are only superseded by tax, employees' claims and the new money privilege.
44 Article L 624-18 of the Commercial Code.

possible by way of seizure. Seizure is a writ for which the use of a bailiff is mandatory. Under Article L 122-1 of the Code of Civil Execution Procedures, a bailiff is the sole authority entitled to make seizures. In addition, and as a prerequisite, the creditor is required to provide to the bailiff an enforcement order or writ of execution against the debtor in order to enforce its rights. This means in practice that recognition of the retention of title must be sought in formal judicial proceedings, whether accelerated proceedings or not, in order to obtain a formal judgment containing such an enforcement order or writ of execution.

3.2 Procedural steps

The seller can claim for the goods in many ways, depending on where the asset is. The seller must first formally ask the purchaser in non-litigious proceedings for the return of the goods. It is only if this formal notice fails that the seller is able to claim the goods from the purchaser in the framework of judicial proceedings and to seize them on the basis of an enforcement order or writ of execution issued by the court.

A creditor with a writ of execution showing an enforceable claim can ask for the seizure of tangible assets possessed by the debtor. In this case, the bailiff must serve on the debtor an order to pay. If the latter fails to pay the debt within eight days, the debtor will be compelled to return the goods sold under retention of title.[45]

Entry into premises can be made in any place where movable assets that are to be seized are located, even if they are held by a third party.[46] The third party's cooperation will however be subject to prior approval by a judge. The judge may also authorise the bailiff to perform a forced entry at a third party's premises. However, this poses some practical problems, including the difficulty for the bailiff of identifying the goods sold under retention of title.[47]

Moreover, the seller and the purchaser can stipulate directly in their contract, or in the applicable terms and conditions, that the purchaser will grant the seller access to the purchaser's premises to recover the goods in the event of default by the purchaser. However, this agreement does not enforce access if the purchaser defaults. The seller cannot enter the purchaser's premises without a writ of execution issued by a judge. In the event that the purchaser is in insolvency, however, the seller cannot recover his goods on the basis of civil law rules, by enforcing the writ of execution against the debtor and by seizing the goods. In this case, the seller has no other choice than to follow the compulsory rules set by insolvency law and lodge a claim for the return of the goods (see further below and the section on insolvency above).

3.3 Formalities

A creditor who wishes to repossess its goods must obtain a writ of execution. A deed drawn up by a notary is enforceable and has the effect of a writ of execution. Moreover, a court decision is enforceable and becomes a writ of execution once the

45 Decree 2012-783 of May 30 2012. Article R 221-2 of the Code of Civil Execution Procedures.
46 Article R 221-9 of the Code of Civil Execution Procedures.
47 In the event that an asset which is subject to seizure does not belong to the debtor, the debtor and the third party can challenge the seizure and request the release of those items not belonging to the debtor.

appeal period has expired and the decision has been served on the opposing party.[48] With the writ of execution the creditor is able to refer the matter to a bailiff. The bailiff proceeds with the execution of the creditors' right through a seizure.

3.4 Identification of goods

The separation of the goods sold under retention of title from the purchaser's other assets is not automatic and must be requested by the seller.[49] In practice creditors enforce their preferential right by asking for an inventory, which should avoid difficulties for the owner of an asset sold under reserve of title in proving that that asset is still present among the assets of the purchaser at the moment of the opening of the insolvency proceedings.[50]

On the opening of the insolvency proceedings, an inventory shall be made of the debtor's estate and of any encumbrances attached thereto.[51] There must be two originals of the inventory, one of which is filed with the register of the commercial court. Copies must be given to the debtor, to the judicial administrator and to the court-appointed creditors' representative.

In the absence of an inventory, the burden of proof that the property claimed remained in the possession of the debtor at the date of the opening judgment is transferred to the liquidator. The judicial administrator can be held liable if the absence of the inventory hinders the seller's claim for the return of the goods.[52]

3.5 Other requirements

The writ of seizure must comply with the conditions as to timing that govern all execution operations as set out in Title IV of Book I of the Code of Civil Execution Procedures. Under these rules, the act of seizure cannot be carried out on a Sunday or a public holiday, unless authorised by the judge of execution as being necessary.[53]

The act of seizure also cannot be carried out before six o'clock in the morning or after nine o'clock in the evening, unless it is necessary and permission is obtained from the judge. Permission cannot be given for execution outside these times in respect of the debtor's place of residence.

3.6 Enforcement in insolvency proceedings

The opening of insolvency proceedings triggers a general stay of payments and obligations, including those applicable to secured creditors. Therefore, the seller is no longer able to seize the reserved goods. However, the seller can claim the return of

---

48 Article L 111-3 of the Code of Civil Execution Procedures gives an exhaustive list of the various writs of execution.

49 Article 879 of the Civil Code.

50 Article L 622-6 of the Commercial Code (safeguard proceeding); Article L 631-4 of the Commercial Code (reorganisation proceeding); Article R 622-4 of the Commercial Code (judicial liquidation proceeding).

51 Unless the opening judgment has appointed a public officer or an accredited commodity broker tasked with drawing up the inventory, the inventory shall be prepared by the debtor and certified by an auditor or witnessed by a public accountant. The debtor shall add to the inventory a statement with respect to assets he holds that may be claimed by a third party and shall give the administrator and the creditors' representative a list of its creditors, the amount of its debts and the main ongoing contracts.

52 Cass Com, July 6 1999, 97-12.613.

53 Article L 141-1 of the Code of Civil Execution Procedures.

the goods from the judicial administrator or liquidator within a time limit of three months[54] from the publication of the opening judgment in the BODACC (*action en revendication*).[55] Between the date of sale and the date of the demand for return of the goods, the goods will often have deteriorated or changed in value, with the result that even where the goods are claimed back successfully, the return of the goods does not cover the price invoiced by the seller at the time of their sale.

In the meantime, the seller is therefore well advised to lodge a claim for the loss of value or for the full invoiced price, to prevent any possible challenge to the validity of the retention of title clause. The time limit for lodging such a claim is two months from the publication of the opening judgment in the BODACC.[56] This claim must be lodged with the creditors' representative, whereas the claim for the return of the goods themselves is to be filed with the judicial administrator.

If the judicial administrator neither agrees to, nor otherwise answers, the claim for return of the goods to the seller within one month from receipt of the claim, the seller must, within one month from the expiry date of the response time, petition the insolvency judge.[57] The administrator could parry this action by paying the total amount of the purchase price in cash or by way of set-off. Should the insolvency judge dismiss his claim, the initial seller can appeal to the commercial court.

Even though no formality of publication is required by French law for the validity of a retention of title provision, a seller benefiting from retention of title is free to publish the contract specifying that fact. Following such publication, the seller is discharged from having to establish its rights to ownership and may directly claim for the return of its property (*action en restitution*).[58] The seller has to claim for the restitution of the goods but is not limited by any time period.

A seller with a published contract is therefore more protected and benefits from other advantages: even if the seller does not claim for restitution, if the liquidator wishes to sell the goods, he must notify the seller of his decision by way of registered letter.[59] The seller is free to take back its goods within one month. However, in the absence of a reply, the liquidator is authorised to sell the goods, but must give the purchase price to the initial seller.

Concerning the new accelerated safeguard proceedings,[60] Article L 628-1 of the Commercial Code asserts that the rules on insolvency proceedings regarding recovery and restitution are not applicable to accelerated safeguard proceedings.

54 There is no time extension for creditors located abroad.

55 Ongoing contracts are subject to the same time limit (see above under heading 2.3).

56 Article L 622-24/R 622-24 of the Commercial Code; the filing of a claim must be lodged within two months for domestic creditors and within four month (as of publication in the BODACC) for creditors located abroad provided that the claim was incurred prior to the opening of insolvency proceedings. As for claims incurred after the opening of insolvency proceedings, under Article L 622-17 (I) of the Commercial Code, covering privileged claims related to expenses necessary for ordinary business activities or required by the procedure, the declaration is to be done immediately as of the due date, within one year after the end of the observation period or after the judgment approving the plan for the sale of assets, and within six months after the publication of the judgment ordering the liquidation (Article L 641-13 of the Commercial Code).

57 Article R 624-13 of the Commercial Code.

58 Article L 624-10 of the Commercial Code.

59 Article R 641-32 of the Commercial Code.

60 Order 2014-36 of March 12 2014 entered into force on July 1 2014.

However, the precise effect of this article currently remains uncertain; there is so far no case law on the question. There is some legal opinion that this measure aims at depriving the creditor of any possibility of claiming for return of the goods, since the creditor would be subject to the abbreviated deadline for the planned sale of assets (ie, two months). The majority of legal opinion, however, thinks, on the contrary, that the creditor could claim the return of the goods under retention of title on the basis of general civil law rules, and would therefore not be limited to the restrictive timetable of the law on insolvency.[61]

61 As a result of the absence of any special provision providing a limitation on the time for claiming the ownership of goods under retention of title.

Germany

Thomas Nicht
Kirsten Schümann-Kleber
GÖRG Partnerschaft von Rechtsanwälten mbB

1. General remarks about retention of title

1.1 Transfer of ownership

The rules for the transfer of legal ownership in movable assets are set out in Section 929 onwards of the German Civil Code. For the transfer of the ownership in a movable asset, it is necessary that the seller physically hands over the asset to the purchaser and both agree that ownership is to pass. If the purchaser is in possession of the asset already, an agreement on the transfer of the ownership suffices. Physical delivery may, under Section 930 of the Civil Code, be replaced by a legal relationship being agreed between the seller and the purchaser by which the seller agrees to hold the asset on behalf of the purchaser. In such a case, German law holds that even though the seller keeps possession, legal ownership passes to the purchaser who would be treated as having indirect possession. If a third party is in possession of the asset, for example on the basis of a leasing contract, delivery may, under Section 931 of the Civil Code, be replaced by the seller assigning to the purchaser the claim to delivery of the asset.

Generally speaking, legal title in an asset therefore passes to the purchaser when the asset has been delivered to him or in cases under Sections 930 and 931 of the Civil Code, when the relevant agreement between seller and purchaser has become legally effective.

The agreement on the transfer of legal ownership can be made subject to conditions including specifying a certain point in time when title shall actually transfer to the purchaser.[1] Therefore, the parties are entitled to agree that the transfer of ownership will take place at a later date than the date of delivery.

1.2 Statutory background rules

As mentioned above, the agreement on the transfer of legal ownership in a movable asset can be made subject to conditions. In particular, German law allows for the seller to retain the ownership of the asset until a specified condition has been met. A retention of title clause contains such a condition.

Retention of title is recognised by statutory law under Section 449 of the Civil Code, which reads as follows:

1 Berger, in Jauernig (ed) *Commentary on the German Civil Code*, 15th edition (2014), Section 929 recital 7.

Section 449
Retention of title
(1) If the seller of a movable thing has retained title until payment of the purchase price, then in case of doubt it is to be assumed that ownership is transferred subject to the condition precedent that the purchase price is paid in full (retention of title).
(2) Retention of title entitles the seller to demand the return of the thing only if he has revoked the agreement.
(3) An agreement on retention of title is void to the extent that the passing of ownership is made subject to the satisfaction by the purchaser of third-party claims, including, without limitation, those of an enterprise associated with the seller.

1.3 Retention of title in insolvency

The treatment of retention of title clauses in German insolvency proceedings is governed by Section 107 of the Insolvency Code.

Section 107(1) provides that if the debtor, before insolvency proceedings were opened, has sold a movable asset while retaining title and transferring its possession to the purchaser, the purchaser may claim performance of the sales contract. The same shall apply if the debtor has undertaken additional obligations with respect to the purchase and those obligations have not been fulfilled or have not been completely fulfilled.

In the event of the insolvency of the seller, this rule excludes the right of the insolvency administrator to choose not to fulfil its obligations under the purchase contract, that is to say to withdraw from the contract and to repossess the asset sold to the purchaser under retention of title. The purchaser of an asset sold under retention of title has an insolvency-proof expectancy right as long as he complies with his contractual obligations.[2]

On the other hand, the seller is entitled to claim repossession of an asset sold subject to retention of title if the insolvency administrator of the purchaser's estate opts for non-performance of the contract. The retention of title therefore protects the seller in the event of the insolvency of the buyer.[3] However, Section 107(2) of the Insolvency Code provides, regarding the legal position of an insolvent buyer, that, if the debtor, before the insolvency proceedings were opened, has purchased a movable asset in which the seller has retained title and whose possession was transferred to the debtor by the seller, the insolvency administrator, if required by the seller to opt for performance or non-performance of the underlying purchase agreement, does not need to opt for performance or non-performance before the first creditors' meeting, which shall be held no later than three months following the opening of the insolvency proceedings.

For the effect of retention of title in insolvency proceedings see further information under heading 2.3(d) below.

2 Andres, in Andres and Leithaus (eds) *Commentary to the German Insolvency Code*, third edition (2014), Section 107 recital 2.

3 Brinkmann, in Uhlenbruck (ed) *Commentary to the German Insolvency Code*, 14th edition (2015), Section 27 recital 25.

1.4 Foreign and international law

According to Article 43(1) of the German Introductory Act to the German Civil Code, the question of whether a retention of title is effectively created is subject to the law of the state in which the relevant asset is located at the point in time when that right is created. Accordingly, the question of whether a retention of title is validly created in respect of a movable asset located in Germany will be subject to German law, even if the purchase agreement is governed by a law other than German law.[4] A different choice of law is not possible in this respect.[5] Regarding the applicable law and legal consequences of a retention of title agreed under German law if insolvency proceedings are commenced against the assets of either a seller or a purchaser located in another country, see under heading 2.3(d) below.

2. Retention of title

2.1 Validity and formal requirements

In general, under German law there are no formal requirements that must be met in order to create a valid retention of title. There is, however, one exception regarding the sale of goods under retention of title to consumers within the meaning of Section 13 of the Civil Code, a category which encompasses any natural person who enters into a legal transaction for purposes that are predominantly outside his trade, business or profession. Such retention of title clauses are subject to a requirement that they must be in written form.[6]

Although German law contains no specific regulations regarding the wording of a retention of title clause, the interpretation of the agreement between the parties must show that the ownership shall pass to the purchaser only upon full payment of the agreed purchase price. Typical wording would be: "The goods remain the property of the seller unless and until paid for in full".

It should be noted that, under German law, retention of title can only be agreed with regard to movable assets, since the transfer of immovable assets cannot, under Section 925(2) of the Civil Code, be subject to conditions precedent.[7] For this reason, it needs to be checked in each case whether the movable asset to be transferred can be the subject of separate rights or if it is an integral part of a plot of land within the meaning of Section 94 of the Civil Code. Furthermore, retention of title cannot be agreed with regard to immaterial goods such as know-how or trade secrets, since such goods are also not classed as movable assets.[8]

A retention of title may be agreed not only by an individual agreement between two parties but also in general terms and conditions. However, the rules set out under Section 305 onwards of the Civil Code, covering restrictions to and prohibitions of

---

4 Prütting, in Gsell, Krüger, Lorenz and Mayer (eds) *Commentary to the German Civil Code* (2015), Section 43 EGBGB recital 42.

5 BGH, decision dated September 25 1996, file number VIII ZR 76/95.

6 Berger, in Jauernig (ed) *Commentary to the German Civil Code*, 15th edition (2014), Section 449 recital 6.

7 HP Westermann, *Munich Commentary to the German Civil Code*, sixth edition (2012), Section 449 recital 8.

8 HP Westermann, *Munich Commentary to the German Civil Code*, sixth edition (2012), Section 449 recital 9.

certain clauses in standard terms and conditions, need to be observed. First of all, for a retention of title clause to be agreed in general terms and conditions, it needs to be incorporated into the purchase contract in accordance with Section 305 of the Civil Code. According to Section 305(2), standard business terms only become a part of a contract if the user (ie, the seller in the present case), when entering into the contract:

- explicitly refers the other party to the contract to them or, where, because of the way in which the contract is entered into, such explicit reference is possible only with disproportionate difficulty, posts a clearly visible notice at the place where the contract is entered into; and
- gives the other party to the contract, in an acceptable manner, which also takes into reasonable account any physical handicap of the other party to the contract that is discernible to the user, the opportunity to take notice of their contents;

and if the other party to the contract agrees to their applying.

Moreover, it must be taken into account that provisions in standard business terms are ineffective under Section 307 of the Civil Code if, contrary to the requirement of good faith, they unreasonably disadvantage the other party to the contract. According to the second sentence of Section 307(1), an unreasonable disadvantage may also arise from the provision not being clear and comprehensible. However, because the agreement of a standard retention of title clause in the terms set out above is legally recognised (in Section 449 of the Civil Code), such a clause should not be deemed ineffective under Section 307.[9]

It is irrelevant for the validity of the retention of title clause whether the goods are delivered directly to the purchaser, or to a third party (such as a warehouse belonging to someone other than the purchaser).[10]

2.2 Scope of retention of title

(a) Sale of goods delivered under retention of title

In the event of a validly agreed retention of title, the purchaser acquires the ownership in the goods sold only once the purchase price has been paid. Although this does not prevent the purchaser from selling those goods to a third party beforehand, he would not be able to transfer the legal ownership to that third party unless and until he has paid the purchase price to the seller. However, once the seller and the purchaser have agreed that the title in the asset shall pass to the purchaser upon full payment of the purchase price and possession in the asset has been transferred to the purchaser in accordance with Section 929 onwards of the Civil Code, the purchaser acquires a so-called 'expectancy right'. The expectancy right is a quasi right *in rem*.[11] The purchaser may transfer the expectancy right to a third party. Once the purchase price has been

---

9 Klink, in Gsell, Krüger, Lorenz and Mayer (eds) *Commentary to the German Civil Code* (2015), Section 929 recital 141.

10 Wurmnest, *Munich Commentary to the German Civil Code*, sixth edition (2012), Section 307 recital 222.

11 Kindl, in Bamberger and Roth (eds) *Beck'scher Online Commentary to the German Civil Code*, Section 929 recital 73.

paid – by the purchaser or the third party – the expectancy right is transformed into full title, without any further measures to be taken.

Since German law recognises a good-faith acquisition of title in movable assets in the possession of a third party, title may however still transfer to the third party. In order to protect the seller, in practice the legal construct of the so-called extended retention of title is used. When such an extended retention of title is agreed, the purchaser is authorised to dispose of the goods at issue in the ordinary course of its business before full payment of the purchase price has been made. In exchange, the purchaser assigns to the seller the purchase price claims against the third party resulting from the resale. Apart from the need for a retention of title agreed with a consumer to be in writing (as mentioned above), there are no specific formal requirements for the agreement of such an extended retention of title.

However, it has to be taken into account that if the purchase agreement between the purchaser and the third party contains a legally valid prohibition of assignment of the purchase price claim, the assignment in advance will be invalid, and the seller would therefore not be secured.[12] In standard contracts, it is therefore usually agreed with the purchaser that his right of disposal will not apply if the contract with the third party contains such a prohibition of assignment.

Moreover, the assignment of the purchase price claim may be null and void in accordance with Section 138 of the Civil Code if it leads to an 'over-collateralisation'. This may be the case if the assignment also covers the purchaser's profits from reselling the goods.[13] To avoid an over-collateralisation, clauses are recommended according to which only receivables in the amount of the original value of the goods are assigned.[14]

Furthermore, problems may arise if in addition to the assignment to the seller the purchaser has made a global assignment to a bank which has made a loan available to him. According to general principles of German law, the earlier assignment to the bank would exclude a later valid assignment to the seller. However, under German case law, a global assignment agreement may be null and void under Section 138(1) of the Civil Code due to inducement of the assignor (the purchaser) to commit a breach of contract if it extends to claims which are customarily covered by an extended retention of title.[15]

(b) Processing/combining/mixing/mingling goods delivered under retention of title

German law contains several rules according to which the combining, mixing or mingling of a movable asset with other movable or immovable assets may lead to a transfer of title by operation of law.

Combining with real property: Section 946 of the Civil Code provides that if a movable thing is combined with a plot of land in such a way that it becomes an

12 Eberl, in Schulze, Grziwotz and Lauda (eds) *German Civil Code-Book of Contract and Procedural Templates*, second edition (2014), Section 449 recital 24.

13 Eberl, in Schulze, Grziwotz and Lauda (eds) *German Civil Code-Book of Contract and Procedural Templates*, second edition (2014), Section 449 recital 25.

14 BGH, decision dated May 11 2006, file number VII ZR 261/04.

15 BGH, decision dated December 8 1998, file number XI ZR 302-97.

essential part of that plot of land, the ownership of the plot of land extends to the movable thing. In such a case any retention of title over the movable asset will lose its effect: the owner of the plot of land will acquire the ownership in the combined asset automatically. If, for example, the seller delivers building materials to a building contractor who incorporates these materials into a building, the seller would lose its ownership to the owner of the building. In order to protect the seller, it is usually agreed that the building contractor assigns his claims resulting from the building contract to the seller up to the amount of the purchase price. In the event that the building contractor has agreed with the owner of the building on a prohibition of assignment, it is disputed whether the seller may claim compensation for its loss of ownership from the owner of the building in accordance with Section 951 of the Civil Code (on reimbursement for loss of rights). Most legal scholars are of the opinion that the seller should have such a claim for compensation at least where the owner of the building acted in bad faith, which would be the case if he knew of the retention of title.[16] In an older decision, the Supreme Court took the position that the seller has no such claim against the owner of the building irrespective of whether the building owner acted in good or bad faith.[17] However, in a more recent decision the Supreme Court has – while leaving the question open – at least indicated that a claim may exist in the event of bad faith.[18]

Combining with another movable asset: In contrast to Section 946 of the Civil Code, Section 947(1) provides that if movable assets are combined with each other in such a way that they become essential parts of a single thing, the previous owners become co-owners of this new asset; the shares of the co-owners are determined by the relative values that the things had at the time of combination. If one asset is deemed to be the main asset, the legal owner of the main asset also becomes legal owner of the combined asset: Section 946(2). Therefore, the seller ceases to be sole owner of the original asset he sold and becomes a co-owner of the new combined asset or loses legal title, irrespective of whether the third party acted in good faith or not.[19] Section 947 of the Civil Code is mandatory law and may therefore not be derogated from by an agreement between the seller and the owner of the other movable asset in such a way that, for instance, another share of the ownership is agreed.[20] However, where the purchaser is the owner of the other asset, he may transfer to the seller legal title in the combined asset in advance, when agreeing on the retention of title.[21]

Processing: If goods delivered under retention of title are processed by the purchaser to become a new asset within the meaning of Section 950 of the Civil Code, the

---

16 Kindl, in Bamberger and Roth (eds) *Beck'scher Online Commentary to the German Civil Code*, Section 951 recital 10; Füller, *Munich Commentary to the German Civil Code*, sixth edition (2013), Section 951 recital 19.

17 BGH, decision dated May 27 1971, file number VII ZR 85/69.

18 BGH, decision dated July 9 1990, file number II ZR 10/90.

19 Schermaier, in Gsell, Krüger, Lorenz and Mayer (eds) *Commentary to the German Civil Code* (2015), Section 947 recital 12.

20 BGH, decision dated January 12 1972, file number VIII ZR 147/70.

21 Schermaier, in Gsell, Krüger, Lorenz and Mayer (eds) *Commentary on the German Civil Code* (2015), Section 947 recital 1.

purchaser acquires ownership of the newly created asset by operation of law and the retention of title covering to the original asset ceases to exist. Through the use of 'processing clauses' it can be ensured that the seller does not lose ownership under this rule. According to case law, the seller may on the basis of such clauses accrue direct ownership in the new asset upon completion of the processing.[22] However, the Supreme Court[23] and certain legal scholars[24] take the position that the ownership stays with the seller only for security purposes. In an insolvency of the purchaser, the seller is therefore not entitled to claim surrender of the asset, but may rather only claim separation of the proceeds accruing from the realisation of the asset.

Intermixture or mingling of assets: If movable assets are inseparably intermixed or mingled with each other, the provisions of Section 947 of the Civil Code apply with some modifications (see Section 948). This means that in general in the case of intermixture or mingling of movable assets, the owners of the assets that are intermixed or mingled become co-owners in the assets which belong to the mixture. The determination of the shares of the co-owners is based on the value of the individual contributions at the time of mixing.[25] Section 948 is mandatory law as well, and may therefore not be derogated from by an agreement between the seller and the owner of the other movable asset(s). As mentioned above with regard to Section 947 of the Civil Code, in the event that the purchaser is the owner of the other assets, however, he may transfer to the seller legal title regarding the other assets in advance, when agreeing on the retention of title.[26]

(c) Retention of title securing further liabilities of the purchaser

A retention of title may secure not only the purchase price, but also further claims of the seller against the purchaser. The condition for the transfer of legal ownership in such a case is not only the complete settlement of the purchase price claim, but also the satisfaction of other claims. In general, such an extended retention of title may be agreed in Germany with legally binding effect between the parties. In contracts between merchants, a retention of title securing further claims in this sense may also be validly agreed in general terms and conditions.[27] Whether such an extended retention of title in a contract with a consumer can be agreed in this form is doubted by the prevailing opinion of legal scholars[28] and the Higher Regional Court of Koblenz.[29] The Supreme Court has not given a ruling regarding this question yet.

However, the agreement of a 'group retention of title', according to which the

22 Kindl, in Bamberger and Roth (eds) *Commentary to the German Civil Code*, Section 950 recital 9.
23 BGH, decision dated March 27 2008, file number IX ZR 220/05.
24 Much, in Ring, Grziwotz and Keukenschrijver (eds) *Commentary to the German Civil Code*, third edition (2013), Section 950 recital 16; Füller, *Munich Commentary to the German Civil Code*, sixth edition (2013), Section 950 recital 30.
25 Schermaier, in Gsell, Krüger, Lorenz and Mayer (eds) *Commentary on the German Civil Code* (2015), Section 948 recital 8.
26 Schermaier, in Gsell, Krüger, Lorenz and Mayer (eds) *Commentary on the German Civil Code* (2015), Section 948 recital 15.
27 BGH, decision dated September 27 2000, file number VIII ZR 155/99.
28 Eberl, in Schulze, Grziwotz and Lauda (eds) *German Civil Code – Book of Contract and Procedural Templates*, second edition (2014), Section 449 recital 37.
29 OLG Koblenz, decision dated April 14 1989, file number 2 U 1874/87.

transfer of ownership is dependent upon the settlement of claims of third parties that belong to the same group as the seller, is ineffective under Section 449(3) of the Civil Code.

2.3 Legal effect of retention of title

(a) Effect towards third parties

Generally speaking, retention of title has automatic effect towards third parties. As long as the agreed condition precedent – the full payment of the purchase price – has not yet occurred, the transfer of the legal ownership is not effected and title therefore remains with the seller. However, by entering into the sale and transfer agreement and handing over the goods, the parties create an expectancy right in favour of the purchaser, which is a special kind of property right which can be separately transferred[30] to, or seized[31] by, third parties. Such third parties will, however, only acquire full legal ownership of the goods when they fulfil the condition precedent, in other words by paying the agreed purchase price.[32] As long as the condition precedent under the purchase contract can be still fulfilled, the seller is not able to invoke the retention of title and claim restitution of the goods, because the expectancy right is a possessory right within the meaning of Section 986 of the Civil Code.[33] Once the purchaser has failed to comply with the obligations under the purchase contract, especially when he has not paid the purchase price as it falls due, the seller may withdraw from the purchase contract so that the expectancy right would cease to exist. After an effective withdrawal, the seller would be entitled to repossess the goods.

German law rules regarding the good-faith acquisition of ownership in movable assets in the possession of the transferor, which are handed over to a transferee, may however apply (Section 932 of the Civil Code). Therefore, there is always a risk that third parties acting in good faith may acquire ownership from the purchaser, if the purchaser does not refer to the retention of title when disposing of the asset.[34] However, a good-faith acquisition is not possible if the acquirer acted in bad faith, which is to say if he is aware, or is not aware only as a result of gross negligence, that the asset at issue does not belong to the transferor (Section 932(2) of the Civil Code). Basically, the acquirer does not have to expect that the seller may have acquired the asset only under retention of title.[35] However, a merchant who acquires goods from a typical distributor is usually deemed to be aware of the fact that goods are delivered to the distributor only under retention of title.[36] A good-faith acquisition would not take place in such cases.

---

30 Reymann, in Gsell, Krüger, Lorenz and Mayer (eds) *Commentary on the German Civil Code* (2015), Section 161 recital 56.
31 Sosnitza, in Bamberger and Roth (eds) *Commentary to the German Civil Code*, Section 1287 recital 8.
32 Reymann, in Gsell, Krüger, Lorenz and Mayer (eds) *Commentary to the German Civil Code* (2015), Section 161 recital 56.
33 Reymann, in Gsell, Krüger, Lorenz and Mayer (eds) *Commentary on the German Civil Code* (2015), Section 161 recital 56; OLG Karlsruhe, decision dated October 29 1965, file number 2 U 144/65.
34 Oechsler, *Munich Commentary to the German Civil Code*, sixth edition (2013), Section 932 recital 10.
35 OLG Frankfurt am Main, decision dated December 8 1998, file number 22 U 110/97.
36 BGH, decision dated June 18 1980, file number VIII ZR 119/79; BGH, decision dated November 3 1988, file number IX ZR 213/87.

(b) *Effect in case of seizure of goods delivered under retention of title*

Creditors of the purchaser are not entitled to seize goods which are subject to a retention of title. If they nevertheless try to do so, the seller may file for third-party proceedings to prevent the execution under Section 771 of the Code of Civil Procedure. As explained above, creditors of the purchaser may, however, seize the expectancy right of the purchaser and the asset itself. The seizure of the expectancy right entitles the creditor to settle the amounts outstanding under the sale and purchase agreement by paying those amounts to the seller.[37]

If the expectancy right and the asset itself have been seized, then once the purchase price has been paid in full the asset can be realized for the benefit of the creditor.[38] If there are any remaining proceeds after the realisation of the seized goods and settlement of the creditors' claims, these would have to be paid out to the purchaser.

In the event that creditors of the seller enforce their claims against the seller by seizing the goods purchased under a retention of title, the purchaser may also initiate third-party proceedings under Section 771 of the Code of Civil Procedure and invoke its expectancy right.[39]

(c) *Effect in case of security right established over goods delivered under retention of title*

There are cases in which an extended retention of title conflicts with other collateral granted to third parties over the same assets. For example, the purchaser may already have assigned any claims resulting from the resale of the goods in a global assignment agreement to a bank in order to secure loan liabilities with the bank. According to case law of the Supreme Court, such an assignment is deemed null and void if the global assignment agreement with the bank did not contain a clause providing that such claims would not be assigned in respect of goods which are usually subject to a retention of title clause.[40] The retention of title will therefore prevail over the assignment to the bank.

In the case of a conflict between an extended retention of title and a factoring agreement entered into by the purchaser and a factor regarding the income from resale of the goods, two scenarios have to be distinguished. If the factoring is constructed as a true sales transaction, where the factor bears the risk of insolvency on the part of the debtor, the case law noted above does not apply, so that the assignment to the factor will prevail over the extended retention of title. However, if a true sale has not been agreed, the assignment will be treated like the security assignment,[41] and the extended retention of title will prevail.[42]

---

37 Smid, *Munich Commentary to the German Code of Civil Procedure,* fourth edition (2012), Section 857 recital 19.

38 Riedel, in Vorwerk and Wolf (eds) *Beck'scher Online Commentary to the German Code of Civil Procedure,* 17th edition, Section 857 recital 12.

39 BGH, decision dated November 11 1970, file number VIII ZR 242/68.

40 Roth, *Munich Commentary to the German Civil Code*, sixth edition (2012), Section 398 recital 148, with further references to the case law of the BGH.

41 BGH, decision dated May 3 1972, file number VIII ZR 170/71.

42 Armbrüster, *Munich Commentary to the German Civil Code*, seventh edition (2015), Section 138 recital 105.

It is also possible that the purchaser has already agreed with a bank on the transfer of (future) ownership in the assets before acquiring them under the retention of title. The retention of title prevails against the transfer of ownership in this case, since the purchaser was not owner when entering into the agreement with the bank and could therefore not effectively transfer the ownership.[43] A good-faith acquisition by the bank will usually not be possible since possession is not being transferred to the bank.

(d) *Effects in case of insolvency*

Insolvency of purchaser: In the insolvency of a purchaser of a movable asset prior to the full payment of the purchase price, the insolvency administrator is entitled either to fulfil the contractual obligations of the purchaser, by paying the agreed purchase price, or to refuse fulfilment in accordance with Section 103(1) of the Insolvency Code. If the insolvent purchaser bought the asset under retention of title, the seller would be able to claim surrender of the sold goods from the insolvency estate under Section 47 of the Insolvency Code. Therefore, if the insolvency administrator refuses payment of the outstanding purchase price, the seller would have a claim for restitution of the goods and would not have to rely on an unsecured damages claim against the insolvency estate as would be the case without the retention of title.

These rules would, however, only apply if and to the extent that the insolvency proceedings are opened in Germany.

Under Article 7(1) of Council Regulation (EC) 1346/2000 of May 29 2000 on insolvency proceedings,[44] the opening of insolvency proceedings against the purchaser of an asset shall not affect the seller's rights based on a retention of title where, at the time of the opening of insolvency proceedings, the asset is situated within the territory of an EU member state other than the state of the opening of insolvency proceedings. This rule would protect also foreign retention of title clauses covering assets located in another member state of the European Union if the main insolvency proceedings are opened in Germany.[45] However, this would not preclude actions for voidness, voidability or unenforceability as referred to in Article 4(2)(m) of Regulation 1346/2000.

If the asset covered by a foreign retention of title is situated in a country outside the applicability of Regulation 1346/2000, then under Section 47 of the Insolvency Code in conjunction with Section 335 of the code and general conflict rules applying to rights *in rem*, the law of the jurisdiction where the asset at issue is located would apply. If the foreign retention of title creates a valid and generally enforceable right *in rem* according to the law of that jurisdiction, that right would be recognised in German insolvency proceedings in accordance with Section 47 of the Insolvency Code.

---

43 Ganter, in Schimansky, Bunte and Lwowski (eds) *Banking Law Compendium*, fourth edition (2011), Section 95 recital 141a.

44 Note that Article 10(1) of Council Regulation (EU) 848/2015 of May 20 2015 on insolvency proceedings, which applies as from June 26 2017, has a comparable provision.

45 Reinhart, *Munich Commentary to the German Insolvency Code*, second edition (2008), Article 7 EuInsVO recital 1.

If insolvency proceedings are opened against the purchaser's assets in a foreign country outside the scope of Regulation 1346/2000, Section 351 of the Insolvency Code would apply. This statutory rule provides that a right of a third party in an asset of the insolvency estate which at the time of opening of the insolvency proceedings was situated in Germany, and which in accordance with German law grants a right to separation or to separate satisfaction, shall remain unaffected by the opening of a foreign insolvency proceeding. The seller would according to this rule be able to enforce his retention of title in respect of an asset located in Germany.

Insolvency of the seller: If insolvency proceedings are opened against the assets of the seller, Section 107 of the Insolvency Code applies. This statutory provision provides that if the seller, before the insolvency proceedings were opened, has sold a movable asset while retaining title and transferred possession to the purchaser, the purchaser may claim performance of the sales contract due to his expectancy right. This means that the seller's insolvency administrator may not choose whether or not the purchase contract shall be fulfilled. The purchaser would be entitled to pay the amounts outstanding under the purchase contract, leading to his acquisition of the ownership in the respective asset.

Section 107 of the Insolvency Code requires that both the conclusion of the purchase contract and the transfer of possession must have occurred before the opening of insolvency proceedings in respect of the seller.[46] However, a transfer by way of 'indirect possession' is sufficient for this purpose.[47] Indirect possession is defined in Section 868 of the Civil Code as follows:

If a person possesses a thing as a usufructuary, a pledgee, a usufructuary lessee, a lessee, a depositary or in a similar relationship by virtue of which he is, in relation to another, entitled to possession or obliged to have possession for a period of time, the other person shall also be a possessor (indirect possession).

Therefore, if the purchaser does not acquire direct possession but nevertheless enters into a legal relationship with the seller or a third party, under which he is entitled to claim possession of the asset (for example a sale-and-lease-back relationship), Section 107(1) of the Insolvency Code would apply.

Again, these rules would only be applied if insolvency proceedings were to be opened in Germany.

With regard to insolvency proceedings opened over the assets of a seller in another member state of the European Union, Article 7(2) of Regulation 1346/2000[48] sets out that the opening of insolvency proceedings against the seller of an asset, after delivery of the asset, shall not constitute grounds for rescinding or terminating the sale and shall not prevent the purchaser from acquiring title where, at the time of the opening of proceedings, the asset sold is situated within the territory of a member state other than the state of the opening of proceedings. According to this

46 Wegener, in Uhlenbruck (ed) *Commentary to the German Insolvency Code*, 14th edition (2015), Section 107 recital 12.

47 Wegener, in Uhlenbruck (ed) *Commentary to the German Insolvency Code*, 14th edition (2015), Section 107 recital 12.

48 In future, Article 10(2) of Regulation 848/2015.

rule, a purchaser who has agreed on a retention of title under the law of another EU member state would be protected even if the insolvency proceedings over the assets of the seller are opened in Germany. Likewise, a purchaser who has agreed on a German retention of title regarding an asset located in Germany would be protected if insolvency proceedings were opened in another member state of the European Union.

If the asset covered by a retention of title is situated in a country outside the applicability of Regulation 1346/2000, Section 351 of the Insolvency Code might apply to any expectancy right of the purchaser if that right is related to the retention of title as a generally enforceable right *in rem* entitling the purchaser to claim separate satisfaction within the meaning of Section 51 of the Insolvency Code. There is, however, no case law or legal literature available regarding this question so far.

(e) Effects in case of partial payment of purchase price

If the seller withdraws from the purchase contract outside an insolvency process, under Section 346(1) of the Civil Code, all things received by the parties to the contract are to be returned. Therefore, on the one hand the seller may enforce its claim to repossess the goods without any restrictions, but on the other hand, he needs to reimburse any purchase price payments already made by the purchaser. The seller would be entitled to offset any damage claims he might have against the purchaser against the purchaser's claim for repayment of the purchase price.

In insolvency proceedings this relationship could be deemed to amount to a contract and, as such, could be subject to the administrator's election rights regarding performance or disclaimer. Once the administrator has effectively opted for non-performance of the purchase contract, the purchaser would have only an unsecured claim against the insolvency estate.

3. Enforcement of retention of title

Regarding the enforcement of retention of title, the general rules of German civil procedures apply. The seller needs to file for compulsory enforcement against movable property in accordance with Section 803 onwards of the Code of Civil Procedure.[49] Compulsory enforcement against movable property is effected by attachment. It may not be extended beyond what is required to satisfy the creditor and to cover the costs of the compulsory enforcement. According to Section 808(1) of the Code of Civil Procedure, the attachment of physical movable objects is effected by a court-appointed enforcement officer taking possession of them.

Compulsory enforcement may not be pursued before the seller has obtained a judgment against the purchaser setting out the obligation of the purchaser to return to the seller the goods sold under retention of title. According to Section 704 of the Code of Civil Procedure, this judgment must be final and binding, or must have been declared provisionally enforceable.

Furthermore, it has to be considered that as long as the seller has not effectively

---

49 HP Westermann, *Munich Commentary to the German Civil Code*, sixth edition (2012), Section 449 recital 33.

withdrawn from the purchase contract, the purchaser has – as mentioned above – an expectancy right which he can invoke against the seller's demand for surrender.[50]

Therefore, the seller first of all needs to withdraw from the purchase contract effectively and needs then to lodge a civil law suit against the purchaser claiming the surrender of the goods sold under retention of title. Thereafter, the seller may pursue compulsory enforcement.

According to Section 89(1) of the Insolvency Code, once insolvency proceedings over the assets of the purchaser have been opened, individual insolvency creditors may no longer seek execution against the insolvency estate or the purchaser's other property during the insolvency proceedings. However, the seller would be entitled to claim surrender of the sold goods from the insolvency estate under Section 47 of the Insolvency Code if the insolvency administrator refuses the payment of the outstanding purchase price. In contrast to compulsory enforcement, the seller does not need to be in possession of an enforcement title against the purchaser in order to claim surrender under Section 47 of the Insolvency Code. If the insolvency administrator disputes the retention of title, the seller would, however, have to pursue his claim in a legal action. The claim must be asserted in normal civil proceedings.[51] The seller can enforce his title against the insolvency administrator by compulsory enforcement according to the principles set out above. The prohibition on enforcement under Section 89 of the Insolvency Code would not apply in this case.[52]

50 Reymann, in Gsell, Krüger, Lorenz and Mayer (eds) *Commentary to the German Civil Code* (2015), Section 161 recital 56; OLG Karlsruhe, decision dated October 29 1965, file number 2 U 144/65.

51 Ganter, in *Munich Commentary to the German Insolvency Code*, Volume 3 (2013), Section 47 recital 473.

52 Ganter, in *Munich Commentary to the German Insolvency Code*, Volume 3 (2013), Section 47 recital 492.

Greece

Constantinos N Klissouras
Christina K Papachristopoulou
KP Law Firm

1. General remarks about retention of title

1.1 Transfer of ownership

Under Greek law[1] in order for title in an asset to pass from the seller to the purchaser, the seller is under obligation to transfer the ownership of and deliver the asset.

Such delivery is effected[2] by means of delivery of the asset with the belief and the mutual agreement of the seller and the purchaser that ownership actually passes on from the former to the latter. Delivery may be physical delivery[3] or constructive delivery,[4] and payment of the price is not a prerequisite for the acquisition of title by the purchaser.

Therefore, under Greek law the agreement to sell has distinct and separate legal effects from the physical action of the transfer of the good sold to the purchaser.

In the agreement to sell[5] the seller promises to deliver the goods and the purchaser promises to pay the consideration (price).

However, until such promise materialises in the actual transfer of title, the seller remains the owner of the goods sold and the goods sold remain part of his property, while the purchaser has only a claim on the agreed transfer of goods.

Furthermore, Article 1034 of the Civil Code on transfer of title is not deemed to be mandatory, and as such it allows the parties to come to a different agreement.

Consequently, the conclusion of the sale and purchase agreement need not necessarily be simultaneous to the actual transfer of title; the parties to a sale agreement are entitled to agree on a different time for the transfer of title.

1.2 Retention of title

Greek law also allows the parties to a sale agreement to agree that the seller will physically deliver possession of the good sold to the purchaser but will retain ownership thereof until the purchaser pays the purchaser price in full.[6]

Such a retention of title clause is additional to the basic agreement (promise) to

1 Article 513 of the Civil Code (PD 456/1984 as in force).
2 Article 1034 of the Civil Code.
3 Article 1034 of the Civil Code.
4 Articles 977 and 978 of the Civil Code.
5 Article 513 of the Civil Code.
6 Given the nature of the retention of title clause as one regulating transfer of title, such a clause may be inserted in any agreement for the transfer of an asset against consideration (sale, exchange etc) or even in gifts when these are made conditional on performance of certain conditions by the recipient thereof (Article 503 of the Civil Code).

sell, regulates matters of delivery and transfer of title, and is allowed under the general principle of contractual freedom[7] on the basis that ownership, possession and possession with the intention of gaining ownership are distinct legal rights. In essence retention of title clauses operate as a security of the seller and constitute a deviation from the basic rule that the parties to a contract perform their obligations simultaneously.

In particular, in respect to sale agreements falling under the scope of Law 4152/2013 (transposing EU Directive 2011/7 on combating late payments in commercial transactions) such a retention of title clause is understood to be valid[8] if expressly agreed between the parties prior to delivery of the goods.

Under the most common form of a retention of title clause, the seller retains ownership of the goods until a certain condition is met despite the fact that he has physically delivered possession of the goods sold to the purchaser; in such a case the full payment of the price is set as a condition precedent (or suspensive condition) to the transfer of title.

However, a retention of title clause may also have a different structure, under which the seller transfers ownership to the purchaser on the dissolving (or resolutory) condition that ownership shall return to the seller in the event that the consideration or price is not fully paid in accordance with the sale terms.

As indicated above, the statutory basis of retention of title clauses under Greek law lies in:

- the legal separation between the promise to sell and the actual transfer of ownership;[9]
- the separation of the rights of ownership, possession and possession with a view to ownership;[10]
- the right to agree that in a sale the price will be credited; and
- the general principle of contractual freedom.[11]

The particular terms of retention of title clauses are left for the parties to decide and agree upon, provided that no agreement of the parties may violate any mandatory legal provisions. In the absence of particular terms detailing the extent of a retention of title clause, or doubt on the exact content of such a clause, it is regulated by Article 532 of the Civil Code. In such a case, Article 532 expressly provides that in a retention of title clause agreed to be conditional upon full payment of the price:

- title passes on to the purchaser upon fulfilment of the condition (payment of the price); and
- if the purchaser defaults, the seller is entitled either (but not both) to claim the price in court or to rescind the agreement and exercise its rights as owner in order to reacquire possession of the asset.

Once the seller exercises one of these options, that choice may not be revoked.

---

7 Article 361 of the Civil Code.
8 Paragraph G11 (Z11).
9 Article 513 of the Civil Code.
10 Article 974 of the Civil Code.
11 Article 361 of the Civil Code.

1.3 Foreign and international law

A retention of title clause governed by a law other than Greek law would be allowed and deemed valid in accordance with its terms and its governing law, save that such terms would not be binding under Greek law if they were deemed contrary to the domestic standard of good morals and public order.[12]

The other law governing the retention of title clause can be chosen by the parties in line with the provisions of EU Regulation 593/2008. Accordingly, under Greek private international law the terms of a retention of title clause, as contractual terms, are governed by the law agreed upon by the parties and in the absence of such an agreement by the law of the country where the seller is domiciled.[13]

On the other hand, under Greek private international law property rights (including security over such rights) are governed by the law of the state where the goods are.[14] Therefore, when the goods subject to a retention of title clause are sold in Greece, transfer of title should be valid under Greek law.

Finally under EU Regulation 1215/2012 (as of January 10 2015) an enforceable judgment given in a member state shall be enforceable in another member state without any declaration of enforceability being required.[15] In such a case the procedure for the enforcement of that judgment shall be governed by the law of the member state addressed and the judgment shall be enforced there under the same conditions as a judgment given in the member state addressed,[16] save that grounds for refusal or of suspension of enforcement under the law of the member state where enforcement is sought shall apply in so far as they are not incompatible with those of the regulation.[17]

1.4 Retention of title in insolvency

The rights of the seller under a retention of title clause are not affected if the purchaser is subject to insolvency proceedings in Greece, provided that the purchaser entered into the sale agreement with the retention of title clause and acquired possession of the asset concerned prior to the declaration of bankruptcy.[18] In such a case, the seller may offer the syndic[19] the option to perform the terms of the agreement.[20] If the syndic refuses to perform the contract, the seller is entitled to remove the asset from the bankruptcy estate, and typically does not need to exercise the right to rescind the agreement. However, the seller may not exercise this right at a time earlier than that of the report of the syndic under Article 70 of the Insolvency Code on the financial condition of the debtor, the causes of the bankruptcy and the survival and recovery prospects.

When a purchaser is subject to bankruptcy procedures outside Greece but within

---

12 Article 33 of the Civil Code.
13 Article 4(1)(a) of Regulation 593/2008.
14 Article 27 of the Civil Code.
15 Article 39 of Regulation 1215/2012.
16 Article 41(1) of Regulation 1215/2012.
17 Article 41(2) of Regulation 1215/2012.
18 Article 35(2) of the Insolvency Code (Law 3588/2007).
19 A syndic is the equivalent of a trustee in bankruptcy under Greek law.
20 Article 29 of the Insolvency Code.

an EU member state,[21] Regulation 1346/2000 will apply. As a matter of exception from the general rule[22] that the law of the state where bankruptcy was declared governs all matters related thereto, Regulation 1346/2000 provides[23] that with regard to reservation of title, the bankruptcy of the purchaser will not affect the rights of the seller, on the same conditions as those applying under Greek law, as outlined above.[24]

Where the purchaser is subject to insolvency proceedings outside Greece and not in an EU member state, the decision of the foreign court would be recognised in Greece under Law 3858/2010.[25] In such a case, from the Greek law point of view and subject to a valid agreement by the parties on governing law providing otherwise, the seller is not released from its obligations under the retention of title, as long as the foreign syndic continues to perform the contract, nor is he deprived of his rights in that contract.

On the other hand, where the seller is the debtor in the bankruptcy and has sold a movable asset subject to a retention of title clause and has delivered possession of the asset to the purchaser, prior to the declaration of the bankruptcy, under Article 35(1) of the Insolvency Code the bankruptcy itself does not constitute a reason to terminate or rescind the agreement, nor does it in any way prevent the purchaser from acquiring ownership of the asset under the terms of the agreement.

When such a seller is subject to insolvency proceeding outside Greece but within an EU member state, again, under Regulation 1346/2000,[26] as with Greek law, the bankruptcy itself shall not constitute grounds for rescinding or terminating the sale and shall not prevent the purchaser from acquiring title.

Finally, when such a seller is subject to insolvency proceedings outside Greece and not in an EU member state, the decision of the foreign court would again be recognised in Greece under Law 3858/2010. In such a case, from the Greek law point of view and subject to a valid agreement by the parties on governing law providing otherwise, the purchaser continues to hold a claim against the seller for the transfer of the title, provided that he continues to perform under the sale agreement (in other words, provided he continues to pay the agreed instalments).

2. Retention of title

2.1 Validity and formal requirements

Under Greek law, in a sale of a movable asset under a retention of title clause neither the sale agreement nor the retention of title clause need be in writing in order to be legally valid. In general, under Greek law, a written instrument is required for the

---

21 That is to say, procedures where the centre of the debtor's main interests is located within the EU (Recital 14 of the preamble to the regulation).

22 In Article 4(1) of Regulation 1346/2000.

23 In Article 7(1).

24 A similar exception applies for the law governing third-party rights in respect of tangible assets belonging to the debtor that are located in another member state on commencement of the bankruptcy proceedings, which would be governed by the private international law of that other member state, so that assets located in Greece would be governed by Greek law (Article 5 of Regulation 1346/2000).

25 Law 3858/2010 introduced into the Greek legal system the UNCITRAL model law of 1997 on cross-border bankruptcy procedures.

26 Article 7(2).

legality and validity of an agreement only in the limited circumstances where the use of such a written instrument is required by statute[27] (such as in the sale and transfer of real property).

Still, in the absence of a general commercial practice that can substitute for any missing parts of such an agreement, it is advisable that the terms governing a retention of title clause are expressly set out in a written instrument. Furthermore, the absence of a written instrument could cause difficulties if the terms of the agreement need be proved in court, in view of Article 393 of the Code of Civil Procedure,[28] which restricts the use of oral evidence in respect of agreements over €20,000 (although there are several exceptions that lie beyond the scope of this analysis).

Given that a written instrument is not required by law, there are also no formal requirements as regards the wording of a retention of title clause. As long as there are provisions stipulating that the seller retains ownership of the goods until full payment of the price is received and providing for the particular terms and conditions of such a clause, these terms prevail. If they are vague, the terms shall be interpreted under the general interpretation principle of Article 173 of the Civil Code, which aims to discern the true will of the parties, as far as it can be determined. Where such terms are absent or in the presence of doubt as to their content, Article 532 of the Civil Code shall apply.

While there may be contractual agreement to a retention of title clause, there are no cases in Greek law where retention of title by the seller until the goods are fully paid for is imposed by operation of law. Quite to the contrary, even Law 4152/2013 (transposing EU Directive 2011/7) provides[29] that retention of title applies only if expressly agreed between the parties prior to delivery of the goods.

Retention of title may be agreed either with respect to a specific one-off sale, or may be included in general terms and conditions applying to all sales involved. However, when the retention of title clause is part of general terms and conditions its terms may be subject to additional scrutiny under specific laws and regulations, such as Law 2251/1994 on sales to consumers.

Furthermore, a retention of title clause will be valid even if the goods are delivered not to the purchaser but to a third party, provided this third party is nominated by the purchaser in the sale agreement, or takes delivery with the consent of the purchaser, or is a person indicated by a court or by law as a person entitled to collect or receive goods on behalf of the purchaser. Such a delivery would be also valid even if the purchaser only approves it after the delivery has been made.[30]

2.2 Scope of retention of title

(a) *Sale of goods delivered under retention of title*

When it comes to the right of the purchaser to resell goods purchased subject to retention of title and before full payment of the price, this is in principle limited,

27 Article 158 of the Civil Code.
28 The Code of Civil Procedure is PD 503/1985 as in force.
29 Paragraph G11 (Z11).
30 Articles 417 and 211 of the Civil Code.

under Article 514 of the Civil Code, which obliges a seller to sell the goods or assets concerned free of any third-party legal rights. Accordingly, in an acquisition with retention of title, the purchaser is on the face of it only entitled to sell on the legal titled vested in it: sole possession of the goods or the future prospect of ownership over the goods, or ownership burdened by the resolutory condition, or a combination of the above depending on the particular circumstance, but not full ownership.

Furthermore when a condition has been agreed upon, even when such condition is met, any sale of the good made while fulfilment of the condition was still pending is void if maintaining the validity of the same would have a detrimental effect on the result of the condition.[31]

On the other hand, as a general rule in the sale of an asset, the purchaser acquires title and becomes the owner of the asset sold, even if the seller had no ownership of that asset, if that purchaser acquired possession with the intention of acquiring ownership and believing in good faith that the seller had ownership of the asset sold.[32] Furthermore there is a presumption that someone who acquires possession of an asset with the intention of becoming its owner is also its owner.[33] The rule in Article 1036 of the Civil Code has two main exceptions, however:

- ownership shall not vest in the purchaser if the latter acted in bad faith; and a purchaser is deemed to act in bad faith when he knows or ignores as a result of gross negligence that the asset was not owed by the seller;[34] and
- Article 1036 does not apply when the asset was removed from the owner as a result of theft or loss.[35]

In the light of the above:

- In the most common form of retention of title clause – where title passes to the purchaser when the price is paid – if the purchaser sells title to the asset before the fulfilment of the condition, this action will constitute embezzlement and Article 1038 of the Civil Code will apply, preventing the passing of title to the new purchaser (unless the original purchaser pays the purchase price after all and so becomes the owner);
- Where the retention of title clause has been structured so that default on payment of the price would constitute a resolutory condition, and the purchaser sells the asset as owner under the resolutory condition, Article 1036 of the Civil Code will still not apply and the third party will not acquire title to the asset even if acting in good faith, on the grounds that Article 1036 regulates matters of ownership only and not of other legal rights on the title.

Consequently, the purchaser will be in a position lawfully to resell ownership of

31 Article 206 of the Civil Code.
32 Article 1036 of the Civil Code.
33 Article 1110 of the Civil Code.
34 Article 1037 of the Civil Code.
35 Article 1038 of the Civil Code.
36 Article 239 of the Civil Code.

the asset only if the seller has authorised the purchaser to do so.[36] In the event of such authorisation, the parties are likely also to have agreed that the price of any such future sale is pre-assigned to the seller. Such agreements are not uncommon in commercial sales, in particular when the purchaser acquires the goods for the purpose of reselling them in the course of its ordinary business.

(b) *Combining/mixing/mingling goods delivered under retention of title*

As a general civil law principle[37] no separate ownership may exist on parts of an object that may not be separated from the whole without damage to either the separated or the remaining part, whether as to substance or to its end-use.

In the event that goods sold under a retention of title clause are combined with other goods, without one becoming attached to the others or to one another within the meaning of Article 953, the rights under the retention of title are on the face of it not affected.

However, when such a combination does result in the separate items becoming parts of one another within the meaning of Article 953:

- If one of the combined goods is deemed to be the main or dominant part of the combination, the retention of title will lapse and the owner of the dominant good shall become the owner of the whole.[38] Case law has also interpreted this rule to apply where there are more than one dominant parts, resulting in the new ownership being divided among the owners of those parts.
- If no part of the combination is main or dominant, the owners of the goods combined become joint owners of the new combined good in proportion to the pre-combination value of each of the goods involved.[39] In such case legal rights under retention of title remain unaffected by the combination.

For the purposes of the above rules, it is irrelevant whether the combination occurred by luck or with the intent of the parties involved, whether the parties had the right to enter into a contract or to undertake the combination, or whether they acted in good or bad faith.

However, acquisition of ownership in these circumstances is not free of consequences. Under Article 1063 of the Civil Code, a party who, as a result of the goods being combined, is deprived of ownership or of another property right has, or may have, a claim in damages against anyone thereby becoming richer at the expense of that previous owner.[40] Such a person can also claim damages in tort[41] and damages for any expenses incurred,[42] or seek restitution of the article previously owned by him.[43]

The same rules apply when goods sold under retention of title are mixed or

---

37 Article 953 of the Civil Code.
38 Article 1058(2) of the Civil Code.
39 Article 1058(1) of the Civil Code.
40 Article 904 of the Civil Code.
41 Article 914 of the Civil Code.
42 Article 302 of the Civil Code.
43 Article 302 of the Civil Code.

mingled with other goods when, as a result of such mixing or mingling, separation of the goods is no longer possible or would incur excessive expense.[44]

(c) Processing of goods delivered under retention of title

Retention of title clauses are treated differently in the event that the goods concerned are processed, that is to say used to create a new product or to transform an existing product into a new product.

In the event of processing of goods delivered under retention of title, any right under a retention of title clause lapses by operation of law[45] and the producer of the new processed product becomes the owner thereof provided that the value of the work involved is manifestly higher than that of the materials used.

In such case a new original right of ownership is created and vests in the person of the producer and all earlier ownership rights (including the rights under a retention of title clause) as well as, in general, all earlier rights are not transferred, but cease to exist; the retention of title lapses.

As exceptions to the general principle outlined above, when the producer acted in bad faith as regards the ownership of the goods used, or when the value of the new product fails to meet the above test, ownership remains with the person who was owner of the goods before they were processed and the retention of title remains unaffected.

If neither exception applies, in a case of processing, the parties are entitled to agree that the seller will retain some rights over the new product until it is sold and the payment of the purchase price is collected. Although the legal nature of such an agreement is disputed, prevailing opinion treats it as an advance (legal, as opposed to actual) transfer by the producer to the seller of possession with the intention of acquiring ownership over the future new product. Under this arrangement, on production the following will occur simultaneously: the seller will lose ownership of the goods he has sold to the producer under a retention of title, and the producer will acquire original ownership over the new product, but this ownership right will in reality vest in the seller by reason of the agreement for the advance transfer of possession with the intention of acquiring ownership of the new product.

Further, in the absence of an agreement of the parties on rights over the new product, the seller can claim damages under Articles 1063, 904, 914, 301 and 302 of the Civil Code, though in such case the seller will have the burden of proof in respect of the damages incurred.

(d) Extension of the retention of title

Though not expressly forbidden by the letter of the law, allowing for extension of the retention of title to debts other than the actual payment of the price of the goods sold would be contrary to the spirit of such a clause, as it is conceived under Greek law. The reason behind this approach lies in the notion of the retention of title clause being additional/ancillary to the agreement for the sale of the particular goods, aimed primarily at serving as security for the seller until the purchaser pays the

44 Article 1059 of the Civil Code.
45 Article 1061 of the Civil Code.

agreed price in full. Therefore, as a legal clause, retention of title is strongly linked to the particular sale agreement and may not extend beyond the limits thereof.

2.3 Legal effect of retention of title

(a) *Effect towards third parties*

Subject to the provisions and limitations on transfer of title outlined above, under Greek law, retention of title clauses have an effect only between the parties[46] to the agreement and in principle have no automatic effect towards a subsequent buyer acting in good faith, other creditors or governmental bodies.

Also, as mentioned above there is a risk of further transfers of the goods sold under retention of title, as a result of the early physical transfer of possession to the purchaser.

To address that risk, the seller may provide that any such further transfer would be a resolutory condition to the delivery of the possession of the goods itself. Under such an arrangement, any further transfer of the goods would fulfil the condition and result in ownership returning automatically to the seller, subject to Article 1036 of the Civil Code (transfer to a subsequent buyer acting in good faith).

(b) *Effect in case of seizure of goods delivered under retention of title*

When the goods sold with a retention of title clause are seized by creditors of the purchaser, the seller has the right to seek the cancellation of that seizure in court[47] on the grounds of its ownership. The seller may exercise this right up until the time of completion of the auctioning off of the goods. Following completion of the auction of the seized goods the seller may claim the proceeds of the auction, in whole or in part, from the party who sold the goods (the creditor of the purchaser) and the purchaser (to the extent that he has received part of those proceeds) on the grounds of unjust enrichment under Article 904 of the Civil Code.

When the goods sold with a retention of title clause are seized in the hands of the purchaser by creditors of the seller, the purchaser, as legal holder of a future expectation of ownership, valid both against the seller[48] and against third parties,[49] is entitled to protection (in his capacity as legal possessor of the goods) or to claim damages as a person benefiting from the retention of title clause (with the right to acquire full title) when the price is paid.[50]

(c) *Effect in case of a security right established over goods delivered under retention of title*

Although a retention of title clause is effectively a form of constructive security held by the seller of the goods sold until payment of the full price by the purchaser, it does not constitute a formal legal type of security interest; in that respect, Greek law acknowledges only the specific rights listed in Article 973 of the Civil Code:

---

46 Article 177 of the Civil Code.
47 Article 936 of the Code of Civil Procedure.
48 Article 109 of the Civil Code.
49 Article 997 of the Civil Code.
50 Articles 204, 206 and 914 of the Civil Code.

ownership, easement (which may be enforceable generally or only against the other party), pledge and mortgage. As regards these specific rights, rem a mortgage may be granted only over real property, airplanes and ships while generally enforceable easements and in most cases easements enforceable only against the other party may also be granted only over real property. Therefore, a pledge is the only security interest commonly available as security in respect of a claim on movable assets.

As a general rule a pledge may be validly established over an asset only when the grantor is the legal owner of the asset.[51]

Therefore, a pledge may be validly granted over goods delivered under retention of title by the legal owner of those goods: the seller. Accordingly, a pledge granted by the purchaser under a retention of title clause will not be valid, or if it is expressly so stated in the pledge agreement only as a lien over the future right of ownership. Other than that, exceptionally a pledge could be held valid if the pledger, if he was a person acquiring the pledge from a pledgee who was not owner of the goods, could acquire good title in the limited circumstances allowed under Article 1036 of the Civil Code, which are outlined above.[52]

(d) Effect in case of insolvency

As indicated above, when the buyer is subject to insolvency proceedings and if, prior to the declaration of bankruptcy, the buyer has purchased a movable asset under a retention of title clause and has acquired possession of the asset, the syndic is, under Article 35(2) of the Insolvency Code, entitled either to pay any price still outstanding and acquire title to the asset or to refuse to perform under the agreement, in which case the seller is entitled to separate the asset from the bankruptcy estate and retake possession of it, without the need to rescind the agreement first.[53]

(e) Effect in case of partial payment of the purchase price

Partial payment of the price would not alter the right of the seller to repossess all of the goods delivered under retention of title unless the parties have agreed the opposite. In practice, such an agreement may reasonably be reached only in the sale of certain divisible goods.

However, in the event of repossession of all the goods sold as a result of only partial payment the seller will have to refund the purchaser that part of the purchase price already paid, as any funds already collected would otherwise constitute unjust enrichment of the seller to the detriment of the purchaser.[54] Furthermore, repossession of all the goods sold under retention of title by the seller in the event of partial payment may in some circumstances not be tolerated on the grounds of excessive exercise of a legal right;[55] for instance, if the seller moves to repossess the goods when the buyer has failed to pay only a small fraction of the price.

---

51 Article 1211 of the Civil Code.
52 Article 1215 of the Civil Code.
53 However, the seller may not exercise this right before the report of the syndic under Article 70 of the Insolvency Code on the financial condition of the debtor, the causes of the bankruptcy and the survival and recovery prospects.
54 Article 904 of the Civil Code.
55 Article 281 of the Civil Code.

Notwithstanding the above, depending on the actual circumstances, the seller may be entitled (in tort or on contractual grounds)[56] to retain part of the price paid as a penalty clause, rent or damages. Again such agreements would not be held valid if found to be excessive.[57]

3. Enforcement of retention of title

When payment of the price is set as a resolutory condition, repossession of the good sold under retention of title is the only recourse for the seller.

On the other hand, under the most common retention of title structure – where the stipulation that title only passes to the purchaser on full payment of the price is merely a condition precedent – when the purchaser defaults, the seller may choose either to claim payment of the price in court or to rescind the agreement and seek to repossess the goods.

In cases of repossession arising under either scenario the purchaser will no longer have a legal right over the goods and will be under an obligation to return them to the seller. However, in the resolutory condition scenario, the purchaser loses his legal right to possession of the goods at the moment of default, while in the condition precedent scenario, the purchaser loses legal right to possession of the goods only when the seller opts to rescind the sales agreement.

In either case, if the purchaser loses the legal right to possession of the goods but refuses to return them to the seller, the seller is entitled to exercise all rights pertaining to ownership and ask in court that its rights be recognised and that the purchaser be ordered to return possession of the goods.[58]

Such court action may be brought as an ordinary lawsuit, but it is much quicker for the seller to opt for the expedited procedure of injunction relief on the grounds of infringement of the right of possession in the expectation of ownership.

In addition, the seller can avoid (significant) delays involved in any court procedure if the parties executed the initial sales agreement (with the retention of title clause) as a notarial deed, as such a deed may be swiftly declared as enforceable title by the notary himself.[59] This option, though more expensive, is advisable when the goods sold under retention of title are of significant value.

The court order or the enforceable copy of the notarial deed will be enforced on the purchaser by a court bailiff.[60]

Consequently, when the purchaser refuses willingly to return the goods, an enforceable court order or other enforceable title is required in order to repossess the goods. Under Article 904 of the Code of Civil Procedure such enforceable instruments are:

- final court rulings;
- arbitral awards;
- court minutes on settlement or allocation of court expenses;

---

56 Article 400 of the Civil Code.
57 Article 281 of the Civil Code.
58 Articles 1094 and 984 of the Civil Code.
59 Provided the deed is drafted in such a way that the default can be proven.
60 Article 941 of the Code of Civil Procedure.

- notarial deeds;
- payment orders or other orders issued by Greek judges;
- foreign titles declared enforceable in Greece; and
- orders and actions acknowledged by statute as enforceable titles.

Such an enforceable title can be enforced not only against the purchaser but also against third parties having possession of the goods (such as when the goods are held on the premises of a third party) provided the action seeking enforceable title was brought against both the purchaser and that third party.

In such a case, the court bailiff will use the same enforceable title to remove the goods and hand them over to the seller[61] irrespective of whether they are in the hands of the purchaser or a third party.

If the action was not brought against the third party as well as the purchaser, the law does still allow for enforcement against third parties under certain limited circumstances set out in Article 919 of the Code of Civil Procedure, which mainly cover cases where a third person acquired possession during, or after the initiation of, the action before the court.

In practice, repossession is much easier when the parties have expressly agreed in advance that in the event of default the purchaser will grant to the seller access to its premises for the purposes of repossessing the goods, as such an agreement is valid under Greek law. However, if, despite such an agreement, the purchaser in default denies access to the seller, the seller has no other alternative but to follow the same course of action outlined above in order to repossess the goods.

In the process of repossession, the bailiff is called on to identify and remove the goods on the basis of the description thereof set out in the enforceable title; there are no formal requirements for identifying the goods subject to retention of title. Consequently, it is of importance that the enforceable title describes the goods at issue in such a manner than they can be readily identified by the bailiff.

On completion of the repossession procedure, the bailiff will draft a report on the process, with copies going to each of the seller and the purchaser (or the third party against which enforcement was performed). This report will include information such as the location, date and action taken, the enforceable title, whether enforcement was performed against the purchaser or a third party and a description of the goods removed and handed over to the seller.

The procedure for repossession differs in the event of the bankruptcy of the purchaser. In such a case, the right of the seller to repossess the goods is provided in Article 35(2) of the Insolvency Code as a right to separate the goods from the bankruptcy estate, and the procedure is governed by Article 37 of the Insolvency Code. Under this provision it would be sufficient for the seller to address a request to the syndic. Upon receiving that request the syndic is under an obligation to hand over the goods to the seller, provided however that before doing so the syndic seeks and obtains the permission of the judge supervising the bankruptcy. In the event that such permission is not granted or that for any other reason the syndic refuses to

61 Article 941 of the Civil Code.

hand over the goods, the seller will have to follow the same repossession procedure outlined above.

Hungary

Attila Jákói
Sándor Németh
Szecskay Attorneys at Law

1. General remarks about retention of title

1.1 Transfer of ownership

The general rule in the Hungarian Civil Code (Act V of 2013) is that acquisition of the ownership of movable property by way of transfer requires a contract for transfer or other legal title and, in that context, possession of the thing must be conveyed.[1]

1.2 Retention of title

In the case of a sale and purchase agreement, the Civil Code allows the parties to make different arrangements, and the general rule is that the title can be retained until the buyer pays the purchase price in full.[2] This rule has existed in Hungarian law for a long time and is widely used in practice.

The parties are also allowed to agree terms that differ from this general rule, and can define the timeframe of the retention of title differently. For example, the title can be retained for a shorter period of time than until the payment of the purchase price, or the retention can be subject to a condition other than the payment of the purchase price (for example a condition relating to another deal, unrelated to the sale of the asset). It should, though, be noted that certain aspects of how contractual arrangements may differ from the general rule established by the Civil Code are not clear yet; in this regard, please see the discussion under heading 2.2 below.

1.3 Foreign and international law

The provisions discussed in this chapter apply if the governing law of the contract is Hungarian law. But Hungarian and EU law also allow the parties to agree on a foreign governing law for the contract. If the parties do not agree on the governing law and the contracting parties are from different countries, then both the Rome I Regulation[3] and the Hungarian Law-Decree on private international law[4] provide that the law of the country of the seller governs a sale and purchase agreement.

It is important to note that agreeing on a foreign governing law has limits.

1 Section 5:38 of the Civil Code.
2 Section 6:216 of the Civil Code.
3 Regulation (EC) 593/2008 of the European Parliament and of the Council of June 17 2008 on the law applicable to contractual obligations (Rome I).
4 Law-Decree 13 of 1979 on international private law.

Regardless of the governing law of the contract, if the seller wishes to enforce a retention of title in Hungary, certain overriding mandatory provisions of Hungarian law are still applicable. The most important of these overriding mandatory provisions is the part of the Civil Code on rights *in rem* (that is to say, rights enforceable against the world at large).[5] This part of the Civil Code regulates, among other things, transfer of title and the establishment and enforcement of security rights (such as a pledge). Retention of the title is however regulated in a different part of the Civil Code (Book Six), most of which is not applicable in the case of a foreign governing law. Therefore, the mandatory provisions of the Hungarian Civil Code do not affect retention of title directly, however they can have indirect effects. For example, if the seller is not the owner of the goods under Hungarian law, then he obviously cannot conclude a sales and purchase agreement either.

Even if a retention of the title is governed by foreign law, if enforcement of that retention takes place in Hungary, then the Hungarian procedural rules are mandatory and must be observed (most importantly the Civil Procedural Code and the Act on judicial enforcement).[6]

1.4 Retention of title in insolvency

Apart from some procedural aspects, in general the insolvency of either the seller or the buyer does not affect retention of the title in Hungarian law. This is because (as explained below) under Hungarian law, the goods are not considered as an asset of the liquidated company if their title is retained.

This, however, may be different in foreign jurisdictions, so if the buyer is subject to foreign insolvency proceedings, then it may affect retention of title, even if the sale and purchase contract is governed by Hungarian law.

2. Retention of title

2.1 Validity and formal requirements

An agreement on the retention of title has to be made in writing. Even though the Civil Code makes it possible to conclude a written agreement electronically, the requirements for that are very strict, for example both parties have to have a secure electronic signature. This means that an exchange of emails for example would not qualify as a written agreement.

If general terms and conditions are also part of the written agreement, placing a clause on the retention of the title in the general terms is permitted. If the retention of the title would be an unusual term in that particular agreement, then the seller has to warn the buyer explicitly that the general terms contain a clause on the retention of title. In the absence of this warning, the retention of title may not be valid. It is also important to note that a retention of the title placed in the general terms and conditions can only be valid if the general terms are part of a written agreement. So if, for example, the parties reach an agreement over the telephone and

---

5 Book Five of the Civil Code.
6 Act III of 1952 and Act LIII of 1994.

the seller refers to his general terms, then this will not qualify as a written agreement and therefore the retention of title will not be valid.

The new Civil Code has also introduced a provision[7] which sets out that, unless the parties agree otherwise, any custom or practice which has been established between the parties or which is a custom or practice which is widely known and used in the relevant industry will become part of the contract. While this is a new provision of the Civil Code and its practice is still unclear, some interpret it to mean that if retention of the title is an established practice between the parties, or in the relevant industry, then it will become part of the contract, even if the contracting parties did not agree on it explicitly.

In Hungarian law we are not aware of any provision which would impose retention of title by the operation of law. While there is no general legal principle in the Hungarian legal system which would prevent the legislator from introducing such rules, currently retention of the title is always based on the agreement of the parties.

The parties are free to determine what the exact wording of the agreement should be, the only requirement is that their intention to that title be retained by the seller must be clear. However, in practice it is recommended to use a wording similar to that of the Civil Code, so that the interpretation of the agreement is easier.

A written agreement makes a retention of title valid between the contracting parties, but further formalities are also necessary in practice. This is because unless the retention is registered with the relevant public registry, a good-faith third-party buyer who provides consideration for the goods (ie, pays for them) can acquire the ownership of the goods or a pledge can be validly established over them. This technically means that unless the retention of title is registered, it is not valid towards third parties.

In the case of movable property, the relevant registry is generally the Security Interest Registry, which is kept by the Notarial Chamber. There are also special registries for certain types of object (cars, aircraft, vessels, etc.) where relevant retentions of title have to be registered.

It is irrelevant for the purpose of retention of title whether the goods are delivered directly to the purchaser or to a third party's premises. This is because, provided the retention of title has been validly concluded, the seller is the owner of the goods no matter who possesses them.

2.2 Scope of retention of title

As explained above, if a retention of title is registered in the relevant registry, then it is valid towards third parties as well. This means that even if the original buyer transfers the goods to a third party, this third party will not acquire ownership of the goods. The seller is still the owner as long as the title is retained, and he is entitled to reclaim the goods from anyone who possesses them. (But again, it should be noted that if the retention is not registered, a good-faith third-party buyer will acquire the ownership and the original seller cannot then reclaim the goods anymore and can only claim damages from the original buyer.)

7 Subsection (5) of Section 6:63 of the Civil Code.

In connection with the Security Interest Registry, without talking about the detailed rules of the system, we would like to note that the registration of the goods means lots of administrative burden for the seller. Our experience is that, in practice, registering all goods sold under a retention of title is close to impossible for those companies who are selling a large number of goods to many business partners (for example wholesalers of consumer goods).

(a) Combining/mixing/mingling goods delivered under retention of title

If the goods get combined, mixed or mingled with other goods, different scenarios are possible, which mostly depend on the nature of the goods. If the goods can be separated without unreasonable effort or without causing large-scale damage to them, then the goods are – from a legal point of view – still considered as separate objects. Therefore, in these circumstances, mixing or combining does not affect retention of title.

If the goods are mixed or combined in such a way that they cannot be separated anymore without unreasonable effort or damage, then the new object will be jointly owned by those whose goods were mixed or combined. This way the original seller will own a part of the goods after they have been combined or mixed in such a way that they cannot be separated anymore.

In the case where one of the mixed or combined goods is to be considered as the main component of the new object, then the owner of that part has the right to take ownership of the object if he compensates the owners of the other goods which became part of it. If the parties do not agree on the amount of the compensation, it shall be the market price of the goods. Alternatively, he has the right to grant ownership of the new object to the owners of the other goods if he gets compensated. The main reason why an object will be considered to be the main component of the new object is its value or function, in comparison to the other goods (for example the body of a car compared to its tyres).

(b) Processing of goods delivered under retention of title

In general, if goods get processed any retention of title will lapse. If the cost of processing the goods is considerably more than the value of the processed goods, then the general rule is that the person who processes the goods will acquire the ownership of the processed goods. However it is possible to circumvent this rule by retaining ownership of the goods which are handed over for processing and by providing that the processor will be mandated to carry out certain works without acquiring ownership of the goods.

It is also possible to agree on a prolonged retention of title where the goods get mixed, combined or processed. One version of this approach is to provide that the seller will acquire the ownership of the new goods after the original goods are processed. The alternative version is that the buyer is allowed to sell, mix or process the goods but the seller will have a pledge over the amount that the buyer receives for the goods. It is important to emphasise that this kind of prolonged retention does not apply automatically under a general retention of the title clause – the parties have to conclude a special agreement for it.

(c) ***Extension of retention of title***

If the seller and the buyer have multiple deals at the same time, the seller may wish to extend the reservation of title until the buyer has paid all of his debt, not just the purchase price of those specific goods. This is an extended retention of the title.

While the validity of a prolonged retention of title is generally accepted, the validity of an extended retention of title agreement is questionable in Hungary. The system of the Hungarian Civil Code is that the parties are allowed to depart from the general rules set out in the provisions of the Civil Code unless it is expressly prohibited. In connection with retention of title, the Civil Code says that the seller can retain title until the purchase price is paid in full. Even though it is not expressly prohibited to agree provisions differing from this rule, some scholars think that this is a mandatory provision of the Civil Code and that the contracting parties are not allowed to depart from it. Since the new Civil Code was only introduced in 2014, court practice is not yet available in connection with this matter.

2.3 Legal effect of the retention of title

(a) ***Effect towards third parties***

As explained above, if a retention of title is registered at the relevant registries, it has full effect towards third parties as well as between the parties to the agreement. This means that subsequent buyers will not acquire the ownership of the goods, and that a security right (which would in practice most likely be a pledge) cannot be validly established without the consent of the seller as long as the title is retained.

(b) ***Effect in case of seizure of goods delivered under retention of title***

If a third party seizes goods the title of which has been retained, then the seller can repossess them, as they are still owned by him. From this point of view, it does not make any difference if the third party who seizes or possesses the goods is a governmental body, since the retention is also enforceable against them. If the goods are seized in enforcement proceedings, the seller can still reclaim them. However, in that case it may be necessary to file an action of replevin[8] against the person who has requested the enforcement proceedings.

The only exception is if the goods are seized by a creditor of the seller. Since the goods delivered under retention of title are still assets of the seller, then creditors of the seller have the right to seize them if they want to enforce a claim against the seller.

(c) ***Effect in case of a security right established over goods delivered under retention of title***

If the buyer establishes a security right over goods (which under Hungarian law is in practice always a pledge over movable property) while the title of those goods is retained (and the retention is duly registered), then the pledge will be invalid – not just invalid towards the seller – because the Hungarian Civil Code requires that the

8 Section 371 of Act III of 1952 on the Civil Procedural Code.

pledger must have the right of disposition over the subject of the pledge. If the title is retained, then the buyer does not have this right.

If the buyer has other creditors who wish to enforce a claim against him, then a retention of title also gives him a stronger position. This is because the ownership of the goods means that the claim of the seller prevails over the claims of other creditors, since the *in rem* right of the seller has precedence over the contractual claims of the other creditors.

(d) Effect in case of insolvency

Retention of title also provides protection if the buyer becomes insolvent. In the event of the insolvency of the buyer, the seller can reclaim the goods, since he is still the owner of them. The Bankruptcy Act[9] provides that only those assets which the insolvent company owns can be sold during liquidation. If the liquidator seizes the assets despite the retention of title, the seller has to lodge a lawsuit with the court to reclaim the goods.

(e) Effect in case of partial payment of the purchase price

Even if the buyer has already paid part of the purchase price, the seller is still the owner of the goods.

In this situation, if the seller wants to terminate the contract or exercise a right of recession it can still reclaim the goods, but it will have to refund the purchase price that has already been paid. However, the parties can also agree on a different solution. For example, if the goods can be separated it is possible to reclaim only the part for which the price has not been paid.

3. Enforcement of retention of title

If the seller wishes to enforce his retention of title he may have different options, but in the end it is likely that he will have to initiate court enforcement proceedings which are conducted by a designated court enforcement officer. This is the case because no other person or organisation actually has the power to do anything else other than to warn the buyer and to request him to give the goods in question back to the seller. A court enforcement officer, however, has the right forcibly to repossess the goods, if necessary with the help of the police.

If the seller wants to repossess the goods, then first he is obliged to request this from the person who possesses them. If the seller expects that this person will not cooperate, then it is advisable to send this request by means of registered mail and get a receipt to prove delivery.

If the person who possesses the goods does not give them back willingly, the seller has to go to court and lodge a lawsuit in which he claims the goods. From this point of view, it does not make any difference whether the buyer has granted a right to the seller to collect the goods from its premises. This is so because, if the buyer does not cooperate with the seller, the seller will have to go to court anyway and follow the same procedure, no matter what the nature of the breach of the contract

9 Act XLIX of 1991 on bankruptcy and liquidation proceedings.

is. It is important that the lawsuit be filed against the person who possesses the goods, who will not necessarily be the seller.

If the seller wins the lawsuit, the court will issue a certificate of enforcement. This certificate serves as the basis of court enforcement proceedings, which are conducted by a local court enforcement officer. The enforcement proceedings have to be initiated by the seller, they will not automatically follow the lawsuit.

Where the buyer is subject to insolvency proceedings, the procedure is slightly different. In that case the seller has to request the goods from the liquidator. If the liquidator is not willing to give the goods back to the seller, it has to lodge a lawsuit against the liquidator.

The repossession of goods is easier if the sale and purchase agreement has been concluded in the form of a notarial deed (a document prepared by a notary public, who certifies the content of that document). In such a case, the notary public who has issued the notarial deed can issue a certificate of enforcement and the seller does not need to go to court to enforce his claim. However, since concluding the contract in the form of a notarial deed has significant costs and is also time-consuming, in practice this is not really a viable option for sellers who conclude a large number of low-value contracts.

Ireland

Frank Flanagan
Mason Hayes & Curran

1. General remarks about retention of title

Retention of title clauses are widely used and, when appropriately drafted, are generally effective in Ireland.

Sales of goods in Ireland are largely governed by the Sale of Goods Act 1893, as augmented by the Sale of Goods and Supply of Services Act 1980.[1] While retention of title was recognised at common law in Ireland,[2] its current statutory basis is found in the 1893 Act.

The 1893 Sale of Goods Act applied to Great Britain and Ireland. It was replaced in the United Kingdom in 1979 but the replacement Sale of Goods Act 1979 re-enacts most of its provisions. Accordingly, the Irish courts, insolvency practitioners and the lawyers advising them all consider United Kingdom case law to be persuasive when adjudicating on retention of title claims, with a slight gloss in relation to the attitude of the Irish courts to *Romalpa*.[3]

In 2008, the government appointed the Sales Law Review Group to review the existing statute and common law regarding the sale of goods and to make recommendations regarding statutory provisions appropriate to modern conditions, among other things. The group delivered its final report in 2011.[4] Following this the Department of Jobs, Enterprise and Innovation consulted on a review of the law relating to consumer contract rights.[5]

On May 25 2015, the department published the draft heads of a bill[6] intended to implement many of the recommendations of the Sales Law Review Group. Accordingly, it is likely that the law relating to contracts for the sale of goods, especially contracts between traders and consumers, will be amended substantially in the relatively near future. However, the Sales Law Review Group did not recommend any substantive amendment to the law relating to retention of title.

---

1 Primarily as regards services and implied warranties in consumer contracts.
2 *Bateman v Green* [1868] IR 2 CL607.
3 *Aluminium Industries Vaassen BV v Romalpa Aluminium Ltd* [1976] 1 WLR 676.
4 Sales Law Review Group, *Report on the Legislation Governing the Sale of Goods and Supply of Services*, www.djei.ie/en/What-We-Do/Consumer-Competition/Sales-Law-Review-Group/Report-on-the Legislation-Governing-the-Sale-of-Goods-and-Supply-of-Services.pdf.
5 www.djei.ie/en/Consultations/Consultations-files/Consulation-Paper-on-Reform-of-the-Law-on-Consumer-Contract-Rights.pdf.
6 www.djei.ie/en/Consultations/Consultations-files/Scheme-of-a-proposed-Consumer-Rights-Bill-May-2015.pdf.

1.1 Transfer of ownership

The Sale of Goods Act provides a set of rules as to when the title to goods[7] is transferred. Section 18 of the act provides:

> *Unless a* different intention appears, *the following are rules for ascertaining the intention of the parties as to the time at which the property in the goods is to pass to the buyer.* [Emphasis added]

Accordingly these rules are simply default rules and can be displaced by the agreement between the parties.

Section 18 contains five rules, as follows.

> *Rule 1: Where there is an unconditional contract for the sale of specific goods, in a deliverable state, the property in the goods passes to the buyer when the contract is made, and it is immaterial whether the time of payment or the time of delivery, or both, be postponed.*

This rule is not as broad in scope as it might at first appear.

First, it applies to specific goods only. Accordingly, if a purchaser enters into an unconditional contract to buy a specific second-hand car, this rule will apply. However, if the same buyer enters into an unconditional contract to buy a new car, specifying all of the features of the car but not uniquely identifying a specific car (for instance by VIN[8] number) this rule will not apply.

Secondly, while there is some lack of clarity in the authorities, commentaries on the act appear to be universally of the view that the use of the word "unconditional" in this rule excludes contracts where there is any condition suspending the transfer of title, for instance a retention of title clause.[9,10] The Sales Law Review Group has recommended that it be made clear in statute that contracts incorporating retention of title do not fall within the scope of Rule 1, and this is included in the draft heads of the bill.

As the application of this rule is dependent on the formation of a contract, it is appropriate to consider when a contract for sale is formed, as to which see below.

> *Rule 2: Where there is a contract for the sale of specific goods and the seller is bound to do something to the goods, for the purpose of putting them into a deliverable state, the property does not pass until such thing be done, and the buyer has notice thereof.*

To take a simple example, if a buyer agrees to purchase a second-hand car that is not roadworthy, and the seller, a motor dealer, is obliged to repair the car to put it into a deliverable state, title to the car will not pass until it has been repaired and the buyer has been put on notice of this.

> *Rule 3: Where there is a contract for the sale of specific goods in a deliverable state, but the seller is bound to weigh, measure, test, or do some other act or thing with reference to the goods for the purpose of ascertaining the price, the property does not pass until such act or thing be done, and the buyer has notice thereof.*
>
> *Rule 4: When goods are delivered to the buyer on approval or "on sale or return" or other similar terms the property therein passes to the buyer:*

---

7 Referred to as the property in the goods.

8 Vehicle identification number, or chassis number.

9 McCormack, *Reservation of title*, 2nd edition (Sweet & Maxwell, London, 1995), p12.

10 Sales Law Review Group: *Report on the Legislation Governing the Sale of Goods and Supply of Services* (*op cit*), footnote 439.

(a) When he signifies his approval or acceptance to the seller or does any other act adopting the transaction:

(b) If he does not signify his approval or acceptance to the seller but retains the goods without giving notice of rejection, then, if a time has been fixed for the return of the goods, on the expiration of such time, and, if no time has been fixed, on the expiration of a reasonable time. What is a reasonable time is a question of fact.

Rule 5: (1) Where there is a contract for the sale of unascertained or future goods by description, and goods of that description and in a deliverable state are unconditionally appropriated to the contract, either by the seller with the assent of the buyer, or by the buyer with the assent of the seller, the property in the goods thereupon passes to the buyer. Such assent may be express or implied, and may be given either before or after the appropriation is made.

(2) Where, in pursuance of the contract, the seller delivers the goods to the buyer or to a carrier or other bailee or custodier (whether named by the buyer or not) for the purpose of transmission to the buyer, and does not reserve the right of disposal, he is deemed to have unconditionally appropriated the goods to the contract.

This rule can create difficulties for buyers where the seller becomes insolvent. For instance, if a buyer agrees to buy a particular model of domestic appliance from a trader, until a specific machine with a known serial number is appropriated to the contract, most likely when it is loaded on the seller's delivery van, no property has passed. Accordingly, if the seller becomes insolvent prior to delivery and the buyer has paid in full, the buyer will only be left with an unsecured claim for debt against the seller.[11]

1.2 Retention of title

The parties are free to agree to change the default rules, in respect of specific or ascertained goods, in any way they see fit. Section 17 of the Sale of Goods Act provides:

(1) Where there is a contract for the sale of specific or ascertained goods the property in them is transferred to the buyer at such time as the parties to the contract intend it to be transferred.

(2) For the purpose of ascertaining the intention of the parties regard shall be had to the terms of the contract, the conduct of the parties, and the circumstances of the case.

The parties can agree that the title to goods transfers on any condition that they consider appropriate, including, without limitation, that the purchase price of the goods has been paid, or that all debts due by the purchaser to the vendor have been paid.

Section 19 of the Sale of Goods Act allows a seller to retain title to goods until any condition set by the seller has been fulfilled. Section 19(1) provides:

Where there is a contract for the sale of specific goods or where goods are subsequently appropriated to the contract, the seller may, by the terms of the contract or

11 See R Bradgate & F White, "Insolvent Sellers and Pre-Paying Buyers" in G Howells et al (eds), *The Yearbook of Consumer Law 2007* (Aldershot, Ashgate, 2007), pp31–85.

appropriation, reserve the right of disposal of the goods until certain conditions are fulfilled. In such case, notwithstanding the delivery of the goods to the buyer, or to a carrier or other bailee or custodier for the purpose of transmission to the buyer, the property in the goods does not pass to the buyer until the conditions imposed by the seller are fulfilled.[12]

While the wording of this section could be redrafted in language that makes its purpose and effect more explicit, the Sales Law Review Group has not recommended any substantive amendment to it.

1.3 Foreign and international law

If the contract between a seller and a buyer, or the retention of title clause, is subject to the law of another jurisdiction, the Rome I Regulation[13] will apply to the contract.[14] With respect to matters falling within the scope of the Rome I Regulation and subject to its provisions, when title passes will depend upon proof of the relevant provisions of the laws of the relevant jurisdiction.[15]

Article 9(1) of the recast Late Payments Directive[16] provides that:

Member States shall provide in conformity with the applicable national provisions designated by private international law that the seller retains title to goods until they are fully paid for if a retention of title clause has been expressly agreed between the buyer and the seller before the delivery of the goods.

The Sales Law Review Group noted that the implementing legislation for the predecessor of this directive did not directly transpose this provision: "presumably on the ground that Irish law already made adequate provision for such clauses".[17]

The law governing the disposition of the goods (including the granting of security over such goods) by a buyer who holds them subject to retention of title will, in general, be the law of the place where the goods are located.[18] Thus, in *re Interview Ltd*,[19] where two German companies sold goods to two Irish companies, under a contract expressed to be subject to German law, the German law clauses were:

- held to be effective as regards reservation of title; but
- could not displace Irish law as regards the granting of security interests in movable property; and
- could not displace Irish law as regards sub-sales.

---

12 Subsections relating to bills of lading and bills of exchange are considered below.

13 Regulation (EC) 593/2008 of the European Parliament and of the Council of June 17 2008 on the law applicable to contractual obligations.

14 Provided that the contract was concluded after December 17 2009. Contracts governed by foreign law entered into prior to that date were generally enforceable but, as it is unlikely that a significant volume of goods supplied prior to that date are still subject to retention of title, that issue is not considered further.

15 If the contract is subject to the jurisdiction of the Irish courts, foreign law must be proved before the Irish courts as a matter of fact, generally on expert evidence.

16 Directive 2011/7/EU of the European Parliament and of the Council of February 16 2011 on combating late payment in commercial transactions; transposed in Ireland by SI 196/2014, the European Communities (Late Payment in Commercial Transactions) (Amendment) Regulations 2014.

17 Sales Law Review Group, *Report on the Legislation Governing the Sale of Goods and Supply of Services* (*op cit*), p54.

18 *Lex loci rei sitae.*

19 *Re Interview Ltd* [1975] IR 382.

1.4 Retention of title in insolvency

While a contract governing the sale of goods may provide that it is subject to the laws of another jurisdiction, the law governing any insolvency will be determined in accordance with the Insolvency Regulation,[20] which will be determined by the insolvent party's centre of main interests.[21]

If the seller is subject to insolvency proceedings in Ireland, the principal issue that generally arises is that where title to goods has not passed, the buyer is limited to a remedy in damages, even if the buyer has paid the purchase price in full.

2. Retention of title

2.1 Validity and formal requirements

Retention of title must be agreed between the parties. While it is not necessary that it be in writing, in practice an oral agreement is likely to be difficult to enforce.[22]

If a retention of title clause is to be governed by a law other than the default law that would apply under the Rome I Regulation, Article 1 of the Rome I Regulation requires that: "The choice shall be made expressly or clearly demonstrated by the terms of the contract or the circumstances of the case."

Moreover, if it is desired to include an agreement as to jurisdiction as provided for in the Brussels Regulation, that agreement must be evidenced as required by Article 25 of the recast Brussels Regulation.[23] In *Dairygold Food Ingredients v Teodoro Garcia SA*[24] the court endorsed the view of the Court of Justice of the European Union in *MSG v Les Gravières Rhénanes*[25] to the effect that:

> *[in a] contract concluded orally in international trade or commerce, an agreement conferring jurisdiction will be deemed to have been validly concluded under that provision by virtue of the fact that one party to the contract did not react to a commercial letter of confirmation sent to it by the other party to the contract or repeatedly paid invoices without objection where those documents contained a pre-printed reference to the courts having jurisdiction, provided that such conduct is consistent with a practice in force in the field of international trade or commerce in which the parties in question operate and the latter are aware or ought to have been aware of the practice in question.*

However, where the contract is made using the web, and the buyer clicks to accept the seller's terms, it is sufficient that there is a hyperlink that permits the buyer to view and print the seller's terms, even if the buyer does not do so.[26]

Accordingly, if it is desired to incorporate a choice of law clause, or a choice of

20 Council Regulation (EC) 1346/2000, noting that the recast Insolvency Regulation – Regulation (EU) 2015/848 – applies only to proceedings opened after June 26 2017.

21 *German Graphics Graphische Maschinen GmbH v van der Schee* (C-292/08) [2009] ECR I-8421.

22 Note that Section 4 of the Sale of Goods Act provides that a contract of sale for the value of €12.70 or more is not enforceable in the absence of a note or memorandum in writing unless the buyer has accepted and received part of the goods or given something in earnest for payment.

23 Regulation (EU) 1215/2012, which is equivalent for present purposes to Article 23 of Regulation 44/2001.

24 High Court, McMenamin J, unreported, April 15 2011.

25 *Mainschiffahrts-Genossenschaft eG (MSG) v Les Gravières Rhénanes SARL* (C-106/95) [1997] ECR I-911.

26 *El Majdoub v CarsOnTheWeb.Deutschland GmbH* (C-322/14) Court of Justice of the European Union, unreported, May 21 2015.

jurisdiction clause in a contract for the sale of goods, the prudent approach is to ensure that the contract is in writing.

There are no formalities to be observed in relation to a simple retention of title clause. Where the clause goes beyond simple retention of title, for instance by purporting to attach to proceeds of sale, it may become a charge requiring registration; we consider this further below.

It would be inadvisable to attempt to incorporate printed general terms and conditions into an oral contract, as certain presumptions arise once a written contract that refers to such terms is signed. In *Noreside v Irish Asphalt,*[27] the court held:

> *On the question of signature, Denning LJ, in* Curtis v Chemical Cleaning and Dyeing Company *[1951] 1 K.B. 805, at p. 808, as ever, put it pithily:*
>
> > *"If the party affected signs a written document, knowing it to be a contract which governs the relations between them, his signature is irrefragable evidence of his assent to the whole contract, including the exempting clauses, unless the signature is shown to be obtained by fraud or misrepresentation:* L'Estrange v Graucob *[1934] 2 K.B. 394."*
>
> *It is important to note the condition of "knowing it to be a contract which governs the relations between them".*

Informal wording of a retention of title clause will suffice in a contract agreed between businessmen to effect a simple retention of title.[28]

However this position must be qualified slightly as, in the English case of *Re Bond Worth,*[29] which is of persuasive authority in Ireland, the court held that where a retention of title clause retained only the "equitable and beneficial ownership" the legal title passed. Accordingly, unless intentional, any attempt to distinguish between legal and beneficial ownership should be avoided.

If it is intended to extend retention of title beyond simple retention of title to include retention in respect of all sums due from the buyer to the seller, manufactured goods, or proceeds of sale, legal advice should be obtained as there are a number of linguistic pitfalls that can undermine the effectiveness of the clause,[30] or have significant adverse consequences.[31]

There is no Irish law that provides for any form of automatic retention of title except in relation to bills of exchange and bills of lading. Section 19 subsections (2) and (3) of the Sale of Goods Act provide:

> *(2) Where goods are shipped, and by the bill of lading the goods are deliverable to the order of the seller or his agent, the seller is* prima facie *deemed to reserve the right of disposal.*
>
> *(3) Where the seller of goods draws on the buyer for the price, and transmits the bill of exchange and bill of lading to the buyer together to secure acceptance or payment of the bill of exchange, the buyer is bound to return the bill of lading if he does not*

---

27 *Noreside Construction Ltd v Irish Asphalt Ltd,* High Court, Finlay Geoghegan J, unreported, October 4 2011.

28 The courts appear willing to distinguish between agreements prepared by businessmen and those carefully drafted by lawyers see: *Hendy Lennox v Puttick* [1984] 1 WLR 485.

29 [1980] Ch 228.

30 *Carroll Group Distributors Ltd v G and JF Bourke Ltd* [1990] ILRM 285, discussed below.

31 *ADM Londis Plc v Ranzett Ltd,* High Court, Hogan J, unreported, February 15 2013, discussed below.

> *honour the bill of exchange, and if he wrongfully retains the bill of lading the property in the goods does not pass to him.*

However, where the governing law of the contract is specified as the law of another jurisdiction, the Irish courts should give effect to that law where it provides for retention of title by operation of law.

(a) Incorporation of terms

It is accepted in Ireland that terms and conditions may be incorporated into a contract by signature, reasonable notice or by a course of dealing.[32]

As regards the incorporation of retention of title clauses in general terms and conditions (typically set out on the reverse of orders, invoices etc), for the retention of title clause to form part of the agreement it must have been incorporated into the contract when the contract was formed.

This raises a number of issues:

- as regards the first, or only, contract between the parties, the clause must have come to the attention of the buyer before the contract is formed;
- there must have been genuine agreement as to which set of terms are applicable to the contract (so there is no 'battle of the forms'); and
- where there is a course of dealing between the parties, even if the clause does not come to the attention of the buyer before a contract is concluded in respect of each sale, it may be incorporated as part of that course of dealing.

(b) When the contract is formed

A contract is formed when the parties reach agreement on its terms; normally this is when one party accepts an offer made by the other party and that acceptance is communicated to the other party. Accordingly, when the contract is deemed to be formed depends on the way in which acceptance is communicated:

- When communicated orally, a contract is formed immediately an offer is unconditionally accepted.
- When a contract is signed face to face, acceptance occurs when the contract is delivered unconditionally.[33]
- When communicated by post, acceptance is deemed to occur at the time the letter of acceptance is posted by the offeree and not the time at which it is received or read by the offeror.
- When communicated electronically, acceptance is deemed to occur when the electronic communication enters an information system outside the control of the originator, unless otherwise agreed between the originator and the addressee.[34] Accordingly, if acceptance is emailed, in the absence of agreement to the contrary it is deemed to have been sent once it passes outside the sender's email system.

---

32 *Noreside Construction Ltd v Irish Asphalt Ltd,* High Court, Finlay Geoghegan J, unreported, October 4 2011.
33 That is, not in escrow and not subject to any conditions precedent.
34 Section 21 of the Electronic Commerce Act 2000.

(c) *Incorporation into the first contract*

The issue of incorporation is best illustrated with two examples:

- Example 1 – A buyer agrees to buy goods from a seller in the seller's premises and contemporaneously signs a delivery note with the seller's standard terms endorsed thereon. In this instance there is little scope for argument that the terms are not incorporated.
- Example 2 – A buyer makes a telephone call to a seller asking that certain goods be supplied and agreeing on price and delivery. The goods are then dispatched by post enclosing a delivery note with the seller's standard terms printed on it. If this is the first contract between the parties, the contract was likely formed during the telephone conversation and, if that is the case, the delivery note cannot then vary its terms. Accordingly, the buyer has a good argument that the terms are not incorporated into the contract, unless perhaps such terms are standard in the relevant industry.[35]

(d) *Battle of the forms*

Technically, a purported acceptance which varies the terms of an offer is a counter-offer, not an acceptance. By way of example:

- a buyer writes to a seller ordering goods and the order states that the sale is subject to the buyer's standard terms;
- the seller sends an order acceptance to the buyer, ignoring the express statement about terms on the order and states that the order is accepted subject to the seller's standard terms; and
- the goods are then dispatched to the buyer who accepts delivery.

While any such case will likely turn on its detailed facts, in this simple example, the order acceptance is likely a counter-offer, not an acceptance. The buyer likely then accepts this counter-offer by accepting delivery of the goods, so the seller's terms prevail.

Moreover, in the absence of terms attaching to various documents, where standard terms are printed on invoices, while the term may come too late for incorporation into the contract of supply in respect of the first invoice, as the contract has likely already been agreed before delivery, where there is a course of dealing between the parties the buyer may be taken as having notice of a term.[36]

Where, or to whom, goods are delivered makes no difference to the effectiveness of retention of title.[37]

2.2 Scope of retention of title

(a) *Sale of goods delivered under retention of title*

A seller of goods is required to give a warranty of entitlement to sell goods, in accordance with Section 12 of the Sale of Goods Act:[38]

---

35 *Mainschiffahrts-Genossenschaft eG (MSG) v Les Gravières Rhénanes SARL* (C-106/95) [1997] ECR I-911.
36 *George Mitchell v Finney Lock Seeds* [1983] 1 All ER 108.
37 Section 19 of the Sale of Goods Act.
38 As substituted by Section 10 of the Sale of Goods and Supply of Services Act 1980.

(1) In every contract of sale, other than one to which subsection (2) applies, there is:

(a) an implied condition on the part of the seller that in the case of a sale he has a right to sell the goods and, in the case of an agreement to sell, he will have a right to sell the goods at the time when the property is to pass, and

(b) an implied warranty that the goods are free and will remain free until the time when the property is to pass, from any charge or encumbrance not disclosed to the buyer before the contract is made and that the buyer will enjoy quiet possession of the goods except so far as it may be disturbed by the owner or other person entitled to the benefit of any charge or encumbrance so disclosed.

(2) In a contract of sale, in the case of which there appears from the contract or is to be inferred from the circumstances of the contract an intention that the seller should transfer only such title as he or a third person may have, there is:

(a) an implied warranty that all charges or encumbrances known to the seller have been disclosed to the buyer before the contract is made, and

(b) an implied warranty that neither:

(i) the seller, nor

(ii) in a case where the parties to the contract intend that the seller should transfer only such title as a third person may have, that person, nor

(iii) anyone claiming through or under the seller or that third person otherwise than under a charge or encumbrance disclosed to the buyer before the contract is made,

will disturb the buyer's quiet possession of the goods.

While some commentators have expressed the view that no breach of the warranty required by Section 12 would arise where a seller with no title conveys good title to a purchaser under one of the exceptions to the rule that one cannot pass title in something that one does not own,[39] the Sales Law Review Group questions this proposition and appears to lean towards the view expressed by Goode[40] that as the seller's disposition is unlawful, as against the true owner of the goods, a breach occurs.[41]

Accordingly, a purchaser of goods subject to retention of title should properly obtain some form of consent to sell from the true owner of the goods.

Such consent is normally granted in one of two forms:

- a licence to sell the goods in the ordinary course of business – generally used with a simple retention of title clause; or
- consent to sell the goods, as agent for the vendor – generally used with more complex clauses where it is sought to render the purchaser a trustee of the proceeds of sale.

Sellers should draft such consents to end automatically on the commencement of any insolvency process and should, as a matter of practice, write to any insolvency practitioner appointed over the buyer notifying him, or her, of the existence of the

39 See under heading 2.3(a) below.

40 R Goode & E McKendrick, *Goode on Commercial Law* (4th edition) (London, Penguin, 2010), pp311–312.

41 Sales Law Review Group, *Report on the Legislation Governing the Sale of Goods and Supply of Services* (op cit), p240.

retention of title clause and terminating the permission to sell promptly on becoming aware of any such appointment.

(b) *Combining/mixing/mingling goods delivered under retention of title*

Where goods are mixed, for instance by goods from multiple suppliers being brought together, where the source of supply cannot be identified, the normal practice is to seek to segregate[42] the goods that are the goods of the seller by reference to the invoices from each supplier and, where a fiduciary relationship can be implied,[43] the application of the rule in *Clayton*'s case.[44]

To take an example:

- if a shopkeeper bought:
  - €10,000 worth of wine from seller A (subject to retention of title); and
  - €1,000 worth of the same wine from another supplier (not subject to retention of title)

  on the same day, but
- when supplier A seeks to recover his goods, the shop contains €9,000 of that wine then, unless the presumption is rebutted, the rule in *Clayton*'s case would imply that the shopkeeper had sold his own wine first and therefore all of the wine in the shop belonged to supplier A.

Where goods supplied subject to a retention of title clause are used in a manufacturing process, the seller may retain title to them if they remain identifiable in their original form and can be detached from the manufactured goods in which they have been used. It is thought that *Hendy Lennox (Industrial Engines) Ltd v Grahame Puttick Engines Ltd*[45] is good law in Ireland although this has not been tested.

(c) *Processing of goods delivered under retention of title*

However, where the goods are altered by manufacturing, or irreversibly lose their identity, a simple retention of title claim will likely fail as an unregistered floating charge.[46]

(d) *Goods affixed to land*

In *Ardfert Quarry Products v Moormac Developments Ltd (In Receivership)*[47] the applicant had provided a large quantity of crushed limestone that had been placed on a construction site in preparation for laying a roadway. The court cited the English decision of Blackburn J in *Holland v Hodgson*,[48] to the effect that "if the intention is apparent to make the articles part of the land, they do become part of the land", and

---

42 *ADM Londis Plc v Ranzett Ltd*, High Court, Hogan J, unreported, February 15 2013, discussed below.
43 *Carroll Group Distributors Ltd v G and JF Bourke Ltd* [1990] ILRM 285.
44 That a trustee disposed of his own property before disposing of property belonging to another (1816) 1 Mer 572.
45 [1984] 2 All ER 152.
46 *Kruppstahl AG v Quitman Products Ltd* [1982] ILRM 551.
47 High Court, Laffoy J, unreported, December 13 2013.
48 [1872] LR 7 CP 328.

found that although it was affixed to the land only by its own weight and could be removed easily, the material had become part of the land and could not be recovered on the basis of the retention of title clause.

However, this should be contrasted with the position regarding equipment that can be regarded as tenant's trade fixtures. In *In the Matter of The Companies Act, 1963 and In the Matter of Galway Concrete Ltd (In Liquidation)*,[49] the court held that the owner of a concrete-making plant affixed to the land had a right to sever it from the land and implied a missing provision entitling it to repossess same.

(e) *Extension of the retention of title*

A simple retention of title clause relates only to the goods purchased, not to the proceeds or sale thereof, or to other amounts that may be due to the seller in connection with some other agreement. It is possible to extend the clause to encompass claims of both types.

All sums due: An appropriately worded retention of title clause can provide that title to goods does not pass until all sums due to the seller on any account whatsoever are paid.[50] However, it needs to be remembered that each time that the buyer clears its account, title to all goods purchased before that date passes to the buyer. Accordingly, merely requiring segregated storage of goods is not sufficient to be able to identify goods which remain the property of the seller where the account is cleared. In such circumstances, the rule in *Clayton's* case,[51] may need to be applied.

Proceeds of sale: *Romalpa* was initially followed in Ireland and the courts were willing to imply a fiduciary relationship, which entitled the seller to trace into the proceeds of sale, even on the basis of relatively simple retention of title clauses.[52]

However, in *Carroll Group Distributors Ltd v G & JF Bourke Ltd*[53] the court appeared to move away from *Romalpa* and held that an assertion of retention of title on the "proceeds of the sale held in trust" in that case was a charge and was therefore void for want of registration in the Irish Companies Registration Office.

To avoid this conclusion and be entitled to trace the proceeds, the seller must be able to establish a fiduciary[54] relationship between the seller and the buyer. For a period of time there was some doubt as to whether this could be accomplished successfully. However, in *Carroll Group Distributors*, the court stated as follows:

---

49 [1983] ILRM 402.

50 *In The Matter of Stokes & McKiernan Ltd* [1978] ILRM 240; as this judgment was delivered before *Bond Worth*, it should no longer be relied on in relation to proceeds of sale.

51 (1816) 1 Mer 572.

52 *Sugar Distributors Ltd v Monaghan Cash and Carry Ltd* [1982] ILRM 399.

53 *Carroll Group Distributors Ltd v G and JF Bourke Ltd* [1990] ILRM 285.

54 Care should be taken where deliberately creating a fiduciary relationship. In *ADM Londis Plc v Ranzett Ltd & Ors* (High Court, Hogan J, unreported, February 15 2013) the court held that a fiduciary relationship, agreed to facilitate retention of title, imposed mutual fiduciary obligations and that if the plaintiff:
wished to extricate itself from agreements which no longer made commercial sense, it was required to do so in a fashion which ensure[d] that its erstwhile partners – in essence, the defendants – were given the maximum opportunity to find new suppliers.
Substantial damages were subsequently awarded in *ADM Londis Plc v Ranzett Ltd (No 2)* (High Court, Hogan J, unreported, July 15 2014).

It seems to me that the question must be asked how does a party come to sell property of which he is not the owner?

- *Is he selling as a trustee in pursuance of a power of sale?*
- *Is he selling as the agent of the true owner?*
- *Does the sale constitute a wrongful conversion?*

If any of those questions were answered in the affirmative it seems to me that the law would impose a trust on the proceeds of sale which would confer on the true owner the right to recover those proceeds from the actual seller or, if the proceeds were no longer in the seller's hands, to trace them into any other property acquired with them. If the new asset was acquired partly with such proceeds and partly with other monies provided by the seller then the right of the true owner would be to a charge on the new asset or mixed fund to the extent of the proceeds of the sale of his property. This is the rule enunciated in In re Hallett's Estate; Knatchbull v Hallett *(1880) 13 Ch D 696."* [Questions reformatted for clarity.]

BHT Group: That at least some draftsmen were paying attention is clear from the 2014 judgment in *BHT Group Limited,*[55] where the High Court found a clause, which appears to have been drafted in light of the recipe set out in *Carroll Group Distributors,* to be effective.

In *BHT Group* the relevant retention of title clause provided as follows:

(a) The property in the goods shall not pass to the Buyer until the price of the goods shall have been wholly paid and until all other sums whatsoever which are due from the Buyer to the Company whether under this contract or howsoever otherwise shall have been paid in full without any reduction or deferment on account of any dispute or cross claim whatsoever.

(b) Pending the payment of all sums aforesaid and the passing of property in the said goods:

(i) A fiduciary relationship shall exist between the buyer and the company and the buyer shall hold the said goods as trustee for and on behalf of the company and shall return the same to the company on demand.

(ii) The buyer hereby licenses the company and its agents to enter on to any premises on which the goods or any of them may be situation for the purpose of inspecting and taking an inventory of the said goods and/or repossessing the said goods.

(iii) If the buyer (being an individual) commits an act of bankruptcy or (being a company) has a Receiver appointed to all or part of its assets or a petition presented or a resolution passed for the winding up of the buyer, the right of the buyer to retain possession of the goods shall automatically cease and the goods shall be returned to the company immediately.

(iv) The buyer shall store the goods separately from goods belonging to the buyer or third parties so as to be clearly identifiable as being the goods of the company.

(v) The buyer shall be entitled to sell the goods to third parties (other than to …

55 *BHT Group Limited & Companies Acts: Unitherm Heating Systems Limited v Wallace*, High Court, Peart J, unreported, April 2 2014.

[group company] in the normal course of the buyer's business (but not otherwise) but the proceeds of any such sale shall be held by the buyer on trust for the company (to be lodged in a separate account by the buyer) and the buyer is hereby deemed to have assigned to the company absolutely the benefit of any claim (including the right to trace the said goods or the proceeds thereof) which the buyer has against any such third party arising from such sale.

(vi) If the buyer mixes or incorporates the goods with any other goods then if the goods used in such mixture or incorporation are capable of being identified the company shall be entitled to dismantle or separate its goods from any other goods comprised in such mixture or incorporation notwithstanding that such dismantling or separation may cause damage to or destruction of those other goods. Where the company's goods mixed or incorporated as aforesaid are no longer capable of being identified the ownership of the product of such mixing incorporation shall be and remain in the companies subject to a charge in favour of the buyer in respect of the value of the other goods comprised in the product of such mixing or incorporation.

(vii) Where goods are worked or cut without the addition of any other goods the property in such goods shall remain in the company.

(c) The risk of damage to the goods shall pass to the buyer on delivery.

BHT Group Ltd had gone into examinership and subsequently into liquidation. It was common cause that the separate bank account was never operated.

The way in which the agreement between the parties operated was as follows:

- Prior to ordering goods from the seller, the buyer sent the end-user's plans to the seller.
- The seller prepared a quotation for the goods, on the buyer's letter-head which set the price that the end-user would pay to the buyer.
- If the quoted price was accepted, the seller supplied the goods to the buyer.
- The seller then invoiced the buyer for the price quoted to the end-user, less an agreed discount which represented the buyer's profit.
- When the goods were delivered to the buyer:
  - they were never mixed with other goods in a manufacturing process;
  - they were by agreement stored separately from the company's goods; and
  - they were readily identifiable through the use of unique serial numbers and other distinguishing features.
- When the end-user paid for the goods the buyer discharged the seller's invoice.

The High Court held that:

All these are consistent with, though not themselves determinative of, an agency relationship, notwithstanding that in another scenario, they would not be sufficient for a court to conclude that an agreement which in reality created a charge, was nevertheless not such an agreement, but was one which created a fiduciary relationship. It is the substance and reality of the parties' relationship that must be considered, and not merely the words used.

One aspect of the retention of title clause gave the court some pause for thought:

I consider that while the requirement to lodge all the proceeds of a re-sale into a separate account may, when combined with all the other facts of the case, indicate a charge and not a fiduciary relationship, one must in the present case understand that the parties expressly agreed that while the end-user would be invoiced with the full amount, the applicant would invoice the seller only for that amount less an agreed discount ... It seems clear, giving business efficacy to the clause, that what was to be lodged to a separate account was the amount due to the applicant on foot of its invoice to the company, rather than the greater amount paid by the end-user to the company. [I]n so far as this is not specifically provided for in the retention clause, I would be prepared to imply such a term...

Accordingly, the High Court held that a fiduciary relationship existed and that the seller was entitled to trace into the proceeds of sale, notwithstanding any difficulty that this might create for the liquidator.

Commenting on the differences between what appears to be the current position in the United Kingdom and Ireland, Peart J stated:

As I have said already, there has certainly been a marked reluctance on the part of courts in the UK to recognise a fiduciary relationship since Romalpa, *including where there is a requirement to keep all proceeds of re-sale in a separate account. In so far as such decisions indicate that under English law a retention of title clause will not be considered to create a fiduciary relationship, such decisions are not binding here.*

The Court of Appeal[56] subsequently overturned the decision of the High Court, holding, amongst other things, that:

Had the standard conditions of sale included a clause that the net proceeds of sale received by BHT had to be placed in a separate bank account and no credit facilities [were to be] afforded to BHT, then, in the absence of all of the other evidence which points in favour of a normal debtor/creditor relationship, one might perhaps consider the possibility that BHT was acting as the agent of Unitherm.

The Court of Appeal was also unwilling to imply a clause restricting the amount to be lodged to the separate account.

The Court of Appeal further noted that *Romalpa* has not been favoured in recent times and, in Ireland, it would appear to have been supplanted by the decision in *Carroll Group Distributors*.

Thus, it remains possible to obtain security over the proceeds of sale, without requiring the registration of a charge, provided that, in light of not only the terms of the contract but also how the contract is in fact operated, one of the questions posed in *Carroll Group Distributors* could be answered in the affirmative.

Special bank accounts: Where it is desired to have the buyer operate a special bank account to deal with the proceeds of sale, the buyer should, in general, be required to agree with the bank holding the account that set-off cannot be applied across that account and other accounts held by the buyer. If this is not done, on an insolvency event, the buyer's bank is likely to set off any positive balance in that account against negative balances in other accounts, reducing the amount available to the seller.

---

56 [2015] IECA 191, Court of Appeal, unreported, July 29 2015, Irvine J (no dissent).

2.3 Legal effect of retention of title

(a) *Effect towards third parties*

The common law position is summarised in the Latin *maxim nemo dat quod non habet*, meaning that one cannot give that which one does not possess – is restated in Section 21(1) of the Sale of Goods Act as follows:

> *Subject to the provisions of this Act, where goods are sold by a person who is not the owner thereof, and who does not sell them under the authority or with the consent of the owner, the buyer acquires no better title to the goods than the seller had, unless the owner of the goods is by his conduct precluded from denying the seller's authority to sell.*

There are however a number of somewhat disjointed exceptions to this basic principle, three of which are of primary importance in the context of reservation of title.[57]

Sale with authority: Where a purchaser sells goods with the authority of the owner, this sale will transfer title under Section 21(1) of the Sale of Goods Act.

Sale under Section 9 of the Factors Act 1889: This permits the transfer of the property and ownership in goods to any person who bought them in good faith and without notice of the reservation of title. Section 9 of the Factors Act 1889 reads:

> *Where a person, having bought or agreed to buy goods obtains, with the consent of the seller possession of the goods or the documents of title to the goods, the delivery or transfer, by that person or by a mercantile agent acting for him, of the goods or documents of title, under any sale, pledge, or other disposition thereof, or under any agreement for sale, pledge, or other disposition thereof, to any person receiving the same in good faith and without notice of any lien or other right of the original seller in respect of the goods, shall have the same effect as if the person making the delivery or transfer were a mercantile agent in possession of the goods or documents of title with the consent of the owner.*

Sale under Section 25(2) of 1893 Act: Section 25(2) provides:

> *Where a person having bought or agreed to buy goods obtains, with the consent of the seller, possession of the goods or the documents of title to the goods, the delivery or transfer by that person, or by a mercantile agent acting for him, of the goods or documents of title, under any sale, pledge, or other disposition thereof, to any person receiving the same in good faith and without notice of any lien or other right of the original seller in respect of the goods, shall have the same effect as if the person making the delivery or transfer were a mercantile agent in possession of the goods or documents of title with the consent of the owner.*

The effect of these provisions is that a sub-purchaser, in good faith, buying goods, with no retention of title in the sub-sale agreement, from a party in possession of those goods and trading goods in the ordinary course of business, acquires good title.

---

57 There is also a protection for sales which take place in a 'market overt'. This is now of limited importance as it relates to old public markets, of which a limited number still operate and there is little clarity on what markets fall within the scope of this provision.

Sale with retention of title and sub-sale with no retention

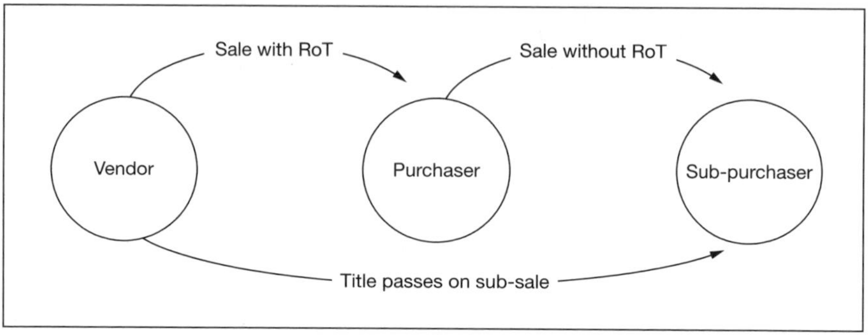

In general, it is not necessary to consider whether Section 9 of the Factors Act or Section 25(2) of the Sale of Goods Act applies as they have almost identical effect. That said, the Factors Act encompasses "any agreement for sale", while the Sale of Goods Act only encompasses "any sale".

Where a sub-sale is expressed to be subject to retention of title there is English case law to the effect that title remains with the original vendor.[58]

Sale with retention of title and sub-sale with retention of title

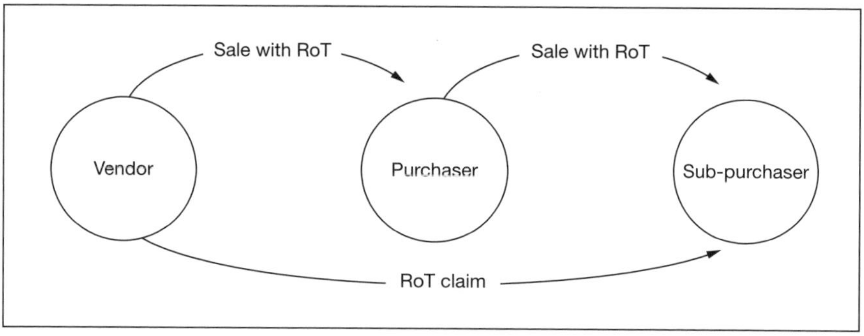

Therefore, if that case law is followed in Ireland, whether or not the original vendor is able to recover against the sub-purchaser is dependent on an event over which the original vendor has no control: whether the sub-sale agreement includes a retention of title clause.

(b) ***Effect in case of seizure of goods delivered under retention of title***

The most common form of seizure of goods in Ireland is by the sheriff, on the basis of a court order for execution. Such an order can only permit the seizure of the goods of the execution debtor (and arguably his or her spouse). Accordingly, at common law the owner of goods which are subject to retention of title can recover those

58 *P4 Ltd v Unite Integrated Solutions plc* [2006] BLR 150.

goods from the sheriff (if unsold) or sue for the appropriate proportion of the proceeds of sale (if the goods have been sold).[59]

There is very little scope for goods to be seized by another creditor in Ireland without a court order. However, there remains, in theory, a remedy of distress for rent, which is very rarely exercised. A landlord exercising distress for rent[60] is entitled to seize a stranger's goods.[61] However, such a creditor should retain goods to secure payment of overdue rent.

(c) *Effect in case of a security right established over goods delivered under retention of title*

Where a buyer purports to grant security over goods that remain subject to retention of title, the security will, in general, be ineffective. This is because the goods are not assets of the buyer.

Possessory security is somewhat different, as common law liens arise in certain circumstances, for instance in relation to common carriers, warehousemen and repairers. If, for example, a buyer verging on insolvency uses its normal carrier to ship goods subject to a retention of title claim back to the seller, the carrier is automatically entitled to a particular lien. This entitles the carrier to be paid for the carriage of the particular goods that are in the course of being shipped, even if the buyer goes into insolvency before the goods are delivered.

A more problematic scenario arises where the buyer is made the agent of the seller, for instance to create a fiduciary relationship to render a proceeds of sale clause effective. If this is not carefully drafted, it may entitle the buyer to grant a general contractual lien over goods shipped as agent for the seller. If this arises, the seller may find itself required to discharge all sums due from the buyer to the carrier in order to recover its goods.

(d) *Effect in case of insolvency*

If a company is in examinership,[62] no steps can be taken to repossess retention of title goods,[63] but the court may make an order permitting the sale of goods subject to retention of title where it is satisfied that such sale would be likely to facilitate the survival of the whole or any part of the company as a going concern.[64] Where a court makes such an order it will provide for the seller of the goods to get the open market value thereof. Accordingly, the court may effectively ignore any ransom value of an all-sums-due retention of title clause, but cannot void simple retention of title.

Retention of title remains fully operative in all other insolvency proceedings in Ireland, except that the insolvency practitioner will adjudicate on the validity of retention of title claims, usually with the benefit of legal advice. Sellers dissatisfied with decisions of insolvency practitioners can have recourse to the courts in this

59 *Jones Bros (Holloway) Ltd v Woodhouse* [1923] 2 KB 117.
60 JCW Wylie, "III: Distress" in *Landlord and Tenant Law* 3rd edn (Bloomsbury Professional, 2014), available at www.bloomsburyprofessionalonline.com/view/landlord-and-tenant-law/LTL-ch12-UID20.xml.
61 Although a number of commentators have questioned the constitutionality of this provision.
62 Broadly equivalent to administration in the United Kingdom, or Chapter 11 in the United States.
63 Section 520(4)(e) of the Companies Act 2014.
64 Under Section 530(2) of the Companies Act 2014.

regard. Insolvency practitioners are required to account for the proceeds of sale of goods subject to retention of title that are sold in the course of an insolvency process.

(e) ***Effect in case of partial payment of the purchase price***

There is a general principle against double recovery in Irish law. Accordingly, if part of the purchase price has been paid, the seller is entitled to repossess all of the goods subject to the retention of title clause, or such part thereof as the seller reasonably believes will realise the sum secured by those goods.

On selling the goods, the seller should refund any surplus over and above the amount due from the buyer and the seller's reasonable costs and expenses of retrieving and realising same.

3. Enforcement of retention of title

There are no formal requirements to repossess goods subject to retention of title. The owner can collect its own goods, or authorise a third party to collect its goods, provided that the buyer is not in an insolvency process. However, it should not use any force or implicit threat of force in so doing.

Subject to certain exemptions for persons registered with an appropriate authority in other EU member states,[65] if a private security company firm is used to collect the goods, it, and its operatives, should be appropriately licensed by the Private Security Authority.

Once a seller decides to repossess goods subject to retention of title, the first step is to write to the buyer, terminating any licence, or agency, to sell the goods, calling on the buyer to make them available for collection, and requiring that any special bank account required in respect of proceeds be operated strictly in accordance with its terms. However, if seller owes a fiduciary duty to the buyer, care should be exercised not to breach this duty.[66]

It is for the seller to prove what goods have been supplied.[67] Accordingly, the seller should amass appropriate evidence to verify the claim. Such evidence would ideally include:

- a copy of a contract between the parties, including the retention of title clause;[68]
- invoices in respect of all goods supplied:
  - referencing the terms, or the written contract, or with the terms endorsed thereon; and
  - serial numbers for high value goods;
- delivery dockets or other written acknowledgement of receipt of the goods in respect of each consignment;
- where an all-sums-due retention of title clause is relied upon, a statement of account from the last time the buyer's account had a zero balance to date;

---

65 Section 44 of the Private Security Services Act 2004.

66 *ADM Londis Plc v Ranzett Ltd (No 2)* (High Court, Hogan J, unreported, July 15 2014).

67 *Blue Monkey Gaming Ltd v Hudson* [2014] All ER (D) 222.

68 If there is a single contract matters are simpler. However, in many instances the terms of the contract need to be determined by reference to the content of order forms, invoices, delivery dockets and so on.

- details of markings on the goods, or their packaging, to show that the goods were supplied by the seller;
- any correspondence from the buyer indicating that particular remittances were to be applied against particular invoices; and
- if the goods are high value and the buyer is known to sell such goods subject to retention of title, as much documentation as possible in respect of such sub-sales.

This level of documentation is highly unlikely to be available except perhaps in cases such as the supply of high-value construction equipment.

If any dispute is likely to occur regarding ownership of the goods, as much of this evidence as possible should be delivered to the buyer, either in advance or when collecting the goods, to assist in resolving any disputes.

Evidence which falls short of this standard will generally be acceptable provided that it proves the necessary facts on the balance of probabilities. For instance:

- the lack of delivery notes has been accepted;[69] and
- serial numbers and indeed labels indicating the source of supply are not used on many classes of goods – sellers often seek to require that their goods be stored separately, or that the buyer buys goods of a particular type only from the seller to overcome the identification issue.

Where the goods are in the possession of the buyer, if the appropriate documentation is available and the buyer is legally advised, it is normally possible to take possession of the goods without recourse to the courts.

Where the goods are in the possession of a third party, for instance in a warehouse owned by a third party, it will likely be necessary to prove the claim to the person who stored the goods and perhaps discharge any particular lien in respect of storage charges.

If it is necessary to have recourse to the courts, an injunction or an order for specific performance is generally available.

3.1 Right to enter premises

Contractual rights to enter a premises are generally enforceable.[70] Accordingly, while there may be some resistance and negotiation between lawyers, such access is normally obtained without recourse to the courts.[71]

Even where a retention of title clause does not contain an express right to enter premises to repossess goods, the courts will imply one provided the buyer is in breach of contract.[72]

69 *Blue Monkey Gaming Ltd v Hudson* [2014] All ER (D) 222.
70 Except where the premises is a dwelling, which is afforded constitutional protection in Ireland.
71 *ADM Londis Plc v Ranzett Ltd* (High Court, Hogan J, unreported, February 15 2013).
72 In *In the Matter of The Companies Act, 1963 and In the Matter of Galway Concrete Ltd (In Liquidation)* [1983] ILRM 402.

3.2 Formal requirements

There is no requirement for any official endorsement to enable a seller to take possession of goods subject to retention of title.

A well-drafted retention of title clause will likely require the buyer to store the goods segregated from the buyer's own goods and those of other suppliers. Accordingly, when taking possession of goods from the buyer, it should theoretically be possible simply to collect the segregated goods.

If this has not been done, damages for breach of contract may be available, as may be a right to trace into the proceeds of sale.[73]

3.3 Enforcement in insolvency

Where an insolvency practitioner stands appointed, the obligation to identify the goods is that of the owner. In the English case of *Blue Monkey Gaming*,[74] the court held that the insolvency practitioner's obligation was:

> *to permit and supervise access to an alleged owner to enable it to identify its own goods and then to adjudicate on any claim arising on the basis of all the evidence supplied.*

It is thought that this is a fair statement of the law in Ireland.

If a buyer is in examinership no steps can be taken to repossess the goods.[75]

Where an insolvency practitioner stands appointed, he will normally seek evidence, and require a period of time to consider that evidence and adjudicate on the claim.

---

73 *BHT Group Limited & Companies Acts: Unitherm Heating Systems Limited v Wallace*, High Court, Peart J, unreported, April 2 2014.

74 *Blue Monkey Gaming Ltd v Hudson* [2014] All ER (D) 222.

75 Section 520(4)(e) of the Companies Act 2014.

Israel

Yuval Horn
Assaf Unger
Horn & Co, Law Offices

1. General remarks about retention of title

1.1 Relevant legislation governing retention of title in Israel

The key legislation regulating retention of title in Israel is as follows:

- the Companies Law 1999;
- the Contracts (General Part) Law 1973;
- the Sale Law 1968; and
- the Pledge Law 1967.

In addition to this legislation, many issues related to retention of title have been settled through rulings and precedents of the Israeli Supreme Court.

1.2 Transfer of ownership

The Sale Law determines that the ownership in an asset passes to the buyer of such asset upon its delivery, unless the parties agree a different date or manner for the transfer of ownership.

When the parties agree to a different arrangement with respect to the transfer of ownership, several questions arise with respect to the rights of third parties to the assets and rights in question. They would typically include market overt issues and the rights of creditors in cases of insolvency.

When the parties to a sale agreement postpone the transfer of ownership to an agreed upon date or milestone of any kind, retention of title is formed.

In addition, Israeli law generally allows sellers to retain ownership in their assets until certain conditions, such as full payment for the asset by the buyer, are met.

The limits of the right, however, are set, like many other legal issues in Israel, by case law of the Supreme Court.

1.3 Retention of title

The Israeli courts have determined that a classic retention of title clause would typically appear in a commercial agreement between a supplier and a retailer which specifically states that the ownership of the goods supplied will be transferred only once the buyer has paid the full purchase price, after the goods have been resold to the end-client.

The goal of such a clause, in the eyes of the Israeli courts, is to allow the retailer first to sell the goods and only afterwards to pay its suppliers. It is thus sometimes referred to as supplier's credit.

Whenever the court suspects a retention of title clause to have goals other than merely protecting the buyer's interest in making payment only after selling the product, the court tends to see the retention of title as a mere charge. Examples include circumstances viewed as aiming to ensure payment to the seller or protecting the goods from the buyer's other creditors.

Another issue that arises in cases of retention of title is the validity of the retention of title under the Contracts Law.

The basic principles considered in order to determine the validity of a contract or any of its provisions are:

- offer – one person's proposal to another constitutes an offer only if it attests to the offeror's intention to enter into a contract with the offeree and is sufficiently definite to enable the contract to be concluded by acceptance of the offer; and
- acceptance – acceptance is tendered either by notice delivered by the offeree to the offeror or by conduct, so long as it attests to the offeree's intention to form a legal contractual relationship.

The tendency of sellers to state the provisions of retention of title in documents that are external to the agreement itself, such as work orders, invoices or certificates of delivery, is generally construed against them.

In the *Vita* case,[1] a significant ruling of the Supreme Court that will be further discussed in detail below, a retention of title clause was specified only on the delivery certificates of the supplied goods.

The Supreme Court ruled that there was no valid acceptance to the retention of title. The employee who signed the delivery certificate had no authority to approve such a provision, and since the retention of title provision itself was not sufficiently explicit and specific, the act could not be interpreted as an offer.

The Supreme Court stated that if the seller honestly seeks to retain ownership of the goods transferred to the buyer, then it does not suffice simply to include a retention of title provision on invoices and shipping documents; the contract or appendices should include strict supervision and control mechanisms, constructed by the seller and agreed upon.

Therefore, since retention of title in Israel is intended to protect the buyer's interest in making payment only after the products are sold, if the seller is aware of that goal it would be in the seller's interest to supervise the chain of supply in order to guarantee that payments are being made subsequent to the buyer's sales.

Without control provisions, the courts would tend to interpret the retention of title clause as a hidden charge. In such cases, the provisions of Section 33 of the Sale Law may conflict with the provisions of the Pledge Law, which limits the scope of the retention of title rights. Such conflicts occur mainly under insolvency situations, as detailed below.

---

1 Civil Appeal 46/11 *Vita Pri Galil Ltd v The Receiver Adv Hanit Nov*, issued on November 13 2013, published on the Nevo legal database.

1.4 Foreign and international law

The rules of private international law allow Israeli courts further discretion to assume jurisdiction over a dispute between parties outside Israel, to the extent that service outside Israel is permissible under Regulation 500 of the Civil Law Procedure Regulations 1984.

Such Israeli jurisdiction would apply in the following cases, among others:

- relief is sought against a person whose regular place of residence is in Israel;
- the subject of the action is real estate in Israel;
- the case concerns a contract executed in Israel or subject to the laws of Israel;
- the action is in respect of an act or omission in Israel; or
- the person abroad is a necessary party or the proper party in an action duly submitted against another person on whom a summons was duly served in Israel.

Israeli courts, typically, exercise their jurisdiction in accordance with the principles that they will not accept jurisdiction if there is a more appropriate forum and that proceedings will be stayed if there is another action on the matter pending in another jurisdiction.

According to Supreme Court rulings, when reviewing agreements that are governed by foreign law, the competent Israeli court must differentiate between procedural provisions and substantive aspects regarding the rights of the parties.

The Supreme Court has ruled that in questions of substantive law, such as matters regarding the validity of a contract and the interpretation thereof, the rules of private international law will apply, and the parties' election of foreign law in the agreement shall prevail. The classification of a legal dispute regarding retention of title would therefore be determined by the way it would be classified by the applicable foreign judicial system.

1.5 Retention of title in insolvency

The position discussed above may not be the case in circumstances of insolvency procedures, during which many of the disputes with respect to retention of title issues arise. Such disputes reflect the inherent conflict between the property rights of the owners of assets under retention of title clauses and the equity rights of other creditors in insolvency proceedings. The most common example of such disputes in Israeli courts is when a purchaser of an asset becomes insolvent following the transfer of that asset into its possession; the seller's right for retention of title in the asset stands in conflict with the rights of other creditors of that purchaser with respect to such asset, if any, under insolvency rules.

1.6 Limits imposed by Pledge Law

The Pledge Law creates a strict mechanism and detailed rules for the creation and enforcement of pledges. Courts are concerned that parties to a sale transaction may try to circumvent the provisions of the Pledge Law by including a retention of title clause in their agreement, even in cases where the nature of the transaction does not justify it.

One requirement for the creation of a pledge which will be valid against third parties as well (and not just the pledger) is the registration of the pledge with a public registry.[2]

Section 2(b) of the Pledge Law specifies that its provisions apply to any transaction intended to charge property as security for an obligation. This section seems to contradict the provisions of Section 33 of the Sale Law and may, in effect, limit the scope of retention of title clauses.

1.7 Evolution of approach by the courts

For many years, retention of title was a common practice. Courts did not impose many restrictions and limitations on the practice, and usually preferred to protect the interests of the owners over those of other creditors. The procedural requirements were very few (if any), and sellers could safely sell goods, while stating in brief in the bills of sale that the transfer of ownership was subject to full payment, knowing that their title over the goods would be reserved.

However, this policy radically changed in 1991. The new governing rule with respect to the legitimacy of the right of a seller to retain title in assets in the possession of an insolvent purchaser was set by the Supreme Court in the precedent established in the *Colombo* case.[3]

Colombo Food and Beverage Ltd provided toys to an Israeli toy store chain, Mama Yokero Toys Ltd, that became insolvent. Following the initiation of insolvency proceedings in respect of Mama Yokero, Colombo argued that it had priority over other creditors with respect to the assets it had provided to Mama Yokero, since the agreement between Mama Yokero and Colombo included a retention of title provision. Colombo argued that the assets remained owned by it, and that Mama Yokero's receiver was not entitled to include them in the liquidation fund.

Mama Yokero's receiver argued that despite the contractual understanding between the parties, the retention of ownership clause was of no effect, and that Colombo did not have any special rights with respect to the assets it had provided to Mama Yokero. The receiver further argued that the court should examine the real nature of the relationship between the parties, and ask whether the parties actually intended that the transfer of ownership of the assets should occur only following payment by Mama Yokero. It was further argued that although Section 33 of the Sale Law provides that parties to a sale transaction are entitled to reach specific agreements which deviate from the statutory default title transfer provisions, such an understanding should not be enforced in cases in which such a mechanism is artificial and meant only to provide the seller an unfair preference over the other creditors if the purchaser becomes insolvent.

The Supreme Court rejected Colombo's arguments, stating that the retention of title clause in the case at issue was indeed artificial, and in reality the parties meant to carry out a transfer of ownership, together with a disguised lien on the assets in favour of Colombo. In the absence of registration, this lien and title retention clause

---

2 Section 4(3) of the Pledge Law.

3 Civil Appeal 455/89 *Colombo Food and Beverage Ltd v Trade Bank Ltd*, Verdicts 45 (1991) (5).

were held invalid, and it was determined that Colombo's status was identical to that of all the other ordinary creditors of Mama Yokero.

The Supreme Court stated further that the intent of the legislator in Section 2(b) of the Pledge Law was to block such attempts to interfere with the legal regime of creditors' hierarchy. To the extent that, in addition to the parties' desire to reserve the title in the assets sold, there are also elements of a standard sale transaction, and in cases in which the general concept of the transaction appears to be an ordinary sale, then the retention of title clause will have no effect, despite the fact that the parties to the transaction agreed upon such a clause. If the parties' intention and commercial logic indicate that the transaction is in fact a sale transaction, it will be treated as such, and the fact that the parties included language with respect to the retention of title might be disregarded.

The Supreme Court's ruling in the *Colombo* case resulted in strong criticism, including by many senior scholars, claiming that the *Colombo* case does not comply with common day-to-day trade experience, in which small merchants do not seek legal advice before entering into sale contracts, and that contractual freedom was being damaged by the court's paternalistic approach.[4]

Thirteen years later, the Supreme Court overruled its precedent in the *Colombo* case, in the revolutionary decision in the *Northern Drilling* case.[5] This detailed and reasoned decision elaborated the difficulties evoked by the *Colombo* case, which may be divided into three major categories:

- The broad interpretation of the Pledge Law applied its procedures on other transactions against the will of the parties to such transactions. Such interpretation stood in contrast to the purpose of the Pledge Law.
- The ruling disproportionately limited the freedom of contracts of the parties, who intentionally chose to include a retention of title clause in their agreement.
- The *Colombo* case ruling did not comply with common practice in the commercial community.

The *Colombo* case ruling was consequently overruled, enabling a resumption of the reasonable enforcement of retention of title clauses, without extensive limitations or the strict, impractical requirement publicly to register a pledge.

According to the *Northern Drilling* case, the tests for the validity of the retention of title should be both subjective – the court should review the agreement between the parties in detail, checking whether their language and the intentions were to reserve title in the goods – and objective – the court should determine whether the

---

4 It should be noted, that in addition to many articles that criticised the Supreme Court's ruling in the *Colombo* case, the Supreme Court itself raised some dissenting voices, questioning the relevance of such ruling to day-to-day trade life, and the implications on freedom of contracts. As examples for such voices, see the minority opinion of Justice Theodor Or in Civil Appeal 196/87 *Ruth Schweiger v Raz Eliyahu Levy Verdicts* 46 (1992) (3), arguing (in another matter, not directly related to retention of title) that the broad interpretation of the Pledge Law may excessively hurt the parties' contractual freedom (while the majority of the judges in that case advocated the approach presented in the *Colombo* case, according to which it is improper to encourage such alternative methods to create pledges under disguise).

5 Civil Appeal 1690/00 *MS Northern Drilling Ltd v Vered Gvily temporary liquidator* Verdict 57 (2003) (4).

circumstances of the transaction between the parties support the retention of title claim from a business perspective. However, as stated above, the threshold established by the *Northern Drilling* case is lower than the one that prevailed during the *Colombo* case era.

Further to the *Northern Drilling* case, the *Vita* case,[6] a more recent ruling by the Supreme Court, elucidated the required formalities and procedure for proper retention of title. This more recent ruling reduced to some degree the liberal approach established in the *Northern Drilling* case.

The Supreme Court clarified that the essence of the *Northern Drilling* precedent was not automatically to validate retention of title provisions and thus grant the seller an unfair advantage over other creditors. Rather, each examination should be made in accordance with Section 2(b) of the Pledge Law, in order to prevent disguised liens, while considering the facts and circumstances of each agreement. The court assisted by providing two rules of thumb:

- When discussing a continuous business relationship, one would assume that the parties should include the provision of retention of title in an explicit clause in their main agreement, and not by mentioning it in ordinary receipts. An explicit clause in the main agreement is not mandatory, but will serve as stronger evidence to the parties' intention, and the court will refer to it accordingly.
- A seller claiming retention of title will be required to prove the use of practical mechanisms of supervision and control attesting to its ownership of the property for an ongoing period. The nature of the supervision mechanisms will be defined by the circumstances, mainly by the essence of the property and the business relations between the parties. Alternatively, the seller claiming retention of title would have to prove that it was not reasonable and logical, from a business perspective, to maintain such mechanisms of supervision.

The Supreme Court did not specify formal requirements regarding the formulation or the specific wording of retention of title provisions. The Supreme Court instead emphasised the essence of the provision and the importance of including the provision in the core agreement between the parties.

In recent years, the Israeli legislator also addressed the matter of retention of title in the 19th Amendment of the Companies Law. The main reason behind the 19th Amendment was to update and improve proceedings relating to corporate recovery. The Israeli legislator specifically referred to retention of title for the first time by including a definition, in Section 350A of the Companies Law, of an "owner of property which is subject to a retention of title provision". The Companies Law determines that "proper protection" for the owner of the property shall be obtained through guaranteeing the full payment of the debt at the time of the beginning of the legal proceedings, taking into account the arm's length value of the protected asset.

6 See Footnote 1 above.

According to Section 350D, the applicable court may appoint an official to a company which is under suspension of insolvency proceedings. According to Section 350E, the company's official may sell or lease the property which is under a retention of title provision, unless the applicable court is convinced that either the sale or the lease of property is not required for the recovery of the company, or the sale or the lease of property will not ensure the owner of the property proper protection as referred to above.

Section 350E further states that the company's official is capable of selling or leasing the property, free of any burden (including a retention of title provision), upon the consent of the owner of the property or the approval of the applicable court.

The applicable court, however, will not approve such action if it is not convinced that the action is vital for the recovery of the company, and that such action will ensure proper protection for the owner.

Reading between the lines, the Israeli legislator has emphasised the importance of corporate recovery by prioritising the recovery of companies over proprietary rights of owners otherwise entitled to retention of title provisions. The legislator is trying to accommodate the interests of all parties, but the grant of such broad discretion to the court in determining whether an owner is sufficiently protected provides the court the freedom and the flexibility to ignore retention of title provisions for the sake of a recovering company.

2. Retention of title

2.1 Validity and formal requirements

The Israeli legal system recognises several specific types of contracts and matters that require formal written expression as a condition for their validity, and without such they will be considered void. Real estate transactions are typical examples of such requirements. In retention of title clauses, the picture is somewhat different.

As stated above, the formal requirements for the validity of retention of title clauses are not substantial, and the major tests applied by the Israeli legislator and by the Israeli courts examine the essence of the clauses rather than their form. Hence, in theory, retention of title clauses do not have to be agreed to in writing in order to be valid. Consent or agreement between the parties on this matter may be sufficient.

However, written expression of the retention of title will help to establish the parties' expectations and support a more accurate interpretation of their original intent, and therefore may encourage the court to validate it. The importance of accurately formalising such understandings increases in the case of a long-term business relationship between the parties. There is no specific formal drafting requirement for such clauses, and as long as the wording clearly expresses the parties' intentions it should suffice. Registration of a pledge in the applicable public register would certainly assist in establishing the validity of the retention of title, but it is not a mandatory term or a very customary practice.

In addition to the declaration of the retention of title itself (whether a written clause, or an oral agreement in the case of an occasional transaction), the courts examine the control and inspection mechanism that the alleged owner applies to the goods while they are in the possession of the buyer. If the alleged owner supervises the goods in the buyer's warehouses, or if that owner is entitled to extensive inspection rights with respect to the goods, the courts would be inclined to declare that the owner reserved title. This would apply, for example, when the goods are stored in a separate location in the seller's storage room, or are labelled in a specific manner aimed at notifying third parties with respect to the owner's claimed rights.

The parties' agreement is a precondition for retention of title, as Israeli law does not set out any mandatory cases in which retention of title shall apply without the parties' consent. There are specific laws which place conditions on the transfer of title (eg, full transfer of ownership in a real estate usually requires registration with the Israeli Land Registry), however, such requirements are not necessarily related to retention of title.

The terms and conditions of the retention of title are determined by the parties to the transaction. When the parties have not determined specific terms and conditions, the court may complete the deficiency in the same way it may do so in the absence of other required details in agreements. However, lack of pertinent details could damage the validity of the claim to retention of title.

There are no formal requirements for the shipping or storage of goods subject to a retention of title. However, as stated above, separate storage or appropriate labelling distinguishing the goods in question from other goods stored at the buyer's warehouse may support the upholding of such a claim.

2.2 Scope of retention of title

It is not uncommon for goods under retention of title to be resold and transferred by the buyer before the buyer has paid the purchase price owed to the seller. In some cases, the parties expressly agree to the resale, while in other cases it is common practice. Both situations are allowed under Israeli law, and the purchasers are merely required to pay the purchase price due to the seller as agreed. However, in such cases, two questions may arise.

First, in the event that the purchaser does not pay the purchase price as agreed, may the seller (the alleged owner) track the ownership in goods that are now in possession of a third party?

In most of the cases, the answer is no. The third-party subsequent purchaser purchased the goods from the buyer (the subsequent seller) who presented himself as the owner of such goods. Such a subsequent purchaser's ownership rights are therefore secured. In order to obtain a retention of title that will have effect upon third parties as well, the seller is required to register a pledge with the applicable registry or to regulate the seller's rights in respect of third parties directly (for example, through an additional agreement with the third party). A third party who entered into a transaction under ordinary market conditions may rely on the buyer's representations, and its rights should not be affected by the rights of the alleged owner.

There may be a claim that the seller (the alleged owner) has proprietary rights over the merchandise, and that such rights, unlike contractual rights, are applicable against third parties as well. However, such a seller may ensure its rights with relative ease through the registration of a pledge with the applicable registry. To the extent that the seller fails to do so, there is no reason to favour the seller's rights over the rights of a third-party purchaser.

The second question that may arise is: to the extent that the title in the goods has already been transferred to the third party and the seller cannot track the actual goods and reserve title, does the seller have the right to track the purchase price paid by the third party to the buyer?

For example, when the buyer becomes insolvent following the transfer of the goods to a third party, before payment of the funds owed to the seller, does the seller have title over those funds, which are in the possession of the buyer, or is his status the same as other creditors, with the retention of title applying only for the goods but not for their consideration?

In cases such as these, the courts consider whether the consideration due for the goods was held separately from other funds in the buyer's accounts, or if it was marked differently, and whether the seller had extensive inspection rights with respect to those funds. If the answers to those questions are no, and the funds due for the goods were mixed in the buyer's accounts together with other non-related funds, then it is very likely that the seller does not have any title over them and will be in the same position as all the other ordinary creditors.

(a) Combining/mixing/mingling goods delivered under retention of title

The goods in respect of which the seller claims to have title may be combined or mixed with other merchandise, unrelated to the seller. What is the result in such cases?

As described above, in order to validate the retention of title, the seller should maintain separation between the goods subject to title retention and other merchandise. To the extent that such separation is not maintained, the seller is likely to face difficulties in protecting its rights and enforcing the title retention provisions. In the event that the goods in question constitute a component within another product (for example, if the seller wishes to retain title in a specific electronic component already integrated into an entire system), it is very unlikely that the validity of a retention of title clause would be upheld.

It should be noted that rulings in these matters are sometimes inconsistent and in some cases the court may resolve to reserve title in the funds although it is difficult to distinguish between them and other general funds in the buyer's accounts.

(b) Extension of retention of title

Another question one may ask is whether parties may add additional conditions to the retention of title, indirectly related to the goods that are subject to the retention of title. For example, may a seller stipulate that title be transferred to the buyer only following full payment of other funds due to the seller with respect to other goods?

Technically, as stated above, the parties may agree in good faith with respect to any conditions they deem relevant, since such conditions are not prohibited by the Sale Law (for example, a clause providing: "property in the goods does not pass to the buyer unless he paid the entire purchase price as well as any other debts due to the seller"). However, it is very unlikely that the courts would validate the retention of title in such cases. The courts would ordinarily decide in these cases that the agreement between the parties is only an attempt to override the requirements of the Pledge Law, and that it is therefore invalid.

2.3 Legal effect of retention of title

As stated above, the automatic, and most common, effect of a retention of title is upon the direct parties to the transaction (ie, the buyer and the seller). However, most conflicts arise when third parties are involved and their interests clash with those of the seller (and alleged owner).

(a) Effect towards third parties

To the extent that the goods subject to the retention of title are sold to a subsequent buyer, and such buyer, in good faith, purchased them in ordinary course, its rights would typically prevail over those of the seller (claiming title by virtue of the clause). The seller may, in such situations, usually seek relief from the first buyer (and under some circumstances as described above, retain title in the funds owed for such goods) but not from a subsequent buyer.

(b) Effect in case of a security right established over goods delivered under retention of title

The tests that the courts will use to determine the validity of a retention of title are directly related to many aspects related to the circumstances in which any lien or charge has arisen. If the seller, for example, did not impose limitations upon the goods, did not separate them and did not label them in a distinct way in the buyer's premises, and a good faith third party could not tell that they were subject to a retention of title and therefore registered a floating charge over the buyer's assets, then the retention of title may not pass the required bar in order to be considered valid. As another example, to the extent that the seller did not supervise the goods that were in the buyer's premises and a third party seized them pursuant to its possessory security right, then the retention of title would again probably not be considered valid.

(c) Effect in case of insolvency

Much more common conflicts, which stand in the centre of almost all of the legal procedures concerning retention of title, are those between the sellers and other creditors under insolvency procedures. In such cases, the seller may not seek relief from the buyer, and the other creditors (typically represented by one general receiver) also claim rights over the goods.

As stated above, in the event that the retention of title is deemed valid, the rights of the seller will prevail over those of other creditors. The meaning of a valid retention of title (that passes all the applicable tests) is that the ownership in the goods was never transferred to the buyer, and therefore none of the buyers' creditors – typically ordinary creditors and creditors with special status (such as the tax authorities, for example) – can obtain ownership over the goods.

In addition, in cases of insolvency, creditors cannot just seize goods that are in the possession of the insolvent party, and the insolvency courts will determine the rights of ownership according to the abovementioned criteria. There is therefore no difference whether the insolvent party is the seller or the buyer; the courts will determine the ownership rights in the goods according to the tests described above, irrespective of the insolvency issues.

The registration of ownership with the applicable public registry (under the Pledge Law, for example) should add validity to the seller's claim and his rights will prevail over the rights of a good faith subsequent purchaser in many cases. However, each such case will be governed by the laws and regulations applicable to the relevant registry, and not according to those of retention of title.

(d) Effect in case of partial payment of the purchase price

Partial payment by the buyer of the purchase price is not likely to affect the legal solution, unless the parties agreed otherwise. Any such terms would be considered part of the retention of title issue; for instance, if the parties agree that title will be transferred to the buyer following payment of 50% of the amount due. In such a case, the seller would probably be required to return the partial funds already paid to it in the event that the goods were returned to its possession, and failure to do so would probably be considered to be unjust enrichment.

3. Enforcement of retention of title

When a seller wants to repossess goods which are subject to a retention of title provision, the involvement of the applicable court is mandatory. The assistance of an execution office is neither applicable nor useful, since a suitable court has to determine whether the retention of title provision is valid.

A seller would typically ask to invoke a retention of title provision and repossess its goods when the seller fears the buyer will not pay its debt, due to bankruptcy or insolvency. As previously mentioned, insolvency proceedings in Israel emphasise the concept of equality between creditors; thus the preference is to solve such disputes in the courts, and not to seek the assistance of entities other than the suitable court, in order to prevent discrimination between creditors.

In order to invoke a retention of title provision, the seller will be obliged to prove to the applicable court that a valid retention of title provision had been agreed between the parties. In the event that the goods are at the premises of a third party, the seller may be entitled to track the goods, and to get the payment from the buyer, but the possibility of tracking the goods is dependent on the circumstances. According to the judgment in *Cosmos Marketing Ltd*,[7] the entitlement to track goods is dependent on the ability of the seller to identify them. The seller will need to prove that the financial receipts received for the goods that are subject to the retention of title provision were separated from other financial receipts received by the buyer.

However, according to a more recent resolution made by the District Court, in

7 Bankruptcy File, Tel-Aviv, 1700/05 *Cosmos Marketing Ltd v Ness*, issued on May 9 2006, published on the Nevo legal database.

the case of *Green Solutions for Printing Ltd*,[8] once the court has validated and approved the authenticity of the retention of title provision, the seller is entitled to track the goods or to be compensated for their value (after deduction of commissions). The decision in *Green Solutions for Printing Ltd* did not stress that the separation of financial receipts is a condition of entitlement for tracking goods.

Moreover, in cases where the parties know that the essence of the agreement is the delivery of goods to a beneficiary, the retention of title provision should be included in the agreement with the beneficiary as well, or else it will only have effect as against the buyer (who no longer possesses the goods).

Additional requirements for identifying and repossessing goods that are subject to a retention of title provision were specified in the *Vita* case. In addition to a valid provision inserted in the agreement between the parties, the seller should ensure mechanisms of supervision attesting to his ownership of the goods. Such mechanisms can include the ability to identify and isolate the goods from other goods, or the ability to separate the financial receipts received by the buyer. Other mechanisms might be the insertion of clauses that enable the seller to visit the buyer's warehouses, or to receive a monthly update with respect to the seller's property.

It is important to note that the vast majority of cases relating to the enforcement of retention of title that were discussed in this chapter are the consequence of insolvency proceedings.

8 168/10 *Green Solutions for Printing Ltd v Excellent Retail Ltd*, issued on January 11 2007, published on the Nevo legal database.

Italy

Elisabetta Caccavella
Legance Avvocati Associati

---

1. General remarks about retention of title

In principle, under Italian law, the transfer of the ownership of an asset is not conditional either on the delivery of the goods, or on the payment of the agreed price.

As a general rule, the ownership of an identified asset is transferred upon the agreement of the parties, once it is legitimately expressed (Section 1376 of the Italian Civil Code): the consensus principle. On the other hand, the ownership of an asset identified by the parties only as to its kind is transferred only upon the identification of a particular asset agreed upon by the parties (Section 1378 of the Italian Civil Code). Such principles, however, are not absolute; under Italian law, the contracting parties are entitled to depart from the basic rule set out above.

The parties to a sale agreement are allowed to agree upon a retention-of-title clause, establishing that the title to the goods remains vested in the seller until payment of the entire purchase price is received from the buyer. The nature and the effects of a retention-of-title clause are highly disputed in Italy among authors and the courts, since Italian law does not provide complete regulation of such kinds of sale agreement and therefore their effects and the differences with respect to a standard sale agreement are still quite controversial.

Regulation of retention-of-title clauses is provided primarily by Sections 1523–1526 of the Italian Civil Code, which govern sale agreements where the purchase price is paid by instalments. Further specific provisions – with specific relevance to the enforceability of a retention-of-title clause against third parties – are contained in Legislative Decree 231/2002, in Section 73 of the Italian Bankruptcy Law (Royal Decree 257/46) and, if the parties agree on the sale of machinery for a price exceeding €258.23, in Law 1329/1965 (see further in section 2.1(b) below).

From an international perspective, the legal framework is complicated by the lack of specific provisions on retention of title in the Italian private international law system, with the consequence that the different aspects of a retention-of-title clause might be governed by the laws of different states. According to the few Italian precedents and to the predominant opinion, based on the Italian private international law system:

- the agreement and the transfer of title are ruled by the law applicable to the relationship between the seller and the purchaser (the law of the contract);
- the possibility of taking security against the goods subject to retention of title, the rank of the retention of title in relation to other rights, and the

enforceability of the retention of title against third parties are governed by the law applicable of the state where the asset is located; and
- the assessment of the existence and the effects of the retention of title with respect to goods exported outside Italy is ruled by the legal provisions of the state of destination of such goods.

Within this legal framework, there are no express rules with regard to several issues that may arise, such as the applicability of a retention-of-title clause to the sale of an immovable asset, the effects of the retention-of-title clause against the seller's creditors or against a good-faith sub-purchaser.

Opinion is even divided on whether a sales agreement with a retention-of-title clause should be classed as a conditional sales agreement, or as a sales agreement with obligatory effects.

Retention-of-title clauses are not particularly common in practice in Italy, due to the fragmentary regulation mentioned above and to the onerous requirements involved in assessing the existence and enforceability of a retention-of-title clause.

2. Retention of title

2.1 Validity and formal requirements

(a) Provisions under the Civil Code

A valid ROT clause under the Italian Law shall be agreed by the parties before or upon the execution of the sale agreement. Once the agreement has been executed, the parties – according to the majority of Authors and of the Case Law – are not allowed to enter into a ROT clause, considering that the ownership of the goods has been already transferred to the purchaser based on the consensus principle.

It is not necessary to use any specific legal wording for a retention-of-title clause, and the clause might refer to movable assets, to assets listed in a public register under Section 1524 of the Italian Civil Code, to immovable assets (see Court of Cassation 3415/99) or to the sale of a going concern. Parties to a sales agreement may even agree on a retention-of-title clause only orally, but in such a case the retention of title is effective only between the contracting parties. A valid retention-of-title clause can also be agreed in the general terms and conditions of sale and, since it is not included in the list of the restrictive clauses, it does not even require specific approval in writing in order to be valid.

Section 1524 of the Civil Code states that, in order to be enforceable against the purchaser's creditors and in the event of the purchaser's insolvency, a retention-of-title clause must meet a double requirement: it must be specified in writing; and it must bear a so-called 'certain date'.

With respect to the requirement for a 'certain date', under Article 2704 of the Civil Code the date of a private document, unless the signature has been authenticated through its notarisation, is not certain and cannot be asserted against third parties:

except from the day on which the private document was registered or from the day of death or supervening incapacity to sign of the person or persons who signed it, or from the day when the content of such document are reproduced in public deeds, or from the day other circumstances occur establishing with equal certainty that the document was drawn up previously.

According to Section 1524 of the Civil Code, it is sufficient that the document with the retention-of-title clause bears a certain date that is prior to the date of any third parties' attachment or seizure of the goods concerned (it being unnecessary that the certain date should be the exact date and hour of creation of the retention of title).

(b) Other statutory provisions

Beside the rules established by the Civil Code, Italian legislation includes other statutory provisions. The result of the combination of such provisions is not always easy to apply.

First, where a retention of title applies to an immovable asset or a movable good subject to specific registration (cars, ships, etc), the retention of title must be recorded in the relevant national public register in order to be effective against third parties.

Additional requirements are provided in Section 1524 of the Civil Code with respect to the sale of machinery at a price exceeding the amount of €15.49. In such a case, in order to be enforceable against a sub-purchaser, the retention of title must also:

- be recorded in a special register kept by the clerk of the court having jurisdiction over the place where the machinery is located; and
- be located – at the time of the sub-purchase – in the same place where it was located when that record was made.

In addition, Law 1329/1965 provides – with specific regard to machinery sold for a price exceeding €258.23 – that a retention-of-title clause will be enforceable against a sub-purchaser only if the machinery bears a plate recording details of the machine and ownership by the seller.

The final relevant statutory provision is Legislative Decree 231/2002 implementing Directive 2000/35/EU combating late payments in commercial transactions (the Late Payment Directive). Section 11 of Decree 231/2002 provides that, in the case of a supply relationship between two commercial enterprises, a retention of title previously agreed upon in writing between the parties is effective against the purchaser's creditors, provided that:

- the retention of title is confirmed in an invoice issued after the sale of goods which bears a 'certain date'; and
- it has been properly recorded in entries in the accounts.

It has been disputed how the provision of Legislative Decree 231/2002 impacts on the provisions of the Civil Code. According to the most conservative authors, in order to be effective, a retention-of-title clause established with respect to a sales agreement has to satisfy both the requirements set out by Section 1523 of the Civil Code and those set out by Legislative Decree 231/2002.

2.2 Scope of retention of title

(a) *General*

By acknowledging retention-of-title clauses, Italian legislation introduced an exception to the basic rule of the free transfer of ownership, aimed at providing a guarantee to the seller with respect to the full payment of the purchase price, while at the same time at financing the buyer, allowing him an immediate use of the good.

Even if it is not mandatory, it is usual that on the execution of the sales agreement, the good is delivered to the purchaser or to a third party nominated by the purchaser. Once the good has been delivered, all the relevant risks, including but not limited to the risk of loss of the good, pass to the purchaser by operation of law, while the ownership of the good will be transferred only upon payment of the last instalment of the purchase price (Section 1523 of the Italian Civil Code).

In the event of the purchaser breaching its obligation to pay the purchase price, or part of it, it is up to the seller either to terminate the agreement or to claim the immediate payment of all the remaining instalments.

Should the seller decide to terminate the agreement, he is also entitled to collect the good and to obtain compensation for its use, as well as indemnification aimed at restoring any damages suffered. The seller, unless a different agreement is made between the parties, is then requested to return to the purchaser the amount of the price so far paid. If the parties agree that any such amount shall not be returned, as a penalty it is always open to the court to amend such an agreement if the amount of the penalty is excessive (as with any other penalty established by the parties) – see Section 1526(2) of the Civil Code. Therefore, in principle, unless a different arrangement is agreed, the seller is allowed to claim back the goods sold under the retention of title, despite the fact that the buyer has paid a significant part of the purchase price and regardless of whether the goods can be split.

As noted, in the event of breach of the purchaser's obligations to pay all or part of the purchase price, the seller may decide to keep the agreement valid and to ask for payment of the entire purchase price (ie, all the remaining instalments) and for compensation for any damages suffered. In order to avoid any possible abuse by the seller, Section 1524 of the Civil Code establishes that the lack of payment by the purchaser of one instalment not exceeding an eighth part to the purchase price does not allow the seller either to terminate the sales agreement or to request the immediate payment of all remaining instalments.

(b) *Combining/mixing/mingling goods delivered under retention of title*

With regard to the purchaser's obligations, even in the absence of express legal provisions the author believes that the purchaser is not entitled to sell goods delivered under retention of title, or to undertake any combining, mixing, mingling or processing of the goods. In fact, according to the majority opinion, consumables intended to be mixed, combined or mingled cannot be sold under a retention-of-title clause unless the purchaser agrees that he will use the goods only after the payment of the entire purchase price or, alternatively, that the retention of title shall be considered to be extended to the goods resulting from the planned process.

Therefore, in principle, a liquid cannot be sold under a retention-of-title clause, with the consequence that – barring specific contractual provisions for the outcome – such a provision would be deemed void.

In the event that the purchaser – despite the absence of specific contractual provisions allowing it – should mingle, mix or combine goods subject to a valid retention-of-title clause, it has been held that the acceleration clause provided by Section 1186 of the Civil Code will apply upon the request of the seller, with the consequence that the seller is entitled to recover payment of the entire purchase price or, alternatively, in the event that the goods are still collectable, to claim the return of the goods together with indemnification for the use of the goods and for the damages suffered.

The effects of such action on a third party acting in good faith are examined in section 2.3 following.

(c) *Extension of retention of title*

Given that a retention-of-title clause is an exception to the general rule regarding transfer of ownership upon the parties' agreement and that the statutory provisions state that such a clause shall be agreed with respect to the purchase price of the delivered good, an extension of a retention-of-title clause with respect to the payment of other claims might be deemed void.

2.3 Legal effects of retention of title

As noted above, the delivery of goods under a retention-of-title clause is considered under Italian law as an exception to the principle of the free transferability of goods. For these reasons, its assessment is subject to special requirements and public formalities (Section 1524 of the Civil Code, Law 1329/1965, Legislative Decree 231/2002) aimed not only at protecting a third-party purchaser acting in good faith but also at avoiding the risk of possible collusion between the seller and the original purchaser.

As previously mentioned, in order to be effective against a third party and (in detail) against the creditors or receivers of the purchaser, a retention-of-title clause has to satisfy the requirements laid down by Section 1524 of the Civil Code and any requirements provided by other laws if they are applicable (see the discussion at section 2.1 above).

Under Section 1524 of the Italian Civil Code, the purchaser's creditors – or the receiver in the event of a declaration of bankruptcy in respect of the purchaser – are not allowed to collect, attach or seize goods delivered under a retention of title, provided that the document attesting the retention of title is in writing and bears a 'certain date' that is prior either to the attachment or seizure of goods, or to the declaration of bankruptcy. In the absence of such formalities, according to some opinion, the retention of title is not effective even against a sub-purchaser who entered into a purchase agreement in bad faith, and who is therefore entitled to start attachment proceedings.

With respect to the seller, there is no express statutory provision, but it is commonly held that he is not allowed to sell the goods. However, if he proceeds with the sale, a retention-of-title clause complying with the statutory requirements is effective against the sub-purchaser unless the latter acted in good faith and obtained possession of the goods (Section 1153 of the Civil Code).

In the event of a declaration of bankruptcy on the part of the seller, provided that the retention-of-title clause bears a 'certain date', the trustee in bankruptcy is not entitled to terminate the sales agreement (Section 73(2) of Italy's Insolvency Law). Should the purchaser fail to provide payment of the agreed price, the trustee in bankruptcy is entitled, as any other seller, to terminate the contract, to collect the goods and to return – unless a different agreement is reached – any instalments of the purchase price already paid by the purchaser.

In the event of bankruptcy on the part of the purchaser, the trustee in bankruptcy is entitled, if authorised by the creditors' committee, to enter into and continue the agreement. If, nevertheless, he decides to terminate the agreement, he is entitled to receive back the price instalments already paid, except for a sum to be acknowledged as compensation for the use of the goods that had occurred in the meantime.

Finally, Section 2762 of the Civil Code provides a non-possessory security interest in favour of the seller of machinery delivered under a retention of title, in the event of termination of the agreement. This interest is limited to the amount of the unpaid price and is guaranteed for three years after the registration of the relevant document in the special register kept by the clerk of the court having jurisdiction over the place where the machinery is located. This charge gives to the seller the right to be paid in priority with respect to the buyer's other creditors, according to the rank established by Section 2778 of the Civil Code – which, however, subordinates that interest to many other statutory preference and security rights.

3. Enforcement of retention of title

In the Italian legal system, there is no special procedural path for an owner wishing to enforce a retention of title and to repossess the relevant goods that are at the premises of the purchaser or of any other third party. In the absence of cooperation from the purchaser or any relevant third party, the owner is obliged – as is any other creditor – to start a lawsuit before the competent Italian court in order to obtain a judicial decree by which the court orders the counterparty to hand over the goods subject to the retention of title.

The owner, provided that the retention of title has been established in writing, might apply for a faster proceeding, an injunctive proceeding, instead of an ordinary proceeding (which may take some years to come to an end). The injunctive proceeding, aimed at obtaining an injunction ordering the repossession of specified goods, under Sections 633 and following of the Civil Procedural Code, comprises two phases: the first necessary, and the second one merely potential.

3.1 First phase of injunction proceeding

During the first phase, the owner may file a petition with the competent court, together with documents proving the retention of title, requesting the court to grant an order requiring repossession of the goods against the purchaser or any other third party. The court usually takes only a few days to deal with the petitioners' request; and if the court is satisfied with the evidence presented for the existence of the claimed retention of title, based on the documents filed, it grants the order. The court may also declare the order to be immediately enforceable if some specific conditions are met, including the existence of a notarised document proving the retention of title and the obligation to hand over the goods, or evidence proving that any delay in collecting the goods may cause substantial damages to the owner.

Once the order requiring repossession has been issued, the owner must serve it (within 60 days) upon the debtor, inviting the purchaser or the third party to hand over the goods, stressing that if they fail to file an opposition against the order within 40 days from the service of the judicial documents, the order of repossession will become final.

If the order of repossession has been declared immediately enforceable by the court, and if then the goods are not returned, the owner is entitled to enforce the order by asking the competent bailiff to proceed by means of attachment of the goods subject to the retention of title. Such an enforcement action is not automatically suspended by the filing of an opposition proceeding by the purchaser or any other third party who might challenge the owner's rights.

3.2 Second phase of injunction proceeding

The opposition proceeding is deemed the second phase of the injunction proceeding. Opposition comprises an ordinary proceeding which may last around two or three years, depending on the activities to be carried out before the judge. The judgment issued at the end of the proceeding is immediately enforceable and is subject to appeal.

3.3 Bankruptcy of party holding the goods

If the purchaser or the third party controlling the goods is declared bankrupt under Italy's Bankruptcy Law, the owner is prevented from taking any enforcement action against the insolvent company (including any enforcement of the retention of title). In such circumstances, in order to enforce its right of ownership the owner – even if he has already obtained a judicial order of repossession or a final judgment – has to file a petition for the return of the goods with the bankruptcy court, asking to be included in the statement of liabilities of the bankrupt company.

The petition will be examined by the trustee in bankruptcy. The bankruptcy judge, having received the opinion of the trustee in bankruptcy in addition to the petition and evidence filed by the alleged owner, might grant or reject the petition. The decision of the bankruptcy judge is subject to appeal before the Bankruptcy Court. Should the petition of the owner be granted, he will receive back the goods according to the terms set out by the court.

Japan

Tomohiro Murakami
Nishimura & Asahi

This chapter will discuss various issues based on the scenario that, in a bilateral agreement, a party sells and delivers a movable asset to another party but retains ownership until that other party has paid the purchase price in full.

Where a seller sells goods to a buyer, the seller will have a lien against the goods owned by the buyer, which are the subject of the sale, to secure the sale price. Such lien is called a lien for sale of a movable under Article 321 of the Civil Code (Law 89 of 1896). This lien is a statutory security interest, which is established by operation of law. However, some sellers may take the view that this lien does not sufficiently protect their interests in some respects. First, a lien for sale of a movable may not be exercised against a movable whose ownership and possession (including constructive possession) are transferred from a buyer to a third party. In addition, a lien for sale of a movable needs to be enforced by auction under the Civil Execution Act (Law 4 of 1979).

In contrast, an arrangement for the retention of title is generally considered to provide a seller with a more favourable means or mechanism for protecting its interests.

1. General remarks about retention of title

1.1 Transfer of ownership

As a basic rule, when a seller and a buyer conclude a sale and purchase agreement in which the seller agrees to sell and the buyer agrees to purchase an asset to or from the other party, the title in the asset passes to the buyer under Japanese law (Article 176 of the Civil Code). Delivery of the asset is not required for the transfer of ownership in the asset.

The parties are entitled to agree on a time of transfer of ownership that differs from this basic rule.

1.2 Retention of title

A sale and purchase agreement between a seller and a buyer may provide that the seller retains the ownership of the asset until a certain condition (such as the purchase price having been paid by the buyer) has been met. This is called an arrangement for the retention of title or retention of ownership.

A retention of title has no statutory basis under Japanese law, but is based on case law and also recognised by legal scholars. There are two contrasting views as to the nature of retention of title, a view that values the form of ownership and a view that emphasises the substance of a security interest. Although some case law conforms to the ownership view, the security interest view prevails among legal scholars and has a greater influence on case law. An authoritative body of case law that covers all important issues pertaining to retention of title has not yet fully emerged in Japan.

1.3 Foreign and international law

Real rights over movables, such as ownership, possession and security interests on movables, are generally governed by the law of the place where the movables are located under private international law in Japan. The Act on General Rules of Application of Laws (Law 78 of 2006) provides that real rights to movables are governed by the law of the place where the movables are located, except for the acquisition or loss of such real rights, which are governed by the law of the place where the movables are located when the events causing the acquisition or loss occur. The prevailing view is that contractual security interests in movables, which are created under an agreement between a collateral provider and a secured party, generally follow this rule. Therefore, in general, acquisition or loss aspects – such as the transfer of ownership, creation of a retention of title, a good-faith acquisition, or acquisition by prescription (which is comparable to the real property concept of "adverse possession") – will be governed by the law of the place where the movables are located when the events causing the acquisition or loss occur, and the other aspects (such as contents and effects of the retention of title, its rank and matters affecting its perfection) will be governed by the law of the place where the movables are located, and should the movables be relocated to another jurisdiction, these matters will be governed by the laws of that jurisdiction.

There are some exceptions to this rule with respect to, among other things, a movable in transit (to which the laws of designation generally apply) and cars, ships and aircraft registered under the respective relevant laws (to which the laws of flag state or the laws of the place where the aircraft or cars are registered generally apply, although there was a case in which the Supreme Court applied the law of the place where a car was located).

1.4 Retention of title in insolvency

Consideration should be given to additional issues arising under insolvency laws, such as the Bankruptcy Act (Law 75 of 2004), the Civil Rehabilitation Act (Law 225 of 1999) and the Corporate Reorganisation Act (Law 154 of 2002) if the debtor (ie, the buyer) is subject to insolvency proceedings in Japan. The first prescribes liquidation procedures, while the second deals with reorganisation procedures. The third of these statutes applies only to stock companies, especially those that are large in size.

As retained ownership is in substance a security interest rather than ordinary ownership, it is recognised as a right of separate satisfaction in the Bankruptcy Act and the Civil Rehabilitation Act, and similarly a basis of secured reorganisation claims in the Corporate Reorganisation Act, rather than as a right of segregation which is typically vested, on the basis of complete ownership, in an owner. Although such rights of separate satisfaction are subject to the Bankruptcy Act or the Civil

Rehabilitation Act, these rights of separate satisfaction may be exercised with respect to assets belonging to a bankruptcy estate or to rehabilitation debtors without going through bankruptcy proceedings or rehabilitation proceedings. On the other hand, the exercise of security interests for secured reorganisation claims is stayed or prohibited after commencement of reorganisation proceedings, and may also be stayed or prohibited after a petition for commencement of reorganisation proceedings.

The Bankruptcy Act provides for ways to discharge a security interest in bankruptcy proceedings. First, a trustee has a right to proceed to auction with respect to the goods, if the holder of the retained ownership does not complete the sale or other disposal of the goods during a period that is fixed, upon the request of the trustee, by a court. The holder of the retained ownership will receive the amount of its secured claim in priority to other creditors from the sales proceeds (from which it is arguable that the costs of the auction can be deducted), and the security interest will be extinguished in the auction process.

Secondly, in certain circumstances, except where the interests of a security interest holder would be unduly prejudiced, the trustee may file a petition at court for permission to sell the collateral in a private manner specifically proposed by the trustee and to cause the security interest to be extinguished by paying to the court the sales proceeds (after deduction of a certain amount, which will be added to the bankruptcy estate, and certain expenses related to the sale and purchase agreement). If the court grants permission to proceed in this way and the net sales proceeds are paid to the court, distribution will be made to the relevant secured creditors following the prescribed procedures. Similar, but separate mechanisms that can cause security interests to be extinguished are also provided in the Civil Rehabilitation Act and the Corporate Reorganisation Act. What differences there are arise from the respective purposes of these statutes.

In the event that a petition is filed for commencement of rehabilitation proceedings, a court may issue an order to stay the execution procedure with respect to security interests for a specified reasonable period if it finds that a stay is consistent with the common interests of the rehabilitation creditors and is not likely to cause undue damage to the secured parties. This order is typically intended to address situations where assets subject to security interests are necessary for rehabilitation of the debtor's business, which would ultimately increase the amounts to be distributed to the creditors as compared with liquidation of the assets.

After commencement of reorganisation proceedings, reorganisation claims (which can include, among other things, a claim on property arising against the company subject to reorganisation from a cause that occurred before the commencement of the reorganisation proceedings, as referred to in the Corporate Reorganisation Act) and secured reorganisation claims may not be satisfied except through the reorganisation proceedings. Commencement of reorganisation proceedings stays and prohibits enforcement of security interests. When considering a petition for commencement of reorganisation proceedings, a court may issue an order, if it finds it necessary, to stay enforcement of security interests even before reorganisation proceedings are commenced provided that doing so is not likely to cause undue damage to the secured parties. Further, a court may issue an order comprehensively to stay and prohibit all enforcement of security interests until a decision is made on the petition for commencement of reorganisation proceedings.

In cases where either the seller or the buyer is subject to insolvency proceedings outside Japan, the Act on Recognition of and Assistance for Foreign Insolvency Proceedings (Law 129 of 2000) may apply. This statute provides procedures for the recognition of foreign insolvency proceedings and assistance to foreign trustees or (if no such trustees exist) debtors in connection with the recognised foreign insolvency proceedings. The types of assistance that a court may render upon or after the issue of a recognition order include an order to stay procedures for exercising security interests and an administration order. A court may issue an order to stay procedures for enforcement of security interests against the debtor's property if it finds that doing so would be consistent with the common interests of the creditors and is not likely to cause undue damage to the secured parties. Further, a court may, if it finds it necessary in order to achieve the purpose of the recognition and assistance proceedings, appoint a recognition trustee (or trustees) and issue an administration order that a debtor's business and property in Japan be administered by the recognition trustee. The administration order vests the exclusive right to carry out the debtor's business in Japan and to administer and dispose of the debtor's property in Japan, in the recognition trustee. Additionally, where a petition is filed for recognition of foreign insolvency proceedings, before a recognition order is issued a court may issue an order to stay procedures for enforcement of security interests, as mentioned above, and a provisional administration order similar to the administration order that could be issued on or after the issue of the recognition order.

In terms of international private law on insolvency, there is no specific provision in the Act on General Rules of Application of Laws or insolvency statutes and no authoritative body of case law. International private law pertaining to insolvency has not been extensively or exhaustively studied by legal scholars in Japan. Some legal scholars have expressed the view that special international law should be applied in the event of insolvency rather than ordinary international law as provided in the Act on General Rules of Application of Laws. According to this view, the law of the place where insolvency proceedings are commenced is generally applied, and is in particular applied to the issues inherently arising in insolvency such as preferred status of security interests and treatment of an executory contract. (Executory contracts in insolvency proceedings in Japan are further discussed in section 2.3(d) below.) The other view is that ordinary international law should be consistently applied to the event of insolvency, which has been recently advocated by some other legal scholars. (See section 1.3 above for an analysis of the impact of ordinary international law on retention of title.)

2. Retention of title

2.1 Validity and formal requirements

Retention of title may be validly established by the oral agreement of the seller and the buyer, but in practice it is usually specified in a written agreement. No registration is necessary for the transfer of ownership, except where there are special registration systems for some movable assets. For instance, the transfer of ownership in certain types of car, ship and aircraft requires registration for perfection purposes.

There are no formal requirements as regards the wording of a retention of title clause in Japan. In general, it is permissible to agree upon retention of title in general terms and conditions in a sale and purchase agreement.

A retention of title is valid even if the goods are not delivered directly to the buyer. However, who is in possession of goods may be relevant for perfection of a retention of title with respect to goods, assuming that the goods are not registered under the relevant statutes. An agent may take possession of the goods for a principal. The taking of possession by an agent suffices for perfection purposes. In practice, however, as a protection against acquisition in good faith by a third party, a seller should make public who holds ownership of the goods. For instance, affixing a name plate to the goods may work.

In general, retention of title will not be put in place by operation of law. However, sale with payment by instalments may, in respect of certain products designated as durable by regulations, be subject to the Instalment Sales Act (Law 159 of 1961). Under this act, with regard to sales by instalment as defined in the statute in respect of designated products, a party that conducts such sales by instalment as its business is presumed to retain ownership of a product sold until the other party has paid the instalment amounts for the product in full.

2.2 Scope of retention of title

(a) Sale of goods delivered under retention of title

In principle, a buyer will not have any power or authority to transfer to a third party goods sold to it subject to retention of title before the buyer has paid the purchase price to the seller. If the buyer is empowered or authorised by the seller, the buyer is entitled to sell the goods before having paid the purchase price to the seller. If the buyer has no such power or authority, the third party will not acquire ownership of the goods subject to retention of title except where it acquires such goods while acting in good faith. A mere agreement between a seller and a buyer that the right to receive the purchase price, which is to be paid by the third party to the buyer, shall be transferred to the seller (who retains title) will not work to bind the third party. In addition to such an agreement, the transfer to the seller of the right to receive the purchase price needs to be perfected in order to bind the third party and require it to pay the purchase price to the transferee (the seller). Instead of a transfer, another way to protect the seller's interest is the creation of a pledge over the sale price receivable from the third party and perfection with respect to the pledge.

There are some Supreme Court cases with respect to car sales by dealers. Designated cars require registration of ownership before they can be driven. The concept of a good-faith purchase by a third party does not apply to sales of registered cars, according to the Supreme Court. In the relevant cases, a dealer sold a car to a sub-dealer on the basis of a retention of title, and in turn the sub-dealer resold the car to an end-user with the sub-dealer being supposed to pay the purchase price to the dealer. The dealer demanded the return of the car from the end-user, who had paid the entire retail price to the sub-dealer, on the basis of its retention of ownership of the car following default by the sub-dealer on payment to the dealer. It was held in one Supreme Court case that the dealer was not allowed to demand the return, on the grounds that it amounted to an abuse of rights, in a situation where the dealer had cooperated with the sub-dealer in the resale transaction to the end-user. However, no authoritative body of case law has fully developed as to whether a seller is allowed to repossess a registered car after a buyer has resold the car to a third party if the buyer is in default of payment to the seller.

(b) Combining/mixing/mingling goods delivered under retention of title

There are situations where goods delivered under retention of title by a seller are combined, mixed or mingled with other goods owned by a buyer.

Where goods are combined with other goods to form composite goods, the situation is governed by Articles 243 and 244 of the Civil Code, among others. Under these provisions, if goods owned by a party are combined with and cannot be separated, without damage or excessive expense, from goods owned by another party, then the resulting composite goods shall be owned by the owner of the principal goods, except where it cannot be determined which is principal and which accessory, in which case the owners shall obtain common ownership of the composite goods in proportion to the prices of goods provided by them at the time of combination. Which is the principal and which the accessory is determined having regard to the goods' respective values, and other matters. The prevailing view is that this rule as to who gains ownership of the composite goods is the default rule, but not a mandatory rule, and therefore the parties may agree otherwise. The same rule applies to situations where goods are mixed or mingled with other goods.

After goods have been combined, mixed or mingled with other goods, the retention of title will in principle no longer be valid with respect to the goods that were combined, mixed or mingled (ie, the goods as they existed prior to their combining, mixing or mingling), as ownership of the composite goods is different from ownership of the goods that have been combined, mixed or mingled. Although it is not explicitly prohibited by Japanese law, it is not common that buyers and sellers use a retention of title which extends to composite goods resulting from combination, mixture or mingling, and therefore the legal character of such a retention of title has not been well developed in the jurisprudence.

(c) Processing of goods delivered under retention of title

There are also situations where goods delivered by a seller under retention of title are processed by a buyer. A party may process goods provided by other parties and create new products, which is governed by Article 246 of the Civil Code, among others. Under Article 246, the owner of the goods that are processed shall obtain ownership of the newly processed products, except where any increase in their value as a result of the processing significantly exceeds the value of the materials provided, in which case ownership of the newly processed products shall vest in the party who processed the materials and created the new products. The prevailing view is that this rule as to who obtains ownership of newly processed products is the default rule, but not a mandatory rule, and therefore the parties may agree otherwise.

The retention of title will in principle no longer be valid with respect to the materials that were processed, as ownership of the newly processed products is different from that of the materials that were processed. As in the case with combination, mixture or mingling, although it is not explicitly prohibited by Japanese law, sellers and buyers in Japan do not commonly use a retention of title which extends to newly processed products, and therefore the legal character of such a retention of title has not been the subject of authoritative case law.

(d) *Extension of the retention of title*

Some goods may be sold by a seller under retention of title in order to secure payment by a buyer not just of the sales price of those goods, but also other debts of the buyer towards the seller.

There are cases from lower courts addressing the validity of such extended forms of retention of title clauses. In one case, a sale and purchase agreement of a bulldozer included a retention of title which was mainly related to the sales price of the bulldozer but also covered the sales price of other machines and machine parts, and left some room to interpret the secured claims as including the seller's other claims against the buyer. The seller demanded, under its retained ownership, return of the bulldozer from the buyer when the latter failed to pay the purchase price for another bulldozer to the seller. The court said that this form of retention of title did not breach public policy and good moral doctrine under certain circumstances, including a situation where the value of a bulldozer decreases rapidly and is not sufficient to secure its sales price, and in reality the secured claims were limited to accounts receivable by the buyer arising from trade by the seller to the buyer of the bulldozer, other machines and machine parts.

On the other hand, another court rendered a contradictory decision in a case where a seller and a buyer agreed in their basic sale and purchase agreement regarding electrical products that ownership of the products was retained by the seller until the buyer paid all current and future debts owing to the seller. It was held in this case that the retention of title was void in the light of the spirit of public policy and good morals doctrine in that the secured obligations for the retention of title extended to all the buyer's debts to the seller. As the above two cases demonstrate, the readiness of a Japanese court to recognise a retention of title is very much dependent on the individual facts of a case.

2.3 Legal effect of retention of title

(a) *Effect towards third parties*

Retention of title can be established in an agreement between a seller and a buyer such as a sale and purchase agreement. In order for the retention of title to have effect towards third parties (which may include subsequent buyers, other creditors and tax authorities), the relevant requirements for perfection need to be met. In the case of a retention of title regarding goods, in general, ownership retained by the seller under a retention of title clause will be perfected when the seller or its agent takes possession of the goods. Therefore, in most cases of bilateral sale and purchase transactions subject to retention of title, a buyer will agree to take possession, on behalf of the seller, of the goods delivered to the buyer, until the purchase price has been paid to the seller, and then such retained ownership will be perfected against third parties. Even once perfected, however, third parties acting in good faith are able, under Article 192 of the Civil Code, to acquire ownership of goods without becoming subject to the retention of title. In this sense, the effect of perfection in respect of the transfer of movable assets is restricted by, and subject to, the possibility of acquisition by third parties acting in good faith. If third parties (for example, subsequent buyers) are aware or only unaware through negligence that the goods were subject to retention of title at the time of the delivery of the goods to them, the subsequent buyers will acquire the goods still subject to the retention of title. Please also see the discussion under heading 2.1 above.

There are special registration systems for certain movable assets such as certain cars, ships and aircraft under the relevant statutes. The transfer of ownership in such movable assets requires registration for perfection purposes. Further, in general, third parties cannot act in good faith to acquire ownership of such movable assets if they have been registered.

(b) Effect in case of seizure of goods delivered under retention of title

Where goods are sold to a buyer under retention of title by a seller, according to a Supreme Court decision, in the event of seizure of those goods by a third party (such as another creditor of the buyer), the holder of the retained ownership of the goods (the seller) is entitled to file, against the third party, a third-party action to prevent the seizure. By the third-party action, the seller is therefore able to thwart the seizure by the other creditor of the buyer, even though retained ownership is not complete ownership. In the case of seizure of the goods by a creditor of the seller, it is unlikely that the creditor of the seller would be able successfully to seize the goods in the possession of the buyer. In the case of seizure of goods possessed by a third party other than a seizure obligor, voluntary submission of the goods by the third party is required under Japanese law. Usually, the buyer would refuse to submit the goods to the creditor attempting seizure.

(c) Effect in case of a security right established over goods delivered under retention of title

A retention of title may cease to be effective in the event that a possessory security right is established over the goods at issue. For instance, where the buyer pledges movable assets in its possession in favour of a creditor (other than the seller), the pledge over the movable assets comes into effect by delivery of the assets to the creditor and is perfected by continuing possession of the assets. Admittedly, a third party, in general, cannot obtain any security interest in assets which are subject to retention of title by the seller (without them remaining subject to such retention of title), unless the creation of the pledge in favour of the third party satisfies the same conditions as an acquisition in good faith. However, if the buyer creates a pledge in favour of a creditor (other than the seller), then the pledge is established over the assets in good faith, unless the creditor was aware or was only unaware through negligence that the assets were subject to retention of title at the time of the creation of the pledge.

On the other hand, the retention of title is not affected by the establishment of a non-possessory security right by the buyer, such as security assignment of movables. The security assignment becomes valid by a constructive transfer of movables in the possession of the assignor to the assignee. Such constructive transfer does not satisfy the requirement of a transfer of possession for an acquisition in good faith. Therefore, a security assignment by constructive transfer of the goods does not supersede the retention of title.

If there are special registration systems for the goods at issue under relevant statutes, the relevant rules lay down an order of priority for conflicting security interests over such registered goods.

(d) *Effect in case of insolvency*

In the event that a buyer is subject to insolvency proceedings in Japan, and goods title to which is retained by a seller are in the buyer's possession then, in addition to the restrictions referred to under the heading "Retention of title in insolvency" above, the retained ownership may be subject to specific rights of a trustee or debtor under the relevant insolvency laws.

It was held in a Supreme Court case that, assuming that retained ownership is a security interest, in principle retention of title must have been perfected as of the commencement of rehabilitation proceedings in order to enforce a retained ownership right against the rehabilitation debtor's goods (in this case, a registered car) in those proceedings. The same rule may apply to bankruptcy proceedings and reorganisation proceedings.

In another Supreme Court case, the court declared void a provision which stipulated that a sale and purchase agreement would terminate on the occurrence of an event that may become a cause for the commencement of reorganisation proceedings with respect to a buyer. There is no analogous case law for bankruptcy proceedings, however the Supreme Court decided in relation to rehabilitation proceedings that a similar termination clause based on a petition for such proceedings against a user in a finance lease agreement was void.

An executory contract may be terminated or affirmed by a trustee or (in the case of rehabilitation proceedings without trustee) the rehabilitation debtor in insolvency proceedings. At issue is whether a sales contract with a retention of title clause is such an executory contract if the seller has completed delivery of the asset but not received the entire sales price as at the commencement of insolvency proceedings against the buyer. Assuming that the transfer of the asset is not subject to registration, the sales contract will not be an executory contract. This is in line with the majority view of legal scholars and lower court decisions. However, in cases where the seller's obligation to register a transfer remains outstanding, lower court decisions have been divided on this issue.

There is less specific discussion on this issue in the event that the seller is subject to insolvency proceedings. Although there is uncertainty where the seller's obligation to register a transfer remains outstanding, the majority view of legal scholars is that a sales contract with a retention of title clause will not fall within the category of executory contracts. To support this majority view, some legal scholars argue further that if a sales contract with a retention of title clause is regarded an executory contract, then the trustee (ie, the seller holding retained ownership) would be able to terminate such a sales contract under which a buyer is not in default of payment, which is an unconscionable result.

(e) *Effect in case of partial payment of the purchase price*

Partial payment of the purchase price by a buyer will reduce the amount of its debt secured by the retention of title. However, ownership of the whole of the goods subject to the retention of title is retained by the seller irrespective of the outstanding secured amount. Therefore, the buyer is not able to acquire complete ownership of the goods sold under retention of title until its debt has been paid in full, even if the outstanding amount of the debt is less than value of the goods subject to the retention of title. If the seller repossesses and then either retains or sells all the goods on enforcement of the retention of title, and the appraised value of the goods or the amount of sales proceeds realised exceeds the outstanding secured amount, then the seller must return the excess to the buyer.

According to legal scholars, the buyer may redeem the goods by tendering the entire outstanding secured amount to the seller until the seller returns such excess to the buyer. There are no Supreme Court decisions on the relationship between the buyer's redemption rights with respect to retention of title and disposal of goods subject to retention of title by the seller. However, if the goods have been sold by the seller because of the buyer being in default of payment, the buyer's right to redeem the goods would lapse when the goods are sold by the seller. This view may be derived from a Supreme Court decision to the same effect on the redemption right of a secured creditor who holds a security assignment as collateral.

3. Enforcement of retention of title

A seller's retained ownership of goods delivered under retention of title is enforced by the seller in a private manner (without auction). Usually, the seller terminates the sales agreement with the buyer when it repossesses the goods delivered. Under the Instalment Sales Act, where a buyer fails to pay an instalment amount to a seller in sales by instalment of certain products identified by statute, the seller, as a person in the business of sales by instalment, may not terminate a sales agreement due to the failure, unless it demands in writing payment of the amount due from the buyer, and specifies in such demand a reasonable period of 20 days or more before the termination. The seller may itself, or through its attorney or debt collection firm, request that the buyer voluntarily return the goods delivered. If the buyer refuses or fails to return the goods, then the seller may bring proceedings demanding the return of the goods in respect of which it has retained ownership.

It may be agreed between a seller and a buyer that the buyer will grant the seller access to the buyer's premises to repossess the goods in the event of default of the buyer, and the buyer may not deny the seller access. This agreement will be void because self-help is prohibited under Japanese law, although self-help is not specifically addressed in the Civil Code. If the seller needs a remedy before bringing an action against the buyer, a provisional disposition order may be available to the seller under the Civil Provisional Remedies Act (Law 91 of 1989) in order, for instance, to maintain the status quo or to demand the delivery of the goods.

After a judgment entitling a seller to repossess the goods, or a provisional disposition order such as an order requiring a buyer to return the goods to the seller, has been rendered in favour of the seller, the seller must file a petition for execution with a competent court under the Civil Execution Act or the Civil Provisional Remedies Act, as the case may be.

There are no formal requirements for identification of the goods subject to retention of title. However, careful attention should be paid to documentation in identifying such goods.

In terms of insolvency proceedings, perfection is important with respect to ownership retained under a retention of title clause. There is a lower court case in which a demand for the delivery of goods (the subject of retention of title) from a rehabilitation debtor was not allowed because of a lack of perfection (in this case, constructive transfer) as of the commencement of rehabilitation proceedings, where the subject matter was not segregated and was not able to be distinguished from other goods provided by other suppliers.

Luxembourg

Paulo Lopes Da Silva
Chan Park
MOLITOR

1. General remarks about retention of title

1.1 Transfer of ownership

Under Luxembourg law, transfer of title takes place when the parties reach agreement on the material elements of the contract, following the principle of consent, unless otherwise agreed by the parties.

This principle is expressly set out in Article 1583 of the Civil Code, according to which the ownership – over movable as well as immovable or immaterial property – is acquired as of right by the buyer as soon as the asset and the price are determined by the parties, even though the asset sold has not yet been delivered nor the price paid.

As an exception to this rule, certain types of contract will require more than an exchange of consent. For example, 'real' contracts are validly entered into between the parties only when there is an effective delivery of the asset (eg, loan, pledge, deposit). Formal contracts require certain formalities for their entry into force between the parties. For certain types of movable asset (ships, aeroplanes), the transfer of ownership requires the registration of the transfer with the relevant register to make it enforceable towards third parties. Similarly, sales of immovable property require a notarial deed in order to be effective against third parties.

Nonetheless, the transfer of ownership between the parties is, in principle, valid upon their mutual consent. As the transfer of ownership of movable assets is primarily based on the contractual freedom of the parties, the parties can freely agree on how and when the transfer of ownership takes place by using a retention of title clause.

1.2 Retention of title

Retention of title under Luxembourg law is essentially based on case law. According to a well-established body of jurisprudence, the immediacy of the transfer of ownership is not the essence of a sale. Consequently, a clause by which the seller retains the ownership of the asset sold until full payment of the purchase price by the buyer is perfectly valid.[1]

Other than through a retention of title clause contractually agreed by the parties, Luxembourg law does not specifically allow the seller to retain the legal ownership of an asset.

1 Diekirch, December 12 1936, Pas 14, p83.

According to Article 2102 4° of the Civil Code, the seller may however claim legal ownership over a movable asset within eight days of its delivery – except in the case where the parties agreed to a forward sale – provided that the asset claimed remains in its original state and has not been paid for by the buyer.

Although the right set out in Article 2102 4° of the Civil Code has been recognised as a rule of public policy,[2] the time limits granted to the seller by this article for enforcing his right to reclaim his goods is far too short, which makes this option largely theoretical. In addition, according to Article 546 of the Commercial Code, the seller loses his right under Article 2102 4° of the Civil Code if the buyer is subject to insolvency proceedings.

It is therefore in the best interests of the seller to organise the retention of title through a contractual retention of title clause which will reserve the ownership to the seller until full payment of the purchase price by the buyer. Such a clause is enforceable against a bankruptcy trustee in the event of the bankruptcy of the purchaser.[3]

In addition, Luxembourg law provides a right of retention which allows a seller who still has the possession of the asset sold not to deliver it if the purchaser does not pay the purchase price,[4] or if, after the sale, the seller went bankrupt and the seller would be in imminent danger of losing the purchase price.[5] A similar right of retention is also recognised in other provisions of the Civil Code[6] and other Luxembourg laws. Luxembourg case law has also largely recognised a right of retention and applies it to circumstances which are not specifically provided for by law.

1.3 Foreign and international law

Under Luxembourg private international law, a retention of title clause governed by a foreign law chosen by the parties is subject to the governing law chosen by the parties. This law will govern the validity, effects, and enforceability of the retention of title clause, including in particular the modalities surrounding the transfer of title. If the contract remains silent as to the applicable law, the law of the contract as determined by the Luxembourg rules of private international law should, in principle, govern all legal aspects of the retention of title clause.[7] However, there is a legal uncertainty in this respect and some authors opine that the law of the place where the asset claimed is located might also determine the legal regime applicable to a retention of title clause since rights over movables are concerned.[8]

Nevertheless, this only applies when the debtor is not subject to insolvency proceedings. If insolvency proceedings are opened in Luxembourg, Luxembourg courts will, in principle, have exclusive jurisdiction to settle any dispute related to these proceedings. Moreover, any effects arising from or related to the insolvency

---

2 Diekirch, December 12 1936, *op cit.*
3 Article 567-1 of the Commercial Code.
4 Article 1612 of the Civil Code.
5 Article 1613 of the Civil Code.
6 Article 1749, in favour of a tenant; Article 1948, in favour of a depositary; Articles 2082 and 2087, in favour of a pledgee.
7 *JurisClasseur – Droit International*, Fasc 569-05, "*Procédure Collective – Loi applicable*", 62.
8 *JurisClasseur – Droit International*, Fasc 552-70, "*Contrats Internationaux – Domaine de la loi du contrat*", 57.

proceedings will be assessed under Luxembourg law. The application of Luxembourg law to the insolvency proceedings must not, however, lead to having a retention of title clause produce effects if this clause does not meet the conditions of validity under the applicable foreign law. Therefore, the implementation and effects of a retention of title clause that a seller seeks to enforce in Luxembourg are subject to Luxembourg law,[9] while its validity has to be assessed in the light of the applicable foreign law,[10] unless it falls within the scope of the more seller-friendly provisions of EU Regulation 1346/2000 (which will be soon replaced by EU Regulation 2015/848 of May 20 2015).

1.4 Retention of title in insolvency

Assuming that insolvency proceedings in respect of the buyer are opened in Luxembourg, Luxembourg courts shall have jurisdiction to hear any claim in connection with such proceedings. As a general rule, any action or claim which is linked to insolvency proceedings pending in Luxembourg falls within the exclusive jurisdiction of the Luxembourg judges,[11] including claims based on a retention of title clause regarding ownership of a movable asset possessed by the insolvent purchaser.[12]

In the event of the bankruptcy of the buyer, the validity of a retention of title clause against the bankrupt estate in Luxembourg is determined either by Luxembourg law (if the retention of title clause is not subject to a foreign law) or by the applicable foreign law governing the claim. However, as already stated above, the effect and enforceability of a retention of title clause against the bankrupt estate must be reviewed under Luxembourg law. Therefore, provided that a retention of title clause governed by a foreign law is compliant with the provisions of Article 567-1 of the Commercial Code, it will be enforceable against the bankrupt estate.

However, under Article 7 of EU Regulation 1346/2000,[13] the provisions set out in Article 567-1 of the Commercial Code will be disregarded if, on the opening day of the insolvency proceedings, the asset sold has been moved from Luxembourg to another EU member state. Under the substantive rule set out in Article 7, the opening of insolvency proceedings against the purchaser of an asset does not affect the seller's right based on a reservation of title where, at the time of the opening of proceedings, the asset is situated within a member state other than the state where the proceedings have been opened. Therefore, the seller will be able to reclaim ownership over an asset located outside Luxembourg according to the general rules of the law governing the retention of title clause, irrespective of the domestic procedures established under Luxembourg law for ownership claims against an insolvent buyer.[14]

9 CA, March 27 1985, 8006.
10 TAL, January 13 1962, Pas 18, p506.
11 TAL, April 24 2003, 75505.
12 CA Douai, June 21 1990, JDI 1992, p187; note Huet, considering that such claims fall within the exception provided for in Article 1(2) 2° of the Brussels Convention on Jurisdiction and the Enforcement of Judgments in Civil and Commercial Matters 1968, an exception which has been since replicated in Article 1(2)(b) of Regulation 44/2001 and Regulation 1215/2012 of December 12 2012.
13 This is reproduced word for word in Article 10 of EU Regulation 2015/848.
14 Ie, Article 567-1 of the Commercial Code.

If the buyer is subject to insolvency proceedings outside Luxembourg, the private international law of the jurisdiction where the insolvency proceedings are opened will determine which law to apply.

However, in a recent case, Luxembourg courts expressly referred to EU case law[15] according to which an action brought by a seller in order to ensure the application of a retention of title clause constitutes an independent claim which is neither sufficiently direct nor sufficiently close to the opening of insolvency proceedings to exclude the application of EC Regulation 44/2001 of December 22 2000.[16] Although the District Court of Luxembourg did not address specifically the issue of retention of title, it nevertheless held that its jurisdiction should be determined according to the provisions of EC Regulation 44/2001 if the action brought is not based on provisions governing insolvency proceedings and could have been raised regardless of the opening of insolvency proceedings.[17] It follows that the national courts of the EU member state where insolvency proceedings were opened might not be considered anymore as having exclusive jurisdiction over retention of title claims raised against the insolvent debtor. However, without further case law, it is certainly too early to say whether this decision will become settled precedent in Luxembourg.

Under Luxembourg law, the validity of a retention of title clause is not affected when the seller is subject to insolvency proceedings. However, as a consequence of the opening of insolvency proceedings, the trustee in bankruptcy will be the sole person entitled to raise an ownership claim.[18]

Under EU Regulation 1346/2000, the opening of insolvency proceedings against the seller of an asset, after the delivery of the asset, shall not constitute grounds for rescinding or terminating the sale, and shall not prevent the purchaser from acquiring title where at the time of the opening of proceedings the asset sold is situated within a member state other than the state in which the insolvency proceedings have been opened. Accordingly, the insolvent seller will not be able to trigger a retention of title clause in order to prevent the buyer from acquiring ownership of the asset sold if the latter has complied with all its obligations under the sale contract (in particular when the price has been paid).

2. Retention of title

2.1 Validity and formal requirements

As regards the validity of a retention of title clause, Luxembourg law does not prescribe any particular form.

However, for evidence purposes and to benefit from Article 567-1 of the Commercial Code, the retention of title clause should be in writing. Other than that, there is no specific requirement as to the wording of the retention of title clause so

---

15 *German Graphics*, Case C-292/08, ECJ, September 10 2009.

16 TAL, January 29 2014, JTL 2014/1, 31, pp 28-32.

17 In this case, the action was based on a pledge contract subject to the Luxembourg Law on Financial Guarantee Contracts of August 5 2005, which explains why the jurisdiction of the Spanish courts in the insolvency proceedings was set aside by the Luxembourg judges.

18 Article 452 of the Commercial Code; TAL, February 13 2009, 117079.

long as its content clearly indicates that the ownership on the asset remains with the seller until the full payment of the purchase price.

There is no retention of title in place by operation of law, and any such right must be explicitly agreed between the parties. The retention of title can be agreed in the body of the sales agreement or included in the seller's general terms and conditions.[19] Luxembourg case law has also recognised the validity of such a clause when it appeared on the seller's invoice.[20]

The parties may agree on retention of title even if the asset is delivered to a third party, and such an arrangement will have no impact on its validity. Similarly, the seller is entitled to assert his ownership over movable property, whether it is held by the buyer or by a third party, provided that the latter has not acquired any ownership right under Article 2279 of the Civil Code which provides that ownership of movable assets results from the physical possession, in good faith, of such assets.[21]

Historically, Luxembourg courts refused to give effect to retention of title clauses when the buyer was placed under insolvency proceedings. It was argued that such clauses aimed at circumventing the provisions of Article 546 of the Commercial Code, which were specifically designed to deprive the seller from privileges and guarantees arising from his sales upon the opening of insolvency proceedings. It followed that the value of the assets that the seller had sold but for which it had not received payment was generally allocated to preferential creditors. As this situation was extremely detrimental to suppliers, the Luxembourg legislators enacted the Law on the Effects of Retention of Title Clauses in Sales Contracts of March 31 2000, which expressly confers on sellers the right to avail themselves of a retention of title clause in respect of insolvent buyers under the conditions set out in Article 567-1 of the Commercial Code.

Regarding the enforceability of the retention of title, if a seller wants to benefit from the regime of Article 567-1 of the Commercial Code in the event of the bankruptcy of the buyer, the retention of title must be in writing and have been concluded prior to the delivery of the asset. The retention of title may be agreed in writing in the sales agreement, set out in the seller's general terms and conditions or indicated in the seller's invoice.

In addition, for the purpose of Article 567-1 of the Commercial Code, the asset sold to the purchaser must be a non-fungible movable asset and must be still available as is (or be capable of being detached from any other asset in which it has been incorporated without damage) at the opening of the bankruptcy proceedings.

Upon fulfilment of these conditions, the seller can claim the asset sold and delivered to the buyer under retention of title within three months following the latest publication of the judgment declaring the bankruptcy (namely the publication in the Memorial B which occurs after the publication in the Commercial and Companies Register and local newspapers, between two to three months after the delivery of the judgment declaring bankruptcy). This does not preclude the seller

19 CA, February 25 2015, 37549.
20 CA, November 8 2007, Pas 34, p125.
21 Cass Fr Com, December 3 1996, 94-21227.

from commencing judicial proceedings for return of the asset after this deadline, provided that an ownership claim in respect of the asset at issue was lodged with the trustee in bankruptcy within the time limits set by Article 567-1 of the Commercial Code.[22]

2.2 Scope of retention of title

There is no rule in Luxembourg law expressly prohibiting the buyer from selling an asset covered by a retention of title clause to a third party. However, doing so would, in fact, deprive the seller from the very purpose of the retention of title clause: reserving the rights of ownership until the full purchase price of the asset sold has been paid. Hence, even if not expressly provided for by law, the principle of consent bars the buyer from reselling an asset falling within the scope of a retention of title clause as long as the purchase price has not been fully paid.

That being said, it is quite common in practice that buyers dispose of an asset before paying for it in full. In such cases, the seller may rely on specific protective provisions. Under the third paragraph of Article 567-1 of the Commercial Code, if a non-fungible asset is sold by the buyer before the opening of bankruptcy proceedings, the seller can claim the amount that the buyer did not pay at the date of the judgment declaring the bankruptcy. As this provision is modelled on the former Article L 621-124 of the French Commercial Code (Article 122 of the French Law of January 25 1985), French case law sheds an interesting light as to the scope of the right conferred to the seller by it. The French Supreme Court ruled that the resale of an asset subject to a retention of title clause shall, as of right, result in a transfer to the original seller of the remaining purchase price to be paid by the sub-purchaser to the initial buyer (up to an amount equivalent to the remaining purchase price agreed between the original seller and the initial buyer).[23] The application of this principle in Luxembourg is not in doubt as the legislators directly referred to Article 122 of the French Law of January 25 1985 prior to adopting the Law of March 31 2000.[24] In general, French case law is fully relevant under Luxembourg law as long as the legal basis underlying the decisions of the French courts does not differ substantially from the applicable rules of Luxembourg law.

(a) Combining/mixing/mingling goods delivered under retention of title

Under Article 567-1 of the Commercial Code, only non-fungible assets can be covered by a retention of title clause. Therefore, a retention of title clause will not produce any effect under Luxembourg law if it concerns fungible goods such as oil or other raw materials. Prevailing legal opinion in Luxembourg was generally reluctant to extend the effects of a retention of title clause to fungible assets when the Law of March 31 2000 was adopted. This is why the text of Article 567-1 does not encompass fungible goods within its scope.

As the position thus adopted is in contrast to French case law, which recognised

---

22 Cass, March 9 2006, BIJ 2006/4, p109; see to the contrary, CA, July 7 2004, 28128.
23 Cass Fr Com, June 16 2009, 08-10241.
24 Parliamentary Work 4470.

ownership claims over unidentifiable fungible assets,[25] there is little chance that an action based on a retention of title clause will achieve a positive outcome if it concerns a fungible asset, even outside the framework of insolvency proceedings (and therefore outside the scope of Article 567-1 of the Commercial Code). At best, although it is not very likely, Luxembourg courts might consider that retention of title rights could apply to fungible goods which are packaged and easily identifiable.

If non-fungible assets are stored with other identical goods, the seller is entitled to enforce his property rights deriving from a retention of title clause provided that the assets sold are identifiable and can be isolated from the other identical assets (by means of an inventory list, serial number, or other means). Otherwise, the seller's claim will fail, since a retention of title clause cannot produce its effects on assets which, albeit identical, belong to the buyer or to other creditors. This being a public policy principle, the parties cannot agree in their contract on a presumption of identity between the assets stored and the assets for which the purchase price has not been paid.[26]

Furthermore, non-fungible goods incorporated into immovable property or combined with other movable assets may be repossessed by the seller under the conditions set out by Article 567-1 of the Commercial Code. More specifically, it is necessary that the asset at issue can be removed without damaging the asset in which it has been incorporated or with which it has been combined.

(b) *Processing of goods delivered under retention of title*

Under Luxembourg law, an asset is deemed to have been processed when it has been transformed into a different product which, as a result, has gained more value.[27] In such a case, exercise of the retention of title clause will be frustrated, as the asset must be of the same nature when it is repossessed as it was when it was initially sold.

However, if the transformation made is minor and does not add significant value to the asset, it is generally agreed that the seller should be able to recover the asset protected by the retention of title clause.[28] If that is the case, the buyer must be indemnified for the difference between the original value of the asset and its increased value after having been processed, however slight it may be.

(c) *Extension of the retention of title*

In principle, retention of title clauses as defined by Luxembourg case law only constitute a means for a seller to preserve his ownership rights until full payment for the asset sold.

However, as the relationship between the seller and the buyer is governed by contractual freedom, the parties may agree on subjecting the transfer of property to additional requirements – such as payment of other debts to the seller which have fallen due but have not been paid – as long as such conditions do not violate imperative provisions of Luxembourg law.

Some uncertainty remains, however, as to the extension of retention of title

25 Parliamentary Work 4470.
26 Cass Fr Com, January 9 1990, D 1991, p130, note G Virassamy.
27 Parliamentary Work 4470.
28 Cass Fr Com, May 17 1988, RTD com 1989, p112, obs B Bouloc; Cass Fr Com, March 6 1990, Rev pr Coll 1991, p227, obs B Soinne.

clauses under Luxembourg law. French case law, which is a steady source of inspiration to Luxembourg courts, ruled that a retention of title clause constitutes a guarantee exclusively attached to the payment of the sale price and cannot be transferred in order to secure another debt.[29] This principle has since been codified in Article 2367 of the French Civil Code which expressly provides that a retention of title clause suspends the transfer of ownership of property under a sales contract until fulfilment of the corresponding obligation, which is payment of the purchase price. This definition certainly excludes any possibility of retention of title based on non-fulfilment of obligations other than the payment of the price for the asset sold.

Given that there is no such provision under Luxembourg law which generally restricts the scope of a retention of title clause (although Article 567-1 of the Commercial Code only refers to payment of the purchase price), Luxembourg courts might be more lenient as to an extension of the retention of title.

Even French courts have recognised the possibility of extending retention of title in certain circumstances. In this regard, it has been held that the seller is entitled to trigger a retention of title clause covering an asset sold within the framework of a procurement contract, even though it has been fully paid by the buyer, insofar as other goods delivered under the same contract remain unpaid.[30] This jurisprudence has opened the way to an extension of retention of title under French law and may in future influence Luxembourg judges towards a broad interpretation of the scope of retention of title clauses.

2.3 Legal effect of retention of title

(a) Effect towards third parties

Retention of title may be enforceable against third parties, depending on whether the third party has acted in good faith or not. If a subsequent buyer acting in good faith purchases an asset subject to retention of title, the retention of title clause will not be enforceable against him, and the seller will not be able to claim repossession of the asset from the subsequent buyer. This results from the protection conferred by Article 2279 of the Civil Code to purchasers acting in good faith, under which, as far as movable assets are concerned, possession gives title.[31] In such circumstances, the seller will only be able to recover the unpaid amount from the original purchaser, or claim the benefit of any remaining purchase price to be paid by the subsequent buyer to the original purchaser (a right of subrogation).

By contrast, if the subsequent purchaser was aware or could not ignore that he has not entered into contract with the real owner of the asset,[32] or knew or could not ignore that the original buyer was subject to insolvency proceedings,[33] the provisions of Article 2279 of the Civil Code will be disregarded.

---

29 CA Colmar, June 20 2001, Act Proc Coll 2002, comm 163.

30 Cass Fr Com, January 16 2007, 05-14452, considering that, in view of the specific nature of a procurement contract, the buyer had a "unique debt" which justified an extension of the retention of title.

31 Parliamentary Work 4470.

32 CA Paris, February 4 1999, Juris-Data 1999-020258.

33 Cass Fr Com, March 5 1996, JCP G 1996, I 3960, 12, obs M Cabrillac.

It should further be stated that third parties who pay for assets covered by a retention of title clause in place of the purchaser shall automatically benefit from a right of subrogation. In this respect, the retention of title clause, as an ancillary element of the debt transferred from the seller to the third party, will be directly actionable by the latter against the defaulting buyer.[34]

However, if a third party acquires physical possession of an asset by any means other than the payment of the buyer's debt, he will have to prove that the retention of title clause covering that asset has been transferred by subrogation.[35]

(b) *Effect in case of seizure of goods delivered under retention of title*

If the asset sold under retention of title and delivered to the buyer is seized by a creditor of the buyer, that creditor will have priority over the seller provided that he has acted in good faith and was unaware of the true owner of the seized asset. Any proceeds resulting from the sale of the seized asset will be paid to the buyer's creditor, unless an action for diversion is raised by the seller prior to the allocation of the proceeds to the buyer's creditor, in which case the seller will be entitled to the proceeds of the enforced sale.[36]

Similarly, a creditor of the seller may seek to seize an asset sold under a retention of title clause from the hands of the buyer, provided that the transfer of ownership has not become definitive, which supposes that the purchase price has not been fully paid or that additional mandatory formalities have not been accomplished.[37]

However, if an action based on the retention of title clause was introduced against the buyer prior to the final court judgment ordering a seizure measure, the seller will be entitled to regain ownership of the asset sold.[38]

Moreover, if a seller cannot in principle interfere with attachment measures ordered by an enforceable court title, it has nevertheless been held that bailiffs shall observe minimal standards of prudence when they carry out such measures. Accordingly, the buyer may seek indemnification from the bailiff if ownership of the seized assets was not verified and claims related to property were ignored prior to the attachment measures.[39]

In the event that the seller is declared insolvent, assets sold under a retention of title clause can no longer be seized, as Article 453 of the Commercial Code provides that the judgment declaring bankruptcy stops any pending actions for seizure of property and prohibits any further actions.

---

34 CA, November 8 2007, Pas 34, p125; Cass Fr Com, March 15 1988, JCP 11, 21348, quoted in Parliamentary Work 4470.

35 TAL, February 13 2009, 117079, holding that a third-party company having among its fleet of vehicles a stolen car could not refuse to return this vehicle to the defaulting purchaser, albeit the latter had not paid the full price of it, insofar as the third party remained unable to demonstrate that the retention of title clause attached to the stolen vehicle had been transferred by legal or contractual subrogation.

36 Cass Fr Civ 2nd, April 8 2004, Juris-Data 2004-023224.

37 CA Rennes, October 4 1989, Juris-Data 1989-048547, validating the seizure by the seller's creditor of a ship since the buyer had not fulfilled the registration formalities which would have made the transfer of ownership enforceable against third parties.

38 CA, October 18 2005, BIJ 2006/4, p122.

39 CA, June 9 1999, Pas 31, p155; in this case, the bailiff was considered liable for the sale of the buyer's asset by public auction.

(c) Effect in case of a security right established over goods delivered under retention of title

Retention of title will not be enforceable by the seller against a third party who has, in good faith, acquired a possessory security right over the asset from the buyer. In the same way as for third-party purchasers acting in good faith, such a security holder will benefit from a right of retention over the asset which is in his possession under Article 2279 of the Civil Code.[40]

This right of retention, however, does not apply to non-possessory security rights which, by their very nature, do not deprive the buyer of possession of the asset, and do not allow any third party to claim ownership on the grounds of Article 2279 of the Civil Code.

(d) Effect in case of insolvency

When the buyer is subject to insolvency proceedings, the trustee in bankruptcy will be the sole person entitled to contest a claim based on a retention of title clause. However, the opening of insolvency proceedings affecting the buyer does not confer on the trustee in bankruptcy specific powers or means of action regarding retention of title claims.

Under Article 567-1 of the Commercial Code, the retention of title will be enforceable against the buyer's bankruptcy trustee if the asset (a non-fungible movable asset) is still in the buyer's possession in its original state at the opening of the bankruptcy proceedings. In this case, as outlined above in greater detail, the seller can claim the return of the asset from the bankruptcy estate and the bankruptcy trustee within three months following the latest publication of the judgment declaring the bankruptcy.

(e) Effect in case of partial payment of the purchase price

If the retention of title provides a requirement for full payment before the transfer of ownership, and the buyer only pays in part, the transfer of ownership will not be deemed to have been completed and the seller will keep the legal ownership of the asset. If the sale is rescinded and the seller repossesses the asset, he must refund the buyer the part of the purchase price paid, without prejudice to any claim for damages.

3. Enforcement of retention of title

Assuming that a defaulting buyer is not subject to insolvency proceedings, the seller has to raise an ownership claim before the Luxembourg courts in order to obtain recognition of his ownership over the asset in respect of which payment has not been made. As with any other judicial action, the seller is first required to summon the buyer to appear before the competent court.

However, such an ownership claim could be jeopardised and deprived of any effect if the buyer has the opportunity to dispose of the asset at issue prior to the completion of the proceedings.

---

40 Cass Fr Com, November 28 1989, Defrénois 1990, p814, obs L Aynès.

Accordingly, the first step of any action aimed at repossessing movable property should be a seizure claim, in order to safeguard the seller's assets with a protective and provisional measure.

Under Article 963 of the new Code of Civil Procedure, the president of a district court may, upon request, grant an order authorising a seizure claim. Naturally, the seller cannot force entry into the buyer's premises and recover the asset sought, whether by his own means or with the help of a bailiff acting beyond his powers. Such actions are strictly prohibited and will entail damages to the buyer. Accordingly, a clause under which the purchaser will grant the seller access to his premises to repossess the goods in the event of default on payment is not sufficient to grant effective access for the seller. In fact, a court order will be required should the buyer deny access to the premises where the asset is stored.

Once completed, seizure allows the seller to retain the seized asset until the outcome of the ownership claim.[41]

The measures outlined above can be ordered whether the unpaid goods are in the hands of the buyer or have been transferred to a third party.

Finally, in view of the provisional nature of a seizure claim, judicial confirmation of the seizure is required,[42] either before the courts of the place where the buyer is domiciled or, if the asset is held by a third party, before the courts of the place where the asset is located.[43]

If the ownership claim has been introduced prior to the latest publication of a judgment declaring the insolvency of the buyer, the action will be suspended until the trustee in bankruptcy is called into the pending proceedings.[44]

Where the ownership claim is raised after the opening of insolvency proceedings, the seller must follow a specific procedure as provided in Articles 567-1 and 572 of the Commercial Code.

Under Article 567-1 of the Commercial Code, the seller must claim the asset covered by the retention of title clause within three months following the latest publication of the judgment declaring the bankruptcy.

However, as stated above, the seller should not be precluded from introducing a judicial action following expiry of that three-month deadline provided that he has made a claim for ownership to the trustee in bankruptcy within three months of the latest publication of the judgment declaring the insolvency.[45]

According to Article 572 of the Commercial Code, the trustee in bankruptcy may accept an ownership claim subject to approval by the supervising judge. It is only when the trustee in bankruptcy and the seller do not reach an amicable solution that the seller will need to start judicial action before the district courts sitting in commercial matters.[46]

Furthermore, by analogy with French case law, a seizure claim can be considered

---

41 TAL, April 30 1986, 71/86.
42 Article 968 of the new Code of Civil Procedure.
43 Cass, April 4 1821, Sirey, 1821, p330.
44 Cass Fr Com, July 9 1996, JCP E 1996, pan 1053, I, 5, obs M Cabrillac.
45 Cass, March 9 2006, BIJ 2006/4, p109, op cit.
46 Article 635 of the new Code of Civil Procedure; TAL, January 13 1962, Pas 18, p507.

as an ownership claim within the meaning of Article 567-1 of the Commercial Code insofar as it does not constitute an enforcement measure.[47] As a result, the prohibition on enforcement measures against persons subject to insolvency proceedings, as provided in Article 452 of the Commercial Code, may not be relevant as far as a seizure claim is concerned.

Therefore, the seller should be able to secure the asset subject to retention of title from any disposal by the trustee in bankruptcy.

47 Cass Fr Com, March 24 2004, Juris-Data 2004-023181; see to the contrary: Cass Fr Civ 2nd, February 18 1999, Juris-Data 1999-000839.

Netherlands

Marcel Willems
Kennedy Van der Laan NV

1. General remarks about retention of title

1.1 Transfer of ownership

According to Paragraph 1 of Article 80 of Book 3 of the Dutch Civil Code,[1] a person may acquire property under universal title or under particular title.[2] Property is acquired under universal title, among other ways, through inheritance by succession, through marriage in a community of property, through a merger of two or more legal persons, or through a split up of a legal person.[3] A person acquires property under particular title through a transfer, a prescription, an expropriation, or through any other way provided by law in order to acquire specific types of property rights.[4]

Ownership rights (as well as limited property rights and debt-claims) are transferable, unless their nature or the law prevents this.[5] The transfer of property requires a formal delivery, pursuant to a valid legal basis, by the person with power of disposition over that property.[6] For the transfer of immovable property formal delivery is performed by drawing up a notarial deed of transfer for this purpose between the parties, followed by its registration in the public registers for immovable property.[7] For the transfer of non-registered movable things[8] that at that moment are in the possession of the seller, formal delivery is performed by transferring the possession of that thing to the purchaser.[9] It is not necessary, however, that the seller be in possession of the property; transfer can also be effected by means of a bilateral declaration, without any physical action, such as where the purchaser is already holding the property for the seller prior to the sale.[10]

Where there is a transfer of ownership rights by way of a formal delivery by the person who has the power to dispose of the property concerned, that person is usually the owner of the property. A sale and purchase agreement is a valid legal basis for the delivery, but does not in itself mean that the purchaser becomes the owner of the property the moment the agreement is concluded. The essential parts of such an

1 In short: Article 3:80(1) of the Civil Code.
2 The English translations of Dutch statutory law are taken from www.dutchcivillaw.com/legislation.
3 Article 3:80(2) of the Civil Code.
4 Article 3:80(3) of the Civil Code.
5 Article 3:83(1) of the Civil Code.
6 Article 3:84(1) of the Civil Code.
7 Article 3:89(1) of the Civil Code.
8 Registered movable things are registered aircraft and ships.
9 Article 3:90(1) of the Civil Code.
10 Article 3:115 of the Civil Code.

agreement are merely that it obligates the seller to deliver the property to the purchaser, and the purchaser to accept delivery and to pay the agreed purchase price to the seller.

The basic rule is that the purchaser becomes the owner of the property upon delivery of the property to him, but this rule is not mandatory; contract law is to a large degree discretionary. The parties may agree, for instance, that the purchase price be paid later or to someone else than the seller; that delivery will not be made to the purchaser but to someone else; or that the risk passes to the purchaser upon conclusion of the agreement instead of upon delivery. Also the parties may agree that the seller retains ownership of the property until the purchase price has been paid in full. It may be concluded, therefore, that parties have great discretionary power to form their contractual relationship the way they deem fit. However, as will be set out in more detail below, there are limits to their freedom as regards the retention of title.

A legal act performed with the intention of transferring property merely to provide security for a debt, or performed without the intention of making the property part of the acquirer's estate, is not a valid legal basis for a transfer of that property.[11] Retention of title is not considered as such a 'security transfer', mainly because for the seller under retention of title not only is security relevant, but also the retention of the ownership itself.

1.2 Retention of title

Retention of title is governed by Article 3:92 of the Civil Code, which reads:

1. *Where an agreement has the intention, in regard of a non-registered movable thing which the alienator has brought in the actual power of another person, that the alienator withholds the right of ownership in that thing until a performance, indebted by that other person, is performed, this agreement is considered to be entered into under a condition precedent of full satisfaction of that indebted performance.*
2. *The alienator can only validly stipulate such a retention of title for things he has to deliver if this is done in relation to the payment of debt-claims on a counter performance due by the acquiring party for things that have been delivered or will be delivered to him by the alienator pursuant to the same or another agreement or for services performed or to be performed for his benefit by the alienator pursuant to such an agreement as well as with respect to compensatory debt-claims indebted by him to the alienator for failing to perform such agreements. As far as a condition in an agreement is null and void because it is not in conformity with the previous sentence, it has never been stipulated according to law.*
3. *A condition precedent, as mentioned in paragraph 1, is regarded to be fulfilled also when the debt-claim of the alienator to obtain the agreed counter performance is settled in another way than through an actual acquisition of this specific counter performance or when the acquiring party is released from his obligation to this end on account of Article 6:60*[12] *or when the right of action of the alienator to claim the*

---

11 Article 3:84(3) of the Civil Code.

12 Article 6:60 of the Civil Code concerns creditor's default and states: "When the creditor is in default, the court may, upon the request of the debtor, discharge the debtor from his obligation, where appropriate, under supplementary conditions to be set by court."

counter performance has become prescribed on account of the expiry of a time-limitation. Unless parties have agreed otherwise, the same applies when the alienator has waived his right to claim the agreed counter performance.[13]

From Paragraph 1 of Article 3:92 it is clear that the parties may agree that the seller remains owner of the property until the purchaser has performed an obligation, usually making the payment of the purchase price. The prevailing opinion is that retention of title constitutes for the seller ownership under the dissolving condition of fulfilment of certain obligations, and for the purchaser ownership under the suspending condition of fulfilment of certain obligations. However, whether this opinion is correct remains to be seen. Only recently, the Court of Appeal in Den Haag[14] expressed the following opinion:

In Article 5:1 [of the Civil Code] the law describes ownership as the most comprehensive right that a person can have to a thing and, because only one right can be the most comprehensive, the court is of the opinion that it follows therefrom that in the view of the legislator only one right of ownership can exist in respect of a thing. Such ownership right can be divided among a number of joint owners, but, in such an event, as parties who, in principle, are equally entitled to the same right of ownership. Also, the right may be incomplete due to limitations imposed upon the owner as regards the way in which he may make use of his right of ownership, or due to the existence of limited rights to the thing, but a division as advocated by the bank [the claimant], is not foreseen by the law.

According to the court, therefore, the notion of the purchaser being owner under a suspending condition is incorrect. The Supreme Court has not yet rendered judgment in this particular case, but is expected to do so shortly. Until then, we hold on to the prevailing opinion as described above.

It should be noted that the parties could also opt for a different construct: a sale under the dissolving condition of default by the purchaser. In that case, should the purchaser default, the ownership returns to the seller as of law. This form of retention of title is also subject to the restrictions mentioned in Article 3:92(2) of the Civil Code.

Article 3:92(2) provides that the retention of title must be limited to claims that are sufficiently connected to the delivery of assets.[15] These are:

- payment for things that have been delivered or will be delivered by the seller under the same or another agreement;[16]
- payment for services performed or to be performed by the seller under such an agreement; and
- payment of compensation by the purchaser for failing to perform such agreements.

13 It should be noted that the causes mentioned in Paragraph 3 are not exhaustive. The seller may, for instance, waive the retention of title, as a result of which the purchaser becomes unconditional owner despite the fact that he has not yet paid the purchase price; see HR November 28 2014, ECLI:NL:HR:2014:3460 (*Snippers/Rabobank*).

14 Hof Den Haag, ECLI:NL:GHDHA:2014:4352, JOR 2015/53 m nt WJM van Andel en ME Brinke.

15 FMJ. Verstijlen, *Groene Serie Vermogensrecht*, comment 12.1 to Article 3:92.

16 Mostly that will be the purchase price, which is the reason why a seller and purchaser are commonly mentioned, but this is not necessary. A retention of title can, for instance, also be agreed upon as regards a barter agreement. In that case, the counter-performance is the other party's obligation to deliver the barter property. In this chapter reference is made only to 'seller' and 'purchaser'.

The words "the same or another agreement" in Article 3:92(2) mean that the property delivered or to be delivered does not have to be delivered on the basis of one and the same agreement. The agreements do not even have to relate to similar goods, as long as the claims they are meant to secure concern the supply of goods or the performance of services in relation to such goods. Think of the supplier of computer equipment who stipulates a separate reimbursement for installing the computer; the retention of title concerning the equipment then also covers this reimbursement.[17] A claim of a totally different nature, such as a claim regarding a bank loan, may therefore not be subject of a retention of title.[18]

The claim for compensation for damages[19] includes interest (whether statutory or contractual)[20] and costs, alternative damages (damages instead of the original performance)[21] and compensation for damages following a rescission.[22]

It is uncertain whether a so-called 'credit retention of title' is valid. Such a retention of title would not terminate as soon as the seller no longer has any claim mentioned in Article 3:92(2) against the purchaser but would serve as a security for the seller as regards any valid claim he might have against the purchaser upon termination of their legal relationship. Possibly such a credit retention of title may be valid, but only in the event that it can reasonably be expected that new claims from the seller against the purchaser will arise due to their lasting relationship.[23]

Although Article 3:92 of the Civil Code expressly mentions movable property, retention of title regarding immovable property is possible as well. This chapter, however, is limited to movable property as the most common subject of retention of title.

(a) Hire-purchase contract

A contract of sale on instalments is a species of the retention of title. The contract of sale on instalments is a sales contract under which parties have agreed that the purchase price is to be paid in instalments two or more of which become due and payable only after the thing being sold is delivered to the purchaser.[24] Any contract to this effect, whatever its form or the name under which it is entered into, is deemed to be a contract of sale on instalments.[25] A contract of sale on instalments cannot relate to immovable property, registered ships or registered aircraft.[26]

A hire-purchase contract is a contract of sale on instalments under which parties have agreed that the right of ownership over the thing being sold shall not pass upon delivery, but only after the fulfilment of the condition precedent that the purchaser has fully paid up what is due on the basis of the contract.[27] It is clear from this that

---

17 FMJ Verstijlen, *Groene Serie Vermogensrecht*, comment 15 to Article 3:92.
18 *PG Boek* 3 (Inv 3, 5 and 6), p1240.
19 Article 6:74 of the Civil Code.
20 Article 6:119 of the Civil Code.
21 Article 6:87 of the Civil Code.
22 Article 6:277 of the Civil Code.
23 AIM van Mierlo in his note under HR December 4 1998, NJ 1999/549 (*Potharst/Serrée*), AA 1999, p288-296.
24 Article 7A:1576(1) of the Civil Code.
25 Article 7A:1576(3) of the Civil Code.
26 Article 7A:1576(4) of the Civil Code.
27 Article 7A:1576h(1) of the Civil Code.

hire-purchase contracts bear a strong resemblance to retention of title. For that reason, in the following discussion the relevant rules applying to hire-purchase contracts will be set out as well when and where they differ from the rules governing retention of title.

(b) *Consumer credit transactions*

Consumer credit transactions fall a little outside the scope of this chapter because of their limited applicability. For that reason they are mentioned only very briefly here.

The Consumer Credit Act and Book 7 of the Civil Code[28] contain specific rules for credit transactions with consumers. These statutory rules form the transposition of the EU Consumer Credit Directive.[29] A credit transaction within the meaning of this act, insofar as relevant here, is any agreement or group of agreements with the intention that the credit supplier provides the borrower (the recipient of the credit) with the enjoyment of a certain good or service and the borrower makes one or more payments to the credit supplier. The Consumer Credit Act is not applicable to credit transactions amounting to more than €40,000.[30] The return of an asset title to which has been retained may be demanded only in certain events mentioned in the act, such as when the borrower has failed to make a payment for more than two months and is in default, or when he has been declared bankrupt.[31] Return of the asset may no longer be demanded when more than 75% of the credit amount has been paid.[32] Return of the asset in conformity with Article 41 of the Consumer Credit Act leads to automatic rescission of the agreement. However, if the borrower, within 14 days after returning the asset to the credit supplier, pays the instalments which are due and payable at that moment plus the agreed upon compensation for his default, then the borrower regains the asset and the rescission is reversed.[33]

1.3 Foreign and international law

The question of which law applies to contractual obligations is governed by the Rome I Regulation.[34] A contract shall be governed by the law chosen by the parties. The choice shall be made expressly or clearly demonstrated by the terms of the contract or the circumstances of the case. By their choice the parties can select the law applicable to the whole or to part only of the contract.[35] The fact that the choice of law must have been made explicitly, or must be otherwise sufficiently clear, implies that the choice of law will in practice be made in writing, although strictly speaking this is not required.

The contractual law aspects (such as whether the retention of title has been validly agreed upon) are governed by the law that is applicable to the purchase

28 Article 7:57 onwards of the Civil Code.
29 Directive 2008/48/EC of the European Parliament and of the Council of April 23 2008 on credit agreements for consumers and repealing Council Directive 87/102/EEC.
30 Article 3 of the Consumer Credit Act.
31 Article 41(1) in conjunction with Article 33 of the Consumer Credit Act.
32 Article 41(2) of the Consumer Credit Act.
33 Article 42(1) and (2) of the Consumer Credit Act.
34 Regulation (EC) 593/2008 of the European Parliament and of the Council of June 17 2008 on the law applicable to contractual obligations (Rome I).
35 Article 3(1) of the Rome I Regulation.

agreement. To the extent that the law applicable to the contract has not been chosen, a contract for the sale of goods shall be governed by the law of the country where the seller has his habitual residence.[36] With regard to the property law aspects (such as the effect of the retention of title against third parties, ownership and enforcing or invoking the retention of title) there are two options:

- In principle, the property law aspects are governed by the law of the state of the territory where the goods are located[37] or, with regard to the real effects of retention of title, by the law of the state of the territory where the goods find themselves at the moment of their legal delivery to the purchaser;[38]
- If it concerns goods that are intended for export, the parties are allowed to let the property law aspects of the retention of title be governed by the law of the state of destination of the goods to be exported,[39] provided that according to that law the seller's right of ownership shall not be lost until the price has been paid fully to him.

Additionally, designating the law of the state of destination shall have effect only if the goods are actually imported into the designated state of destination. Choice of the law of the importing state is an exception to the main rule on applicability of the law of territory where the goods are located, and gives the parties the possibility to avoid 'mobile conflicts': where, by moving an asset (across the border), the location of the asset changes and as a result the applicable law changes as well. The parties can rule out any such change of law.

1.4 Retention of title in insolvency

In the event of an insolvency with cross-border consequences, the European Insolvency Regulation[40] applies. In the event that the purchaser is subject to insolvency proceedings in the Netherlands, the retention of title will, in principle, be governed by the law that applies to the insolvency proceedings, under Article 4 of the regulation. As regards assets delivered under retention of title, however, Article 7 of the regulation contains a special rule for the event that the assets are not located in the same Member State as the state where the insolvency proceedings are opened.

According to this Article 7, presuming that the retention of title is valid:[41]

- The opening of insolvency proceedings against the purchaser of an asset shall not affect the seller's rights based on a reservation of title where at the time of the opening of proceedings the asset is situated within the territory of a Member State other than the state of opening of proceedings;
- The opening of insolvency proceedings against the seller of an asset, after delivery of the asset, shall not constitute grounds for rescinding or terminating the sale and shall not prevent the purchaser from acquiring title,

---

36 Article 4(1) of the Rome I Regulation.
37 Article 10:127(1) of the Civil Code.
38 Article 10:128(1) of the Civil Code.
39 Article 10:128(2) of the Civil Code.
40 Council Regulation (EC) 1346/2000 of 29 May 2000 on insolvency proceedings.
41 Whether that is the case must be established according to the law that is applicable to the retention of title; in the Netherlands Article 128 of the Civil Code.

where at the time of the opening of proceedings the asset sold is situated within the territory of a Member State other than the state of the opening of proceedings; and

- The rules mentioned in the previous two paragraphs shall not preclude actions for voidness, voidability or unenforceability as referred to in Article 4(2)(m) of the regulation.

The purpose of the second of these provisions is to protect the purchaser in the event that the law of the state of the opening of proceedings were to consider the asset as forming part of the estate of the debtor and to oblige the purchaser to return it or to allow the contract to be rescinded.[42]

In the event that the asset sold under retention of title is located in a jurisdiction that is not a Member State, the rules of foreign and international law outlined above would apply. If the retention of title is valid according to the applicable foreign law, this would be recognised under Dutch law as well. If, for example, goods were sold in Germany under a valid (German) retention of title and subsequently moved to the Netherlands, the scope of the retention of title, which may be wider than allowed under Netherlands law, will most likely[43] be accepted. If, therefore, the retention of title is securing not only the purchase price but also a loan from the seller to the purchaser, transfer of ownership will not be effected until both the purchase price and the loan are paid.[44] The question of whether a seller under retention of title remains owner in the event of the goods becoming affixed to other property, being intermixed with other property or processed so as to create new things (see under heading 2.2 below) is to be answered by the law of the state where the goods are located at the time when the fixture, intermixture or creation occurs.[45]

2. Retention of title

2.1 Validity and formal requirements

Article 3:92(1) of the Civil Code speaks of an agreement having the intention that the alienator (the seller) withholds the right of ownership in the property until a performance, owed by the other party (the purchaser), is performed. An agreement, under Dutch law, generally does not have to be in writing; an oral agreement is legally as valid as a written one. Obviously, however, proof of the agreement and what exactly the parties have agreed upon is much easier delivered when it is in writing.

That it is important (under Dutch law) to be able to establish what the parties agreed upon follows from the so-called Haviltex-criterion, which plays a pivotal role

42 M Virgós and F Garciamartín, *The European Insolvency Regulation*, 2004, 171.

43 M Virgós and F Garciamartín, *The European Insolvency Regulation*, 2004, 172, remarks that "The majority of commentators deduce from the tenor of Article 7 that it only applies to simple reservations of title, not to more complex figures such as 'prolonged' or 'extended' reservation of title."

44 XE Kramer and HLE Verhagen, *Asser 10-III Internationaal Privaatrecht: Internationaal Vermogensrecht*, 2015/526.

45 Article 10:127(5) of the Civil Code; Kramer and Verhagen, *Asser 10-III Internationaal Privaatrecht: Internationaal Vermogensrecht*, 2015/528.

in Dutch contract law. This criterion is named after a judgment of the Dutch Supreme Court bearing the same name,[46] in which the court held that, when interpreting a contract, one should not only pay attention to the literal wording of it but also to what the parties meant to agree upon and what they could reasonably have expected from one another.

Not only does the retention of title not necessarily have to be in writing in order to be valid, but also there are no other formal requirements to be observed. Registration of the retention of title is not required. As a matter of fact, in the Netherlands there is no public register in which the retention of title could be registered, even if one would wish to do so.

From the fact that the retention of title does not need to be in writing it follows automatically that there are also no formal requirements as regards the wording of a retention of title clause. It is, for example, permissible simply to stipulate in the agreement that "the goods remain the property of the seller unless and until paid for in full". Moreover, the retention of title clause may be incorporated in general terms and conditions.[47] In that case it is essential that the seller makes sure that these apply. Article 6:233 of the Civil Code states that a stipulation from the general terms and conditions is voidable if the seller has not given his counterparty a reasonable opportunity to take cognisance of their content. The rules regarding validly agreeing to the applicability of standard terms and conditions must be carefully observed, because non-applicability of the terms and conditions will imply also that any retention of title contained therein will not be applicable. These rules will be determined by the law that governs the contractual relationship between the parties.

For the validity of the retention of title it is irrelevant whether the goods are delivered directly to the purchaser; they may be delivered to a third party (such as a warehouse belonging to someone other than the purchaser) if the parties have so agreed or the seller has been so instructed by the purchaser. Also they may be delivered directly by the seller's supplier to the purchaser.[48]

(a) *Hire-purchase contracts*

A hire-purchase contract is entered into by authenticated (notarial) or private deed.[49] It must mention the entire purchase price, a scheme for regular payment and the stipulations with respect to the retention of title and the transfer of ownership. In the absence of a deed which meets all these requirements, the contract is deemed not to be a hire-purchase contract but a contract of sale on instalments without the stipulation that the right of ownership of the thing being sold shall not pass merely by delivery.[50]

(b) *Seller's right of reclamation*

As follows from the above, retention of title must be agreed upon by the parties and does not exist by operation of law. However, there exists a somewhat comparable

46 HR March 13 1981, NJ 1981, 635.
47 According to Van der Weide, T&C BW, comment 1 to Article 10:128, this is almost standard.
48 HR December 4 1998, NJ 1999/549 (*Potharst/Serrée*).
49 Article 7A: 1576i of the Civil Code.
50 Article 7A:1576j of the Civil Code.

right by operation of law, which is called the right of reclamation.[51] It is outside the scope of this chapter to explain this right in detail. Therefore, let the basics suffice.

The seller who has transferred a movable thing, not being registered property, to the purchaser, may reclaim it as his own property by means of a written declaration addressed to the purchaser for this purpose, if the purchaser has failed to pay the purchase price and the requirements for a rescission as referred to in Article 6:265 of the Civil Code[52] are met. Through this declaration the sale agreement is rescinded and the right of ownership of the purchaser and possible real property rights of third parties derived from it are lost. The right of reclamation may, however, be exercised only to the extent that what has been transferred to the purchaser is still in the same condition as it was when it was supplied to him. In addition, it is assumed that the law of the place where the asset is located determines whether or not the right of reclamation may be exercised.[53]

Where only the price of a certain part of what has been transferred to the purchaser has not been paid, the seller may only reclaim this part as his own property. If, with respect to the whole contract, just a part of the price has not been paid, then the seller may reclaim a proportional part of what has been transferred to the purchaser as his own property. In both cases the sale agreement is only rescinded for the reclaimed part of what has been transferred to the purchaser. In all other cases of a partial payment of the purchase price, the seller may only reclaim as his own property all that has been transferred to the purchaser if he reimburses what has already been paid to him.

The seller may no longer exercise his right of reclamation, under Article 7:39 of the Civil Code, when both:

- six weeks have passed since payment of the purchase price has become due and enforceable; and
- 60 days have passed since the day that the thing was stored by the purchaser or by someone who has been appointed by him for this purpose.

In this regard the right of reclamation is much more limited than retention of title.

In addition, unless the asset concerned remains in the hands of the purchaser, the seller loses his right of reclamation when the purchaser transfers the asset for consideration to a third party who could not reasonably have expected that such a right of reclamation would be exercised. The same applies where the asset, after it has been transferred to the purchaser, has been encumbered for consideration with a usufruct or a pledge.[54]

---

51 Article 7:39 onwards of the Civil Code.

52 This article reads:
1. *Every failure of a party in the performance of one of his obligations, gives the opposite party the right to rescind the mutual agreement in full or in part, unless the failure, given its specific nature or minor importance, does not justify this rescission and its legal effects.*
2. *As far as performance is not permanently or temporarily impossible, the right to rescind the mutual agreement only arises when the debtor is in default.*

53 Kramer and Verhagen, *Asser 10-III Internationaal Privaatrecht: Internationaal Vermogensrecht*, 2015/534.

54 Article 7:42 of the Civil Code.

2.2 Scope of retention of title

(a) Sale of goods delivered under retention of title

The seller of goods under retention of title is the owner of those goods under the dissolving condition that the purchaser fulfils his obligations under the agreement; the purchaser holds the goods for the seller.[55]

Being the owner, the seller is entitled to dispose of this conditional ownership, for instance by transferring it to a third party.[56] Obviously, in such a case the third party obtains an ownership that is subject to the same condition. The third party will mostly not be able to claim that he obtained unconditional ownership due to the fact that he acted in good faith (see below), because the goods will be in the possession of the purchaser and not of the seller.

It is quite common that the seller grants the purchaser the right to sell the goods in the ordinary course of his business; thus the scope of the condition under which the goods are sold to the purchaser is in fact limited. This is also in the seller's own interest: it enables the purchaser to obtain the purchase price (plus profit) and thus to pay the seller. In such an event, the third-party purchaser becomes the owner of the goods. The sole fact that the goods are intended to be used in the ordinary course of the purchaser's business does not imply that the purchaser is entitled to transfer them.[57] Even if the purchaser has not been granted such a right and merely holds the goods for the seller, however, that does not mean that he cannot dispose of his property law position as conditional owner, for instance by transferring the conditional ownership[58] to a third party. It is not necessary that the purchaser does so in the ordinary course of business (although that may be relevant when determining whether the third party acts in good faith), or that the parties expressly agree that the purchaser is entitled to do so. In this case, however, should the purchaser not pay the purchase price to the seller, the condition is not fulfilled and the purchaser does not become the owner. As a consequence, the seller could invoke the retention of title and claim his property from the third party who has obtained conditional ownership from the purchaser.

It should be noted, however, that despite the fact that the purchaser lacks the power of disposition before having paid the purchase price, a third party might be inclined to think that the purchaser is the owner because he is in possession of the property. In the event that the purchaser transfers the property despite lacking the power of disposition Article 3:86 of the Civil Code comes into play, which provides that a transfer of a movable thing by an alienator without power of disposition is nevertheless valid if the transfer was not performed gratuitously and the acquiring party acted in good faith.[59]

---

55 HR June 1973, NJ 1974/346 (*Nationaal Grondbezit/Kamphuis*).

56 HR April 28 1989, NJ 1990/252 (*Puinbreekinstallatie*).

57 HR December 14 1992, NJ 1993, 623 (*Hinck/Van der Werff & Visser*).

58 Coming from the Roman law adage of *nemo plus iuris ad alium transferre potest quam ipse habet*: (no one can transfer a greater right than he himself has).

59 Article 3:86 of the Civil Code also applies in the situation where the seller sells the property to a third party, but due to the fact that the seller has already delivered the property to the purchaser, he will not be able to deliver it to the third party as well.

'Good faith' is defined in Article 3:11 of the Civil Code:

A person has not acted in 'good faith' as a condition for a certain legal effect if he knew or in the circumstances reasonably ought to have known the facts or rights from which his good faith depends. The impossibility to conduct an inquiry does not prevent that a person, who had good reason to doubt, is to be regarded as someone who ought to have known the relevant facts or rights.

There is no hard and fast rule to determine when exactly the third party does not act in good faith, that is to say whether he has investigated with enough care whether the other party has the power of disposition. This depends on the circumstances in the specific case, in which the profession and the experience of the third party may play an important role. In a case concerning a pledge, where a bank (being a professional party who should have known that in the type of business concerned the use of general terms and conditions is customary) should reasonably have foreseen that a retention of title could have been agreed and demanded the handing over of the pledged property from the pledger because of his bad financial situation, the bank was considered not to have acted in good faith. These circumstances (especially the financial position of the pledger) should have given the bank reason to assume that the purchase agreement may not have been executed in a straightforward manner.[60]

Under Dutch law, even when the seller allows the purchaser to transfer the property subject to retention of title to a third party before the purchaser has paid the purchase price, it is not allowed to agree that the purchase price which the third party will have to pay to the purchaser is to be assigned to the seller. This would be considered a security transfer within the meaning of Article 3:84(3) of the Civil Code.[61] Instead, in order to give the seller some sort of security, the seller and the purchaser could agree that the purchaser grants the seller a right of pledge over the purchaser's claim against the third-party purchaser.

Hire-purchase contracts: In respect of a thing that has been delivered under a hire-purchase contract, Article 7A:1576m of the Civil Code expressly states that the purchaser may use it, even before he acquires the right of ownership thereof, in accordance with its intended purpose, but may not change its shape or arrangement, and is also not allowed to lease it out or to grant someone else the possibility to enjoy or use it. The seller and the purchaser are, however, allowed to derogate from these provisions by agreement.

Furthermore, according to Article 7A:1576l of the Civil Code, a transfer by the seller of the thing after it has been delivered under the hire-purchase contract shall have no effect to the detriment of the purchaser. Because the purchaser has the thing under his control, a third party cannot assume that the seller was still entitled legally to dispose of it, so he will not be deemed to have been acting in good faith.

60 Hof Den Bosch August 11 2015, ECLI:NL:GHSHE:2015:3184. See also HR January 6 1961, NJ 1962, 19 (*Seneca/Forum Bank*) and HR June 29 1979, NJ 1980, 133 (*Hoogovens/Matex*).

61 See under heading 1.1 above.

(b) *Combining/mixing/mingling goods delivered under retention of title*

As regards combining, commingling and processing of movable property, Articles 5:14 onwards of the Civil Code contain the following rules.

Article 5:14 Accession to property

1. *If a movable thing becomes a component of another movable thing, which has to be regarded as the principal thing, then the ownership of the movable thing passes over to the owner of the principal thing.*
2. *If none of the movable things can be pointed out as the principal thing and they belong to different owners, then these owners will become co-owners of the new thing, each of them for a share proportionally to the value of the movable thing he owned before.*
3. *The principal thing is the thing of which the value exceeds the value of the other thing considerably, or the thing that is regarded by generally accepted views (common opinion) as the principal thing.*

Article 5:15 Intermixture (intermingling) of movable property

When movable things which belong to different owners are intermixed (intermingled) in such a way that they have become one single thing, the previous Article shall apply accordingly.

Article 5:16 Creation of a new thing

1. *If someone creates a new thing out of one or more different movable things, then this newly formed thing is owned by the owner of the original things. Where these things belonged to different owners, the previous two Articles shall apply accordingly.*
2. *If someone creates a new thing for himself or if he lets another person make a new thing for him, and the new thing is created entirely or partially from one or more movable things that did not belong to him, then he becomes the owner of the new formed thing, unless this is not justified because of the modest costs involved in the creation of the new thing.*
3. *The previous paragraphs apply accordingly to the processing of different substances into a newly created substance and to the cultivation of plants (vegetation).*

Retention of title therefore lapses when the thing concerned loses its independence through one of the circumstances outlined in the articles set out above.

When two things are combined, the question is whether one of those things becomes a component of the other. Article 3:4 of the Civil Code provides that:

- everything that, according to generally accepted views, forms a part of a thing, is a component of that thing; and
- a thing that is attached to another principal thing in such a way that it cannot be separated from it without causing meaningful damage to one of the things, becomes a component of the principal thing.

Because the fact that a thing is considered to have become a component of another thing is detrimental to the owner (who loses ownership), it should not be accepted too readily that there is a general accepted view.

If, because of the difference of value, one of the things that are combined is to be considered as the principal thing, the owner of the principal thing also becomes the owner of the thing that is combined with the principal thing. So if the purchaser owns a car into which he places a motor which was delivered under retention of title, the purchaser remains the owner of the car including the motor (assuming it is not a scrap car and a brand new motor) because according to the common opinion a car will be incomplete without a motor. The seller of the motor, therefore, loses ownership; the retention of title lapses.

If no principal thing can be discerned (which will generally be the case when commodities, such as quantities of oil or grain, are commingled), the retention of title lapses as well. In this case, however, the owners of the goods that have been commingled become joint owners of the new thing, being the total quantity of the goods, in proportion to the value of the things they owned before the commingling took place.

If a thing that was delivered under retention of title does not become a component of another thing within the meaning of Article 5:14 of the Civil Code, the retention of title does not lapse and it may be repossessed by the seller in the event of default by the purchaser.

(c) *Processing of goods delivered under retention of title*

As a result of the strict character of Articles 5:14 onwards of the Civil Code, it is not possible validly to agree that the retention of title extends to things that are created out of one or more different movable things in contradiction of these rules. According to Article 5:16(2), if the purchaser creates a thing for himself[62] or has someone else create a thing for him out of things that have been delivered under retention of title, the retention of title lapses and the purchaser becomes the owner of the newly created thing.[63] An exception applies when the value of the things that are being used to create the new thing considerably exceed the costs of creation (the processing costs).

(d) *Extension of retention of title*

As we have seen above, Article 3:92(2) of the Civil Code states:

> *The alienator can only validly stipulate such a retention of title for things he has to deliver if this is done in relation to the payment of debt-claims on a counter performance due by the acquiring party for things that have been delivered or will be delivered to him by the alienator pursuant to the same or another agreement or for services performed or to be performed for his benefit by the alienator pursuant to such an agreement, as well as with respect to compensatory debt-claims owed by him to the alienator for failing to perform such agreements. As far as a condition in an agreement is null and void because it is not in conformity with the previous sentence, it has never been stipulated according to law.*

---

62 Paragraph 1 of this article is about the situation where the purchaser does not create the new thing for himself. This situation occurs less often than the situation described in Paragraph 2 because it is not usual that a purchaser creates new things for the account and at the risk of the seller.

63 HR December 5 1986, NJ 1987, 745 (*Gescheurde orchideeën*).

So, according to this article, the retention of title need not be confined to the purchase price for the goods delivered, but can be somewhat extended. A retention of title may be validly stipulated with respect to:

- claims for the counter-obligation (usually the purchase price) for goods delivered or to be delivered by the seller to the purchaser under an agreement;
- work performed or to be performed for the benefit of the purchaser under an agreement; and
- claims for failure to perform such an agreement.

This list is exhaustive, meaning that a stipulation with a wider scope (such as an 'all monies' clause) is invalid, as is a retention of title with regard to a claim based on tort. It should be noted, however, that, should the retention of title clause have a wider scope than allowed by Article 3:92, this does not render the entire clause invalid. The clause is deemed not to exist only insofar as the scope is wider than that allowed. This follows from the words 'as far as' in the last sentence of Article 3:92(2). In other words: an all monies clause is legally considered a retention of title for the claims mentioned in Article 3:92(2).

It should be noted, however, that a seller of goods under retention of title who also has claims that cannot be validly covered by the retention of title, may strengthen his position by agreeing with the purchaser that any payment which the seller receives will in the first place be used to settle claims that are not covered by the retention of title. By doing so, the retention of title remains intact as long as there are other uncovered claims allowed under Article 3:92(2).

Another option for the seller to optimise his legal position is by combining the retention of title with a so-called retained right of pledge. This follows from Article 3:81(1) of the Civil Code:

A person to whom an independent and transferable property right belongs, is able to establish – within the limits of that right – the limited property rights which the law has made available for this purpose. He may also transfer his property right under reservation of such a limited property right, provided that he observes all legal requirements for a transfer as well as for the creation of this type of limited property right.

In this case the seller sells the property under retention of title, at the same time retaining a right of pledge on the property in respect of claims that are not covered by Article 3:92(2) of the Civil Code. As soon as the claims that are covered by the retention of title are paid, the retention of title comes to an end. The seller then, however, still has a right of pledge on the property as security for the payment of any uncovered claims (such as a claim based on tort). Such a right of pledge automatically ranks first because, due to the retention of title, the purchaser has no power of disposition, being just a conditional owner and not the full owner. A right of pledge granted by the purchaser to a third party does not become valid until the purchaser has become the owner, but in this case he becomes owner of a property that is already encumbered by the retained pledge. As regards the right of pledge, two rules must be observed that do not apply to retention of title:

- the right of pledge must be established by notarial deed or by registered[64] private deed;[65] and
- if the purchaser defaults, the seller as pledgee is not allowed to repossess the pledged asset, but must sell it and recover his claim from the proceeds.[66]

The parties are not allowed to agree in advance that a newly processed good is to be delivered to the seller under retention of title. Such a security transfer is void on the basis of Article 3:84(3) of the Civil Code. Retaining a right of pledge on the new good is also not possible, because the seller does not transfer the newly processed good to the purchaser.

2.3 Legal effect of retention of title

(a) Effect towards third parties

A seller who has sold an asset under retention of title is still the owner, albeit under the dissolving condition of the purchaser paying the purchase price. The purchaser on the other hand lacks the power of disposition before having paid the purchase price, but may give the impression that he is the owner because he is in possession of the asset. Unless the purchaser transfers the asset for value to a third party who acts in good faith (see under heading 2.2(a) above), the retention of title also has effect towards the third party and the seller may reclaim the property from the third party in the event of default on the part of the purchaser.

The seller under retention of title may, however, not only be confronted with a third party in good faith, but also by a third party who has a claim for costs made to preserve the asset that was sold under retention of title.[67] According to Article 3:284 of the Civil Code such a claim is secured by a privilege attached to the asset. The third party may recover his claim from that asset regardless of the rights of third persons in that asset, including those of the seller, unless these rights have been created after the moment at which the preservation costs were incurred.

As regards movable goods that are intended to be used by a tax debtor and meant to remain permanently on his premises (being a premises which he uses and has at his actual disposal independently of any other person), the tax collector has a special and very strong position in relation to a secured creditor like a pledgee or the seller under retention of title as regards these goods. The tax claim is privileged, ranks higher than a right of pledge and keeps this rank in the insolvency of the tax debtor.[68] Since January 1 2013, a pledgee or another person who has a right in movable goods

---

64 As mentioned before, there is no public register for retention of title or security rights on movable property. The registration meant here means sending the private deed of pledge to the tax office, which puts a date stamp on it and returns it to the sender, and only aims at ensuring that the exact date of the creation of the pledge can be established.

65 Article 3:237(1) of the Civil Code. Stipulating a retained right of pledge in general terms and conditions will, therefore, not create a valid right of pledge.

66 Article 3:248 of the Civil Code.

67 Additionally, in general, a creditor with whom the purchaser entered into an agreement may refuse to hand over the asset to the seller in the event that the purchaser was entitled to enter into this agreement or the creditor had no reason to doubt that the purchaser was so entitled.

68 Article 21(2) of the Tax Recovery Act 1990.

of this type (such as a hire-purchase seller or a seller under retention of title) must give notice to the tax collector when he intends to execute his right in respect of the goods,[69] unless the value of the goods does not exceed €10,000 at the time when the agreement between the tax debtor and the pledgee or other person is concluded.[70] During a period of four weeks after having given this notice, the pledgee or other person may not exercise his rights if, as a result, the right of the tax collector would be impaired.[71] The tax collector can use this period to decide whether or not he will seize the goods. If the tax collector decides not to seize the goods, he must inform the pledgee or other person as soon as possible. During four weeks after the date of such a notice from the tax collector, the pledgee or other person may exercise his right in respect of the goods.[72] Should the pledgee or other person fail to inform the tax collector, he is obligated, upon demand, to give the tax collector documentary evidence of the execution value of the goods.[73] The tax collector himself then determines the execution value of the goods, and the pledgee or other person is obligated to pay this value to the tax collector up to the amount of the tax claim.[74] These rules also apply in the event that a cooling-off period has been ordered in insolvency.[75]

Hire-purchase contract: As mentioned above (under heading 2.2(a)), in the case of a hire-purchase contract, a third party to whom the seller transfers the property delivered to the purchaser under the hire-purchase agreement is not acting in good faith. Such a transfer has no effect to the detriment of the purchaser.

(b) Effect in case of seizure of goods delivered under retention of title

A creditor of either the seller or the purchaser may seize the goods delivered by the seller to the purchaser under retention of title.

In the event that a creditor of the seller does so, the seizure has effect only if the purchaser defaults and the seller repossesses the goods. In that case, the seller is the owner and his creditor can take recourse against the seller by seizing his assets, selling them and recovering his claim (and the costs of the execution) from the proceeds. Any surplus must be paid to the seller. In the event that the purchaser fulfils his contractual obligations, the seizure does not affect him.

In the event that a creditor of the purchaser seizes the goods, the seizure has effect if the purchaser pays the purchase price to the seller and thus becomes the owner. The conditional ownership then evolves into full ownership. In this case, obviously, the purchaser shall be entitled to any excess proceeds from the execution. Should the seller repossess the goods because the purchaser defaults, the seller has full ownership and the seizure is without any consequence.

69 Article 22*bis*(2) of the Tax Recovery Act 1990.
70 Article 22*bis*(17) of the Tax Recovery Act 1990.
71 Article 22*bis*(5) of the Tax Recovery Act 1990.
72 Article 22*bis*(6) of the Tax Recovery Act 1990.
73 Article 22*bis*(7) of the Tax Recovery Act 1990.
74 Article 22*bis*(10) of the Tax Recovery Act 1990.
75 Article 22*bis*(18) of the Tax Recovery Act 1990.

(c) Effect in case of security right established over goods delivered under retention of title

As outlined above, the purchaser of an asset under retention of title is entitled to sell the asset to a third party who obtains ownership under the same suspending condition of the purchaser paying the purchase price to the seller. According to Article 83(1) of the Civil Code, ownership rights, limited property rights and debt-claims are transferable, unless their nature or the law prevents this. Article 81(1) of the Civil Code states (insofar as is relevant here):

> *A person to whom an independent and transferable property right (asset) belongs, is able to establish – within the limits of that right – the limited property rights which the law has made available for this purpose.*

In order validly to grant a security right over a movable asset, one needs to have the power of disposition over that asset. A purchaser of an asset under retention of title does not have such power. If he nevertheless grants a third party a security right over the asset, such as a right of pledge, that security right is conditional. Upon the purchaser becoming unconditional owner – by paying the purchase price to the seller – the has the power of disposition and the security right immediately and automatically becomes valid.[76] However, if the purchaser grants a security right to a third party who acts in good faith at the moment when the asset is brought under his control, or under the control of a third party who has been appointed by him for this purpose, the third party is protected and the retention of title lapses.[77]

On the other hand, after having handed over the asset to the purchaser but before full payment of the purchase price has been obtained, the seller is still the owner thereof and may establish a pledge or usufruct on it for the benefit of a third party. Such an encumbrance does not harm the rights of the purchaser. Because he already has the asset under his control, the third party cannot assume in good faith that the seller was entitled legally to encumber the good.

Hire-purchase contract: What has been said above regarding retention of title also applies to hire-purchase contracts. In respect of a sale or encumbrance by the seller of the asset after it has been delivered under the hire-purchase contract, Article 7A:1576l of the Civil Code expressly states that this shall have no effect to the detriment of the purchaser.

(d) Effect in case of insolvency[78]

The moment an insolvency proceeding[79] is opened in respect of a person, the rights of third parties, such as creditors, are frozen. This also affects the right to transfer (title to) assets.

---

76 See HR November 28 2014, ECLI:NL:HR:2014:3460 (*Snippers/Rabobank*).

77 Article 3:238(1) of the Civil Code; Hof Den Bosch August 11 2015, ECLI:NL:GDSHE:2015:3184.

78 Articles 212v and 213q of the Insolvency Act, respectively, and Article 3:342 of the Financial Supervision Act contain special provisions on retention of title in the event that a bank or an insurer, respectively, in insolvency is the seller or purchaser of goods under retention of title. These provisions fall outside the scope of this chapter.

79 Meaning here a liquidation proceeding, comparable to the US Chapter 7, and not a suspension of payments (comparable to Chapter 11) or a debt repayment scheme for natural persons.

According to Article 35(1) of the Insolvency Act, if, on the date of the declaration of bankruptcy, not all acts required for a transfer by the debtor have been performed, the transfer can no longer be validly completed. If the seller has sold an asset under retention of title and delivered it to the purchaser before the seller goes bankrupt, the transfer of ownership is dependent only on the performance by the purchaser of the counter obligation. As a result, Article 35(1) of the Insolvency Act does not apply, because all acts required for the transfer have taken place.

The Insolvency Act sets a limit to the protection of persons (purchasers or pledgees) even where they act in good faith: after the bankruptcy order has been published in the official Dutch government gazette, such a person is deemed to be aware of the debtor's lack of legal capacity.[80]

An insolvency does not, in principle, change an agreement that the debtor concluded before the insolvency. The opening of insolvency proceedings, therefore, is in itself no ground for rescission of a purchase agreement including retention of title. However, if an agreement has, at the time of the declaration of bankruptcy, not been performed in full by either party, and the liquidator does not state, within a reasonable period set for this purpose in writing by the counterparty, that the insolvency estate will perform its obligations under that agreement, then the liquidator will lose his right to claim performance of the agreement.[81] If the liquidator states that the insolvency estate is prepared to perform the agreement, then he must provide security for such performance.

This rule does not apply when goods have been delivered under retention of title, since the seller has fully performed his part under the agreement. If the purchaser performs as well, ownership passes to him. If the purchaser goes bankrupt, the liquidator may choose to perform and thus make the insolvency estate owner of the goods, or not to perform. In the latter case, the seller may repossess the goods as set out below (see section 3 below) and submit any claim for damages as an unsecured claim in the bankruptcy.

Hire-purchase contract: A special rule governs the insolvency of the purchaser under a hire-purchase agreement. When the bankrupt debtor is a purchaser under a hire-purchase agreement, both the liquidator and the seller may rescind the hire-purchase agreement.[82] Such a rescission has the same legal effects as the rescission of an agreement on the ground of non-performance of his obligations by the purchaser.

The seller may submit an unsecured claim in the bankruptcy for the amount due to him.[83] This claim can be calculated by comparing the situation as a result of the rescission with the situation that would apply had the agreement been executed.

When the seller under a hire-purchase agreement[84] goes bankrupt, the general rule of Article 37 of the Insolvency Act applies. In short: if, at the time of the

80 Article 35(3) of the Insolvency Act.

81 Article 37(1) of the Insolvency Act.

82 Arguably the liquidator can prevent rescission by the seller by paying to the seller the full remainder of the purchase price; see B Wessels, *Wessels Insolventierecht* II 2012/2507.

83 Article 38a of the Insolvency Act.

84 The Temporary Act on Hire-Purchase of Immovable Goods has a special provision regarding insolvency of the seller under a hire-purchase agreement, which falls outside the scope of this chapter.

declaration of bankruptcy, the agreement has not been performed in full by either party, and the liquidator does not state, within a reasonable period set for this purpose in writing by the counterparty, that the insolvency estate will perform its obligations under that agreement, then the liquidator will lose his right to claim performance of the agreement.

Seller's right of reclamation: The seller's right of reclamation was mentioned above (under heading 2.1(b)). According to Article 7:40 of the Civil Code, where the purchaser has been declared bankrupt or where a judicial suspension of payment under a moratorium has been granted to him, a rightful reclamation by the seller of what has been transferred to the purchaser has no effect, if the court-appointed liquidator or, in the case of a judicial suspension of payment under a moratorium, the purchaser and the court-appointed administrator jointly pay the full purchase price or give security for that payment within a reasonable period of time to be set by the seller in his declaration.[85]

(e) ***Effect in case of partial payment of purchase price***

When goods have been delivered under retention of title, it is in principle irrelevant whether the purchaser has not performed his side of the agreement at all or has paid the purchase price only partially. In either case the seller can rescind the agreement and demand the return of the goods. As a result of the rescission the parties are obligated to return what they have already received under the agreement, so the purchaser must return the goods and the seller must return to the purchaser any payments so far received. The seller is, however, entitled to set off against this repayment obligation any damages he may incur due to the purchaser's default, including any depreciation of the goods.[86] In the event that the goods delivered are divisible (for example, 100 pairs of identical shoes) and the purchaser has partially paid the purchase price, the seller may opt for a partial rescission of the agreement, so that he has no obligation to repay the purchaser but still gets back the goods for which payment has not been received.

As regards hire-purchase contracts, these rules are laid down expressly in Article 7A:1567t of the Civil Code, which states that if a rescission on account of non-compliance by the purchaser has the result that the seller enters into a better financial position than he would have been had the contract remained in force, the purchaser must be compensated in full for such advantage.

It is unclear whether the liquidator in an insolvency of the purchaser is entitled to sell goods that have been delivered to the purchaser before the insolvency under retention of title. The liquidator is charged with the administration and winding-up of the insolvency estate,[87] but has no power of disposition over goods that are owned by third parties and, therefore, do not belong to the insolvency estate.

Obviously, the seller may agree to a sale by the liquidator, usually under the

85 This rule applies also if the purchaser falls under the Law on a Debt Repayment Scheme for Natural Persons, unless the sales agreement has been concluded after the court order which made the debt repayment scheme applicable.

86 Any increase in value should be taken into account as well, but that will not often be the case.

87 Article 68(1) of the Insolvency Act.

condition that the liquidator pays the originally agreed purchase price. It can be argued that the liquidator may also sell the goods that are owned by the seller, if there is a cooling-off period (a stay),[88] the liquidator continues the business of the purchaser, and when weighing up the interests of the seller and the insolvency estate (including public interests, such as continuity of the business and preservation of jobs)[89] the interests of the estate prevail.[90] The liquidator will then, however, have to pay damages to the seller, which will ordinarily amount to the purchase price that was agreed with the purchaser. The seller's claim in this respect has super-priority.

If the seller wishes to prevent the liquidator from selling the goods, the seller will have to rescind the agreement with the purchaser before the liquidator has sold the goods, and make a repossessory attachment.

3. Enforcement of retention of title

Under Dutch law a bailiff is a public official with special authority and powers, such as enforcing court orders and (forcefully) gaining access to the premises where goods under retention of title are stored in order to seize these goods. When seizing goods, the bailiff will draw up an official report listing the goods that are being seized, which report may be used as evidence in court.

In the event that the purchase price is not paid, the seller may want to invoke his retention of title. If and under what circumstances he is entitled to do so, depends primarily on what the parties have agreed upon in this respect. Generally, the purchaser must be in default before the seller may reclaim his property. According to Article 6:82(1) of the Civil Code:

> *The debtor is in default when he is held liable for his non-performance by a letter of formal notice, in which the creditor grants him a reasonable period of time during which he still may perform in conformity with his obligation, and he nevertheless fails to accomplish the performance owed within that period.*

The parties may, however, agree that such formal notice is not required and that the seller may reclaim the property as soon as the purchaser does not comply with any of his obligations under the agreement.

In addition, the purchaser may be held to be in default immediately, without the necessity of a prior letter of formal notice to perform or an announcement in which he is held responsible for his non-performance, in certain circumstances, such as when the creditor must conclude from a statement of the debtor that he will not act in conformity with his contractual obligations, or when the obligation is subject to a fixed time for its performance and he has failed to accomplish the required performance within that specified period.[91]

---

88 Article 63A of the Insolvency Act. During a cooling-off period, the right of third persons, with the exception of creditors with an estate claim (being a claim directly against the insolvency estate instead of against the insolvent debtor), to take recourse against the assets of the insolvency estate or to claim the handing over of assets which are under control of the bankrupt debtor or liquidator, may be exercised only with the authorisation of the supervisory judge.

89 HR February 24 1995, NJ 1996, 472 (*Sigmacon II*); HR April 19 1996, NJ 1996, 727 (*Maclou*).

90 CM Harmsen, "De afkoelingsperiode", in *Praktijkboek Insolventierecht, Deel 2, Lopende overeenkomsten en afkoelingsperiode* (Kluwer, Deventer 2007), pp92–95.

91 Article 6:83 of the Civil Code.

The seller can in any case reclaim the property when the requirements for rescission of the agreement[92] are met. Upon rescission of the agreement, the purchaser holds the property without any legal basis. Rescission of an agreement has no retroactive effect,[93] but releases the parties from their obligations under it, which (unless the agreement is rescinded only partially) encompasses all the obligations created by the rescinded agreement. As far as these obligations have been performed already, the legal basis for performance remains effective, but the law imposes an obligation on the parties to undo what has been done under the rescinded agreement.[94] This means that the seller will have to repay to the purchaser that part of the purchase price already paid, but the seller may set off the repayment obligation with any damages incurred as a result of the purchaser's default. The amount of damages are calculated by making a comparison between the situation in which the seller would have found himself had the agreement been properly executed and the situation he is in following rescission.[95]

The seller is under no obligation to sell the repossessed property; by rescission the seller assumes full ownership again and may keep it or dispose of it as he deems fit.

It should be noted, however, that rescission of the agreement is not always necessary.[96] Sometimes, the seller may not wish to rescind the agreement because rescission, as mentioned, obliges the parties to undo the performance that has already happened, or because a third party is prepared to pay what is due by the purchaser but wishes to assume the secured position of the seller.[97] Besides, especially in insolvency situations, a stalemate might arise. In the event of an agreement where neither party has entirely fulfilled their contractual obligations, the solvent party (in this example, the seller) may request the insolvency liquidator to declare whether he wishes to execute the agreement. If the liquidator does not declare that he does, or does not make a declaration within the stipulated reasonable time, then according to Article 37 of the Bankruptcy Act he loses the right to claim performance from the seller. The agreement is hardly ever rescinded; the liquidator is not entitled to rescind,[98] and the other party mostly has no reason to do so. Ordinarily, in such a situation the liquidator hands over the property to the seller, who then submits his claim for the difference between the agreed purchase price and the residual value of the property (plus any part of the purchase price already received by him) as an unsecured claim in the insolvency.

In principle, the goods delivered under retention of title can be repossessed by

92 Article 6:265 of the Civil Code; see footnote 53.

93 Article 6:269 of the Civil Code.

94 Article 6:271 of the Civil Code.

95 Parl. Gesch. Boek 6 BW, p. 1036.

96 As regards a hire-purchase contract this follows from Article 7A: 1576s of the Civil Code, which says that: If the thing that has been delivered to the purchaser under the hire-purchase contract is taken back by virtue of a stipulation made for this purpose in the event that the purchaser has not complied with his obligations, then this shall result in the rescission of the contract, unless the parties have agreed otherwise.

97 In that case it must be clear that the third party does not pay the purchaser's debt under the agreement, otherwise the retention of title will terminate, the purchaser will become owner and the third party will have no security.

98 Hof Amsterdam January 15 2004, JOR 2004/89 with a note by JJ van Hees, held that the liquidator was entitled to rescind, but this judgment has no statutory basis.

the owner (the seller) himself, or by an agent of the owner, in the event that the purchaser defaults and holds the goods without right or title.[99] However, if the debtor (the purchaser) does not cooperate and hand over the goods to the seller voluntarily, a bailiff should be involved. With the permission of the president of the district court the seller can instruct the bailiff to make a pre-judgment attachment[100] of the goods, followed by either summary proceedings or proceedings on the merits in which the seller reclaims his property. Also with the permission of the president of the district court the bailiff may be instructed to store the attached goods with a custodian (known as 'sequestration'). Should no pre-judgment attachment be made, the seller may, as soon as the court has acknowledged the retention of title and granted the claim of the seller, instruct the bailiff to make an attachment and so force the purchaser to hand over the goods.[101]

Even when the parties have agreed that the seller shall have access to the premises of the purchaser when he wants to exert his right to repossess the property, he is dependent on the cooperation of the purchaser. If the purchaser (or the owner of the warehouse in which the property is stored) denies the seller access, contrary to the agreement, the seller will have to obtain permission from the court and will need the help of a bailiff. Self-help is not allowed. In the event that the purchaser is in insolvency, the court-appointed liquidator will normally cooperate (assuming he accepts the validity of the retention of title). If he does not, the seller may request the supervisory judge in the insolvency to order the liquidator to hand over the property, or demand such an order in summary proceedings before the (ordinary) court. Requesting an ordinary court order requires the involvement of a lawyer and the payment of court fees and is, therefore, much more costly than requesting an order from the supervisory judge.

(a) *Hire-purchase contracts*

The statutory rules for hire-purchase contracts contain some specific rules for this type of contract that are stricter than the rules set out above regarding retention of title in other cases. Without discussing these rules at length, the most important ones are mentioned below.

Article 7A:1576q of the Civil Code states that:

A rescission of the hire-purchase contract or the return of the thing that is under control of the purchaser under the hire-purchase contract, invoked by the seller by virtue of a stipulation made for this purpose in the event that the purchaser has not performed his obligations in time, cannot be invoked or claimed, unless the purchaser, after having been formally notified to perform, still remains negligent in the compliance with his obligations.

When the seller has the right to claim the rescission of the hire-purchase contract or the return of the thing that has been delivered to the purchaser under the hire-purchase contract, then the court may, upon request by the seller, order the return

99 Article 5(2) of the Civil Code.
100 Article 730 of the Code of Civil Procedure.
101 Article 491 onwards of the Code of Civil Procedure.

of the thing. Such an order may also be given by way of a preliminary relief which is enforceable immediately.[102] The judgment ordering the purchaser to return the thing that was delivered to him under the hire-purchase contract may establish the financial value of the thing to be returned. In that case the enforcement by the seller could also be an action for the recovery of the established value.[103] The situation where the purchaser under the hire-purchase contract is in insolvency is described above under heading 2.3(d).

If a rescission of the hire-purchase contract on account of non-compliance by the purchaser has the result that the seller enters into a better financial position than he would have been had the contract remained in force, then this advantage must be compensated for in full.[104] If the purchaser, as a result of the rescission, has a right to any repayment, he may be authorised by the court to withhold the return of the thing he has to give back, until the seller has paid to him what is due to him or has provided sufficient security for this debt.[105]

If the thing that has been delivered to the purchaser under the hire-purchase contract has been taken back by the seller because one or more due and enforceable instalments have not been paid, and this has occurred without any prior intervention of the court, then the purchaser is entitled to regain the thing within 14 days after it was taken from him by paying up the instalments which are due at that moment and by paying the interest, financial penalties and costs incurred at that moment. If the hire-purchase contract has already been rescinded, any payment as described in the previous sentence shall have the effect that the rescission is undone. Should the same situation occur again, the purchaser shall only have the right to pay up once more against payment of the entire purchase price.[106]

(b) Identification of goods concerned

There are no formal requirements for identifying the goods subject to retention of title. From a practical point of view, though, it is recommended that goods under retention of title be shipped or delivered in easily identifiable packaging, which can be connected to the relevant (purchase) agreement, for example by clearly marking them with the owner's logo or an order tracking number, and shipping information.

From the words "the same or another agreement" in Article 3:92(2) of the Civil Code it follows that the property secured by the retention of title does not have to be delivered in execution of one and the same agreement. As a result, where a seller has sold and delivered to the purchaser similar goods under subsequent agreements, some of which have been paid for by the purchaser and in respect of which he would otherwise become the owner, the seller is not required to prove exactly which goods have not been paid for, but is considered to have remained the owner of a part of the goods that corresponds to the unpaid amount, provided the retention of title covers goods that have not been paid for under the subsequent agreements. Should a third

102 Article 7A:1576r of the Civil Code.
103 Article 7A:1576x of the Civil Code.
104 Article 7A:1567t of the Civil Code.
105 Article 7A:1576u of the Civil Code.
106 Article 7A:1576v of the Civil Code.

party claim to have a security right on some of those goods, this party will have to identify those goods exactly.[107]

(c) Insolvency proceedings

During insolvency proceedings, the owner of goods delivered under retention of title is considered to be a secured creditor who may enforce his rights regardless of the insolvency proceedings to which the debtor is subject. The court-appointed liquidator will have to be notified by the owner in a similar way as set out above. If the liquidator accepts the retention of title and is not prepared or able to pay (the remainder of) the purchase price due from the insolvent debtor, the common practice is that the agreement is not officially rescinded, but the seller and the liquidator act as if this were the case (ie, the liquidator returns the goods to the seller and the seller submits a claim in the amount of the purchase price less the actual value of the goods). Notification of the liquidator and subsequent repossession of the goods should, unless a moratorium has been granted, be done as quickly as possible in order to ensure that the liquidator is aware of the retention of title and does not transfer the goods to a third party in ignorance of it. If the liquidator refuses to cooperate, either the owner can request the supervisory judge in the insolvency proceedings to order the liquidator to return the goods, or the owner can start interim proceedings or proceedings on the merits to have the court acknowledge the retention of title and to order the liquidator to cooperate accordingly.

As mentioned above under heading 2.3(a), the position of the tax collector is very strong. The obligation of the seller under retention of title to notify the tax collector that he intends to take back the goods delivered to the purchaser also applies in insolvency, and even when a cooling-off period has been ordered. Because it is quite rare that a debtor in insolvency has no tax debt, it may be assumed that the tax collector will, upon receipt of the notification, seize[108] the goods delivered under retention of title. In that case the liquidator is not allowed to return the goods to the seller (unless the tax collector gives him permission to do so, notifies the seller that he will not seize the goods, or does not notify the seller within four weeks after the seller has informed the tax collector of his intention to repossess the goods).

---

107 See JJ van Hees in his note under HR December 4 1998, JOR 1999/94.

108 Goods owned by the insolvent debtor may not be seized after the opening of the insolvency proceedings, but the debtor is not the owner until he has paid the purchase price.

Poland

Jan Kieszczyński
Michał Kocur
Kocur & Partners

1. General remarks about retention of title

1.1 Transfer of ownership

The general rule for transfer of title of specific goods (movable assets) under Polish law is that the title passes upon conclusion of the sale agreement. With regard to unascertained or future goods (goods to be manufactured or acquired by the seller after the conclusion of the sale agreement), the title to such goods passes in the moment in which those goods are handed over to the buyer or at a later moment agreed by the parties.

Subject to the rules on transfer of ownership of unascertained and future goods, the parties to a sale agreement may freely agree on the moment at which the title to the goods shall pass to the buyer. The parties may agree that the transfer of title shall occur at a specific date or be subject to a condition precedent or condition subsequent.

1.2 Retention of title

Polish law permits a seller to retain title of the sold goods until payment of the purchase price has been made in full. Retention of title clauses are regulated in Articles 589 to 591 of the Polish Civil Code. Article 589 of the Civil Code provides that if the seller has retained the title to the goods until the price is paid in full, the payment of the full price of the goods is to be construed as a condition precedent to the passing of title of goods to the buyer. Article 590 of the Civil Code provides that if the goods have been handed over to the buyer, the retention of title clause shall be evidenced in writing. Article 590 further provides that if such a clause is to be enforceable towards third parties, the written document containing it should have a certified date (how a certified date can be obtained is discussed under heading 2.1 below). Article 591 of the Civil Code establishes the right of a seller, who moves to repossess the goods delivered under retention of title, to claim reimbursement for wear and tear and damage to those goods.

Case law does not have a direct influence on the operation of a retention of title clause, as Poland is a civil law jurisdiction in which there are no binding precedents. However, case law, particularly that of the Supreme Court, has significant authority and serves as an important point of reference for the lower courts.

1.3 Foreign and international law

In accordance with the Private International Law Act, the law governing a sales agreement that contains a retention of title will be determined according to the Rome I Regulation (EC Regulation 593/2008 of June 17 2008 on the law applicable to contractual obligations).

According to Article 41(2) of the Private International Law Act, the creation and the expiry of retention of title is governed by the law of the country in which the goods concerned were situated in the moment at which that creation or expiry occurred. Those aspects of retention of title such as transfer of title, rank of securities and the possibility to taking security over goods which are subject of retention of title, shall be governed by the law of the location of the goods (Article 41(1) of the Private International Law Act).

Under these rules, in a case where the security right in a movable asset was created under foreign law, but the goods are currently situated in Poland, the Polish court will examine if this security should be treated as a retention of title (or as another security right, such as a fiduciary security transfer of title). If it comes to the answer that the security right is a retention of title, then Polish rules on retention of title will apply and determine the legal situation of the seller, as well as remedies that are available to him under Polish law.

1.4 Retention of title in insolvency

The Polish insolvency law regime consists of two types of insolvency proceeding: bankruptcy and restructuring. In bankruptcy proceedings, a trustee is appointed by a competent court with a view to liquidating the bankruptcy estate and distributing the proceeds to the creditors. Restructuring proceedings aim to restructure the business of an insolvent debtor, who generally maintains management and control of his business. From January 1 2016 these two types of proceeding will be regulated by two separate acts, the Bankruptcy Act and Restructuring Act respectively.

With regard to bankruptcy of the buyer, Article 101 of the Bankruptcy Act provides that retention of title does not expire due to the bankruptcy provided that it is valid and enforceable against other creditors of the buyer in accordance with the provisions of the Civil Code. This means retention of title will not expire if the agreement in which it was granted has a certified date as provided for in Article 590 of the Civil Code (see further under heading 2.1 below).

With regard to restructuring of the buyer, Article 249 and Article 168 of the Restructuring Act provide that the retention of title clause remains effective during the restructuring proceedings.

If the buyer is subject to insolvency proceedings outside Poland, the validity of the retention of title will be determined according to the laws of the jurisdiction in which insolvency was declared.

The validity of a retention of title clause is unaffected if it is the seller who is subject to proceedings under the Bankruptcy Act or the Restructuring Act. However, in bankruptcy proceedings the trustee of the bankruptcy estate will have a right to rescind the sales agreement (see under heading 2.3 below).

If the seller is subject to insolvency proceedings outside Poland, any issues with regard to the validity of the retention of title clause will be determined according to the laws of the jurisdiction in which the insolvency was declared.

2. Retention of title

2.1 Validity and formal requirements

Retention of title does not have to be agreed in writing in order to be valid. However, a retention of title arrangement should be made in writing for the sake of avoiding any potential disputes with the buyer, as well as to have the possibility of establishing a security effective against other creditors of the buyer (see below).

If the retention of title is to be effective against other creditors of the buyer, it has to have have a certified date (Article 590 of the Civil Code). The retention of title is then effective against other creditors of the buyer from the certified date. The form of the certified date is regulated by Article 81 of the Civil Code. The most practical way to obtain the legal effect of a certified date is to have a notary certify the date on the agreement containing the retention of title clause. The date may also be certified by a public body. The certification of the date may be performed on the date on which the agreement is concluded or at a later date. Article 81 of the Civil Code also provides for other situations in which retention of title will be deemed to have a certified date: in the event that the document containing a retention of title clause is referenced in a public document (the effective certified date being the date of issue of that public document), or in the event that a person who signed the agreement has deceased (the effective certified date being the date of death).

The wording of the retention of title clause can be freely agreed by the parties and there are no specific legal phrases to be observed. The wording must state, in an unambiguous manner, that the title to the assets being sold remains with the seller unless the whole price is paid. Polish law does not provide for a retention of title by operation of law.

It is also possible to agree on retention of title in general terms and conditions. In this case the rules outlined above with regard to written form and certified date still apply.

The parties are free to agree on the place where the goods are to be delivered, including agreement that delivery will take place by handing over of the goods to a carrier or by delivery to a warehouse belonging to a third party.

2.2 Scope of retention of title

(a) Sale of goods delivered under retention of title

The buyer is not allowed to sell goods that are delivered under retention of title. The right to sell the goods is vested with the seller. The parties may agree that the seller authorises the buyer to sell the goods to a third party on behalf of the seller (as the seller's agent) and provide for appropriate mechanisms of settling the proceeds of any such transaction. In such a case, the parties can agree that the price (or part of it) will be paid directly by the third party to the seller.

(b) Combining/mixing/mingling goods delivered under retention of title

The effect of combining, mixing or mingling of goods depends on the circumstances of any such event, the nature of the other goods involved and their value.

If the goods delivered under retention of title (such as building materials) are affixed to real property then the retention of title becomes void and the title passes to the owner of the real property (Article 191 of the Civil Code). This rule cannot be amended by the parties' agreement.

If the goods have been combined or mixed, the seller generally has the right to restoration of the goods to their previous state, that is to say the state they were in before combining or mixing occurred. However, if the goods have been combined or mixed in a manner that would make it too difficult or too costly to restore them to their previous state, the seller becomes a co-owner of the whole lot of goods, his share in the lot determined by the value of the goods he owned (Article 193 of the Civil Code). The parties may also agree that in such a case the seller will become the owner of the whole lot.

If one of the combined or mixed goods has a value much higher than the other goods, the goods of lesser value are treated as attached to the goods of much higher value and any retention of title to the goods of lesser value would lapse. In this case the owner of the goods of much higher value becomes the owner of the combined thing. The parties may agree that the seller of goods delivered under retention of title will become owner (or co-owner) of any product created by the buyer with the use of those goods, regardless of their value in relation to the other goods involved. Such an agreement will be effective if the combined, mixed or mingled goods belong to the buyer. If the buyer has also used goods belonging to third parties, the seller could acquire ownership of goods belonging to the buyer and those third parties if the seller concluded agreements to this effect with all those entities.

(c) Processing of goods delivered under retention of title

If the buyer processed the goods delivered under retention of title and the work he has invested in the creation of the final product had a higher value than the goods involved, the retention of title will lapse and the buyer will be an owner of the final product. However, if buyer processed the goods in bad faith or the goods had a higher value than the work involved in their processing, the seller of the goods will be the owner of the final product (Article 192 of the Civil Code). Opinion is split over the issue of whether the parties are allowed to agree that the seller will retain title to the product resulting from the processing of the goods even if the work involved in the creation of the product is of higher value than the goods.

(d) Extension of retention of title

The issue of whether retention of title can extend to debts other than the purchase price has been a controversial topic in the discussion of Polish legal doctrine. The currently prevailing view is that the passing of title to the goods may be made conditional upon payment by the buyer of debts other than the purchase price.

2.3 Legal effect of retention of title

(a) Effect towards third parties

Retention of title will not have automatic effect towards other creditors and governmental bodies. In order for a retention of title to be invoked successfully against other creditors and government bodies, the retention of title has to be effective towards such parties, which means that it must have a certified date, as explained in detail above (under heading 2.1). If this condition is satisfied, the seller may effectively bring an action to secure his right under retention of title against those parties (and may therefore move to exclude the goods from enforcement proceedings or the bankruptcy estate, as explained below).

Retention of title will not have any effect towards a subsequent buyer acting in good faith. According to Article 169 of the Civil Code a valid retention of title will not prohibit the buyer from fraudulently selling the goods to a third party before he has paid the whole purchase price to the seller. The condition for such a transfer to be valid, however, is that the third party must act in good faith, both at the moment of concluding the sales agreement with the original buyer and at the moment of taking delivery of those goods from the buyer. Acting in good faith means that the third party must, considering the circumstances and terms of the sale, not have any objective doubts as to the fact that the buyer is the owner of the goods.

(b) Effect in case of seizure of goods delivered under retention of title

If the goods delivered under retention of title are seized, the aggrieved party has the right to initiate anti-enforcement proceedings, demanding that the goods are excluded from enforcement. However, the situation will differ depending on whether enforcement proceedings are started against the buyer or the seller.

Where the third party is a creditor of the buyer and starts enforcement against the buyer, the enforcement body will seize the goods if they remain at the buyer's disposal. In this case the seller may bring anti-enforcement proceedings to exclude the goods from enforcement by arguing that he is the owner of the goods. The seller must then prove that his retention of title has a certified date and is effective against third parties (see heading 2.1 above).

Where the third party is a creditor of the seller, and enforcement proceedings are started against goods still belonging to the seller under a retention of title clause but already delivered to the buyer, the situation is different. The goods may be seized if the buyer consents to the seizure or admits that the title to the goods actually still belongs to the seller (Article 845(2) of the Civil Procedure Code). Also, the goods may be seized if the enforcement order provides for the seizure of goods held by the buyer. It is a controversial issue whether the buyer can initiate anti-enforcement proceedings and argue that the seizure compromises the rights that he has under the sales agreement with the seller. Some scholars express the view that the buyer (where he is not in default as regards payment of the purchase price) has a right that is effective against the seller: an expectation that he will acquire title to the goods once the price is paid.

(c) Effect in case of a security right established over goods delivered under retention of title

The effect of a retention of title clause on any security rights established over goods delivered under that retention of title depends on the good faith of the creditor for whom the security rights are established. If the creditor acts in good faith, the security rights will be validly established despite the retention of title.

The rules set out in Article 169 of the Civil Code, described above in relation to a subsequent buyer in good faith, will apply subject to the necessary alterations. The notion of good faith will however be construed differently as regards possessory and non-possessory rights.

In the case of possessory rights (such as a pledge), establishment of a security right will require handing over the goods to the creditor. If at this stage it can be proven that the creditor knew or should have known (for instance due to labelling of the goods) that the buyer did not have title to the goods then the security would not be validly established.

In the case of non-possessory rights, such as a registered pledge (or a floating charge, which under Polish law is one of the forms of a registered pledge), the creditor will usually not be in a position directly to examine the goods and so discover any potential labelling. This means that in the case of a registered pledge, if the creditor has objective reasons to believe that the buyer has title to the goods in the moment of signing the pledge agreement and its entry in the pledge register (the mere entry of the pledge in the pledge register is treated as equivalent to handing over the goods within the meaning of Article 169 of the Civil Code), the creditor will impose a valid registered pledge over the goods delivered under retention of title.

(d) Effect in case of insolvency

In the event that the buyer is declared bankrupt under the Bankruptcy Act and the purchase price has not yet been fully paid, the seller may initiate an action to exclude the goods delivered under retention of title from the bankruptcy estate (Articles 70 to 74 of the Bankruptcy Act). In order to bring such an action successfully against the bankruptcy estate, the seller will then have to prove that his retention of title has a certified date and is effective towards the creditors of the bankrupt buyer (see above).

Also, in the event that the buyer is declared bankrupt and the goods delivered under retention of title have already been disposed of by the buyer, then under Article 71 of the Bankruptcy Act, the seller will be entitled to claim the consideration that has been received in exchange for those goods. However, if the proceeds from the sale of the goods delivered under retention of title became mixed in the bankruptcy estate (as in the case of money), the seller only has an ordinary monetary claim on the bankruptcy estate.

The seller will be in a better situation if the goods delivered under retention of title are disposed of by the trustee. In that situation, the seller will always be entitled to claim the consideration received in exchange for those goods.

If the price has not been paid before the seller filed any of the above claims, the claim for the purchase price will as of law be transferred to the seller.

The trustee of the bankruptcy estate also has additional rights with regard to an unperformed sales agreement. If the sales agreement has not yet been fully performed (in other words, if the price has not yet been paid in full), the trustee may rescind the contract for the sale of the goods, in which case the seller will be obliged to return that part of the price that he has received (if any) and at the same time will be allowed to take back the goods to which he has a valid title (for further explanation of the mechanism of rescission see below).

(e) ***Effect in case of partial payment of purchase price***

In the event that the buyer does not pay the purchase price in due time, the seller may call for payment and declare that if the buyer does not pay in a fixed period of time, the seller will rescind the contract. If the fixed period of time passes without payment, the seller will be entitled to rescind the agreement and move to repossess the goods. The parties may agree that the seller has the right to rescind without issuing a prior call for payment.

The general rule is that once the agreement is rescinded the parties are obliged to return to each other all that they received in performance of the agreement. Generally, if an agreement containing a retention of title clause is rescinded, the seller will be entitled to repossess all the goods while the buyer will be entitled to a return of all of the purchase price he has paid. The seller, however, will also have a potential claim for reimbursement for wear and tear or destruction of those goods (Article 591 of the Civil Code) and a potential damages claim for non-performance of the contract against the buyer (Article 494 of the Civil Code). The mutual monetary claims of the buyer and seller may be subject to a set-off.

If the goods sold under retention of title are separable and the seller has received only part of the purchase price, the seller also has the right only partially to rescind the agreement and to repossess only the goods that have not been paid for.

3. Enforcement of retention of title

3.1 Enforcement methods

In order to repossess the goods delivered under retention of title where the buyer does not voluntarily give them back, the seller must obtain an enforcement title for his repossession claim (a court order or the buyer's declaration of voluntary submission to repossession of the goods) and start enforcement proceedings with a court bailiff. It is not possible to authorise a commercial or private enforcement agency to act on the seller's behalf, or for the seller to act on his own motion to take back the goods.

3.2 Repossession

If the buyer or a third party at whose premises the goods are stored declines voluntarily to return the goods to the seller, it is necessary for the seller to obtain a repossession enforcement title. To do that the seller must file a statement of claim with the court in order to initiate repossession proceedings against the person on whose premises the goods are stored, regardless of whether it is the buyer or a third party. During these proceedings, the court examines the seller's title to the goods. Once the proceedings are completed the court issues a judgment in which it grants or rejects the seller's claim to repossess the goods.

If the goods are at the buyer's premises, an alternative to the court proceedings is obtaining the buyer's declaration of voluntary submission to repossession of goods (Article 777 of the Civil Procedure Code), which serves as an enforcement title, a substitute of the judgment of the court. This declaration must be made in front of a notary and is a practical and effective security for the agreement. The shortcoming of voluntary submission is that it will be effective only against the party who issued it: the buyer.

It is not possible validly to agree that the seller will be entitled to enter on to the buyer's premises and take possession of the goods delivered under retention of title.

3.3 Formal requirements for repossession

An enforcement title, whether it comes from the court or from the buyer (in the form of a declaration of voluntary submission as explained above), must be submitted to the court in order to have a writ of execution appended to it. Once the enforcement title and the writ of execution have been prepared, the seller may file a motion to initiate enforcement proceedings with an appropriate bailiff (preferably a bailiff active in the district where the goods are stored). The bailiff then moves to repossess the goods.

3.4 Identification of goods

There are no formal requirements regarding identification of the goods to be repossessed. However, the clearer the identification of the goods, the easier it is to enforce the retention of title. In the case of specific goods it is desirable to describe the brand, model, type, specifications, serial number, colour and so on. An effective description will most likely prove to be a challenge with regard to unspecified goods, but in this case all due care should be exercised by, for example, labelling the bags or boxes in which any such goods are delivered.

3.5 Insolvency

If the buyer is declared bankrupt, then as described under heading 2.3 above, the seller may move to exclude the goods delivered under retention of title from the bankruptcy estate. If his claim is rejected by the magistrate in charge of the bankruptcy proceedings, then a claim to exclude the goods from the bankruptcy estate may be filed with the court.

Portugal

Miguel de Avillez Pereira
Tiago Castanheira Marques
Filipe Portela do Valle
Abreu Advogados

1. General remarks about retention of title

1.1 Transfer of ownership

In Portuguese law, the basic rule governing the transfer of ownership of any asset is laid down in the Portuguese Civil Code, which determines that ownership is transferred upon conclusion of the applicable sale and purchase agreement. Usually, transfer of ownership of an asset is an immediate effect of the sale and purchase agreement. Therefore, the transfer of ownership and of property rights over the asset occurs on conclusion of the agreement.

Despite this basic rule regarding the transfer of ownership of an asset on the conclusion of the sale and purchase agreement, under the Civil Code, parties are allowed to agree on a different time for the transfer of ownership over an asset.

The main example of this possibility is a sale with reservation or retention of title, in which the seller may delay the transfer of ownership over an asset until the price of that asset is fully paid by the debtor or until the occurrence of some other specified event.

1.2 Retention of title

In line with the principles outlined above, Article 409 of the Civil Code expressly allows the seller to retain the ownership of an asset until a specified condition is met, by inserting a retention of title clause in the sale and purchase agreement.

Specifically, the Civil Code allows the seller of an asset to retain ownership of that asset until the buyer fulfils all of its obligations or until the occurrence of any other event.

Generally, title is reserved until full payment of the acquisition price to the seller, but given the wording of the Civil Code, other situations may be included in the expression "any other event". For example, the transfer of ownership may occur when a third party – a financial institution for example – is reimbursed an amount agreed in the financing agreement entered into with the buyer regarding an asset.

As a consequence, it is clear that retention of title has a statutory basis in Portugal, since it is expressly foreseen in Article 409 of the Civil Code.

Despite this statutory basis, the fact is that current commercial reality has forced the Portuguese courts to produce several decisions related to retention of title clauses in recent years, developing the legal regime and adapting it to different situations. Most decisions are related to the need for interpretations of Article 409 of the Civil Code in the light of commercial practice.

Presently, one situation that requires further discussion and attention from the Portuguese courts is the possibility for a financial institution to retain title over a vehicle, the acquisition of which was financed by the bank, but which was not sold by that financial institution.

1.3 Foreign and international law

In the event that a retention of title clause is governed by another law other than Portuguese law, it is necessary to bear in mind that the previously stated principles depend on the application of Portuguese law. If the parties have previously chosen the application of another law to apply to their agreement or the retention of title clause, rather than Portuguese law, then those provisions must be interpreted in accordance with the chosen law.

If the parties do not choose a specific law to be applicable to a bilateral contractual obligation, the Civil Code (Article 42) provides that the applicable law is that of the domicile or common residence of the parties.

If the parties do not share the same domicile or common residence, EC Regulation 593/2008 of June 17 2008 on the law applicable to contractual obligations (Rome I) provides that the applicable law is that of the seller's habitual residence.

1.4 Retention of title in insolvency

If the debtor (the buyer) is subject to insolvency proceedings in Portugal, the principles outlined above will also be applicable, although with some additional features. One of the most important of these concerns the period of time given to the receiver to decide whether to perform the sale and purchase agreement or to refuse its performance.

In the event that the receiver refuses the performance of the sale and purchase agreement, the Insolvency Code also provides special rules for the calculation of compensation to be paid to the seller, as a result of the breach of contract.

When the receiver refuses the performance of the sale and purchase agreement neither one of the parties can ask for the reimbursement of what has been given during the agreement, so that the seller will not have to reimburse the amounts already received. Furthermore, the seller may demand from the buyer payment of the difference between the amount of the instalments received, as at the date of the insolvency, and the value of the asset as at the date of the refusal to perform the contract, as a priority over the insolvency.

Moreover, due to the breach of contract, the seller will be entitled to compensation for the damages suffered as a result of the breach, from which will have to be deducted the amount to which he is entitled under the previous paragraph.

If the receiver does not make a decision regarding the performance of the sale and purchase agreement, then the seller may fix a reasonable time limit for such decision to be made. If the receiver does not reply within the time limit given, it will be considered that he has refused to perform the agreement. If the creditors' meeting, which decides the future of the insolvent buyer, has not yet been held then the time limit set by the seller may not end before five days after the day on which the creditors' meeting takes place.

This means that the seller cannot himself rescind the agreement before the receiver has made a decision regarding the future of the agreement.

It is also important to note that under Article 104(4) of the Insolvency Code, when the buyer is declared insolvent, the retention of title clause must fulfil two conditions in order to be enforceable against the bankrupt estate: first, the buyer must have the possession of the asset, and secondly the retention of title clause must have been agreed in writing before the delivery of the asset to the buyer.

However, if the buyer is subject to insolvency proceedings in a foreign jurisdiction and the assets sold subject to a retention of title clause are physically located in that foreign jurisdiction, the applicable law will be the one of the jurisdiction where the assets are located.

Under Article 280(2) of the Insolvency Code, if the seller is subject to insolvency proceedings in Portugal, the validity of a sale and purchase agreement with a retention of title clause will not be affected. In fact, a buyer to whom the asset has already been delivered may claim full performance of the agreement, as long as it pays the amounts still owed.

If the seller is subject to insolvency proceedings in a foreign jurisdiction and the assets sold subject to a retention of title clause are physically located in that foreign jurisdiction, the applicable law will be the one of the jurisdiction where the assets are located.

However, taking into consideration the statutory basis under Article 280 of the Insolvency Code, there is no reason for the retention of title clause to be affected if the buyer intends to perform the sale and purchase agreement and the asset is located in Portugal.

2. Retention of title

2.1 Validity and formal requirements

Under Article 409 of the Civil Code, there is no legal general requirement for retention of title to be agreed upon in writing in order to be valid, but it must respect the form of the overall contract or agreement being entered into.

For example, under Portuguese law a real estate purchase must be entered into through a public deed in order to be valid; therefore, in such a case if the parties want to include a retention of title clause in their agreement they must respect that form, namely to agree upon the retention of title in the public deed.

Therefore, when the retention of title is related to real estate or movable assets subject to registration (vehicles, boats and aeroplanes) the clause must be part of the registered agreement in order to be enforceable against any third party.

Furthermore and as previously mentioned, in the cases when the buyer is subject to insolvency proceedings, retention of title over an asset needs to be put in writing before delivery of that asset, in order to be enforceable against the bankrupt estate.

Under Portuguese law, there are no formal requirements as regards the wording of a retention of title clause. However, although it is not mandatory to observe any specific wording in such a clause, the intention to retain the ownership of the asset until either full payment or the occurrence of some other specified event must be clear and objective.

Retention of title can only result from agreement between the purchaser and seller of an asset, and cannot arise from the operation of law in Portugal.

However, although that is the current position, the sale of cork by the Portuguese state was regulated by a specific decree-law in 1980 (Decree-law 99/80, revoked one year later), which stipulated that the cork had to be sold with a retention of title clause until the buyer paid the price and collected the cork.

Under Portuguese law it is possible to agree on retention of title in general terms and conditions, as long as the intention to retain the property until a specified event occurs is clear and objective, and the agreement does not violate any mandatory law.

The validity of retention of title does not depend on the delivery of the assets directly to the purchaser. Therefore, the assets may be delivered to a third party, for example a warehouse belonging to someone else other than the purchaser. Delivery of the goods is only relevant in cases where it is necessary to determine who bears the risk of their loss.

2.2 Scope of retention of title

(a) Sale of goods delivered under retention of title

In the event of a validly agreed retention of title clause, the purchaser is not entitled to sell and transfer the goods to a third party before he has paid the purchase price to the seller. If the purchaser sells the goods subject to a retention of title, the sale (if none of the parties is a trader or merchant) will be null and void, because the asset belongs to a third party, namely the initial seller (Articles 892, 939 and 956 of the Civil Code).

When the sale of the goods under retention of title is made by a party whose ordinary business is that of a trader or merchant in that type of goods (and it may be either the initial seller or the initial buyer), the subsequent buyer's position is safeguarded as long as he acted in good faith, because if the original seller asks for the return of the goods he will have to pay to the subsequent buyer the price the latter paid for the goods (Article 1301 of the Civil Code).

Under the Civil Code, if the parties agree on a retention of title, the property of the goods will only be transferred when payment of the full price (or another event stipulated by the parties) takes place. Until the purchase price is paid in full to the seller, the seller is still the owner of the goods. The only exception to this rule is where the sale is a 'sale of future goods'. The purchaser may agree with a third party on a sale of future goods, through which the purchaser is required to take the necessary steps for the third party to acquire ownership of the goods. This situation is provided for in Article 880 of the Civil Code. The validity of such an agreement depends on a covenant between the purchaser and the third party, under which the third party must be informed that the agreed sale is a sale of future goods.

The purchaser is also entitled to negotiate an assignment of his contractual position, through which he negotiates, with a third party, the substitution of his position in the agreement for the sale of goods. In this case, the third party occupies the purchaser's position in the sale and purchase agreement, and takes over the obligation to pay the full purchase price to acquire the ownership of the goods. However, such an agreement is subject to a valid consent from the seller.

According to some Portuguese authors, it is also possible to agree that the purchaser is entitled to sell the goods before having paid the purchase price to the seller. Such an agreement depends on a complex contractual structure, through which the seller provides the purchaser with an authorisation to sell and simultaneously the purchaser assigns to the seller the future credit resulting from that sale (the price to be paid for the goods by the third party), along with an authorisation to collect the purchase price directly from the third party.

(b) Combining/mixing/mingling goods delivered under retention of title

When goods that are subject to a retention of title are combined, mixed or mingled with other goods in such a way that it is impossible to distinguish between them (for instance when oil is mixed with oil, or tyres with other tyres), the retention of title lapses as the goods lose their individuality. The consequences are the same whether the goods were delivered or not by a third party other than the seller, and whether the goods were already paid for or not. It is not possible to agree on a retention of title over non-specified goods.

This being so, it is not possible validly to agree that the seller will retain his rights over the delivered goods in such a scenario, since it is no longer possible to identify which ones were the goods delivered by the seller.

A classic discussion in Portuguese case law concerns whether a retention of title is still valid and effective when a lift sold subject to retention of title is installed in a building. In this case, court decisions have been unanimous in finding that after the installation of the lift in the building, the lift becomes part of it and therefore the retention of title becomes ineffective; in other words it lapses.

This conclusion arises from a specific rule of the Civil Code according to which goods that are materially and permanently connected to a building are treated as if they were a part of the building. Therefore, the result will differ in cases of the combination of movable goods (for example, where tyres are attached to a car), because there is no similar rule for movable property. In the example of tyres being attached to a car, the seller (and owner) would be allowed to demand their separation from the car, taking into consideration that the retention of title is enforceable even against any third parties.

The Civil Code also provides for the situation where something that belongs to a person gets mixed with something that does not belong to this person, and where such a situation is caused either by an act done in good faith, or by an act done in bad faith.

When someone acting in good faith mixes his goods with someone else's goods, in a way that the separation is not possible or prejudicial for one of the owners, the goods resulting from the mix belong to the owner of the one with higher value, as long as he compensates the other owner, or gives him goods of equivalent value. If both the original goods have an equal value and the owners do not agree on who should be owner of the resultant goods, bidding will take place and the goods will be attributed to the higher bidder, with compensation for the other owner.

When someone acting in bad faith mixes his own property with goods that do not belong to him, then, if it is possible, the goods will be returned to the owner, together with due compensation. If it is not possible to return the goods, because they cannot be separated, the party responsible must compensate the owner for the value of his goods. The owner may also opt to retain all the goods and pay the party responsible for mixing them a price calculated according to the rules of unjust enrichment.

These solutions apply if the goods subject to retention of title are mixed with other goods of the same type and it is not possible to separate them once they are mixed together; that is to say where the retention of title becomes ineffective.

(c) *Processing of goods delivered under retention of title*

In the event that goods delivered under retention of title are meant to be processed and actually are processed, the retention of title does not lapse if the newly processed product's value does not exceed the value of the goods before the processing. In such a case, the seller and original owner would have to compensate the person responsible for the processing, according to Article 1336 of the Civil Code.

If the processing is carried out by a party acting in bad faith then, after being processed, the new goods become the property of the seller and original owner, in their current state, with due compensation from the person responsible, and the seller has no obligation to compensate the party responsible unless the added value resulting from the processing is more than one third of the value of the goods before processing. If the added value is in fact higher than this figure, the owner must pay the party responsible the amount by which it surpasses one third of the goods' original value, according to Article 1337 of the Civil Code.

According to some Portuguese authors, the parties may also agree that, in the event of processing, the retention of title does not lapse. Again, such an agreement would depend on a complex contractual structure through which the seller provides the purchaser with an authorisation to process and sell the goods and simultaneously the purchaser assigns to the seller the future credit resulting from such sale (the price to be paid for the processed goods by the third party), along with an authorisation to collect the purchase price directly from the third party.

(d) *Extension of retention of title*

In Portugal, retention of title does not have to relate exclusively to the payment of the purchase price for the goods delivered, as it is possible for the parties to stipulate a retention of title that is dependent on other events.

As the Portuguese rule accepts a retention of title based on other events, in principle it is possible that retention of title may be extended to cover other claims, such as other debts owed to the seller, as long as the arrangement does not violate the prohibition on unreasonableness and is not contrary to public policy.

3.3 Legal effect of retention of title

(a) Effect towards third parties

In the case of movable assets not subject to registration, the effect of a retention of title clause towards third parties is automatic. However, if the assets concerned are immovable assets or movable assets subject to registration (vehicles, aeroplanes and ships) only a retention of title clause registered in the public register is enforceable against third parties.

In the case of immovable assets and movable assets subject to registration, provided the retention of title clause is duly registered, a subsequent buyer cannot be considered to be acting in good faith since there is a public registry in which he may obtain all the information about the true owner of the assets.

The most complicated situation concerns movable assets not subject to registration, as the subsequent buyer does not have the means to know if the goods belong to the seller.

In cases where the original seller or buyer in a sale and purchase agreement with a retention of title clause is a trader or merchant dealing in the type of assets concerned, the position of a subsequent buyer in good faith is always safeguarded, because if the original seller wants to demand the return of the asset, he will have to pay to the subsequent buyer the price he paid to the seller (the initial buyer).

Therefore, when this happens, the most common situation is for the initial seller to try to collect the amount still owed on the goods from the initial buyer. In such a situation, the holder of the retention of title has relatively little protection.

(b) Effect in case of seizure of goods delivered under retention of title

Seizure by a third party (a creditor of the seller or of the purchaser) of goods subject to a retention of title clause is normally only temporary, because the parties who agreed to the retention of title may always react to that seizure and request the return of the goods.

Since the property in such goods is not definitively transferred until the respective agreement is performed in full, or until there is a termination of the agreement by the default of one of the parties, the goods cannot be seized by a third party without notice to the party who is in debt (whether the seller or the purchaser), who may then enforce the retention of title.

Where goods are seized by creditors of the buyer, the seller may react by opposing that seizure. In fact creditors of the buyer can only claim against the expectation of acquisition of the goods by the buyer. This means that goods sold under a retention of title clause cannot be seized.

On the other hand, if creditors of the seller seize the goods, the buyer, who owns the expectation of acquisition of the goods as well as the right to use and enjoy the goods, can also react to that seizure by opposing it. In any event, whether or not opposition to the seizure is filed, when the buyer pays the outstanding purchase price, the seizure lapses.

(c) *Effect in case of a security right established over goods delivered under retention of title*

Under Portuguese law, a retention of title clause prevails over any possessory or non-possessory rights. If the goods being used as security are subject to registration, and the retention of title clause is duly registered at the competent registry, the clause is enforceable against third parties.

This means that a seller with a retention of title clause cannot see its position usurped by a possessory or a non-possessory security right.

(d) *Effect in case of insolvency*

If the purchaser in an agreement that includes a retention of title clause is subject to insolvency proceedings in Portugal, the liquidator has the power to demand the delivery of the assets burdened by the retention of title and include those assets in the bankruptcy estate as long as the buyer has already fulfilled its obligations under the sale and purchase agreement.

However, if the agreement has not been completely fulfilled by both parties, the liquidator has the choice to perform the sale and purchase agreement subject to the retention of title (and consequently, on fulfilment of the agreement, acquiring ownership of the asset for the insolvency estate), or to refuse to perform the agreement. If the liquidator chooses the latter option, the seller may request the separation of the asset from the insolvency estate and its return to his possession and has the possibility of demanding damages from the bankruptcy estate to compensate for the non-performance of the agreement.

(e) *Effect in case of partial payment of purchase price*

In the situation where the purchaser has obtained goods from the seller and then defaults having only paid part of the purchase price, the seller may repossess the goods and is entitled to compensation calculated on the difference between the value of the goods as new and the value of the goods when repossessed.

If the part of the price paid is greater than the amount of compensation to which the seller is entitled, then the seller will have to refund the purchaser the amount by which both the repossessed goods and the instalments paid exceed the value of the goods as new.

3. Enforcement of retention of title

In the event of default, if the purchaser refuses to return the goods subject to retention of title to the seller, it is not possible to authorise any commercial collection or enforcement agency to act on behalf of the seller. Nor is it possible for the seller to enforce the retention of title himself, unless the purchaser voluntarily agrees to collection of the goods.

If the purchaser does not agree to repossession, the seller has to apply to the courts to obtain a decision ordering the delivery of the asset to him. If the buyer does not deliver the asset voluntarily, the seller will then have to enforce the court decision through an enforcement procedure, whereby the enforcement is conducted by a bailiff appointed by the court.

3.1 Procedure

To repossess the goods in the event of default, first of all the seller has to terminate the contract, which can be done through a simple declaration to the other party, preferably by a registered letter with acknowledgement of receipt, in order for the seller to have proof of delivery to the purchaser of the notification.

After termination, if the seller does not return the goods voluntarily and the goods are kept on the premises of the purchaser, the only solution is to file proceedings for the recovery of possession and recognition of ownership of the goods.

In order to file such proceedings, the following documents would have to be presented with the initial petition: the contract with the retention of title clause, proof of ownership by the seller, all documentation related to the breach of contract or the absence of the event stipulated in the retention of title clause, and proof of termination of the contract.

If the goods are on the premises of a third party (such as a warehouse owned by a third party), in the event either the purchaser or the third party gives permission, the seller can recover them immediately. If neither the purchaser nor the third party give permission to enter the premises, once again, the only solution will be to file proceedings for the recovery of possession and recognition of ownership of the goods.

Once a judgment has been given recognising the seller's ownership of the asset and ordering its return, it becomes enforceable. If the purchaser does not comply with this decision voluntarily, the seller has to initiate an enforcement procedure, asking for the repossession of the goods, which will be carried out by a bailiff in coordination with the court.

It is possible for the seller and the purchaser to agree (either expressly or through the applicable terms and conditions) that the purchaser will grant the seller access to the purchaser's premises to collect the goods in the event of default by the purchaser.

However, despite any such agreement, if the purchaser (when in default) denies the seller access to his premises and to the goods, the seller cannot enforce access without a court judgment ordering repossession and recognising ownership of the asset to the seller.

Additionally, it should be noted that the above will not change in the event of the purchaser being subject to bankruptcy, as a court judgment will always be necessary to enforce the retention of title.

3.2 Identification of goods

If the asset subject to retention of title is immovable property (buildings) or movable property subject to registration (such as a car), then under Article 409(2) of the Civil Code, the retention of title must be registered in order to be valid against third parties. This means that when the asset concerned is immovable property or movable property subject to registration, the asset can be correctly identified by its individual number in the register or its licence plate.

When the retention of title concerns movable property not subject to registration, the only requirement is that the goods are sufficiently accurately described for it to be possible to identify them.

There are no other formal requirements for identifying goods subject to retention of title.

3.3 Other formal requirements

Other than the termination of the contract and the subsequent filing of proceedings for the recovery of possession and recognition of ownership of the goods, outlined above, which are required in order to obtain a judgment that is then enforceable by the bailiff, there are no additional formal requirements for the repossession of the goods.

3.4 Insolvency

If the buyer is subject to insolvency proceedings, the procedure outlined above does not change, as the only feature affecting retention of title in insolvency proceedings that does not exist in the enforcement of the retention of title outside insolvency, is the period of time given to the receiver to decide whether to perform or to refuse performance of the sale and purchase agreement.

It should also be noted that the fact that the buyer is insolvent does not preclude the possibility of the receiver, acting on behalf of the insolvent buyer, voluntarily returning the goods sold under a retention of title clause.

Russia

Evgenia Evdokimova
Sergey Strembelev
Egorov Puginsky Afanasiev & Partners

1. General remarks about retention of title

1.1 Transfer of ownership

Generally under Russian law ownership title passes to the purchaser upon receiving physical possession of the asset (Articles 223(1) and 224(1) of the Civil Code of the Russian Federation). However, if there is no obligation of the seller to deliver the asset to the premises of the purchaser the latter becomes the owner at the moment the asset is handed to the carrier. Furthermore, transfer of physical possession may be substituted by transfer of a bill of lading.

If at the moment of concluding the contract the asset is already in possession of the purchaser, title transfers to the purchaser at the moment the parties conclude the contract.

Nevertheless, the parties may freely agree on a time for the transfer of title that differs from the rules outlined here (for instance, they may agree that the title transfers upon conclusion of the purchase agreement, or upon receipt of full payment by the seller).

1.2 Retention of title

Article 491 of the Civil Code expressly provides for the possibility of the seller retaining ownership until a certain condition stipulated by the contract is fulfilled (in particular, until the purchase price has been paid by the purchaser). Therefore, retention of title is valid if the parties agreed upon it in the contract.

Moreover, Article 491 states that where the seller retains title the purchaser may not dispose of the asset unless the parties have agreed otherwise, or the possibility of disposal derives from the properties of the asset (such as where the asset is a perishable item), or there is a specific law that allows the purchaser to dispose of the asset. In the event that the purchaser does not pay for the asset according to the contract (or some other condition for the transfer of title does not occur) the seller may request the return of its asset unless the parties agreed otherwise. These are the only specific provisions regarding retention of title in the Civil Code.

1.3 Foreign and international law

Under Article 1206 of the Civil Code transfer of title is generally governed by the law of the country in which the asset is located at the moment of transfer. However, the parties may agree that transfer of ownership shall be governed by the law that governs the contract itself. Therefore, the timing of the transfer of title will depend upon the location of the asset and/or the agreement of the parties.

Under Article 1205(1) of the Civil Code, other aspects of title to a movable asset (in particular its content, effect as regards third parties, and so on) is governed by the law of the country where the asset is located. Therefore, the legal position of a seller who retains ownership to an asset located in Russia will be governed by Russian law.

1.4 Retention of title in insolvency

All the principles outlined above are also applicable in a situation where either the seller or the buyer is subject to Russian insolvency proceedings. There are no special provisions regarding retention of title in insolvency proceedings in Russia.

If the buyer is subject to insolvency proceedings outside Russia then its legal position will depend upon the conflict of laws rules applicable in the country of the insolvency proceedings and the treatment of retention of title in that country.

2. Retention of title

2.1 Validity and formal requirements

In Russia a retention of title clause is deemed to be a part of the purchase agreement. Consequently, requirements regarding the form of the purchase agreement apply to the retention of title clause as well.

Based on the general Civil Code requirements regarding the form of agreements, retention of title has to be agreed in writing if:

- one of the parties to the agreement containing the retention of title clause is a legal entity; or
- the purchase price is higher than Rb10,000.

The requirement that an agreement be in a written form is deemed to be complied with when there is a document in text form signed by the parties.

Where, in violation of these rules a retention of title clause is not in writing, then it is still valid, but the parties may not use witness testimony in a court to prove that retention of title exists. They may, however, use any other evidence (such as any correspondence between the parties).

There are no other formal requirements for effectiveness or perfection of retention of title or as regards the wording of the retention of title clause in the contract.

Where retention of title is agreed by the parties it has effect both between them and as regards third parties (with some exceptions that will be described below). Moreover, a retention of title clause may be also included in general terms and conditions, the application of which is agreed upon by the parties. But it is not possible to have retention of title in place by operation of law.

For retention of title to be valid, it is not essential that the goods concerned be delivered directly to the purchaser; the goods may be delivered to a third party (such as a warehouse belonging to someone other than the purchaser) as well.

2.2 Scope of retention of title

(a) *Sale of goods delivered under retention of title*

In the event of a validly agreed retention of title, the purchaser is not entitled to sell and transfer the goods to a third party before he has paid the purchase price to the seller, unless (Article 491 of the Civil Code):

- the seller and the purchaser have agreed that the purchaser may sell and transfer the goods;
- a specific law entitles the purchaser to sell and transfer the goods; or
- the properties of the goods imply that the purchaser may sell and transfer the goods.

If the purchaser is entitled to sell the goods before having paid the purchase price to the seller, the parties are not allowed to agree (with effect as regards third parties) that the purchase price to be paid by the third party to the purchaser is as of law to be transferred to the seller. At the same time, in this situation, the seller retains the right to receive the purchase price from the initial purchaser. However, the purchaser may agree with the third party acquiring the goods that the latter will pay the price directly to the seller and the latter is entitled to require direct payment.

Where the purchaser is not entitled to sell the goods held under a retention of title clause, but nevertheless sells them, the rules regarding acquisition of ownership in good faith are applicable. If the third party acquiring the goods acts in good faith (in other words, it did not know and was not in a position where it should have known that the goods were subject to a retention of title) it becomes the owner of the goods and initial seller loses its title. In such a case the latter may claim damages from its purchaser.

(b) *Combining/mixing/mingling goods delivered under retention of title*

There are no express provisions in Russian law that regulate what happens with the ownership in a case of combining, mixing or mingling of goods (such as oil being put into a tank which already contains other oil belonging to the purchaser). Two main positions may be highlighted:

- the seller's title is terminated and the purchaser becomes the owner of all the combined, mixed or mingled goods (in such a case the seller may claim damages for unjust enrichment if the purchaser does not pay for the goods); or
- the seller and the purchaser become joint owners of the combined, mixed or mingled goods.

Therefore, in order to preserve the sole title of the seller with regard to assets supplied under retention of title it is necessary to individualise those assets, such as by storing them in a separate tank with proper labelling. Where the goods are combined, mixed or mingled with other goods sold by the same seller under a retention of title clause before the transfer of title to the earlier goods to the buyer, the seller remains the owner of all the goods. However, when the condition for the transfer of title under which the goods were sold is fulfilled with regard to the part of the goods, the seller and the buyer most likely become joint owners of all the entire mass of goods. Contractual provisions according to which the seller retains its title in spite of combining, mixing or mingling with the goods of another owner are null and void.

Let us take another example: car tyres sold under a retention of title clause are attached to a car. According to the prevailing conservative opinion, in such a case, as the goods sold under the retention of title clause become part of an indivisible item, the seller loses its ownership of them and may claim only damages if the purchaser does not pay for the goods. However, according to Article 133(3) of the Civil Code (which has been recently amended) the court may order the separation of certain parts from an indivisible item where that is possible. This provision may be considered as an argument in favour of a position that the seller does not lose its ownership of the tyres. However, the provision is new for Russian legislation, rather imprecise, and needs to be further clarified by the courts.

(c) *Processing of goods delivered under retention of title*

Under Article 220(1) of the Civil Code the ownership of a newly processed product belongs to the owner of the material, unless:

- the value of work on processing the material is substantially higher than material itself;
- the party that processed the material acted in good faith; and
- the party that processed the material acted for itself.

However, a purchaser who has processed the goods cannot be deemed to have been acting in good faith, as it in any case should know that it is processing material which belongs to the seller. Therefore, in the case of processing by the purchaser of goods sold under a retention of title clause, the seller acquires ownership of the newly processed product.

(d) *Extension of retention of title*

In general, Russian law does not prohibit extending retention of title to claims other than claims arising out of the purchase agreement itself. Under Article 491 of the Civil Code the parties may agree upon retention of title until the purchaser has paid the price in full or until any other condition is fulfilled. At the same time, court practice on this issue has not yet been established, and there is a substantial risk that a Russian court will not give legal effect to such an extension.

2.3 Legal effect of retention of title

(a) *Effect towards third parties*

Retention of title has automatic effect towards third parties, except a subsequent buyer or secured creditor acting in good faith (or where the purchaser is entitled to dispose of the assets by the purchase agreement). Other creditors of the purchaser cannot seize and sell the goods, because the purchaser does not own them.

Retention of title is also effective against the tax authorities with regard to any corporate profits tax to be paid by the purchaser: the purchaser, not being the owner, does not have to pay corporate profits tax in respect of the goods.

However, there are no practical and effective measures which can make retention of title enforceable against a subsequent buyer or secured creditor acting in good faith, except notifying potential subsequent buyers and secured creditors that the purchaser does not own the goods.

(b) Effect in case of seizure of goods delivered under retention of title

The seller's ownership title with regard to assets sold under a retention of title clause is an ordinary ownership title. Therefore, a bailiff acting with a court's permission may seize an asset sold under a retention of title clause in order to satisfy creditors of the seller. The excess proceeds in such a case shall be returned to the seller.

In contrast, a bailiff may not seize the asset in order to satisfy creditors of the purchaser. However, if in the latter case the asset is seized, the seller may ask the court to release the property.

(c) Effect in case of a security right established over goods delivered under retention of title

Retention of title does not have effect against the holder of a security right acting in good faith (in other words, where the security holder did not know and was not in a position where it should have known that the security provider did not own the asset) regardless of whether the secured creditor has a possessory or non-possessory security interest. However, in our opinion, such rules do not apply in case of a floating charge, as in this case only assets that are owned by the purchaser are deemed to be encumbered. Nevertheless, the Civil Code provision regarding good-faith acquisition of a security interest (Article 335(2)) was adopted only in 2014 and, therefore, it is not clear yet how it will be interpreted by the courts.

(d) Effect in case of insolvency

In the event that the debtor (the initial buyer) is subject to insolvency proceedings in Russia, in spite of the fact that the goods are in the debtor's possession, they shall not be included into the bankruptcy assets.

The liquidator or trustee in bankruptcy has no specific rights over such assets that the debtor itself did not have.

(e) Effect in case of partial payment of purchase price

The situation where the buyer has paid for goods acquired under retention of title only in part is not directly regulated by Russian law. Generally the rights of the seller in such a situation will depend upon the provisions of the contract. Where, under the contract, ownership of all the assets passes to the buyer only after the full payment of the purchase price and the price has not been paid in full, the seller may request the return of all the assets provided it returns the part of the price received less any damages.

3. Enforcement of retention of title

Under Article 491 of the Civil Code, in the event that the purchaser does not pay for the asset according to the contract (or any other condition for the transfer of title does not occur) the seller may request the return of its asset unless the parties have agreed otherwise. However, Russian legislation does not contain specific provisions regarding enforcement of a retention of title clause. The seller may repossess the assets itself only if the buyer does not object. Otherwise it is necessary to sue the buyer (with an action in contract) and then enforce the judgment with help of a bailiff. It is not possible to use a commercial collection or enforcement agency to enforce the retention of title should the purchaser object to repossession.

If the assets are on the premises of a third party and that third party objects to repossession by the seller then it is necessary to sue the third party.

There are no specific requirements as to identifying to the court and the bailiff the assets sold under retention of title, but, of course, the seller has to prove to the court that the assets are subject to retention of title. As mentioned above, if the retention of title clause was not executed in writing in a case where it should have been, the seller may not refer to witness testimony in order to prove the retention of title clause.

All the principles regarding enforcement outlined here are also applicable if there are bankruptcy proceedings against the purchaser. However, in such a case the bankruptcy trustee acts on behalf of the debtor and may, therefore, return the assets to the seller. But if bankruptcy trustee objects, the seller has to sue the debtor as the party to the retention of title clause and not the trustee.

South Africa

Hans Klopper
Independent Advisory (Pty) Limited

1. General remarks about retention of title

1.1 Transfer of ownership

The most comprehensive private right that a person can have in terms of South African law with regard to property is ownership.[1] We draw a distinction between original and derivative acquisition of ownership. Where ownership is acquired independently and not derived from the ownership of a predecessor it is viewed as original. Derivative acquisition of ownership occurs if ownership is derived from or depends on the ownership of the previous owner. In the case of movable assets, the most important element in the acquisition of ownership is delivery of the specific asset. In order to transfer ownership two main requirements must be satisfied.

First, there must be an agreement between the parties to transfer ownership and then there must be a form of conveyance of ownership. Consequently, failure to deliver the movable asset means that ownership does not transfer.

Furthermore, where movable assets are sold ownership does not pass, notwithstanding delivery, unless the purchase price is paid or security or credit for its payment is given. A sale of movables is usually a cash sale unless circumstances clearly indicate the existence of a credit sale such as, for example, a failure by the seller to reclaim the object, non-payment of the purchase price, failure to demand cash immediately on delivery, or where a cheque is post-dated. If a credit sale is intended or it is apparent that credit was extended to the buyer, ownership passes on delivery.

To summarise, therefore, ownership of movables is transferred by delivery and payment in a normal cash transaction and upon delivery in a credit transaction.

Unlike in some other jurisdictions, ownership in the case of movables therefore does not pass on the mere agreement between the parties.

In South African law, the agreement, such as for example a contract of purchase and sale giving rise to transfer, being the reason for the transfer, is strictly separate from the juristic act of transfer.

The underlying agreement relates only to personal rights and obligations and an additional legal transaction relates to the transfer of ownership. Consequently, there are two separate legal acts, each with its own requirements.

1 CG van der Merwe (ed) "Ownership" in Francois Du Bois (general ed) *Wille's Principles of South African Law*, ninth edition.

The question that arises is whether in terms of South African law the parties are entitled to agree on a time of transfer of ownership other than as is provided above.

Even though the agreement which gives rise to the personal obligation to transfer and the actual agreement to transfer ownership of the movable property[2] may take place simultaneously it is possible to distinguish between them.

In principle, two requirements[3] must be satisfied for the transfer of ownership of movables: the parties must, in the first place, intend to transfer ownership, and, secondly, they must give effect to that conveyance by delivery of the asset.

The real agreement is distinguishable from the contractual agreement that gives rise to the obligation to transfer.[4] Two requirements for a valid to real agreement are as follows. The property must be capable of being held in private ownership, and the transferor must be capable of transferring ownership.

The parties to an agreement for the sale and transfer of movables may therefore enter into an agreement to sell movables, but may also agree to a delay in payment under which the seller agrees to provide credit for the payment of the purchase price and agrees that the transfer of ownership may follow later or at a specific date.

Insolvent persons cannot transfer ownership. Minors, insane persons and fiduciaries can transfer ownership only with the assistance of their guardians, curators and beneficiaries respectively.

The transferee must be capable of acquiring ownership. Infants and insane persons are legally incapable of having the intention to possess, and therefore need the assistance of their legal representatives to comply with the necessary registration formalities.

At the moment of transfer, the transferor must have the intention to transfer ownership and the transferee must have the intention to accept ownership. Where a contractual party takes the law into his or her own hands and takes possession of the object in the absence of an intention to transfer ownership on the part of the transferor, the usurper does not become owner, but a possessor in bad faith, open to a 'mandament of spolie' (a type of order for restitution) or other remedy.

1.2 Retention of title

It will now be examined as to whether South African law allows for the seller to retain the ownership of an asset until a certain condition (like the full purchase price having been paid by the purchaser) has been met.

Agreements under the terms of which movables are sold are often entered into on the basis that ownership of the asset is retained or reserved until the full purchase price has been paid by the purchaser. Such agreements are referred to as instalment sale agreements or suspensive sale agreements.

An instalment sale agreement[5] is defined in the National Credit Act[6] as the sale of property in terms of which:

---

2 Van der Merwe, *Sakereg*, p300.
3 *Wille's Principles of South African Law*, ninth edition, p520.
4 *Wille's Principles of South African Law*, ninth edition, p521.
5 Mars, *The Law of Insolvency in South Africa*, ninth edition, p230.
6 Act 34 of 2005.

- all or part of the price is deferred and is to be paid by periodic payments;
- possession and use of the property is transferred to the purchaser; and
- ownership of the property either:
  - passes to the purchaser only when the agreement is fully complied with; or
  - passes to the purchaser immediately but subject to the right of the credit provider to repossess the property if the purchaser fails to comply with all his financial obligations under the agreement.[7]

In the latter instance, ownership passes to the purchaser upon delivery, but the seller may reclaim the good sold if the purchaser is in default.

The case law on this issue was initially decided under the repealed provisions of the Credit Agreements Act[8] (repealed with effect from June 2006 by the National Credit Act), and it was not clear whether an instalment agreement that provides for deferred payment of the price in one lump sum was covered by the definition. This uncertainty continued under the provisions of the National Credit Act.

Although some authors and commentators argued that the purchase price should be payable in at least two instalments before the transaction could be an instalment sale transaction in terms of the repealed provisions,[9] transactions in terms of which the purchase price was payable in a single lump sum in the future have been held to be included in the definition of an 'instalment sale transaction'.[10]

Statutory recognition is therefore afforded to agreements complying with the terms of the National Credit Act relating to instalment sale agreements.

However, any agreement under which a seller reserves ownership of an asset is permissible, and the strength of the rights of the seller depends on the level of detail provided for in terms of the agreement and the nature of the asset.

In instances where a valid agreement has been entered into but where the assets subject to the reservation of ownership are not identifiable, for example by way of serial numbers or specific markings, the seller will have difficulty in enforcing his or her rights irrespective of what the agreement provides.

Where the nature of the asset is such that it loses its identity once it is transferred from the seller to the purchaser, a reservation of ownership clause, no matter what the agreement provides, would serve no purpose.

A proper record-keeping system that provides for which assets have been paid for and which not is also essential for the purposes of the seller enforcing his or her

7 Provided for in Section 1 of the National Credit Act. This section also contains as a fourth requirement that interest, fees or other charges are payable to the credit provider in respect of the agreement or the amount that has been deferred, but this requirement is not referred to in Section 84(1) of the Insolvency Act.

8 Act 75 of 1980.

9 Otto, (1985) TSAR 11 at 19-20; van Rooyen, (1985) TSAR 22 at 228. Forder (1986) 103 SALJ 83 at 84 n10 disagreed and submitted that a transaction providing for a lump sum payment in the future was included in the definition. The definition in Section 1 of the Credit Agreements Act referred to payment of money "in whole or in part in instalments".

10 *Sandoz Products (Pty) Ltd v van Zyl* 1996 (3) SA 726 (C); referred to with approval in *Ukaubona 2000 Electrical CC v City Power Johannesburg (Pty) Ltd* 2004 (6) SA 323 (SCA).

rights in terms of reservation of ownership clauses contained in the sales agreements.

As will become apparent from the remainder of this chapter, the concept of reservation of ownership is fully recognised in South African case law.[11]

1.3 Foreign and international law

A further question is what the position would be if the agreement containing the reservation of ownership clause is governed by another law other than South African law.

It would in fact be irrelevant as to whether the agreement containing the reservation of title or ownership is governed by the laws of a jurisdiction other than South Africa or not.

The same challenges outlined above that prevail under South African law would apply to contracts entered into in any other jurisdiction.

Likewise, whether any seller can enforce his or her rights under an agreement that contains reservation of ownership provisions, irrespective as to whether the agreement or the reservation of ownership clause is governed by another law or not, will depend on the same ability clearly to identify the assets subject to the reservation of ownership as set out above.

Further issues, such as whether the agreement was properly entered into by parties duly authorised by the respective entities entering into the agreement, as well as whether the seller would be able to identify the assets not as yet paid for, as opposed to those that have been paid for, will also determine the validity and practical enforceability of the reservation of ownership clause, as is the case in South African law.

In terms of South African private international law, the agreement containing the reservation of ownership clause determines the legal position. Where the agreement clearly provides that title or ownership will be reserved until the goods have been paid for the reservation of ownership will be respected. The seller, as the creditor having reserved ownership or title, will rank as a secured creditor in terms of Section 84(1) of the Insolvency Act irrespective of the jurisdiction under whose laws the agreement was entered into in the event that the debtor becomes subject to insolvency proceedings.

A creditor or seller having validly reserved ownership will therefore be able to enforce any agreement containing a reservation of ownership clause, irrespective of whether the parties are South Africans or foreigners.

The enforceability of the agreement will furthermore depend on the nature of the assets and the ability of the seller to prove that certain specific assets, capable of identification by way of serial numbers or unique markings, have not as yet been paid for under the terms of the agreement containing the reservation of ownership provisions.

Surrounding circumstances, such as whether the seller truly intended for a reservation of ownership to be established will often be determined by what is contained in the seller's own financial statements.

It has been argued that in circumstances where the seller in fact identifies the purchaser as a debtor in its financial statements under accounts receivable and thereby acknowledges that credit has been granted, the purported reservation of title could be viewed as a sham or a simulated transaction.

1.4 Retention of title in insolvency

South African law regulating insolvency is substantially provided for in the Insolvency Act.[12] The common law of insolvency as contained in Romano-Dutch sources also applies in so far as it is not inconsistent with any legislation.

The effect of insolvency is, however, not unified in a single piece of legislation. The Insolvency Act essentially governs the relationship between creditors and debtors where natural persons, trusts or partnerships become subject to insolvency proceedings.[13] Insofar as legislation governing corporate entities such as companies and close corporations does not provide otherwise, the Insolvency Act also applies to such entities, as further explained below.

South African corporate entities are companies and close corporations. Companies are incorporated in accordance with the company laws of South Africa, and close corporations in accordance with the Close Corporations Act.[14] The Companies Act 2008[15] came into effect on May 1 2011 and replaced the previous Companies Act 1973,[16] which was repealed. The Companies Act 2008, however, provides, as a transitional arrangement, that Chapter 14 of the Companies Act 1973 continues to apply with respect to the liquidation (or winding-up) of companies[17] and close corporations.

In accordance with the Companies Act 2008, the Close Corporations Act was amended and close corporations that existed as at May 1 2011 were permitted to remain in existence but no new close corporations could be formed thereafter.

Therefore, upon the liquidation of a company, the provisions of Chapter 14 of the Companies Act 1973 apply. Even so, where Chapter 14 of the 1973 Companies Act does not deal with any specific set of circumstances, the provisions of the Insolvency Act apply subject to any necessary alterations.

Furthermore, where the Close Corporations Act also does not provide for any specific set of circumstances, the provisions of Chapter 14 of the Companies Act 1973 may apply; and where Chapter 14 of the 1973 Companies Act does not apply, the provisions of the Insolvency Act will apply.

The Insolvency Act applies to a situation where a purchaser under an instalment sale agreement, as described above, becomes subject to insolvency proceedings; in other words where there is an instalment agreement under the terms of which possession and use of the asset was transferred to the purchaser subject to reservation of ownership, and where the purchaser becomes subject to insolvency proceedings.[18]

Section 84(1) of the Insolvency Act will apply to any transaction that meets these

---

11 *Pellow NO v Club Refrigeration CC* 2006 (1) SA 230 (SCA).
12 Act 24 of 1936.
13 Referred to as 'sequestration' in the Insolvency Act.
14 Act 69 of 1984, which was repealed with effect from May 1 2011.
15 Act 71 of 2008.
16 Act 61 of 1973.
17 Schedule 5, Paragraph 9 of the Companies Act 2008.
18 Section 84(1) of the Insolvency Act.

requirements even if the National Credit Act itself does not apply to the transaction.[19]

Special rules apply[20] where the party subject to insolvency proceedings bought goods under an agreement falling within paragraphs (a), (b) and (c)(i) of the definition of 'instalment agreement' in Section 1 of the National Credit Act which provides as follows:

"instalment agreement" means a sale of movable property in terms of which–

(a) all or part of the price is deferred and is to be paid by periodic payments;

(b) possession and use of the property is transferred to the consumer;

(c) ownership of the property either–

(i) passes to the consumer only when the agreement is fully complied with; or

(ii) passes to the consumer immediately subject to a right of the credit provider to re-possess the property if the consumer fails to satisfy all of the consumer's financial obligations under the agreement; and

(d) interest, fees or other charges are payable to the credit provider in respect of the agreement, or the amount that has been deferred.

The most interesting aspect of Section 84 of the Insolvency Act, however, is that the seller, despite reserving ownership, loses ownership upon the commencement of insolvency proceedings in respect of the buyer. Ownership in fact passes to the buyer's estate upon the commencement of the insolvency proceedings. This follows from the wording of Section 84(1), which provides that, in circumstances where the buyer becomes subject to insolvency proceedings, the seller automatically acquires a security (in the form of a 'hypothec') over the goods, whereby the balance outstanding under the agreement is secured. Since it is not possible in law, for any party, to have a hypothec over his own property, ownership in the goods passes from the seller to the buyer's insolvent estate to be administered by the trustee or liquidator.[21]

If the seller validly reserved ownership of the assets under the agreement and is able to identify the assets and, as a result, can prove which assets have been paid for and which not, then the seller will be afforded the protection provided for in the Insolvency Act.

Where a buyer entered into an agreement under which the seller has validly reserved ownership of assets which are in the possession of the buyer, and that buyer is subject to insolvency proceedings that are outside South African jurisdiction but recognised in South Africa, the seller will be afforded the protection of the South African laws on insolvency in that it will be recognised as a secured creditor. The proceeds to be derived from the assets subject to the reservation of ownership provisions in the agreement will be the subject matter of the seller's security.

Where a seller who reserved the ownership of assets sold to a buyer under a valid agreement is subject to insolvency proceedings, the trustee or liquidator of the insolvent seller will have the right to elect whether to abide by the agreement or not.

---

19 *Potgieter v Daewoo Heavy Industries (Pty) Ltd* 2003 (3) SA 98 (SCA) at 100-102.

20 Sharrock, van der Linde, Smith, *Hockley's Insolvency Law*, ninth edition, p95.

21 *Williams Hunt Vereeniging Ltd v Slomowitz* 1960 (1) SA 499 (T) at 501; see also *van der Burgh v van Dyk* 1993 (3) SA 312 (O); *Standard Bank of South Africa Ltd v Townsend* 1997 (3) SA 41 (W) at 50.

In other words, the seller's liquidator or trustee cannot force the buyer to do anything other than what is provided for under the terms of the instalment sale agreement or agreement containing a valid reservation of ownership clause.

In practice, the buyer will either arrange to obtain finance to settle the claim with the seller's liquidator or trustee by paying in full for the assets that are subject to the reservation of ownership provisions, or the buyer may continue or perform the terms of the original agreement and continue paying the trustee or the liquidator in accordance with the agreement.

Where a seller is subject to insolvency proceedings outside the jurisdiction of South Africa which have been recognised in South Africa, the duly appointed South African liquidator or trustee will have to make an election whether to abide by the agreement or not as described above.

2. Retention of title or ownership

2.1 Validity and formal requirements

Under South African law an agreement may be made orally or in writing except where agreements are required by statute to be in writing.[22] It is, however, necessary that each party knows what the other's intention was.

In circumstances where a seller alleges that ownership of assets sold under the agreement has validly been reserved, it is possible for such an agreement to be oral but the onus will be on the seller, where a reservation of ownership is alleged, to prove the existence of the reservation of ownership provisions.

It is therefore unlikely that an agreement containing reservation of ownership provisions will be verbal, and it is fairly safe to say that such an agreement would have to be in writing and entered into by parties duly authorised by the buyer and a seller respectively, especially in cases where the buyer and seller are corporate entities.

It is often alleged by sellers that invoices relating to assets sold to the buyer contained provisions under the terms of which the seller reserved ownership of the assets until such time as they had been fully paid for by the buyer. There can have been no agreement on such terms in circumstances where the invoice and delivery note were, for instance, handed to a storeman in the employ of the buyer who signed the delivery note and thereby acknowledged the terms contained on the invoice.

In such a case, and in order for a valid reservation of ownership agreement to come into existence, a duly authorised representative of the buyer must acknowledge receipt and sign the delivery note.

The mere existence of a valid written agreement is sufficient in order for a valid reservation of ownership clause to become enforceable. There is no public registration or authentication required of either party in order for the exact time and date of the reservation of ownership to be determined.

---

22 *Goldblatt v Fremantle* 1920 AD 123: "Subject to certain exceptions, mostly statutory, any contract may be verbally entered into; writing is not essential to contractual validity. And if during negotiations mention is made of a written document, the Court will assume that the object was merely to afford facility of proof of the verbal agreement, unless it is clear that the parties intended that the writing should embody the contract."

For the sake of absolute clarity, however, it is necessary that the terms of the written agreement be absolutely clear and unambiguous insofar as the provision for the reservation of ownership is concerned. The agreement should also be absolutely clear as to the identity of the assets subject to the reservation of ownership. In circumstances where the nature of the assets is such that it will be difficult to identify the assets paid for and those unpaid for, reservation of ownership will, most probably, be unenforceable.

The parties to an agreement containing a reservation of ownership clause are not subject to any formal requirements as to the wording of the agreement. As long as the agreement is clear and the assets subject to the reservation of ownership are clearly identifiable, an agreement of this nature will be enforceable.

There are no known circumstances under which a reservation of ownership provision will automatically be in place by operation of law in South Africa.

It is perfectly in order to agree upon a reservation of ownership of assets in general terms and conditions, but the enforceability thereof, as noted above, will depend on the ability of the seller to identify the assets which have not yet been paid for as opposed to those assets that have already been paid for.

As was stated above, delivery of the goods from the seller to the purchaser will ordinarily be the manner in which ownership is intended to be transferred between the parties.

However, by virtue of the English law concept of attornment[23] having been adopted into South African law,[24] it is possible for a seller to deliver goods, being sold to the purchaser, to a third party under a tripartite agreement between all the parties involved.

Consequently, where delivery of goods under an agreement containing a reservation of ownership clause is made to a third party on behalf of the purchaser, and by agreement with and at the instance of the purchaser, the validity of the reservation of ownership clause is not affected by the fact that the goods or assets were not delivered directly to the purchaser.

2.2 Scope of retention of title

(a) Sale of goods delivered under retention of title

It is common in the ordinary course of business for sellers to sell to third parties assets which have been acquired from a supplier subject to a reservation of ownership clause. The obligation to pay the debt owing to the supplier will remain that of the seller in such circumstances. However, in the event of the seller failing to pay his supplier and if the asset is capable of identification in the hands of the purchaser, the owner or supplier who reserved ownership under the agreement with the seller may, by *rei vindicatio*[25] (an action for repossession), reclaim its asset, even from a purchaser who had been acting in good faith. The purchaser's only recourse is to pursue the party with whom he contracted for damages.

---

23 'Attornment' is an agreement by the tenant of land to hold the land for the transferee of the owner.

24 *Page Automation (Pty) Ltd v Profusa Properties CC t/a Homenet OR Tambo* 2013 (4) SA 37 (GSJ).

25 Derived from the maxim *ubi rem meam invenio ibi eam vindicio* which means "where are my thing is found, there vindicate it".

As ownership only passes where the owner delivers it to another party, with the intention of transferring ownership, and the other party takes the asset with the intention of acquiring ownership,[26] the seller in the circumstances described above will immediately have to settle the debt owed to his supplier, failing which the new purchaser will not acquire ownership.

(b) Combining/mixing/mingling goods delivered under retention of title

Where goods or things are joined or combined to each other or mixed with each other the manner in which such goods are joined or mixed will be important.[27] This will govern how the specific scenario will be treated in law. If, for instance, goods subject to a reservation of ownership clause are joined or mixed with other goods in such a manner that the goods subject to reservation of ownership lose their identity by becoming part of the other goods, the owner of those other goods acquires ownership of the joint goods.

In determining whether, by operation of law, new rights have been created, the separability of the mixture and whether a new thing has been created will be decisive. It would, in the case of mixing, be important as to whether the mixed things retained their identity or not.

It would appear that where goods are combined, in the absence of a subsequent agreement with the seller of the goods to the contrary, the rules of confusion (mingling), specification (manufacture) and commixtion (mixing) will apply and that a reservation of ownership clause will not be capable of being enforced in respect of individual goods that have lost their identity.

It has however been held in a case where bulbs subject to retention of ownership were planted in the ground as bulbs and were intended to be removed from the ground as bulbs (in contrast to seeds which root and bear crops), that such bulbs remained movables and did not become property of owner of land.[28]

In circumstances where assets subject to a reservation of ownership provision are delivered into a warehouse containing similar goods belonging to another supplier the problem of identification, alluded to above, arises. In such circumstances one might very well be able to argue that the reservation of ownership clause is invalid and incapable of implementation by virtue of the vagueness thereof and the inability of the seller to identify the assets subject to that clause.

The general principle in cases of accession or the combination of goods, in South African law, is that the owner of the principal thing becomes the owner of the accessory.

What is important, therefore, is to determine the principal object. When considering an asset or thing formed by the combination of components, a decision must be reached as to which component gives it its identity. In other words, which component is the principal and which components are accessories.

---

26 *Trust Bank van Afrika Bpk v Western Bank Bpk en Andere NNO* 1978 (4) SA 281 (A).
27 *Wille's Principles of South African Law*, ninth edition, p493.
28 *Gore NO v Parvatas (Pty) Ltd* 1992 (3) SA 363 (C).

One example that arose in case law[29] concerned a motor vehicle consisting of a rear portion, including the interior, which could positively be identified as having been stolen. The engine and inner front portion could positively be identified as belonging to the applicant in the court proceedings. There were some other components of the vehicle, some of which were probably from the same stolen vehicle as the rear portion of the car and others which had been obtained from a different source. In this case it was held that the identity of the vehicle was conferred by the stolen rear portion, and that the components belonging to the applicant and others had accordingly been appended to the stolen vehicle. Based on this principle, a seller of accessories subject to reservation of ownership will have difficulty enforcing its ownership where those accessories have been added to a principal asset belonging to a third party.

However, in a further case,[30] relating to the determination of ownership and the principle of accession, the plaintiff in the matter sold six tyres to X. X also bought a truck from another party. Both cheques written by X, being the purchase price for the six tyres and the purchase price in respect of the truck, were dishonoured by X's bank. As a consequence the owner of the truck repossessed the truck, with the six new tyres fitted to it, from X.

The plaintiff in the matter immediately endeavoured to obtain possession of the tyres from the owner of the truck. The owner of the truck initially agreed to purchase the tyres from the plaintiff but then failed to pay and upon being pursued for payment contended that the transaction between the plaintiff and X was a credit transaction and contended that X became the owner of the tyres upon delivery thereof. The owner of the truck furthermore contended that the tyres became his property by accession. The court held that, although the two objects formed an economic unit in terms of the economic unit test, the nature and manner of fitting was such that accession had not taken place. In terms of the principle arising from this case, the owner of clearly identifiable assets such as the tyres in question will be able to enforce its reservation of ownership.

In a further case relating to ownership and accession[31] pumps, pipes and ancillary equipment were installed in a pumphouse as part of the irrigation system for a farm. All these items were purchased individually by the installer from a wholesaler under an agreement according to which the wholesaler reserved ownership of the items pending payment of the full purchase price. The court had to decide whether the purchaser (the landowner) became the owner of the equipment through accession before the purchase price was paid in full.

The court held that the modern approach is that the subjective intention with which the attachment of the goods was made takes precedence over the nature of the articles and the degree and manner of annexation. The court had to decide whether the relevant intention was that of the seller of the goods or that of the purchaser. The court found that the test set out in the leading case, that the intention of the owner

29 *Khan v Minister of Law and Order* 1991 (3) SA 439 (T).
30 *J L Cohen Motors SWA (Pty) Ltd v Alberts* 1985 (2) SA 427 (SWA).
31 *Konstanz Properties (Pty) Ltd v Wm Spilhaus en Kie (WP) Bpk* 1996 (3) SA 273 (A).

of goods is decisive, was still applicable and that the wholesaler never intended to part with ownership before every item had been paid for in full, and that accession therefore did not take place.

In summary therefore, assets subject to a reservation of ownership and capable of identification may always be recovered with a court order in favour of the owner. However, the owner may not simply pursue the matter himself and apply self-help.

A reservation of ownership provision will lapse in circumstances where the description of the assets is so vague that a court order to restore possession to the owner is incapable of being implemented.

(c) *Processing of goods delivered under retention of title*

The general principle of specification (manufacture) has been stated as follows[32] in case law:

> *Specification occurs when a person creates a nova species (a new product) out of materials which belong wholly or partly to another without there being any legal relationship between the parties. The maker only becomes the owner of the new product if it cannot be reduced to its original form.*[33]

Where a manufacturer, in good faith, uses goods or materials subject to a reservation of ownership clause in favour of the seller and processes them in order to create a new product, and the goods or materials subject to the reservation of ownership cease to exist and are no longer recoverable, the reservation of ownership clause would be unenforceable.

The owner who has been deprived of the goods or materials can possibly be compensated in full on the basis of unjust enrichment, and if the final product is reducible to its former state, the owner of the goods or materials remains their owner.[34]

It has subsequently also been stated that examples where the new product would not be reducible to its original form include olive oil produced from olives, wine from grapes, bread from wheat or corn, margarine from lard, clothes fashioned from wool, planks from trees, a statue sculpted from marble or wood, and a patchwork quilt fashioned from pieces of cloth.[35]

It was also determined in a criminal matter[36] that before the maker of an article can be said to have acquired ownership of it by specification, it is essential that a new thing or product should have been manufactured, that the material used has ceased to exist as such and cannot be restored to its original form, and that, as a general rule, the maker thought in good faith that the materials belonged to him.

In that case, R had been charged with the theft of a table from his employer, and had been convicted of the theft of the table-top only. In an appeal it appeared that R had made the table on the complainant's property. The legs of the table were his own. The remaining material from which it had been made, though the property of

---

32 *Frank & Hirsch (Pty) Ltd v A Roopanand Brothers (Pty) Ltd* 1993 (4) SA 279 (A).
33 CG van der Merwe in *Wille's Principles of South African Law*, eighth edition.
34 *Wille's Principles of South African Law*, ninth edition, p506.
35 *Wille's Principles of South African Law*, ninth edition, p505.
36 *S v Riekert* 1977 (3) SA 181 (T).

the complainant, was in the nature of scrap. R was leaving the employ of the complainant and had previously told the complainant that he would return to take his things. This he had done quite openly, stating that he was going to take "his table". It was held that as R had regarded himself as entitled to take the table, the state had not discharged the onus on it of establishing that he had the intention to steal.

(d) *Extension of the retention of title*

A reservation of ownership clause can only relate to the purchase price of the goods delivered as provided for in the agreement, and the operation of such a clause cannot be extended to other claims.

The seller may, however, enter into an arrangement with the purchaser under which additional security is provided to the seller, which may be in the form of an assignment of other book debts (in South Africa known as a cession of book debts), but only by agreement with the purchaser.

2.3 Legal effect of retention of title

(a) *Effect towards third parties*

As already mentioned above, where goods subject to a reservation of ownership clause are delivered to a third party and are capable of being identified, then if they are paid for the seller will at all times be entitled to reclaim possession of his assets even if they are in the hands of third parties.

An owner of an asset must institute legal action and must allege and prove in the pleadings that he is entitled to ownership of the asset (whether movable or immovable property)[37] and that the third party was in possession of the asset when the legal action was instituted.[38]

The plaintiff (the owner) in such an action has the following relief available: either the return of the property or, in lieu thereof, payment of its value calculated on the day of the trial. The owner may also claim delivery of all fruits of the use of his property (or payment of the equivalent value) that have accrued to the party in possession in the event that this party was acting in bad faith. If the possessor acted in good faith, the owner may claim delivery of the fruits of use (or payment of their value), only to the extent that they have accrued to the possessor since the commencement of legal proceedings.[39]

In order to succeed with this action the owner must prove his ownership of the property and the property must furthermore clearly be identifiable and not have been destroyed or consumed.

The third party's only recourse is to pursue the other party in the transaction by which it acquired the asset.

---

37 *Goudini Chrome (Pty) Ltd v MCC Contracts (Pty) Ltd* 1993 (1) SA 77 (A); *Concor Construction (Cape) (Pty) Ltd v Santambank Ltd* 1993 (2) SA 930 (A).

38 *Graham v Ridley* 1931 TPD 476; *Chetty v Naidoo* 1974 (3) SA (A).

39 *Mlombo v Fourie* 1964 93) SA 350 (T).

(b) Effect in case of seizure of goods delivered under retention of title

Assets subject to a valid reservation of ownership clause may not be seized by a third party and in such circumstances the owner would be entitled to institute proceedings to prevent the third party who had seized the assets from selling them.

When a creditor has seized or attached goods subject to a reservation of ownership clause, other than an instalment sale agreement within the meaning of the National Credit Act, and has done so by way of a court order after having obtained judgment, the owner of the goods may again institute proceedings to retain possession of his assets.

However, it should be noted that a lessor of immovable property obtains an immediate security right (a hypothec) in respect of any rent due to him,[40] which attaches to all goods brought on to the leased premises whether they belong to the lessee, a sub-tenant or a third person.

It was decided in one case[41] as follows:

A landlord's claim on a hypothec in respect of goods belonging to a third party is dependent, inter alia, *on the landlord being unaware of the fact that the goods do not belong to the tenant. Although the landlord usually acquires knowledge of the true position as a result of having received notice to that effect from the owner, a lessor may become aware of the true position by a method other than the receipt of a communication from the owner.*

Legislation provides that the lessor's hypothec excludes[42] movables subject to an instalment agreement[43] as defined in the Credit Agreements Act (which has been repealed and replaced by the National Credit Act).

(c) Effect in case of a security right established over goods delivered under retention of title

The rights of an owner with a valid reservation of ownership clause in an agreement are absolute, and assets subject to such reservation of ownership clauses cannot validly be offered to third parties as security for any indebtedness.

(d) Effect in the case of insolvency

The effect of the buyer becoming subject to insolvency proceedings, under Section 84(1) of the Insolvency Act, is that the seller loses his right of ownership in the property and simultaneously becomes a creditor with a security right over the property that was subject to retention of ownership.

The trustee or liquidator of the buyer's estate must, if required by the seller, deliver the goods to him, and thereafter the seller is deemed to hold them as security for his claim, and has the right of a secured creditor to realise his security as provided for in the Insolvency Act.

The trustee or liquidator of any buyer who is subject to insolvency proceedings

---

40 *Wille's Principles of South African Law,* ninth edition; *Webster v Ellison* 1911 AD 27; *Bloemfontein Municipality v Jacksons Ltd* 1929 AD 266.

41 *Paradise Lost Properties (Pty) Ltd v Standard Bank of South Africa Ltd* 1998 (4) SA 1030 (N).

42 Security by Means of Movable Property Act 57 of 1993, Section 2(1)(b).

43 *Janse van Rensburg v Mahu Exhaust CC* 2014 (3) SA 431 (NCK).

in South Africa will therefore be duty bound to treat the seller as a secured creditor in respect of the proceeds of any assets that had been acquired under a validly entered into agreement falling within the scope of Section 84(1) of the Insolvency Act.

In such a case, the seller, as a secured creditor, may give notice to the liquidator or trustee to the effect that he intends to realise or sell his security, this being the assets or goods subject to the reservation of ownership clause, and the seller will thereafter be duty bound in law to pay the net proceeds from the sale of the assets or goods (after deduction of costs such as an agent's commission)[44] over to the liquidator or trustee.

The liquidator or trustee must then place the proceeds in a liquidation and distribution account, further deduct the costs of liquidation such as liquidators' and other fees, and then award the net amount to the secured creditor.

(e) Effect in case of partial payment of purchase price

Where a valid reservation of ownership clause exists and only a portion of the purchase consideration has been paid to the seller by the buyer, the assets would, in the event of the insolvency of the buyer, still fall to be dealt with by the liquidator or trustee in insolvency subject to the secured claim of the seller for the unpaid balance.

The assets would be realised as encumbered assets and dealt with as such in the liquidation and distribution account operated by the trustee or liquidator.

Following payment in full of the seller's claim from the net proceeds of the sale of the assets, after all the costs have been deducted,[45] any remaining balance will be transferred to the free residue to be distributed to the general body of unsecured creditors together with the net proceeds of all other unencumbered assets.

3. Enforcement of retention of title

There is no specific body or organisation in South African law that is authorised or empowered to be involved in the process of repossessing assets subject to reservation of ownership clauses.

The only party who may attach and sell goods or assets subject to a reservation of ownership is the sheriff of the court, who may only do so in execution proceedings upon having been directed to do so by a court order.

In order to invoke the provisions of a reservation of ownership clause the owner may only, irrespective of where the goods are situated, approach the court for an order under which it may take possession of the goods in question.

If the seller was granted specific permission by the purchaser, in their agreement, to collect the goods in the event of a default by the purchaser, and the purchaser does default then, in the absence of a voluntary surrender of the goods by the purchaser, the seller will still only be entitled to obtain possession of the goods pursuant to a court order.

---

44 Insolvency Act, Section 89.
45 Insolvency Act, Section 89.

Where the purchaser is subject to insolvency proceedings, possession of the goods in question will pass to the trustee or liquidator appointed in the proceedings who must deal with the assets in terms of the provisions of the Insolvency Act, as described above. By virtue of the seller's security rights, provided for under the Insolvency Act, the seller will become a secured creditor over the proceeds of the goods in question upon realisation thereof by the trustee or liquidator.

There are no formal requirements for the identification of the assets sold under retention of title other than that the application to the court must be for an order to repossess specific assets, which must be clearly identified.

South Korea

Sang Jin Ahn
Hai Jin Park
Steve Sunghwa Song
Kim & Chang

1. General remarks about retention of title

1.1 Transfer of ownership

The Civil Code adopts a formalistic approach regarding transfer not only of title to real property, but also of title to movable assets. To acquire[1] title to real property from the original title holder, there must be public disclosure by way of court registration and legal action. Meanwhile, to obtain title to a movable asset, there must be public disclosure by way of physical delivery of the asset, as well as a legal action. In cases where the law requires the transfer of title to a movable asset to be publicly disclosed by way of registration with the court or other type of registration, then any change to title will be effective only if such court registration or other applicable registration is complete. For example, change of title to motor vehicles or aircraft must be registered with the applicable registrar, while change of title to vessels requires court registration.

It is widely accepted that the 'legal action' required means an act concerning a proprietary right, or to be more precise, an agreement to obtain or transfer title. Actions related to claims (for example, executing a sales and purchase agreement) and acts concerning proprietary rights are generally conducted simultaneously, but there are cases in which the two acts are clearly separated such as in the case of the sale of a third party's asset.

In addition, 'delivery' refers to the transfer of possession, that is to say the transfer of actual control, and this includes not only actual delivery, but also 'summary delivery', 'agreement as to possession', and 'delivery based on a claim of return' as provided in the Civil Code.[2]

1 Proprietary rights can be changed through either transfer by legal action or transfer without legal action (ie, by operation of law).

2 According to the Supreme Court of Korea, 'actual delivery' refers to the surrender of possession (where the transferor effectively has control) from the transferor to the transferee while maintaining the identity of the content. 'Summary delivery' refers to cases in which the transferee already has possession of an object and the transferor and transferee agree to deliver the title. In this case, the transferee's possession changes from possession for the benefit of the transferor to possession for its own benefit. 'Agreement as to possession' refers to cases in which the transferor agrees to possess the object for the benefit of the transferee. In this case, the transferor would grant the transferee summary possession, and the transferor would continue the possession of the object as an intermediary possessor. 'Delivery based on a claim of return' refers to cases in which the transferor indirectly possesses an object by utilising an intermediary third party. In this case, the delivery of title is realised when the transferor conveys its claim for the return of possession to the transferee.

1.2 Retention of title

Title transfer of movable assets, unlike the title transfer of real property, may be subject to certain conditions or time limitations (which is often the case). For example, it is possible to execute a sale subject to retention of title, which means that full payment of the sale price is the condition precedent to the conveyance of title.

There are many cases in which the title to an asset remains with the seller until full payment is made, at which time the title will be automatically transferred to the buyer. This type of transaction is called transaction subject to retention of title. In practice, continuous and flexible transactions subject to retention of title are frequently carried out.

A transaction subject to retention of title can be considered as the most secure and convenient type of collateral for the seller because the seller reserves the title based on a special agreement, and may enforce the collateral by retaking possession of the subject item of the transaction in the event that the buyer does not pay in full or the buyer's credit rating deteriorates. Thus, a transaction subject to retention of title supplements a weakness of the current Civil Code's collateral system, which does not accept the pledging of property without a transfer of possession. Transactions subject to retention of title have been recognised by the Korean Supreme Court.

Usually, transactions subject to retention of title are used in respect of movable assets. The conditions for the transfer of title in real property require registration with the court, and because the Registration of Real Estate Act only allows conditions subsequent to be registered, conditions precedent such as sales subject to retention of title cannot be registered. The Supreme Court has confirmed that real estate cannot be subject to retention of title. Similarly, although automobiles, heavy machinery or construction machinery are movable assets, because transfer of their title also requires registration, such assets cannot be subject to retention of title.

1.3 Foreign and international law

If the contract for a sale subject to retention of title is validly governed by laws other than Korean law, the interpretation of claims between the parties shall be determined according to the governing law chosen by the parties to the contract in accordance with the Korean Private International Law Act.

However, unlike contracts regarding claims, the Private International Law Act provides that proprietary rights in respect of movable assets or real property (including any change of such rights) are governed by the laws of the jurisdiction in which the subject item is located at the time the action causing the change, or the completion of the change, of proprietary rights occurs. Therefore, proprietary rights such as the acquisition or loss of a possessory right shall be determined by the laws of the jurisdiction in which the movable asset is located at the time of such acquisition or loss.

---

3 A rehabilitation proceeding under Korean law is similar to a Chapter 11 reorganisation proceeding under US bankruptcy law. Its purpose is to rehabilitate a debtor facing financial difficulty by adjusting the debtor's debt under a rehabilitation plan approved by the creditors and the court. It is different from a bankruptcy proceeding the purpose of which is to liquidate the debtor's assets and distribute the proceeds amongst creditors in a fair manner.

1.4 Retention of title in insolvency

In the event of a buyer being subject to rehabilitation proceedings,[3] in practice, reservation of ownership has been considered as a rehabilitation security interest because it was characterised as collateral to secure unpaid claims. Therefore, the seller was not able to exercise the right of repossession for a subject item that was a movable asset. The Supreme Court recently reaffirmed that the seller holds a rehabilitation security interest and that the seller cannot exercise the right of repossession.

In the event of a buyer being subject to bankruptcy proceedings, there is no clear court precedent on whether the seller is a person having the right to foreclose outside bankruptcy, or the right to repossess. While it would be more consistent with the position under rehabilitation proceedings to consider the seller as a person having the right to foreclose outside bankruptcy, unlike a secured rehabilitation claim which can only be paid under a rehabilitation proceeding, exercising the right to foreclose outside bankruptcy need not be the result of bankruptcy proceedings, so regardless of whether the seller (as the buyer's creditor) has a right to foreclose outside bankruptcy or a right to repossess, as a practical matter, the seller will be able to dispose of the subject item and recover its outstanding claim against the buyer.

If a foreign insolvency proceeding has been commenced against a buyer, the foreign insolvency proceeding must be approved by the Korean court for that court to apply the law of the jurisdiction where the insolvency proceedings are taking place. Assuming the Korean court approves the foreign insolvency proceeding, the two prevailing approaches are:

- including the movable assets subject to retention of title in the insolvency estate, but applying the laws of the jurisdiction in which the collateral is located; and
- including the movable assets subject to retention of title in the insolvency estate, but applying the laws in which the collateral is located or the law of the jurisdiction where the insolvency proceedings are taking place, whichever is more favourable to the seller.

At this time, there are no court precedents to clarify this matter.

Meanwhile, if an insolvency proceeding has been commenced against a seller either in Korea or a foreign jurisdiction (whether or not the foreign proceeding is approved in Korea), that proceeding would not become a basis on which to nullify the transaction or to prohibit the buyer from obtaining ownership, thereby protecting the buyer's expectation.

2. Retention of title

2.1 Validity and formal requirements

Because retention of title constitutes a special agreement in connection with a sales agreement, there must be an agreement on retention of title between the buyer and seller.

Retention of title does not require any special method or formality. However, the

Instalment Transactions Act[4] requires the retention of title to be in writing. The purpose of the Instalment Transactions Act is the protection of consumers, and does not apply to instalment contracts regarding commercial activities where the buyer is a merchant. In other words, as long as the buyer is not entering into an instalment contract in connection with his commercial activity the Instalment Transactions Act will apply, so the seller in an instalment contract must:

- notify the terms of the contract to the buyer so that the buyer understands the terms of the contract;
- put the retention of title provision in writing; and
- promptly issue a copy of the contract to the buyer.

If the agreement between the buyer and seller is not in writing, the contract shall still be valid, but the seller must convey the subject item to the buyer without any right of repossession.

Even when retention of title is required to be in writing, there are no requirements for notarisation or registration, and there is no specific wording for a retention of title provision under Korean law.

The special agreement for retention of title can be made at the time of entering into the sales agreement (which is an action regarding claims), or it can be made at the time that an act regarding proprietary rights is made. Thus, if the seller was silent on retention of title throughout the negotiation but unilaterally notifies a retention of title to the buyer at the time of delivering the subject item, the buyer must consent to this notification for the retention of title to be valid. If the buyer does not agree, there is no agreement on proprietary rights covering the transfer of title, so the buyer cannot obtain title. Once a movable asset is conveyed to the buyer, the title to the asset is transferred to the buyer barring special circumstances, so there will be no valid retention of title agreement.

If the parties enter into a sales contract that has no express retention of title provision, the issue is whether the conveyance of the subject item signals the transfer of title to the buyer or whether retention of title can be implied. A seller in a commercial transaction generally includes a retention of title provision regarding the subject item until payment is made in full. However, in the absence of such a specific provision, the conveyance of the subject item shall be considered as the transfer of title. On the other hand, for instalment transactions that frequently include retention of title provisions, the Instalment Transactions Act requires the retention of title provision to be in writing and issued to the buyer. In addition, the Instalment Transactions Act requires any provision that is ambiguous on its face to be interpreted in a manner favourable to the buyer. Therefore, without a specific retention of title provision, it will be difficult for the seller to argue that there is an implied retention of title against the buyer. Rather, the title to the subject item shall have transferred to the buyer without any right of repossession.

Under the Regulation of Standard Contracts Act, a 'standard contract' is a form

4 The Instalment Transactions Act is only applicable when the seller is a merchant engaging in an instalment sale.

of contract unilaterally prepared by one party for its customers. In order to have an enforceable standard contract, the customer must agree to the terms and conditions provided therein. Only then will the terms and conditions become a part of the contract, a process which is referred to as 'incorporation of contract'. The Regulation of Standard Contracts Act requires the seller (the party that prepared the standard contract) to explain material provisions of the standard contract, in order to protect the customer's interests before the standard contract is incorporated. Therefore, a standard contract that includes a retention of title will become valid only if it is incorporated, which requires the seller expressly to provide for retention of title in the standard contract and explicitly to explain that provision to the buyer, and requires the buyer to agree to the standard contract.

2.2 Scope of retention of title

(a) Sale of goods delivered under retention of title

Because title is reserved to the seller until buyer pays the purchase price in full, the buyer cannot sell the subject item as a title holder. In principle, such a sale is invalid.

However, a third party who subsequently purchases the subject item from the buyer may obtain complete title to the subject item if it satisfies all conditions as a good-faith purchaser under the Civil Code. For example, a subsequent purchaser would not be able to obtain complete title if he obtains possession even if he was not aware that the subject item was subject to a retention of title if he acted negligently.

Meanwhile, for cases in which the buyer subsequently sells the subject item (which it purchased subject to retention of title) after the seller has granted the buyer in advance the right to sell the subject item, the seller can obtain an extended retention of title by obtaining rights to the proceeds resulting from the subsequent sale as security to compensate his loss of title to the subject item. Such an agreement to obtain an extended retention of title can be made at the time the initial retention of title is agreed.

(b) Combining/mixing/mingling/processing goods delivered under retention of title

There are situations in which an item sold under retention of title may be affixed to, or mixed or processed with other items. Articles 256 and 261 of the Civil Code address situations where such affixation, mixture or processing (collectively referred to as 'annexation') of real estate and movable assets results in an original acquisition of title. Such a possibility is provided for cases where it is socially unacceptable or too costly to separate the goods that have been annexed, and it is more efficient to have one party have full ownership over the entire combination of goods rather than enforcing a restoration that would be socially or economically inefficient.

'Affixation' refers to combining several goods that originally belonged to separate persons into one item, thereby making the combined item appear to be a single item under accepted social conventions and making it impossible or extremely difficult to separate so that the combined item belongs to one person. When an item is affixed to real property, the owner of the real property acquires the title to the item affixed (Civil Code, Article 256). When a movable asset is affixed to real property, the

Supreme Court has held that even if the price of the movable asset is greater than that of the real property, the owner of the real property has title over the affixed movable asset as well. In cases of affixation involving only movable assets, the owner of the main asset acquires the title to the combined asset. However, when it is difficult to distinguish the main asset from the subordinate asset, the owners of the original assets own the newly created asset jointly in proportion to the value of their respective original assets at the time of affixation.

'Mixture' refers to the mixing of the same type of solid or liquid, so that the original matter no longer becomes identifiable. Mixture is a type of affixation of movable assets, so the rules for affixation also apply to mixture (Civil Code, Article 258). Therefore, in principle, although the owner of the main movable asset acquires the title to the mixed item, in the event that it is impossible to distinguish the main asset from the subordinate asset, the owners of the original assets would own the newly created asset jointly in proportion to the value of their respective original assets at the time of mixture.

'Processing' refers to creating a new item by utilising another person's raw materials or by changing an item owned by another person. The new item must be created by combining the item with labour. In principle, the title to the processed item belongs to the owner of the raw material, but if the increase in value resulting from the processing is much larger than the value of the raw material, the item belongs to the processor (Civil Code, Article 259, Clause 2). The value of any raw material provided by the processor shall also be included in the increase of value resulting from the processing (Civil Code, Article 259, Clause 2).

If the seller loses his title through annexation, his retention of title will no longer be valid.

In this case, the one who has acquired the title to the goods through affixation, mixture, or processing will have been unjustly enriched, so the profit resulting from obtaining title must be returned. Article 261 of the Civil Code provides that a person suffering a loss due to annexation may request compensation under provisions regarding unjust enrichment, and that the requirements for restitution following unjust enrichment must be satisfied for the agreement on compensation to be recognised.

When goods sold subject to retention of title are processed by the buyer with the approval of the seller (usually where the approval is comprehensively granted in advance), in order to compensate the seller's loss of retention of title, the seller's right may extend to the processed goods by way of agreement on possession or assignment of receivables for the purpose of obtaining a security interest.

(c) *Extension of retention of title*

There are no court precedents or discussions in Korea regarding an extended form of retention of title in which the title to the subject item is transferred to the buyer only upon both paying the purchase price and discharging all other debts owed by the buyer to the seller or any other third party.

2.3 Legal effect of retention of title

(a) Effect towards third parties

Since the seller reserves title until the buyer makes full payment, the buyer cannot freely dispose of the subject item as its owner. However, as an exception, a third-party purchaser acting in good faith will be protected.

Meanwhile, the seller, as owner of the subject item, may subsequently transfer it to a third party prior to receiving full payment, and that third party may validly obtain title to the subject item. However, to sell the subject item when it is in the possession of the original buyer, the third-party purchaser must exercise its right to claim for its return. The rules concerning the transfer of receivables are applied by analogy, so if the original buyer pays the purchase price for the subject item in full to the seller, the buyer may argue that the conditions for acquiring title to the subject item imposed by not only the seller but also the third party have been fulfilled. On the other hand, if the seller sells the subject item by actually transferring it when it is not in the possession of the buyer, then while the third-party purchaser would validly acquire title, the buyer would also retain a contractual right to purchase it. Therefore, the seller would be liable for damages to the buyer for failure to perform its obligation under the Civil Code.

(b) Effect in case of seizure of goods delivered under retention of title

When a creditor of the buyer seizes the subject item, the seller may prevent its being foreclosed by filing a third-party action based on the retention of title (Civil Execution Act, Article 48). This also applies to cases where the creditor is the Republic of Korea (such as the National Tax Service).

If a creditor of the seller seizes the subject item, the buyer may not file a third-party complaint. However, foreclosure is only possible when the movable asset is in the hands of the debtor or when a third party who holds the asset does not object to its release (Civil Execution Act, Articles 189 and 191). Therefore, when an unsecured creditor tries to foreclose on a subject item based on the seller's retention of title, the buyer will not be subject to foreclosure unless the buyer voluntarily relinquishes the subject item.

(c) Effect in case of a security right established over goods delivered under retention of title

If the buyer provides the subject item to a creditor as a non-possessory security interest, then the subject item will be delivered by way of agreement as to possession, and the legal relationship in this agreement depends on the legal characteristics of the non-possessory security interest. If it is approached as a transfer of ownership in trust, the creditor cannot acquire title from the buyer as he does not hold title, so the only issue under that approach is the possibility of purchase in good faith. However, the Supreme Court rejected the argument that the security holder cannot become a purchaser in good faith by way of agreement as to possession.

If the creditor tries to acquire the subject item by means other than an agreement as to possession (such as transferring the claim for return of the subject item), the creditor may acquire title to the subject item as a purchaser in good faith. In that case, the seller can ask for the payment of the unpaid purchase price and default interest against the buyer. The seller may also terminate the sales contract and can claim return of the full monetary value of the subject item (given that the title to the actual subject item has already been transferred to the purchaser in good faith), as well as claim for monetary damages.

(d) *Effect in case of insolvency*

As mentioned above, when the buyer is subject to rehabilitation proceeding and the subject item is under the buyer's possession at the start of such proceedings, the seller would be treated as secured creditor of the rehabilitation and the receiver would be considered as the owner of the subject item. Although there is no clear precedent, the same principle will likely apply to bankruptcy procedures.

(e) *Effect in case of partial payment of purchase price*

Even in cases where the buyer has partially paid the purchase price, the validity of the retention of title would be the same as in cases where the price was not paid at all, provided the condition for the transfer of title was full payment of the purchase price.

3. Enforcement of retention of title

Retention of title is enforced by claiming return of the subject item under the reserved title after rescinding the relevant sales contract. Usually, the standard contract incorporated into the relevant sales contract provides acceleration and the right to rescind. However, even when the right of rescission is not provided for, the buyer would be in default due to acceleration unless the buyer is able immediately to pay the full purchase price, and the seller is allowed by statute to rescind the sales contract. Since the buyer has the right to possess the subject item, the claim for its return cannot in principle be made without first rescinding the sales contract. Meanwhile, the seller must return to the buyer any portion of the purchase price the buyer had already paid, less any damages.

Foreclosure on tangible movable assets is commenced by requesting foreclosure in writing from an executor[5] and providing an original document that has executory power such as a final and conclusive court judgment.

If the subject item that must be returned is in the debtor's possession, the executor may seize it from the debtor and transfer it to the creditor. The executor may take any necessary action, such as searching the debtor's home, warehouse and other places, or opening locked doors or equipment. If the debtor resists, the executor may seek police or military assistance.

In principle, when the subject item is in the possession of a third party other than the debtor, foreclosure is not allowed. However, in cases where the buyer has

---

5 An executor is a person who is attached to the district court and handles the execution of court orders, delivery of documents and other administrative matters under the law. An executor is appointed by the chief judge of the relevant district court from persons who have previously worked as public servants at a court for at least 10 years.

stored the subject item in a warehouse owned by a third party and has a claim for delivery of the subject item against the third party, the creditor may seize the debtor's claim, which is referred to as a seize and transfer order. When there is a seize and transfer order and the third party cooperates with the foreclosure, the foreclosure process is completed upon the transfer of the subject item to the creditor. However, if the third party does not cooperate, then the creditor must bring a lawsuit against the third party for the delivery of the subject item. Then the creditor can carry out foreclosure based on a court judgment in his favour.

If the location of the subject item is unclear, foreclosure will be impractical. Even if the debtor is aware of the location of the subject item, there is no method to force the debtor to disclose the location.

Additionally, self-help is prohibited even for the owner of the subject item. Thus, the owner may be subject to criminal sanctions for interference with the exercise of another party's rights if he removes a subject item that is in the possession of the buyer or a third party.

Sometimes the buyer and seller enter into an agreement that allows the seller to enter the buyer's premises to recover the subject item. When the purchase contract is rescinded because of the buyer's default, the buyer no longer has any right to retain possession of the subject item. Therefore, the seller may directly recover the subject item under such an agreement.

To make such an arrangement enforceable, the seller may consider filing for a preliminary injunction against the buyer to prevent him from interfering with the seller's right of entry. However, because there is no effective means to enforce an act of omission (such as not to interfere with entering the premises), such a preliminary injunction is unlikely to provide practical protection to the seller. However, if the parties can agree in advance to reconciliation before any court proceeding or to notarisation of the buyer's obligation to return the subject item, then the seller may be able to exercise immediate foreclosure as soon as the ground for rescission occurs.

Parties also frequently agree in advance to separate the subject item from other items or to affix a name tag that cannot be detached from the subject item in order specifically to designate the subject item. This type of agreement is intended to make direct recovery or foreclosure easier by identifying the subject item.

When the buyer enters into a rehabilitation proceeding or bankruptcy proceeding, the seller may retrieve the subject item as a person with a right of repossession, as long as the sales contract was lawfully rescinded.

Spain

Agustín Bou
Jausas Legal

1. General remarks about retention of title

1.1 Transfer of ownership

Transfer of ownership under Spanish law is based in the theory of title and manner, which means that validly to acquire the ownership of an asset, or other rights over an asset, requires:

- a contract or agreement (title); and
- the formal transfer of the asset (manner).

In an ordinary sale and purchase transaction, the exchange of the assets and the purchase price take place simultaneously.

The parties may agree on the time of transfer of ownership. It is possible to postpone (or make conditional) transfer of ownership until full payment of the purchase price, making both events happen at the same time.[1] This possibility is based on Article 1255 of the Civil Code, which, in line with the basic criterion of the parties' freedom of choice, establishes that:

The contracting parties may establish any covenants, clauses and conditions deemed convenient, provided that they are not contrary to the laws, to moral or to public policy.

1.2 Retention of title

Spanish law does not contain any specific provision governing the retention of ownership of an asset until a certain condition has been met, except from specific legislation dealing with the acquisition of non-consumable movable property, namely Law 28/1998 of July 13 1998.

However, retention of title has been unanimously accepted in jurisprudence and by scholars as a consequence of agreeing a condition precedent to the transfer of title to the relevant asset.

1.3 Foreign and international law

The principles outlined above may obviously be different in the event that foreign law is applicable instead of Spanish law.

When we speak about retention of title we are in the field of sales of assets and, therefore, of contractual obligations. Hence, where the Spanish courts have before

1 Resolution of the Supreme Court, dated June 10 1958.

them a matter related to retention of title, they apply EC Regulation 593/2008 of June 17 2008, on the law applicable to contractual obligations (Rome I) to determine the law applicable to the case.

The basic criterion of this European regulation is the parties' freedom of choice and, consequently, any retention of title would be governed, first, by the law the parties have freely chosen. Parties can choose the law of a non-member state under the regulation, and may even opt for a *dépeçage* whereby different issues within the case are governed by the laws of different states.

In the absence of a choice of law by the parties, the regulation establishes a list of rules depending on the nature of the contract. Contracts subject to particular rules are divided into four categories, one of which includes contracts for the sale of assets and the provision of services. In this area, and in the absence of a contrary choice by the parties, the regulation applies the law of the country where resides the party to the contract responsible for performing the obligation that is characteristic of the contract type, that is, the seller or the service provider.

The connecting criterion used by the regulation is the habitual residence of the seller of assets or the provider of services. It is assumed that this party is responsible for the performance that gives the contract its character, because the other party does the same in either type of contract (in that he pays a price).

Consequently, if the seller is habitually resident in Spain the contract would be subject to Spanish law. As has been stated above, in Spain there is no law exclusively governing retention of title, and therefore Law 28/1998 on deferred purchase of chattel property, the Civil Code and other trade regulations could all apply.

1.4 Retention of title in insolvency

In the event of the buyer's insolvency, those sellers with retention of title will benefit from a security similar to that of creditors who have been granted a real guarantee. In this sense, Article 90.1.4 of the Act 22/2003, dated July 9 2003, on insolvency considers as debts with special preference those debts arising from financial leasing arrangements or the instalment purchase of movable or immovable assets, where they are in favour of the lessors or sellers and, when appropriate, the financers, and where they relate to assets leased with retention of title, with a prohibition on disposal or with a termination condition in the event of failure to pay.

However in accordance with Article 56.1 of the Insolvency Act, creditors with a security over assets that are required for the continuation of the debtor's professional or business activity may not foreclose or forcibly execute the security until a composition is reached whose content does not affect exercise of that right, or until one year has elapsed from declaring the insolvency proceedings open without the winding-up having commenced. During that same period there may also be no actions aimed at recovering assets sold by instalments or financed under a reservation of ownership by a contract registered at the Register of Moveable Assets.

Regarding the possibility of attachment, retention of title will be effective against the creditors of the party actually possessing the encumbered property, provided the title holder is able to show conclusively that the retention of title was agreed and effective prior to the enforcement action being initiated or the attachment sought (Articles 1218 and 1227 of the Civil Code).

In the event that the buyer is subject to insolvency proceedings outside Spanish jurisdiction, the laws of the jurisdiction where the proceedings have been opened will be applied.

In the event of the seller's insolvency, the retention of title arrangement will continue in force and the buyer should continue to fulfil his obligations. Accordingly, seller's creditors may not expect direct benefits from the sale of the assets concerned, which are not going to be part of the aggregate assets. However, there are two scenarios where the assets may be attached to the aggregate assets and, therefore, be sold for the creditors' benefit. First, if the buyer does not fulfil his obligations. In this case, the seller or the insolvency administrator may terminate the contract and recover possession of the goods. Secondly, according to Article 61.2 of the Insolvency Act, the insolvency receiver may request the rescission of the contract if he deems it convenient for the benefit of the insolvency proceedings.

In the event that the seller is subject to insolvency proceedings outside Spanish jurisdiction, the laws of the jurisdiction where the proceedings have been opened will be applied.

2. Retention of title

2.1 Validity and formal requirements

Other than in the circumstances where Law 28/1998 applies, retention of title clauses are not regulated by any legislation in Spain.

Relevant case law and the opinion of legal scholars suggest that for an agreement containing a retention of title clause to be valid and enforceable, it must fulfil certain necessary conditions:

- It must concern the sale of non-consumable movable or immovable property;
- It must defer full payment of the purchase price;
- The retention of title clause must be specifically spelled out; and
- It must be registered at the Property Registry.

Also according to the case law and legal scholars, the wording of the retention of title clause does not need to contain any specific legal phrase, but it should be specifically agreed in writing.

A retention of title clause can be contained in general terms and conditions, but they must be signed.

Since retention of title is not specifically provided for under Spanish statute law, a retention of title cannot apply by operation of law and has to be claimed by the interested party.

If the parties so agree, the assets may be delivered to a third party instead of to the purchaser of such assets. Direct delivery of assets to the purchaser is not essential to retention of title.

2.2 Scope of retention of title

(a) *Sale of assets delivered under retention of title*

According to the case law and legal scholars, the party purchasing assets subject to retention of title does not have the authority to transfer the assets acquired, essentially because its title is not complete.

The purchaser may transfer his position as purchaser of assets subject to a retention of title, and the new purchaser would thereby acquire the obligation to pay the full price owed to the seller. In order to transfer the obligation to pay the purchase price to a third party, it is necessary for there to be a formal agreement and express acceptance by the seller.

The purchaser may also transfer assets subject to retention of title by sale, despite not holding the title, and satisfy his debt with the original seller with the paid price for the assets.

In the event that the purchaser is permitted to sell the assets subject to retention of title, the purchaser just transfers his possession of those assets.

Since retention of title is not expressly regulated under Spanish statute law, it is important that the contract considers all possible scenarios and sets out the parties' rights and obligations.

(b) *Combining/mixing/mingling assets delivered under retention of title*

Under Spanish law, retention of title is only regulated for non-consumable, distinguishable, movable assets.

The buyer may not transform the asset during the existence of the retention of title, because the asset must retain its identity as a guarantee of the sale and for the eventual execution of a recovery action by the seller.

Until payment of the purchase price, the seller retains his rights in the delivered assets. The seller may retrieve an asset that has been incorporated into another asset owned by the purchaser, even where the resultant composite has been transferred to a third party, as long as it is physically separable without detriment to the object or property to which it has been attached. In the event that it cannot be separated, the seller will be entitled to damages.

Notwithstanding the above, under Article 464 of the Civil Code, a third party who has purchased the resultant composite item should be protected.

In the event that assets delivered under retention of title are meant to be combined and they are actually combined with other assets, then under Spanish law the value of the assets they combined with is irrelevant. The seller retains the right to be paid the outstanding amount, with reference to the moment when the retention of title was established.

Where the assets are generic, the seller may be paid with assets of the same nature and value as the assets that have been attached to or mixed or combined with other assets. However, in these circumstances the seller does not retain his rights over the combined assets until payment of the purchase price is received.

Notwithstanding the above, the seller also retains the right to be paid in cash for the value of the assets subject to retention of title in the event that the purchaser does not fulfil his obligations.

(c) ***Processing of assets delivered under retention of title***

Under Spanish law, retention of title is only foreseen for non-consumable, distinguishable, movable assets.

In the event that assets subject to retention of title are processed, the retention of title does not cover the newly processed product. When the assets subject to retention of title are generic, the seller retains the right to be paid either with assets of the same nature and value as the assets that have processed, or in cash.

(d) ***Extension of retention of title***

As mentioned before, retention of title is not specifically regulated under Spanish statute law, other than Law 28/1998.

Law 28/1998 only refers to the purchase price for the assets delivered and does not provide for the retention of title to be extended to other of the purchaser's assets or to other debts owed to the seller of any nature. Relevant case law and legal scholars also do not support extension of retention of title.

2.3 Legal effect of retention of title

(a) ***Effect towards third parties***

Retention of title arrangements are valid contractual provisions and create valid and binding rights and obligations between the parties, although they are not specifically provided for under Spanish statute law and, therefore, do not have automatic effect.

In the event that assets subject to a retention of title clause are transferred, then under Article 464 of the Civil Code, a third party acquiring those assets in good faith (even though they were acquired from someone other than the owner of title to them) is entitled to be regarded as legal owner of those assets in respect of all legal effects.

This legal principle is only non-applicable in respect of:

- lost movable property;
- property which has been illegally seized from its owners; and
- movable property which has been properly registered at a public registry.

(b) ***Effect in case of seizure of assets delivered under retention of title***

When an asset is sold and the legal title is retained by the seller, only the creditor of the seller may use that asset as a guarantee. Notwithstanding the above, under Article 464 of the Civil Code, third-party rights must be protected.

Under Article 15 of Law 28/1998, in the event of seizure or enforcement of movable assets, all proceedings regarding such assets will be dismissed as on the production of evidence, certified by the relevant registrar, that the assets are subject to registered rights in favour of third parties.

(c) ***Effect in case of a security right established over assets delivered under retention of title***

According to Spanish law, assets subject to retention of title cannot also be subject to a possessory or non-possessory right as, from a legal point of view, the debtor is not yet its owner as possession has not been transferred. In the event that there is a floating mortgage over the purchaser's assets, it will not affect the goods that are subject to retention of title.

(d) *Effect in case of insolvency*

In the event of the buyer's insolvency, those sellers with retention of title will benefit from a security similar to that of creditors who have been granted a real guarantee. In this sense, Article 90.1.4 of the Insolvency Act considers as debts with special preference those arising from financial leasing arrangements or instalment purchase agreements for movable or immovable assets, in favour of the lessor or sellers and, when appropriate, the financers, where they relate to assets leased with reservation of title, with a prohibition on disposal or with a termination condition in the event of failure to pay.

However in accordance with Article 56.1 of the Spanish Insolvency Act, creditors with a security over assets that are required for the continuation of the debtor's professional or business activity may not foreclose or forcibly execute the security until a composition is reached whose content does not affect exercise of that right, or until one year has elapsed from declaring the insolvency proceedings open without the winding-up having commenced. During that same period there may also be no actions aimed at recovering assets sold by instalments or financed under a reservation of ownership by a contract registered at the Register of Moveable Assets.

Regarding the possibility of attachment, retention of title will be effective against the creditors to the party actually possessing the encumbered property, provided the title holder is able to show conclusively that the retention of title was agreed and effective prior to the enforcement action being initiated or the attachment sought (Articles 1218 and 1227 of the Civil Code).

(e) *Effect in case of partial payment of purchase price*

The seller has the right to seek the fulfilment of all contractual obligations and, therefore, the right to be paid the full amount agreed. Therefore, the seller is entitled to initiate the appropriate actions in an ordinary declaratory proceeding or in an insolvency proceeding, under the Civil Procedure Act or the Insolvency Act, even when the purchaser has already paid part of the purchase price.

If the debtor neither pays the outstanding amount claimed nor delivers the assets for sale by public auction, the creditor may ask the competent court for summary custody of the assets. The seller may seek enforcement through a public auction or may choose to recover the property to extinguish the debt without recourse to public auction.

Acquisition of the assets, either by public auction or recovery, does not settle the claim for the amounts due if the value of the assets is lower than the debt claimed.

On the other hand, in the event that the value of the assets (or the proceeds of the sale) is higher, the surplus (after deduction of damages and execution costs) has to be paid to the debtor, if the court declares such a duty.

3. Enforcement of retention of title

There is no specific organisation that is solely authorised or needs to be involved to repossess assets subject to retention of title.

The owner of the assets has an action against the holder and possessor of the claimed asset under Article 348 of the Civil Code.

First, though, the owner of the assets should proceed according to the provisions of the contract regarding default and repossession of the assets.

Where the contract does not include clauses regarding this event, the interested parties should start an action for declaratory proceedings as provided for in the Civil Procedure Act in order to repossess the assets subject to retention of title.

The owner of the claimed assets does not need additional permission or documentation from any specific authority to repossess assets delivered under retention of title.

However, the owner of the assets should provide a valid and enforceable title to the assets that are subject to retention of title where enforcement is sought in the form of:

- a public instrument (such as a public deed); or
- a commercial agreement signed by the parties and authorised by a notary public.

Moreover, where Law 28/1998 applies, in the event of a breach of a properly registered and formalised contract, the creditor may act directly and exclusively in respect of the assets purchased in instalments, under Article 16.2 of the law, according to the following procedure:

- The creditor, through a notary public, requests the outstanding payment, stating the total amount claimed and the event causing the maturity of the obligation. Also, the debtor shall be informed that in the event of not settling the obligation, the creditor may proceed to recover the asset at issue;
- The debtor, within three working days from the date on which the request is received, must pay the outstanding amount or deliver possession of the claimed asset to the creditor or other specifically designated person;
- Where the debtor does not pay the outstanding amount but voluntarily delivers the asset, that asset shall be sold by public auction; and
- Where the debtor fails to pay the claimed amount and does not deliver the asset for sale by public auction, the creditor may ask the competent court for summary custody of the asset.

According to the case law, the requirements for the success of this action are as follows:

- The plaintiff needs to prove its ownership of the property claimed. A public document is not essential, since the plaintiff's rights can be demonstrated by any form of evidence admissible under Spanish law;
- The defendant has to have possession of the claimed asset without title or right to do so; and
- The asset should be specific and definite.

Based on case law, and in accordance with Article 217.2 of the Civil Procedure Act, it is for the plaintiff to show that each and every one of these requirements is fulfilled.

In the event that the buyer is subject to insolvency proceedings in Spain, under the Insolvency Act, the assets whose recovery is sought will not be part of the aggregate assets since the buyer is not their owner, and the seller may therefore claim the repossession of them in the insolvency proceeding. The one exception is that the seller will not be able to repossess assets required for the continuation of the professional or business activity of the insolvent buyer.

Switzerland

Benedict F Christ
David Jenny
Vischer AG

1. General remarks about retention of title

Swiss law recognises the concept of retention of title, but provides for restrictive requirements. Namely, the retention of title must be registered in a special registry to become valid and, irrespective of the registration, the retention of title cannot be enforced against a good-faith acquirer of the asset. Due to this registration process and the prevailing rights of a good-faith third party, retention of title has only limited practical relevance in Switzerland. For instance, in the Canton of Zurich with a population of around 1.5 million and a gross domestic product of roughly CHF140 billion, only 521 new retentions of title for an aggregate value of CHF33,767,815 were registered in 2014. Starting at CHF25 for assets with a value of CHF1,000 or less and CHF50 for assets between CHF1,000 and CHF5,000, the minimum registration fees are relatively high, making retention of title expensive for assets of minor value, although the maximum fee cannot exceed CHF150. Accordingly, to the extent that retention of title is used, the registered assets mainly comprise movable assets of significant value such as machinery and cars sold in a business-to-business context.

1.1 Transfer of title

As a basic rule, under a purchase contract, ownership of a movable asset passes to the purchaser upon delivery, that is, upon the transfer of the asset's possession from the seller to the purchaser. The parties can agree on a retention of title and, thereby, postpone the transfer of title from the time of transfer of possession to any later moment. Typically, the transfer of title will be delayed until the payment of the purchase price, but other conditions may be agreed on as well. A retention of title can be agreed on in connection with purchase contracts and any other contract that has a delivery of asset component, such as contracts for work and labour that include the delivery of an asset as work product.

1.2 Retention of title

In Switzerland, retention of title is governed by statutory law. The key rules are set out in Article 715 and following of the Swiss Civil Code. Article 715 of the Civil Code provides that a retention of title is only valid if it is registered in a public register at the domicile or corporate seat of the purchaser. No retention of title is permitted for cattle (livestock). Also, the rules regarding retention of title only apply to movables (chattels), while the transfer of ownership of immovable property (real estate) is governed by different rules.

Further statutory rules relevant in connection with retention of title are:

- two ordinances governing the procedural and administrative aspects of registration in the retention of title register and its maintenance – the Ordinance Regarding the Registration of the Retention of Title dated December 19 1910 and the Ordinance Regarding the Maintenance of the Retention of Title Register dated March 29 1939;
- the Federal Consumer Credit Act, which refers in Article 10(d) to retention of title;
- Articles 102 and following of the Federal Act on Private International Law which govern the rules applying to retention of title in the international context, in particular regarding goods in transit through, imported to, or exported from Switzerland;
- Article 214(3) of the Code of Obligations, confirming the principle that a seller may only reclaim an asset sold from a defaulting purchaser if a retention of title has been expressly agreed on; and
- Article 884 of the Civil Code (see also Article 717 of the Civil Code) providing for the general principle that a pledge over movable assets in the debtor's possession is not valid under Swiss law. This general principle explains the very restrictive, mandatory rules applying to the retention of title.

1.3 Foreign and international law

As a basic rule under Swiss private international law, the transfer of movable property is governed by the law of the jurisdiction where the asset is located at the time of transfer of title. Therefore, the retention of title for assets located in Switzerland at the time of transfer from the seller to the purchaser is governed by Swiss law. Accordingly, a choice of law is not permitted for any *in rem* aspects of the retention of title (such as the transfer of title, the rank of the retention of title in relation to the rights of other preferred or secured creditors, the possibility to take security over the goods which are subject to a retention of title) while the contractual agreement regarding the retention of title could be governed by foreign law.

Special rules apply to assets in transit through, or being imported to, or exported from Switzerland:

- Rights *in rem*, including any retention of title, regarding an asset in transit through Switzerland from a foreign origin to a foreign destination are governed by the laws of the jurisdiction at the asset's destination.
- An asset entering Switzerland from abroad that has been subject to a valid foreign retention of title prior to entering Switzerland will remain subject to such foreign retention of title in accordance with the foreign rules, even if the requirements for a valid retention of title in Switzerland are not met. The foreign law governed retention of title will lapse within three months of the asset having entered Switzerland. However, even during that period, the retention of title cannot be enforced against a good-faith purchaser of the asset.
- Retention of title regarding an asset leaving Switzerland for a foreign destination is subject to the laws of the jurisdiction at the asset's destination.

1.4 Retention of title in insolvency

If the retention of title is not registered in the competent official register prior to the opening of Swiss insolvency proceedings concerning the purchaser then a subsequent registration of retention of title has no effect in the pending proceedings. If insolvency proceedings concerning the purchaser are opened outside Switzerland and no proceedings concerning the Swiss establishment or Swiss assets of the purchaser have been opened in Switzerland, then a registration of retention of title may still be effective in subsequent Swiss proceedings.

If the seller is subject to insolvency proceedings in Switzerland, then the estate will exercise all rights with regard to a retention of title. If the seller is subject to insolvency proceedings outside Switzerland, then the foreign officeholder has no power to assert any rights concerning retention of title on Swiss territory. To exercise such rights foreign proceedings will have to be recognised in accordance with Article 166 and following of the Private International Law Act unless an international treaty applies.

2. Retention of title

2.1 Validity and formal requirements

There are no formal requirements for entering into an agreement regarding a retention of title outside consumer credit agreements, but any retention of title must be registered in an official register to become effective against third parties. There is no retention of title by operation of law.

Retention of title is entered into by way of agreement (that is by mutual consent). The retention of title must be agreed on prior to the delivery of the assets. Under Swiss law, as a general rule, there are no formal requirements (such as an agreement in writing) for a retention of title and, therefore, it could be entered into by way of oral agreement. Also, there is no specific wording that must be used to agree on a retention of title. As long as the parties' intention to defer the passing of title is evident from the agreement, there will be a valid retention of title. However, for practical purposes, it is recommended to use clear language in the agreement by referring explicitly to a retention of title (in the languages of Switzerland, *Eigentumsvorbehalt, pacte de réserve de propriété* or *patto di riserva della proprietà*) and by making provision for the seller to be entitled to register the retention of title. A retention of title can also be agreed to validly in general terms and conditions (provided the general terms and conditions become part of the contract between the parties in accordance with the general rules applying to general terms and conditions).

There is one exception and one practical consideration to the general rule that a retention of title agreement requires no particular form:

- If the retention of title is agreed on as part of a consumer credit agreement, the Consumer Credit Act requires in Article 10(d) that the agreement be in writing and disclose the identity of the original owner and the conditions under which title to the assets passes to the purchaser. Upon registration of the retention of title in the register, in the case of a consumer credit contract, the registrar is required to check whether all formal requirements under the Consumer Credit Act have been complied with. In practice, retentions of title are rarely registered in connection with consumer goods given the comparatively small amounts involved and the high registration costs for assets of minor value.

- A written document evidencing the retention of title will be necessary unless the parties jointly appear in person at the registry for the registration to declare the retention of title.

Once agreed, to perfect the retention of title, it must be registered in the official register of retention of title. The filing for registration can be made at any time even after the delivery of the assets as long as payment for the assets has not occurred, but it becomes effective only upon registration and will have no effect if made after bankruptcy. The request for registration can be filed in writing or submitted in person either by both parties jointly or one party with written confirmation from the other party. There is no national register; the registries are organised on a cantonal level as part of the debt enforcement and bankruptcy administration. Depending on the structure in the respective canton, there may be one cantonal register or several registries at district level, but never more than one per municipality. The filing must be made with the competent registry of the purchaser's domicile (in the case of individuals) or registered seat (in the case of corporations). Typically, the registries have standard forms that can be used for the registration, but there is no online filing available. If filed in writing, the filing itself or the attached agreement should set out:

- the identities of the parties;
- a description of the assets subject to the retention of title;
- the location of the assets;
- the amount of the unpaid part of the purchase price for which the assets serve as security; and
- details regarding any down-payments.

The filing or the documents creating the retention of title must be signed by all parties not physically present at the registry and must be filed as an original or as a certified copy. In addition, in the case of a consumer credit agreement, the items required by the Consumer Credit Act must be contained in the written agreement to be submitted with the filing.

If the debtor (purchaser) changes its domicile or registered seat, the retention of title must be re-registered in the registry at the new domicile or registered seat and a new registration fee must be paid. The former registration survives only for a period of three months from the change of domicile or registered seat.

Normally, in the context of a retention of title, the asset is directly transferred from the seller to the purchaser. However, the asset could also be delivered to a third party (such as a warehouse company). In this case the third party could be instructed to hold the asset on behalf of the purchaser and a retention of title could be created. Alternatively, the third party could be instructed to hold the asset on behalf of the seller until delivery to the purchaser. In this case, the seller could retain its property rights without need for a registered retention of title until such delivery. Thereafter, a retention of title needs to be registered if a continued retention of title is required.

2.2 Scope of retention of title

Under Swiss law, a retention of title has the following scope. Even in the absence of a specific clause or agreement (and provided there are no special circumstances or an agreement to the contrary), the retention of title agreement includes an implicit covenant by the purchaser not to frustrate the retention of title. Therefore, the purchaser is liable to avoid any act that could compromise the property rights of the seller such as selling the asset, processing or changing the asset, or commingling or combining the asset with other goods.

In the event of a breach of this implicit covenant (or any explicit covenant in this respect), the purchaser becomes liable for any damages caused thereby to the seller (including any damages caused by forfeiture of the retention of title). The *in rem* effects of such a breach on the retention of title depend on the circumstances and are determined by the general rules regarding movable property. The following rules apply independently of whether the purchaser or a third party is processing, commingling or combining the assets, and independently of whether the combined or commingled assets belong to the purchaser or a third party:

- In the event of a sale of an asset subject to a retention of title, the purchaser cannot validly transfer the property to a third party as it has no title. Therefore, while a contractual agreement to sell is possible, the purchaser is not able to perform. However, a third party that is, in good faith, not aware of the retention of title can still acquire the property and obtain title. In the event of a transfer to a good-faith third party, the retention of title will be forfeited and the seller can only claim damages. Further, the parties can agree that the purchaser may sell the asset subject to the original retention of title and subject to entering into a second retention of title with the third-party purchaser. This second retention of title again must be registered in the register of retention of title with the original seller as owner. In addition, the original seller may request an assignment from the purchaser of its claims against the third-party purchaser.
- In the event of processing (involving alteration or change) of the asset, the allocation of property will depend on the value of the asset and the value of the effort used for the processing. The property will belong to the party that has contributed the higher value, be it the asset or the processing. If the processing has the higher value, the retention of title will be forfeited. In the event of a person processing an asset subject to a retention of title in bad faith, the court may allocate the property to the owner of the asset regardless of the values contributed. Furthermore, the parties could agree that, despite the processing's higher value, the processed asset becomes subject to the retention of title. However, in the absence of any case law on the issue, it is disputed in the legal doctrine whether such a retention of title is enforceable (even if registered).
- In the event of a combination, that is a mixing of assets where the asset can

be separated easily, the parties contributing will remain owners of their respective assets. In this case, the retention of title remains valid.

- In the event of a commingling, that is a mixing of movable assets where the asset cannot be separated easily, the parties contributing will become joint owners of the commingled assets (unless one asset becomes a minor accessory of the other asset). Consequently, where one of the assets is subject to a retention of title, the seller will have a surrogate retention of title in the joint ownership of the combined assets. In the event of a commingling where one asset becomes a minor accessory of the other asset, the property of the entire combined assets remains with the owner of the main asset. In this case, if the minor asset was subject to a retention of title, the retention of title will be forfeited or, inversely, if the main asset is subject to a retention of title, the retention of title will apply to the entire asset.
- In the event of attaching an asset that is subject to a retention of title to immovable property (real estate), the asset becomes part of the real estate. Consequently, the retention of title is forfeited.

Apart from the exceptions mentioned, the rules regarding sale, processing, combination and commingling are strict *in rem* rules that cannot be changed by way of contract and, therefore, apply regardless of what the parties have agreed among themselves or with any third parties. To the extent that the retention of title is forfeited there is no surrogate right *in rem* over the asset, the only remedies remaining being claims for damages.

Where the retention of title survives, but the combination or commingling changes the description of the asset, the respective entry in the retention of title register must be amended to reflect the new situation and a new registration fee must be paid.

Retention of title serves as security for the payment of the purchase price. In the absence of any case law, it is disputed in the legal doctrine whether a retention of title can secure further claims of the seller against the purchaser.

2.3 Legal effect of retention of title

To be effective, retention of title has to be properly registered in the competent public register. As there is no general duty to consult these registers, third parties acting in good faith may acquire property (title) or other rights over the asset despite proper registration (Article 933 of the Civil Code). A third party does not act in good faith if it does not exercise the degree of diligence which is required under the given circumstances. Merchants of certain goods which are regularly sold subject to retention of title have a duty to check the register: for example used car dealers are subject to such a duty. Furthermore, a landlord wishing to be able to exercise rights granted by the landlord's special lien (Articles 268 and following of the Code of Obligations) should check the register to see whether objects in commercial premises are subject to a retention of title.

If goods subject to a properly registered retention of title are subject to an enforcement of debts proceedings initiated by a third-party creditor (including governmental bodies such as tax authorities), then the seller will be treated as if the goods had been pledged to the seller. The seller has to assert its right in the third party's claim proceedings in accordance with Articles 106 and following of the Debt Enforcement and Bankruptcy Law. If the rights of the seller are recognised, then the seller is entitled to the proceeds from the realisation of the goods up to the amount of its claim. Such goods cannot be sold in a public auction, unless the "amount realised exceeds the sum of any secured claims having priority over the claim of the applicant creditor" (Article 126(1) of the Debt Enforcement and Bankruptcy Law). Alternatively, the seller has the possibility of reclaiming the goods. The seller can do so as long as the purchase price has not been fully paid. If the Federal Consumer Credit Act (Article 18(1)) is applicable then this option is not available if 90% or more of the cash purchase price has already been paid. In the event of reclaiming the goods, the seller has to reimburse any payments made for the goods by the purchaser after deduction of an appropriate rental charge and compensation for wear and tear (Article 716 of the Civil Code).

As a general rule, Swiss law does not allow non-possessory security rights like floating charges.

Conflicts between the rights of the seller and those of third parties are resolved by applying the rules regarding the acquisition of rights *in rem* by good-faith third parties.

3. Enforcement of retention of title

The seller may ask the purchaser or third parties in possession of the goods directly to hand over goods subject to a retention of title. Should the purchaser or a third party refuse to do so then the seller has to resort to the civil courts. Whether a third party can invoke better rights is determined by applying the rules regarding acquisition of rights *in rem* by third parties acting in good faith, as described above.

If the purchaser is in default then the seller may either withdraw from the contract and request the return of the goods (Article 214 of the Code of Obligations) or may ask for performance of the contract. If performance is requested then the seller has to set an appropriate time limit for the subsequent performance unless it is evident that a time limit would serve no purpose. If performance has not been rendered by the end of the time limit then the seller may either compel performance in addition to suing for damages or may forego subsequent performance and either claim damages or withdraw from the contract (Articles 107 and following of the Code of Obligations).

Goods subject to retention of title are identified by their entry in the relevant register. A purchaser reclaiming such goods has to prove that the relevant goods have been entered into the register. Such an action can also be directed against third parties in possession of goods subject to retention of title. The third party may assert that they have acquired title in good faith.

If the purchaser is subject to insolvency proceedings, then the seller has to assert its title to goods under retention of title. Should the administrator of a Swiss bankruptcy estate reject such a claim then the seller has to commence proceedings with the court at the location of the insolvency proceedings within 20 days after having received notice from the bankruptcy administration (Article 242 of the Debt Enforcement and Bankruptcy Law). The administration may also opt to perform the contract between the seller and the purchaser. It will usually do so if most of the purchase price has already been paid. In this event the goods subject to a retention of title cannot be repossessed and the seller's claim for payment becomes a claim against the estate. Whether performance by the estate can be prevented by a provision to this effect in the purchase contract has not yet been finally decided. The seller also has the option not to repossess the goods and to file its claim for the outstanding payment of the purchase price, which will then be admitted as a claim of the third class as with claims of other trade creditors (Article 219 of the Debt Enforcement and Bankruptcy Law).

Turkey

N Can Artüz
E Sevi Fırat
Fırat-Izgi Attorney Partnership

1. General remarks about retention of title

1.1 Transfer of ownership

In Turkish law, transfer of title is regulated separately for movable and immovable goods. As regards the acquisition of title to movable goods, it is apparent that initial acquisition of title and acquisition by transfer are distinct concepts. Accordingly, where there is an agreement for title to be transferred from one person to another, the concept of acquisition by transfer is relevant. In order for title to a movable asset to be transferred between parties, in principle the actual transfer of possession is required.

If no agreement to the contrary is present between the parties, the buyer should receive possession of the asset being sold immediately. However the parties can decide on another time for the asset to be delivered to the buyer by mutual agreement. Similarly, it is also possible to agree on the transfer of title being contingent upon a condition, even though delivery takes place immediately and possession changes hands.

1.2 Retention of title

In Turkish law, a retention of title agreement is defined as an agreement where the parties agree for the ownership to remain with the seller of the movable asset received by the buyer until a certain condition is satisfied. In the literature, there is debate whether such a condition is a condition precedent or a dissolving condition. Majority opinion states that the agreement between the parties should be examined, and if the parties did not explicitly state the contrary, the condition should be accepted as a condition precedent.

Underlying an agreement on retention of title is an agreement for the acquisition of title, and the retention of title can be effected by including a provision within the sales agreement or by a separate agreement. Prevailing opinion among Turkish experts is that an agreement on retention of title is a contingent real contract. The act of disposal effecting the transfer of the movable title is contingent. The promissory transaction that underlies this act, on the other hand, is not contingent.

The conditions for a valid agreement on retention of title are set out in general terms in Article 764 of the Turkish Civil Code (Law 4721). In addition, retention of title is used extensively in sales by instalments, and Article 765 of the Civil Code specifically provides that retention of title agreements can be applied to sales by instalments. Furthermore, Article 263 of the Code of Obligations, which regulates the enforcement aspects of instalment sales, states that the provisions regarding instalment sales shall also be applied to other agreements having the same intent, and in the event that title is retained in loan agreements, the provisions with regard to instalment sales shall be applied by analogy. Finally, there is a prohibition on retention of title agreements in sales of animals under Article 764(2) of the Civil Code, and a prohibition on registering a retention of title in sales of immovable property is provided explicitly under Article 243 of the Code of Obligations.

1.3 Foreign and international law

Since an agreement on retention of title is essentially about transfer of a generally applicable property right, under Turkish international private law the laws of the country where the asset at issue is located during the moment of the transaction shall be applied. On these grounds, an agreement on retention of title validly made under the laws of the location where the asset is should be deemed valid under Turkish law. However some authors in Turkey state that in order for this right to be claimed in Turkey in respect of a movable asset sold with a retention of title agreed validly under the laws of the country where the asset was located at the time but later brought to Turkey, conformity to the conditions set out under Turkish law is also required. The Court of Appeals has also adopted this opinion and in one of its decisions stated that, in the event that the former jurisdiction's law of property provisions do not conform with Turkish law on this point, the position under Turkish law shall replace the position under the law of the former country and agreements that do not conform to Turkish requirements shall be invalid.

On the other hand, debtor-creditor relationships born out of agreements with foreign elements are explicitly subject to the parties' choice of law (where such a choice is made in the agreement). For this reason, the law chosen by the parties shall be applied to the promissory transactions underlying the agreement on retention of title, and in the event no choice of law was expressed in the contract, the law to be applied will be that which has the closest relationship with the agreement.

The standing of the seller's rights over an asset sold with retention of title, as against the rights of third parties, is most significant in enforcement and bankruptcy procedures. The position of the holder of the retention of title against other pledgees and privileged creditors in enforcement and bankruptcy procedures in Turkey, and the means of enforcing these rights, are exclusively determined according to Turkish law.

1.4 Retention of title in insolvency

Restrictions on the power of disposition for persons subject to insolvency proceedings are not absolute under Turkish law. With the commencement of insolvency, all the insolvent party's goods that can be seized are registered to the bankruptcy estate and the insolvent party's power of disposition over such goods is removed. However no restrictions or prohibitions are foreseen for the insolvent's power of disposition in respect of goods and rights excluded from the estate.

For this reason, an insolvent seller is still able to sell an asset excluded from the estate with a retention of title. Likewise, there are no obstacles for an insolvent buyer in buying goods subject to retention of title. There is no difference in this respect if the buyer or seller is subject to insolvency procedures outside Turkey. The effects of insolvency on the part of the seller or the buyer on goods subject to retention of title where the insolvency arises after the agreement for retention of title has been made are examined separately below.

2. Retention of title

2.1 Validity and formal requirements

Turkish law makes sales subject to retention of title contingent upon the parties' agreement to such an outcome. Under Article 764 of the Civil Code and Article 89 of the Public Notary Code, in order for an agreement on retention of title to be valid, it needs to be officially drafted by a notary public and registered to a special register held by the notary public of the buyer's place of residence. In other words, it is not sufficient for the parties to sign the agreement among them and certify it before the notary public, but must be properly registered, which is subject to different fees based on the value of the transaction. In the event that the buyer's place of residence changes, the agreement is required to be registered to the notary public in the new place of residence.

Registration of the agreement, therefore, does not have a merely declaratory function, but an establishing one. An agreement on retention of title that does not conform to the compulsory requirements explained above shall be invalid, and title in the asset concerned shall be transferred to the buyer. In other words, the invalidity of the agreement on retention of title does not invalidate the underlying sales transaction. On the other hand, registration does not have a publicity function that nullifies acquisition by third parties acting in good faith as does the land registry. For this reason, where an asset delivered to the buyer subject to retention of title is subsequently acquired by a third person acting in good faith, his acquisition is valid.

There are no specific statements that are required to be included in the content of agreements on retention of title. It is sufficient for the agreement to show the parties' will in this regard. Provided the parties agree that retention of title is a condition of the agreement being made, the condition's validity shall not be affected by including it only within the general terms and conditions of the agreement. In agreements where the buyer is a consumer, in particular, it may be thought that such a condition may be claimed to be unfair, however as it does not excessively disrupt the balance of interests between the parties and acts as a security, retention of title should not be held to be an unfair condition.

It is permissible, under an agreement on retention of title, for delivery to be made to a representative authorised by the buyer or by law, rather than directly to the buyer.

2.2 Scope of retention of title

(a) Sale of goods delivered under retention of title

The essence and purpose of agreement on retention of title is that goods subject to the agreement are left at the disposal of the buyer. The further sale of goods that are subject to retention of title to a third person who is, or should be, aware of this fact is invalid, unless the buyer acquires title. However if the third person is not aware, and has no reason to be aware, that the goods are subject to retention of title, the sale to him confers title, and the original seller can only claim against the original buyer. It is possible, though, for the parties to agree beforehand that the buyer may sell the goods to third parties. Additionally the parties can add conditions to such an agreement, stating that the full purchase price shall become due with the sale of the goods to a third person or that the third person shall pay the sale price to the original seller. In our opinion, however, the latter condition cannot be enforced against the third person.

(b) *Combining/mixing/mingling goods delivered under retention of title*

Under Article 776 of the Civil Code, if goods belonging to more than one person are merged or mixed and cannot be separated without incurring substantial damage or spending excessive effort or money, those persons shall have joint ownership of the resultant goods in a ratio equivalent to the value of their original goods at the moment of merger or mixture. In such circumstances, an agreement on retention of title in respect of any goods that were merged or mixed shall terminate, and it is not possible to agree that the seller retains his rights in the goods after they are mixed or combined.

In the event that an asset subject to retention of title is merged with another movable asset as a complementary part thereof, title to the entire resultant asset shall belong to the original owner of the main asset. Accordingly, the agreement on retention of title shall terminate and it is not possible to agree that the seller retains his rights in such a case. On the other hand, if another asset becomes a complementary part of an asset sold with retention of title, the seller who holds the retention of title shall acquire title to the entire asset including the new complementary part. A 'complementary part', in this context, means a part that is inseparable from an asset without destroying, damaging or changing the structure of the asset, and that constitutes a fundamental element of the main asset.

On the other hand, movable goods that are "continuously allocated to the main asset for operating, protecting or providing a benefit, and are bound to the main asset while in use through connecting, affixing or other means" are defined as 'accessories' in Turkish law, and accessories can be subject to right to title separate from the main asset. For this reason it is possible to have agreements on retention of title in respect of these goods and the seller's retained title is not harmed in the event such goods are attached to another asset.

(c) *Processing of goods delivered under retention of title*

Under Turkish law, in the event that a person processes goods owned by another person, and in the event that the value of the effort involved is more than the value of the goods, the person who undertook the processing shall own the newly created asset. However, if such a person processes the goods being aware that this will be the outcome, the court can decide that the resulting asset belongs to the owner of the original goods rather than the person who undertook the processing. These provisions are equally applicable to goods subject to an agreement on retention of title as well. However it is possible for the parties to decide beforehand on who shall own the new asset.

(d) ***Extension of the retention of title***

In principle, an agreement on retention of title constitutes security only with respect to the promissory transaction subject to this agreement. However, this principle should be explicitly enforced only in the event that no agreement to the contrary exists between the parties. Although there is no consensus in this regard, in our opinion, it should be possible for the effect of a retention of title to be expanded to constitute security against other debts owed to the seller by the purchaser by adding a provision to this effect to the agreement.

2.3 Legal effect of retention of title

(a) ***Effect towards third parties***

Provisions of Turkish civil law that protect third parties acting in good faith have effect in respect of sales made subject to retention of title. The primary reason for this is that the register, in which agreements on retention of title are registered, does not have a publicity function. For this reason, third parties acting in good faith who acquire goods that were originally sold subject to retention of title are fully protected and acquire ownership of the goods. However circumstances are different as regards creditors of the buyer. The seller retains the title to goods sold under retention of title until the condition precedent is fulfilled. On these grounds, by relying on its right to title in the goods, the seller can file an action for recovery against the buyer's creditors. Even in the event that the creditor is a public body, the rules do not change. It is explicitly provided in Article 12 of Law 6183, the principal law with respect to pursuing public debts, that an action for recovery in respect of assets sold subject to retention of title can also be filed against public authorities.

(b) ***Effect in case of seizure of goods delivered under retention of title***

It is possible for goods sold subject to retention of title to be seized by creditors of either the buyer or the seller between the time the agreement on retention of title is made and the fulfilment of the condition to which the agreement is subject. Each scenario is examined separately.

Seizure by creditors of the buyer: In this case, within the scope of the execution procedure, it is possible for either the buyer or the seller to claim that the seller owns the goods within seven days of learning of the seizure. If the creditor does not object to this claim, or does object but the seller files and wins an action for recovery, the seized goods shall be returned. However, there are two possible avenues by which the buyer's creditor may still recover its debt. The first of these is ensuring the passing of the title to the goods to the buyer by the creditor fulfilling the condition for the completion of acquisition, if the creditor is in a position to do so. An example for this can be payment of the remaining instalments by the creditor of the buyer in case of instalment sales. The other possibility, in the event that the creditor cannot or does not wish to fulfil the condition for acquisition, is that the seller can withdraw from the agreement. In this case, the seller will be required to return any part of the purchase price so far obtained to buyer up to the moment of withdrawal. Then, it will be possible for the buyer's creditor to seize those fees.

Seizure by creditors of the seller: There are also two possible approaches to seizure by creditors of the seller. If the buyer is in fact performing the obligations under the sales agreement, for example if the buyer is paying the instalments on time, the seller's creditors cannot interfere with the buyer's rights under the agreement, and it will not be possible for the goods to be seized or sold. However if the buyer is in default, the seller can withdraw from the agreement and request the return of the goods from the buyer, and the seller's creditor can then seize the goods. Alternatively, if the seller does not withdraw from the agreement the creditor can seize the purchase price.

(c) Effect in case of a security right established over goods delivered under retention of title

In principle, according to Turkish property law, a pledge contingent upon delivery is valid for movable assets. As a natural result of this, in order for the pledge over such an asset to be validly established, possession of the asset has to be transferred to the pledgee. Creditor organisations (especially banks) establishing commercial enterprise pledges on movable assets owned by commercial enterprises without receiving delivery of the goods (contingent upon registration) constitute an exception to this rule. However, under this form of pledge the pledged goods must be assets of the pledger enterprise at the moment that the commercial enterprise pledge is established. A separate registration action is required for any assets added later to the enterprise's existing assets.

In the event that goods subject to retention of title are pledged as explained above, a pledgee acting in good faith shall be protected as in the acquisition of ownership. However if it is known by the pledgee that the asset to be pledged is subject to an agreement on retention of title, the seller can claim its title.

(d) Effect in case of insolvency

In sales under retention of title, in the event that the buyer becomes insolvent prior to fulfilment of the condition precedent, the full purchase price receivable by the seller becomes due. However since the condition is yet to be fulfilled and the title of the good has not transferred to the buyer, the goods at issue should not be included in the bankruptcy estate. Liquidation in insolvency is performed by the administrator in bankruptcy. If the administrator is of the opinion that including the goods in the estate would be beneficial for the creditors, it may take over the agreement in order to fulfil the condition precedent and include the goods in the estate by paying the outstanding purchase price to the seller. However, the seller has two options if the administrator does take this action. The first of these is that the seller may withdraw from the agreement and request that the goods be delivered back to him. In this case, the seller shall pay the estate any part of the purchase price so far paid by the buyer, less any damages or extraordinary depreciation on grounds of usage of the good. The other option is not withdrawing from the agreement and registering the debt as bankruptcy debt with the estate.

(e) Effect in case of partial payment of purchase price

The essence of a retention of title provision is to provide security over the price receivable by a seller making a sale on credit. It is frequently the practice for a buyer who cannot immediately pay the full sale price of goods to pay the price within an agreed term and in instalments. In the event that the buyer defaults on paying its debt in this manner, the seller has the right to withdraw from the agreement and request the return of the goods. The effects of this circumstance on third parties seizing the good are examined above. Once the seller withdraws from the agreement, it must return all amounts received from the buyer up to the point of withdrawal and request the return of the goods. However the seller may claim a fair usage fee on the grounds that the buyer used the good during the life of the agreement, and also claim damages due to depreciation.

3. Enforcement of retention of title

Under Turkish property law, the owner of an asset is entitled to file an action for recovery to protect its title against those who are in possession of the asset with no right to be so. This is also valid and applicable for goods sold subject to retention of title. This is because the requirement to register the agreement on retention of title with the notary public only enables such an agreement to be validly established. In fact, not registering such agreements in a registry which would be kept by an execution office, which is the practice in Swiss law, has become a point of criticism in the literature. On the other hand, it is not possible for a seller of goods under retention of title to take advantage of the special administrative protection provisions established under Turkish law, rather than the regular course of legal actions for protecting ownership. This is because such administrative protection applications can only be used for preventing infringements in respect of immovable possession.

While the sales agreement is still being performed, albeit that its completion is contingent upon a condition that is yet to be fulfilled, the seller cannot infringe the buyer's anticipatory right. This means that the seller can only exercise its right to request the return of goods if the buyer is in default. The conditions under which the buyer can be considered to be in default are determined according to the general principles of the law of obligations. Accordingly, in order to put the buyer in default, it is necessary for the seller to issue a warning. Along with this, where it has agreed that the debt shall be paid within a specific term – which is usually the case in sales subject to retention of title – the buyer shall be in default automatically on the agreed date. In order for the seller to exercise its right to withdraw from the agreement against the defaulting buyer, in principle, a certain amount of time should be granted to the buyer. However if it is apparent from the agreement that the performance can no longer be accepted following non-performance within the set term of the contract, the seller is not required to grant such time. This circumstance is established where a definitive term is set, and it is explicitly set out under the agreement that non-performance within the definitive term shall not be accepted.

In the event that the seller is required to put the buyer in default or to grant time before withdrawing from the agreement, if the parties are merchants, the notification must be made in a warning letter sent through a notary public, registered mail, telegram or a registered email system using a secure electronic signature. Sending a warning letter through a notary public is the common practice.

There will not be any problems in the event the buyer or the third person gives its consent to returning the goods in the event that seller withdraws from the agreement. However, if the buyer or third person does not return the goods despite the withdrawal of the seller, the seller will have to file an action for recovery. In the event that the action is decided in favour of the seller, but the buyer or third person still does not return the goods, it is possible to force the delivery by proceedings through an enforcement office.

If the buyer is insolvent and the goods have been included to the insolvency estate, the action for recovery should be filed against the administrator of the bankruptcy. If the administrator rejects the seller's claim, the conflict shall be resolved via an action for recovery under the recovery procedures discussed above.

United Kingdom[1]

Ken Titchen
Gateley Plc

1. General remarks about retention of title

1.1 Transfer of ownership

A retention of title agreement is a mechanism designed to protect a seller of goods from the buyer's failure to pay. It is most useful in circumstances where the buyer becomes insolvent and the seller would otherwise be left as an unsecured creditor ranking behind payment of the expenses of the insolvency, and behind the secured and preferential creditors.

Under a retention of title agreement the seller retains ownership of goods it has delivered even though possession has been handed over to the buyer. Retention of title is not a perfect solution. Goods supplied may be perishable, be of little value to the seller, be dispersed far and wide, and recovery may incur significant costs. A small-scale seller to a large-scale buyer may not have the commercial strength to include retention of title terms in a supply agreement. The seller may lose title whatever the supply agreement says, and the validity or effectiveness of retention of title terms are often challenged. Nevertheless a retention of title agreement is a useful tool for a seller. As a minimum it may provide him with a negotiating position if the buyer does not pay, and at best it can provide the seller with the opportunity to receive substantial payment of an unpaid balance if the buyer becomes insolvent. Credit insurers may require a retention of title clause to be included in terms and conditions of sale before they will provide cover. Taking all these factors into account the use of retention of title clauses is widespread throughout UK business.

The general rules about the transfer of ownership of goods sold by a seller to a buyer are found in the Sale of Goods Act 1979. It is necessary to look first to the statutory provisions to determine when title in goods passes from a seller to a buyer.

Section 16 of the Sale of Goods Act provides that:

Subject to section 20A below where there is a contract for the sale of unascertained goods no property in the goods is transferred to the buyer unless and until the goods are ascertained.

Section 20A applies to certain contracts for the sale of a specified quantity of unascertained goods.

Section 17 of the act provides that:

(1) Where there is a contract for the sale of specific or ascertained goods the property in

1 This chapter is based on the law of England and Wales only.

them is transferred to the buyer at such time as the parties to the contract intend it to be transferred.

(2) For the purpose of ascertaining the intention of the parties regard shall be had to the terms of the contract, the conduct of the parties and the circumstances of the case.

Section 18 sets out rules for ascertaining what the parties intended:

Unless a different intention appears, the following are rules for ascertaining the intention of the parties as to the time at which the property in the goods is to pass to the buyer.

Rule 1

Where there is an unconditional contract for the sale of specific goods in a deliverable state the property in the goods passes to the buyer when the contract is made, and it is immaterial whether the time of payment or the time of delivery, or both, be postponed.

Rule 2

Where there is a contract for the sale of specific goods and the seller is bound to do something to the goods for the purpose of putting them into a deliverable state, the property does not pass until the thing is done and the buyer has notice that it has been done.

Rule 3

Where there is a contract for the sale of goods in a deliverable state but the seller is bound to weigh, measure, test, or do some other act or thing with reference to the goods for the purpose of ascertaining the price, the property does not pass until the act or thing is done and the buyer has notice that it has been done.

Rule 4

When goods are delivered to the buyer on approval or on sale or return or other similar terms the property in the goods passes to the buyer:-

(a) when he signifies his approval or acceptance to the seller or does any other act adopting the transaction;

(b) if he does not signify his approval or acceptance to the seller but retains the goods without giving notice of rejection, then, if a time has been fixed for the return of the goods, on the expiration of that time, and, if no time has been fixed, on the expiration of a reasonable time.

Further rules apply for unascertained or future goods.

Section 19(1) deals with the situation where goods are sold and the right of disposal is reserved by the seller:

Where there is a contract for the sale of specific goods or where goods are subsequently appropriated to the contract, the seller may, by the terms of the contract or appropriation, reserve the right of disposal of the goods until certain conditions are fulfilled; and in such a case, notwithstanding the delivery of the goods to the buyer, the property in the goods does not pass to the buyer until the conditions imposed by the seller are fulfilled.

In summary, the general rule is that where there is a contract for the sale of ascertained goods, title in the goods passes when the parties intend it to pass. Without an intention to the contrary, title will pass from the seller to the buyer when the contract is made. The parties can agree otherwise, but any intention to postpone the transfer of title must be ascertainable or the statutory presumptions in Section 18 of the Sale of Goods Act will apply.

Specific rules sometimes apply with regard to the form that a contract for sale must take. For example an agreement to transfer an interest in land must be made in writing, incorporating all the terms which the parties have expressly agreed in one document or, where contracts are exchanged, in each.[2] A transfer of legal title in land must be by way of a deed.[3] Specific rules as to registration of ownership may also apply, for example in relation to land and ships.

1.2 Retention of title

It follows from the statutory rules set out above that a seller can retain ownership of goods until payment is made providing that this is what the parties intend when the contract for sale is made. Although permitted by statute, retention of title is not created by statute. It is simply a matter of agreement between the parties. The effectiveness of retention of title provisions was confirmed by the Court of Appeal in the case *Aluminium Industrie Vaassen BV v Romalpa Aluminium Ltd*.[4] The court upheld a contract term by which the seller retained title to goods until all sums due to it from the buyer were paid. This case led to retention of title clauses becoming known as "Romalpa" clauses.

The courts have considered retention of title provisions in a number of situations. They have approved not only simple retention of title clauses where the seller retains title to goods until the price for those goods has been paid, but also more complex all monies clauses. In an all monies clause, the seller retains title until all amounts due to it from the same buyer have been paid, even though the other sums may have fallen due under different contracts.[5] It does not matter that the buyer may have an actual or implied permission to consume the goods or to resell them in the ordinary course of business.[6] However if a retention of title clause retains merely beneficial ownership of goods, with legal title passing to the buyer, or seeks to provide for the buyer to pay the proceeds of sale of goods to the seller, then it is likely to create a charge. Such a charge would be invalid against an administrator, liquidator or creditor of a company unless it is registered under Section 860 of the Companies Act 2006.[7]

There are some other limits to the effectiveness of retention of title clauses which will be considered below.

1.3 Foreign and international law

If the agreement containing the retention of title clause is subject to a governing law clause, that named jurisdiction will usually apply and be upheld by the court. Where there is no governing law clause, or the clause is not clearly drafted, determining the applicable law can be complex, costly and uncertain.

---

2 Section 2(1) of the Law of Property Act (Miscellaneous Provisions) Act 1989.

3 Section 52(1) of the Law of Property Act 1925.

4 [1976] 1 WLR 676.

5 For example *Aluminium Industrie Vaassen BV v Romalpa Aluminium Ltd* [1976] 1 WLR 676; *Borden (UK) Ltd v Scottish Timber Products Ltd* [1981] Ch 35.

6 For example *Aluminium Industrie Vaassen BV v Romalpa Aluminium Ltd* [1976] 1 WLR 676; *Re Bond Worth Ltd* [1980] Ch 228; *Hendy Lennox (Industrial Engines) Ltd v Grahame Puttick Ltd* [1984] 1 WLR 485; *Re Peachdart Ltd* [1984] Ch 131; *Borden (UK) Ltd v Scottish Timber Products Ltd* [1981] Ch 35.

7 For example *Re Bond Worth Ltd* [1980] Ch 228; *Borden (UK) Ltd v Scottish Timber Products Ltd* [1981] Ch 35.

For contracts made on or after December 17 2009 where at least one of the parties is based in an EU member state, the Rome I Regulation[8] will apply with regards to the choice of law. Where parties to a contract have explicitly stated their choice of law the Rome I Regulation will generally not affect the agreement the parties have made. In the absence of a choice made by the parties the Rome I Regulation states that the applicable law will (subject to certain specific exceptions) be the law of the country where the party performing the main obligations under the contract is resident. It is therefore necessary to determine where the party selling the goods is based.

Article 9 of EU Directive 2011/7 on combating late payment in commercial transactions[9] provides:

Retention of title

1. *Member States shall provide in conformity with the applicable national provisions designated by private international law that the seller retains title to goods until they are fully paid for if a retention of title clause has been expressly agreed between the buyer and the seller before the delivery of the goods.*

English courts have long recognised retention of title clauses found in agreements subject to the jurisdiction of foreign courts where the claim relates to goods located within England and the clause would be valid in the overseas jurisdiction. The most common ground on which the court has declined to recognise a retention of title clause in favour of overseas sellers has been inadequate offers of translations of relevant terms into English, or inadequate translations themselves.

In a cross-border insolvency falling within the scope of the EC Regulation on insolvency proceedings,[10] Article 7 of that regulation contains specific rules about reservation of title:

1. *The opening of insolvency proceedings against the purchaser of an asset shall not affect the seller's rights based on a reservation of title where at the time of the opening of proceedings the asset is situated within the territory of a Member State other than the State of opening of proceedings.*
2. *The opening of insolvency proceedings against the seller of an asset, after delivery of the asset, shall not constitute grounds for rescinding or terminating the sale and shall not prevent the purchaser from acquiring title where at the time of the opening of proceedings the asset sold is situated within the territory of a Member State other than the State of the opening of proceedings.*

Under the United Nations Commission on International Trade Law's Model Law on Cross-Border Insolvency, where office holders have been recognised in a state other than the state of the main proceedings, Article 22 requires the court to satisfy itself that the interests of creditors are adequately protected. That requirement specifically includes creditors with retention of title agreements. The UNCITRAL model law was given force in England with effect from April 4 2007 by the Cross-Border Insolvency Regulations 2006.[11]

8 Regulation (EC) 593/2008 of the European Parliament and of the Council of June 17 2008 on the law applicable to contractual obligations (Rome I).

9 Directive 2011/7/EU of the European Parliament and of the Council of February 16 2011 on combating late payment in commercial transactions (recast).

10 Council Regulation (EC) 1346/2000 of May 29 2000 on insolvency proceedings.

11 SI 2006/1030.

1.4 Retention of title in insolvency

A company can become subject to various insolvency procedures in England and Wales, and different procedures may have different impacts on a supplier with a retention of title clause in its terms of supply.

There is a statutory definition of retention of title agreement set out in Section 251 of the Insolvency Act 1986, as follows:

"Retention of title agreement" means an agreement for the sale of goods to a company, being an agreement–

(a) which does not constitute a charge on the goods, but

(b) under which, if the seller is not paid and the company is wound up, the seller will have priority over all other creditors of the company as respects the goods or any property representing the goods.

Typical insolvency procedures a company may enter are:

- administration;
- liquidation;
- receivership; and
- company voluntary arrangement.

In administration the debtor is placed under the control of one or more administrators, who are bound to achieve one of the statutory purposes set out in Paragraph 3 of Schedule B1 to the Insolvency Act. The objectives are:

- to rescue the company as a going concern;
- to achieve a better result for the company's creditors as a whole than would be likely if the company were wound up (without first being in administration); or
- to realise property in order to make a distribution to one or more secured or preferential creditors.

Administration is a tool used to restructure and preserve an insolvent company and/or its business and assets as a going concern. To assist an administrator to achieve the statutory purpose a moratorium arises on commencement of the administration process. This protects the company from certain actions that creditors might otherwise take.[12] One of the important features of the moratorium is that no step may be taken to repossess goods in the debtor's possession under a retention of title agreement without the consent of the administrator or the permission of the court. The supplier does not lose ownership of the goods or any other of his rights under a retention of title clause. However a supplier's ability to enforce those rights is suspended by the moratorium until consent or permission to rely on them is given. Consent or permission is unlikely to be granted if to do so would impact on the administrator's ability to achieve a statutory purpose. Further, an administrator can apply to court for permission to sell goods that are subject to an effective retention of title clause as if the goods were vested in the company. Permission will only be granted on condition that the administrator applies the net

12 Paragraphs 42, 43 and 44 of Schedule B1 to the Insolvency Act 1986.

proceeds of sale, or the market value of the goods if that is greater, towards payment of monies due under the retention of title agreement.[13]

Liquidation is a different process altogether. A liquidator's duty is to realise the company's assets to pay its debts and liabilities in accordance with the status and ranking of the creditors. Liquidation is usually a procedure of last resort where there is no going concern business to protect and preserve. No moratorium arises and there is no impact on a seller's ability to enforce a retention of title clause.

In receivership, a secured creditor will appoint a receiver over an asset subject to a fixed charge, usually land. Again there is no moratorium and a retention of title creditor of the company may rely on his clause without limitation.

A company voluntary arrangement is a mechanism under which a company enters into a binding agreement with its creditors under the supervision of an insolvency practitioner to compromise its debts. Typically creditors agree to receive payment of a proportion of their debts over time while the company continues to trade. This is on the basis that in doing so they will recover a greater amount than if the company went into immediate liquidation. Once approved, a company voluntary arrangement is binding on all creditors of the company whether they voted in favour of the proposal or not.[14] A company voluntary arrangement cannot affect a secured creditor without his consent.[15] The definition of 'security' for this purpose means a mortgage, charge, lien or other security and it does not refer to rights under a retention of title agreement.[16] There is usually no moratorium in relation to a company voluntary arrangement and a retention of title creditor will be able to rely on an effective retention of title agreement with the company. However for a small company[17] a moratorium may be created while the proposal is under consideration.[18] This is not however commonly seen in practice.

The effectiveness of a retention of title clause is often challenged by an administrator or liquidator appointed over an insolvent buyer, usually on the ground that it is not incorporated into the contract of supply. The law as to incorporation of a supplier's terms and conditions is complex. It is often difficult for sellers to provide office holders with sufficient evidence to persuade them that their retention of title terms form a part of the sale agreement. Administrators often purport to transfer ownership of goods that are subject to retention of title terms to an acquirer of the insolvent buyer's business. They take care only to transfer such right, title and interest as the buyer may have in the goods, and attempt to avoid a claim for conversion for dealing in property owned by a third party (the seller). This is problematic for a seller as he will often find his goods have been handed over to a third party the seller did not contract with. He may have to pursue his retention of title claim against the third party, who will hold his goods. This often leads to commercial negotiations and settlements which still put the seller in a better

---

13 Paragraph 72 of Schedule B1 to the Insolvency Act 1986.
14 Section 5(2) of the Insolvency Act 1986.
15 Section 4(3) of the Insolvency Act 1986.
16 Section 248(1)(b) of the Insolvency Act 1986.
17 A company which satisfies two of the following three requirements: turnover not more than £6,500,000; a balance sheet total of not more than £3.26 million; and no more than 50 employees (Sections 382 and 465 of the Companies Act 2006).
18 Pursuant to Schedule A1 to the Insolvency Act 1986.

position than he would have been in had he not had a retention of title clause in place at all. However he may not achieve the level of protection and recovery he anticipated on an insolvency of the buyer.

If the seller, rather than the buyer, is subject to an insolvency process then the office holder appointed to the seller will be able to continue to rely on the benefit of the retention of title clause. The insolvency of the seller will not have any legal impact on the clause, assuming it was valid and effective before insolvency. However as a practical matter it may be more difficult for the seller to rely on the clause as the buyer is likely to seek to apply set-offs and counterclaims against the debt which the seller seeks to recover. In an insolvency situation the seller may not have the funding to pursue a retention of title claim if that would require litigation.

If the seller or the buyer is an overseas entity subject to a foreign insolvency proceeding, the first thing for the parties to consider is which law governs the contract, and whether disputes are allocated to a specific jurisdiction.

As noted above, in a cross-border insolvency subject to the EC Regulation on insolvency proceedings, Article 7 contains specific rules about reservation of title:

1. *The opening of insolvency proceedings against the purchaser of an asset shall not affect the seller's rights based on a reservation of title where at the time of the opening of proceedings the asset is situated within the territory of a Member State other than the State of opening of proceedings.*
2. *The opening of insolvency proceedings against the seller of an asset, after delivery of the asset, shall not constitute grounds for rescinding or terminating the sale and shall not prevent the purchaser from acquiring title where at the time of the opening of proceedings the asset sold is situated within the territory of a Member State other than the State of the opening of proceedings.*

If the insolvency is not subject to the EC regulation then the provisions of the UNCITRAL model law may apply.

2. Retention of title

2.1 Validity and formal requirements

In order to be effective, a retention of title clause must, for all practical purposes, be in writing. Generally (outside certain specific cases such as land) contractual terms do not need to be written to be valid as a matter of English law. However, without sufficient evidence to rebut the statutory presumptions on the intentions of the parties as to the passing of title[19] it is unlikely that a court would find that a retention of title clause had been incorporated into a contract to supply goods if it was not set out in writing. It would not be necessary for a court to imply such a term into a supply contract to make the overall agreement effective, even in a business sector where retention of title was usual. Without a written clause the statutory presumptions on when title pass will generally apply. An administrator or liquidator appointed to an insolvent buyer would almost certainly not accept that an unwritten term was incorporated and effective.

19 As set out in Section 18 of the Sale of Goods Act 1979.

There is no requirement for a retention of title clause to be registered (unless it goes further than seeking to retain title with the seller and creates a charge). That is one of the concerns that many suppliers, credit insurers and commentators have around retention of title terms. Without registration, a supplier who gives credit to a company cannot find out if stock or other goods which the buyer appears to own, and which might be available to creditors generally on an insolvency, are in fact owned by the company. Instead he may find they are all recovered by suppliers in satisfaction of their own debts. The process of registering a retention of title agreement every time goods are supplied to a company would be cumbersome, expensive and does not work at a practical level in real commercial situations. Where the buyer is not a company or limited liability partnership the question of whether retention of title agreements should be registered is even more difficult to resolve. There is no register as readily accessible for non-corporate traders as the register that appears at Companies House for companies and limited liability partnerships. The register maintained at court under the Bills of Sales Acts 1878 and 1882 is the only current potential solution. The entire issue of registration of retention of title agreements and how a workable solution could be achieved is a topic that has been debated from time to time, and is likely to be considered further as a matter for future reform.

Retention of title clauses can take different forms:

- simple clauses, where the seller retains title to goods supplied under a particular contract until those goods have been paid for;
- all monies clauses, where the seller retains title to all goods supplied to the buyer until all sums due to the seller have been paid, not just goods and sums due under the contract in question;
- proceeds of sale clauses, where the seller claims to retain an interest in the proceeds of sale of goods it has supplied; and
- mixed goods clauses, where the seller purports to retain an interest in items that have been created or manufactured by mixing or combining goods supplied with other goods in a process designed to create something more complex, or in the proceeds of sale of such items.

The more complex a clause is, the more likely the courts will find it is a charge which must be registered under Section 860 of the Companies Act 2006 to be effective.

There is no specific form of wording required to create an effective retention of title agreement, save that the wording must make the intention of the parties clear. Simple and all monies retention of title clauses have been upheld by courts on many occasions,[20] whereas a proceeds of sale clause or a mixed goods clause may not be upheld if not registered.[21]

Many disputes over retention of title provisions arise on the question of

20 For example *Aluminium Industrie Vaassen BV v Romalpa Aluminium Ltd* [1976] 1 WLR 676; *Borden (UK) Ltd v Scottish Timber Products Ltd* [1981] Ch 35.

21 For example *Re Bond Worth Ltd* [1980] Ch 228; *Borden (UK) Ltd v Scottish Timber Products Ltd* [1981] Ch 35.

incorporation, and whether a clause that the seller seeks to rely on forms part of the contract of supply. Retention of title provisions are typically found in standard terms and conditions, and it is often not clear if they have been validly incorporated. This is a matter of contract law. A well-advised seller will have a written supply or credit agreement with a buyer which includes the retention of title terms the seller seeks to rely on. He should require the buyer to sign the terms to signify agreement to them. Once a signed agreement is in place there should be little doubt that the retention of title clause is incorporated. Clauses can also be incorporated effectively by way of unsigned standard terms provided there is sufficient evidence that they were brought to the buyer's attention before the contract was formed. Alternatively the buyer must have reasonable notice of the terms, or they must be reasonably available either in writing or electronically. Standard terms can be incorporated if there has been a course of dealing between the parties on the same terms over a period of time. This may often apply in relation to incorporation of industry-specific trade association terms. Difficulties arise for a seller where retention of title terms are found only on invoices and/or delivery notes. These are documents that arise after the contract between the parties has been formed, and it will then be too late for them to be incorporated into the agreement (other than by way of a course of dealing). Whether or not unsigned standard terms have been incorporated, or whether it is the seller's or buyer's terms that take precedence, is commonly known as the 'battle of the forms'. The seller must win that battle if its retention of title claim is to succeed.

Retention of title terms must also be consistent with the general purpose of the contract. For example the court has found that a retailer had permission to resell goods in the ordinary course of its business notwithstanding that the goods had been supplied under retention of title terms.[22] That was the nature of the buyer's business and the seller knew that to be the case. Any other interpretation would have been inconsistent with the buyer's business. The seller failed to withdraw permission to resell the goods on the buyer going into administration and its retention of title claim failed.

There are other practical matters a seller must deal with if it is to make a successful retention of title claim against a buyer, even if it has a valid and legally effective clause incorporated into the terms of sale.

(a) *Identification*

A supplier can only recover goods which it can identify as those it has supplied. A well-drafted retention of title clause will require the buyer to keep the seller's goods separately from goods supplied by others. It may also require the buyer to retain the seller's identity markings on them, or to label the goods itself as supplied by the seller. However this may not be practical for a buyer, and any such terms are often breached. For that reason identification can be difficult where there is more than one seller supplying the same goods to a buyer, or stock is not well labelled with unique means of identification.

The buyer's own records may help a seller identify its goods (for example an electronic point of sale system can be invaluable in checking and locating stock

---

22 *Bulbinder Singh Sandhu v Jet Star Retail Ltd (in administration)* [2011] EWCA Civ 459.

supplied to a retailer operating from multiple sites). Nevertheless it is the seller's obligation to identify its stock and prove its retention of title claim. The duty of an administrator of an insolvent buyer is limited to providing the seller with access to goods to allow identification to take place.[23]

(b) ***Simple clauses***

Where the seller relies on a simple retention of title clause it must be able to allocate goods supplied to a specific unpaid invoice.

(c) ***All monies clauses***

Under an all monies clause, title to goods will pass once the buyer has paid all sums due to the seller. For a clause to be effective, the seller will need to show that a credit account has never been repaid in full or has never had a credit balance. Alternatively, it must show that goods it seeks to recover were supplied after the date on which a nil or credit balance arose.

(d) ***Access***

A seller will need a right of access to a buyer's premises to recover goods supplied under retention of title terms. A right of access should be included as one of the provisions of the overall retention of title clause. Without a specific right of entry, a seller may be deemed a trespasser when seeking to recover its goods. If the buyer prevents the seller from exercising a contractual agreement to access premises to recover his goods, the seller will need to obtain a court order to enforce his right of entry.

Goods do not need to be supplied directly to the buyer for retention of title to be effective. However title will be lost where the buyer resells the goods to its customer, unless the later sale is also made subject to an effective retention of title clause,[24] and the later buyer is aware of the prior seller's claim.

2.2 Scope of retention of title

(a) ***Sale of goods delivered under retention of title***

Section 21(1) of the Sale of Goods Act 1979 provides that:

> *... where goods are sold by a person who is not their owner, and who does not sell them under the authority or with the consent of the owner, the buyer acquires no better title to the goods than the seller had, unless the owner of the goods is by his conduct precluded from denying the seller's authority to sell.*
>
> Section 25(1) of the same act provides:
>
> *Where a person having bought or agreed to buy goods obtains, with the consent of the seller, possession of the goods or the documents of title to the goods, the delivery or transfer by that person ... of the goods or documents of title ... to any person receiving the same in good faith and without notice of any lien or other right of the original seller in respect of the*

---

23 *Blue Gaming Monkey Ltd v Hudson* [2014] EWHC (Ch).

24 *W Hanson (Harrow) Ltd v Rapid Civil and Engineering and Usborne Developments* (1987) Build LR 106; *Re Highway Foods International Ltd* [1995] BCLC 209.

goods, has the same effect as if the person making the delivery or transfer were a mercantile agent in possession of the goods or documents of title with the consent of the owner.

Section 2(1) of the Factors Act 1889 provides:

Where a mercantile agent is, with the consent of the owner, in possession of goods or of the documents of title to goods, any sale, pledge, or other disposition of the goods, made by him when acting in the ordinary course of business of a mercantile agent, shall, subject to the provisions of this Act, be as valid as if he were expressly authorised by the owner of the goods to make the same; provided that the person taking under the disposition acts in good faith, and has not at the time of the disposition notice that the person making the disposition has not authority to make the same.

Under these provisions, a third party acquiring goods in good faith from a buyer where title has been retained, but the buyer has resold the goods on terms where title is to pass at the point of the resale, will obtain good title. It does not matter whether the buyer has paid the seller for the items. Further, in many circumstances the buyer will have express or implied permission to resell the goods, and title passes as the resale takes place with the authority of the original seller.[25]

However where the resale itself takes place under terms including retention of title, title may not pass to the third party as the resale is characterised as an agreement to sell, not an actual sale.[26]

The original seller will not have any claim to the proceeds of sale of the goods to the third party, even if his retention of title agreement includes a proceeds of sale clause, unless he has registered the retention of title agreement as a charge under Section 860 of the Companies Act 2006.

(b) Combining/mixing/mingling goods delivered under retention of title

If goods supplied under retention of title clauses are mixed with other goods by the buyer then title will pass to the buyer. The seller will no longer be able to identify the goods he has supplied if, for example, his oil has been stored by the buyer in a tank with oil from other suppliers, or his books have been stacked on a store shelf with the same titles obtained from other suppliers.[27] If the seller seeks to retain his rights to goods that have been combined, mixed or mingled with others in this way, the retention of title clause will create a charge that will be void unless it is registered under Section 860 of the Companies Act 2006.

It makes no difference to the seller's retention of title claim if the goods were supplied with the intention that they would be combined, mixed or mingled with others. Once the seller is no longer able to identify the goods he supplied as against other goods, title to the goods will pass to the buyer (save in exceptional circumstances such as seen in *Hachette UK Ltd v Borders (UK) Ltd*).[28] The seller will have no claim to any part of the mixed goods.

---

25 For example *Bulbinder Singh Sandhu v Jet Star Retail Ltd (in administration)* [2011] EWCA Civ 459.

26 *Re Highway Foods International Ltd* [1995] BCLC 209.

27 Although see *Hachette UK Ltd v Borders (UK) Ltd* [2009] EWHC 3487 (Ch), in which the court allowed a retention of title claim where the supplier could demonstrate he had supplied the vast majority of the goods.

28 [2009] EWHC 3487 (Ch).

(c) Processing of goods delivered under retention of title

Where goods supplied under a retention of title agreement are used by the buyer to manufacture other goods, or are used as a component of other more complex items, the seller may lose title to the original goods. In *Borden (UK) Ltd v Scottish Timber Products Ltd*[29] the seller supplied resin that was used by the buyer to manufacture chipboard. The Court of Appeal found that once the resin had been used in the irreversible manufacturing process it had lost its identity and so title to the resin was also lost. It could not be traced into the chipboard, and the seller's retention of title claim failed. In *Re Peachdart Ltd*[30] the seller supplied leather to the buyer to make into handbags. The court found that it must have been the intention of the parties that once the buyer had started to work on the leather and had appropriated it to a specific handbag by cutting it, the leather no longer belonged to the seller. Title was lost. Other similar examples include cardboard made into boxes,[31] cloth that was cut to be worked on,[32] and processed food.[33] In *Clough Mill Ltd v Martin*[34] the court found that where goods supplied by the seller were lawfully used by the buyer to create new goods, whether or not the buyer incorporated other goods of his own, title to the new goods generally vested in the buyer, at least where the new goods were not reducible to the original components.

This contrasts with a situation where goods have been used to make a more complex item but can be removed from the new item in the same form as when they were supplied. In *Hendy Lennox (Industrial Engines) Ltd v Grahame Puttick Ltd*[35] the seller supplied diesel engines that were incorporated into generating sets. The process did not alter or destroy the engines and they could readily be removed from the sets. In the circumstances, the court found that title had not passed to the buyer and the seller had retained ownership of the engines.

The courts have also considered cases where the retention of title clause states that where the seller's goods are used to create new products, title to those new items vests in the seller in place of the goods that have been used. It is unlikely that such a term will be effective unless it is registered as a charge. For example in *Borden (UK) Ltd v Scottish Timber Products Ltd*[36] the court noted that if the clause in question had purported to grant the seller an interest in the chipboard or its proceeds of sale, that would appear to be security for payment of the debt due to the seller. The clause would then be registrable as a charge. Similarly in *Re Peachdart Ltd*[37] wording that attempted to give the seller rights in the handbags that were manufactured were found to create a charge. So was the clause in *Clough Mill Ltd v Martin*[38] which purported to give the seller an interest in new goods manufactured from yarn that it supplied to be made into fabric.

---

29 [1981] Ch 5.
30 [1984] Ch 131.
31 *Modleboard Ltd v Outer Box Ltd* [1993] BCLC 623.
32 *Ian Chisholm Textiles v Griffiths* [1994] BCC 96.
33 *Re Highway Foods International* [1995] BCLC 209.
34 [1985] 1 WLR 111.
35 [1984] 1 WLR 485.
36 [1981] Ch 5.
37 [1984] Ch 131.
38 [1985] 1 WLR 111.

Title to goods supplied may also be lost where they are attached to land so as to become fixtures.[39]

A retention of title clause does not of itself impose any obligation on the buyer to account to the seller for the proceeds of sale of the goods. A clause may specifically impose an obligation on the buyer to hold the proceeds of sale on trust for the seller. In *Re Bond Worth Ltd*[40] the court noted that unless the buyer is obliged to hold the proceeds of sale in a separate account and not mingle them with his own monies, that trust will fail and the buyer is merely a debtor of the seller, not a trustee of the monies in question. However, even with a purported trust arrangement, it is likely that the seller is creating a security interest for payment of his debt. That charge will fail unless it is registered as such under Section 860 of the Companies Act 2006.

2.3 Legal effect of retention of title

(a) Effect towards third parties

As noted above, a third party acquiring goods in good faith from a buyer will obtain good title where title to the goods has been retained but the buyer has resold them on terms where title is to pass at the point of the resale. That applies whether or not the buyer has paid the seller for the goods. Further, in many circumstances the buyer will have express or implied permission to resell the goods, and title passes as the resale takes place with the authority of the original seller.[41]

However where the resale itself takes place under terms including retention of title, title may not pass to the third party as the resale is characterised as an agreement to sell, not an actual sale.[42]

A retention of title agreement will be effective against other creditors, whether they are willing suppliers or involuntary creditors such as public bodies with taxation powers. Some public authorities have the right to distrain over goods owned by a debtor to recover unpaid tax. They can take possession of goods, remove them from the site and sell them. However that right does not extend to goods owned by third parties, and where a seller has an effective retention of title agreement any purported distraint over its goods must be withdrawn and the items returned to the seller.[43]

As there is no requirement to register a retention of title agreement, no seller of goods has visibility as to such arrangements the buyer may have made with other suppliers. This is a common source of concern as it can make it difficult for a seller to make an informed judgement on giving credit to a buyer.

(b) Effect in case of seizure of goods delivered under retention of title

As noted above, goods in the possession of the buyer may be subject to seizure by third parties. HM Revenue and Customs or local authorities may exercise rights of

39 For example *Melluish v BMI (No 3) Ltd* [1996] AC 454; *Aircool Installations v British Telecommunications* [1995] CLY 821 Cty Ct; *Bennet and Davis* (1994) 110 LQR 448.
40 [1980] Ch 228.
41 For example *Bulbinder Singh Sandhu v Jet Star Retail Ltd (in administration)* [2011] EWCA Civ 459.
42 *Re Highway Foods International Ltd* [1995] BCLC 209.
43 For example see www.hmrc.gov.uk/manuals/dmbmanual/DMBM655250.htm.

distraint for unpaid taxes; landlords may exercise rights of commercial rent arrears recovery[44] for unpaid rent over goods; and agents instructed by a judgment creditor may carry out execution of a judgment debt.

If goods delivered under a retention of title agreement are subject to seizure by or on behalf of a third party, the seller should contact the agent who has seized the goods as soon as possible and put him on notice of its rights in the goods. Distraint, commercial rent arrears recovery and execution do not destroy effective retention of title agreements and title will remain with the seller. A seller with a retention of title agreement can apply to court to prevent the sale of his goods under a distraint, commercial rent arrears recovery or execution, but will often need to act swiftly and effectively.

If a sale takes place, the seller may be able to bring a claim for conversion of goods in order to recover the proceeds of sale or value of the goods.

(c) Effect in case of a security right established over goods delivered under retention of title

Under a fixed charge, assets charged as security for a debt are permanently appropriated to the payment of the sum charged, in such a way as to give the chargee a proprietary interest in the assets.[45] The debtor will usually need to give full title guarantee in a fixed charge, which means that he has the right to charge the property and that it is not subject to any adverse rights. Goods that are subject to a retention of title agreement will often take the form of stock or movable items, and a lender will not have sufficient control over the goods to have the benefit of a fixed charge security. While a security instrument may purport to take a fixed charge over movable items, it is likely that the purported fixed charge will be characterised as a floating charge due to the nature of the goods. If the goods supplied are more permanent in form they may, for example, become fixtures to land and title will pass to the buyer on that basis.[46] Competing claims to assets between a retention of title creditor and a fixed charge creditor are not common in practice.

A floating charge over the assets of a company or limited liability partnership creates a security right over the assets of the debtor in favour of the beneficiary of the charge. However, the floating charge only applies in relation to assets owned by the debtor, and it is subject to the rights of a seller under a retention of title agreement. On enforcement or crystallisation of a floating charge, an equitable assignment of the debtor's interest in its assets takes place to the beneficiary of the charge, but there is no assignment of goods that belong to a third party that are merely in the possession of the debtor.[47] The security interest does not defeat a seller's rights under an effective retention of title agreement.

---

44 Part 3, Chapter 2 of the Tribunals, Courts and Enforcement Act 2007 and the Taking Control of Goods Regulations 2013, SI 2013/1894.

45 *In re Spectrum Plus Ltd* [2005] UKHL 41.

46 See the description of a fixture in *Elitestone v Morris* [1997] 1 WLR 687.

47 *In the matter of Interview Ltd* [1975] IR 382, in which the High Court in Ireland made reference to *Re Samuel Allen & Sons Ltd* [1907] 1 Ch 575 and *Re Morrison, Jones and Taylor Ltd* [1914] 1 Ch 50.

(d) *Effect in case of insolvency*

When an administrator or liquidator is appointed to a company, he often has little knowledge of the business or assets over which he is appointed. An administrator will frequently want to sell the buyer's business as a going concern, and the acquirer will need stock from the outset to carry on the business. There is often a need to determine urgently whether a retention of title clause is valid or not. A buyer of a business from administrators is often left in a position whereby he acquires goods from the administrator on terms that if they are subject to a retention of title claim, he will have to deal with the seller of the goods. If the retention of title claim is valid he may lose the goods without any compensation, or have to pay the full price for them. Alternatively the parties may reach a commercial agreement whereby, for example, the new owner pays a reduced price for the goods on condition that he will carry on trading with the same supplier. That can make good business sense for both parties.

Under Schedule B1 to the Insolvency Act 1986, an administrator can apply to the court under Paragraph 72 to sell goods free of a retention of title agreement. In practice such applications to court rarely take place. Instead retention of title goods are handed over to the acquirer of the buyer's business on terms that the acquirer will only get whatever right, title and interest the insolvent company had in the goods. It will usually have to deal with the original seller of the goods who claims it has retained title, and either return the stock to the original seller if the claim is valid, or pay for the goods as noted earlier.

The seller of the goods to the insolvent buyer may seek to bring a claim for conversion against administrators who have unlawfully dealt with his property. There is no statutory definition of conversion. It may be summarised as an act whereby a person without authority does something which interferes with the title of the owner of goods in a manner which is inconsistent with the rights of the owner. An administrator may have a statutory defence to a claim for conversion under Section 234 of the Insolvency Act 1986 whereby:

> *(3) Where the office-holder–*
> *(a) seizes or disposes of any property which is not the property of the company, and*
> *(b) at the time of seizure or disposal believes, and has reasonable grounds for believing, that he is entitled … to seize or dispose of that property,*
> …
> *(4) … the office holder–*
> *(a) is not liable to any person in respect of any loss or damage resulting from the seizure or disposal except in so far as that loss or damage is caused by the office holder's own negligence …*

(e) *Effect in case of partial payment of purchase price*

If the buyer has paid part of the purchase price for the goods, title to the goods will remain with the seller under a typical retention of title clause. It will usually say title does not pass until all amounts due are paid, whether the retention of title clause is a simple or all monies clause. It would seem the effect of this is that there will have been a total failure of consideration under the supply contract, as the buyer will have paid part of the price but received nothing in return. This gives rise to a claim on the part of the buyer against the seller in restitution, and the seller may well be required to repay that part of the purchase price that it received.[48] However that is not a uniform view. In *Armour v Thyssen Edelstahlwerke AG*[49] the court noted that it was consistent with the finding that an all monies clause did not create a charge, that a seller who recovered goods under a retention of title agreement need not account to the buyer for any part or the value of those goods. The seller would be able to retain any profit that was made if the resale price exceeded the sum due under the original contract.

3. Enforcement of retention of title

When a retention of title claim is successfully made by a seller, it is usual for the seller to arrange with the buyer (acting through its administrator or liquidator if the buyer is in an insolvency process) to recover its goods. There is no need for the seller to appoint an agent to act on its behalf, although it may do so in practice.

It is vital for a seller to act quickly on becoming aware of circumstances that entitle it to enforce a retention of title agreement. Quick action not only signifies a serious intention by the seller to rely on its rights, but it puts any administrator or liquidator of the buyer on immediate notice of a retention of title claim. Notice will prevent an administrator or liquidator from claiming ignorance of the seller's rights. Notice can also operate to terminate any express or implied right for the buyer to resell goods sold subject to retention of title, whether in the ordinary course of business or otherwise.

If the buyer is insolvent, the administrator or liquidator will often supply the seller with a retention of title questionnaire to be completed and returned. It will ask for information and documents including:

- a copy of the seller's terms and conditions including the relevant retention of title clause;
- how the seller claims that the retention of title clause is incorporated;
- a statement of account;
- a copy of relevant purchase orders, invoices and delivery notes;
- details of the place of delivery and where the seller believes the goods are now located; and
- details to assist in identification, including details of packaging, unique branding or other forms of identification, and photographs.

If the buyer is not insolvent the seller should supply the same information to the buyer in any event.

The seller should arrange to attend at the buyer's premises to inspect the goods, often by itself setting a time and place when it will attend at the premises to do so. On inspection the seller should take an inventory of its goods signed by representatives of the buyer or its administrator or liquidator. It should photograph

---

48 *Clough Mill Limited v Martin* [1985] 1 WLR 111.
49 [1991] 2 AC 339.

and mark the goods, and may, for example, arrange for them to be removed from retail store floors, or be moved to a segregated part of the warehouse as appropriate. The buyer, or its administrator or liquidator, ought to be satisfied that goods have been identified if the seller can demonstrate that the goods have unique markings, bar codes or distinctive packaging as the case may be, that the seller alone used. Similarly it will be sufficient to demonstrate that the seller is the only supplier of the goods in question.

As noted earlier, the obligation to carry out the identification process falls on the seller even if it is a difficult or costly process. All an administrator is obliged to do is to provide the seller with access to goods to allow identification to take place.[50]

There is then often a negotiation between the seller and the buyer as to what happens next. An administrator or liquidator, or a third-party buyer of the insolvent business, may reject the retention of title claim on any of the grounds noted earlier. The most usual ground asserted is lack of incorporation. The parties may come to commercial terms depending on the bargaining position each has. Or the seller may simply recover its stock and resell it to mitigate its loss. The result often depends on several factors:

- how much the stock is worth to the buyer or its administrator/liquidator – if the answer is very little the buyer may be willing to release the goods, preferring to pass the costs of removal to the seller;
- if:
    - the goods are vital to complete work in progress to realise value from contracts; or
    - to keep the buyer's business trading until a sale; or
    - they are needed by a buyer of the insolvent business;

  then the administrator may well be more willing to pay for the goods, but will seek to negotiate on the amount paid so it is less than the full invoice value;
- how much the stock is worth to the seller – if the goods are perishable then the seller is unlikely to press its claim strongly as time goes on. If the goods can be sold elsewhere for full value then the seller may pursue its claim aggressively to recover the stock. On the other hand if the costs of removal are high and the resale value is low, the seller may be more willing to allow the buyer or its administrators to retain the goods in return for payment of part only of the invoice value; and
- if the buyer is in administration, the seller will not be able to enforce its retention of title rights without the consent of the administrator or the permission of the court because of the moratorium that arises.[51]

An administrator or liquidator will usually want to come to a commercial arrangement with a supplier to agree a retention of title claim. If no agreement can be reached, a seller can make an application to court to restrain the buyer from

50 *Blue Gaming Monkey Ltd v Hudson* [2014] EWHC (Ch).
51 Paragraphs 42, 43 and 44 of Schedule B1 to the Insolvency Act 1986.

reselling the goods, or for their recovery. It may consider a claim for conversion against the administrator or liquidator, who will be insured and usually able to pay any judgment that is awarded against them.

One issue that can be problematic to a seller is obtaining access to the goods it seeks to recover under a retention of title agreement. A well-drafted clause will permit the seller to access the buyer's premises to inspect and recover its goods if they are not paid for. If the buyer refuses access despite the terms of the agreement, the seller can apply to court for an order to enforce his right to enter. However, if the buyer is insolvent that right may not be enforced without the consent of the administrator or the permission of the court in an administration, as the moratorium will be in place.

Access can be particularly problematic where goods are on the premises of a third party. Relevant contractual terms may be included by the seller giving a right of access to goods wherever they are found. However they may not be enforceable against a third party who is not a party to the agreement. The seller can easily fall foul of the laws of trespass if it seeks to enforce rights of access it does not have. It has no right to force entry to a premises.

Goods in the possession of a third party may also be subject to other claims made over them, such as a lien exercised by a warehouseman or carrier. Access to premises may also be restricted by health and safety issues, for example if goods have been delivered to a construction site. These matters may all lead to three-way negotiations between the seller, the buyer and the party in possession, failing which the seller may have to resort to the court to enforce its rights against the buyer to require it to make the goods available.

Any of these issues will add to the expense and delay in enforcement of the retention of title agreement.

United States of America

Steven L Harris
Chicago-Kent College of Law, Illinois Institute of Technology

One can think of the American legal system as comprising 51 jurisdictions, each of which has its own law: the 50 states and the United States.[1] Insolvency proceedings, whether for liquidation or reorganisation, are conducted under the US (federal) Bankruptcy Code and are typically referred to as 'bankruptcy cases'.[2] Outside bankruptcy, the legal rights of the buyer, seller, and third parties with respect to a title-retention transaction are ordinarily governed by state law.

The state law governing a title-retention transaction is found in that state's enactment of the Uniform Commercial Code. Each state's enactment of the Uniform Commercial Code is unique. In any given case, one would need first to apply the applicable choice-of-law rules to determine which state's law governs and then to consult the Uniform Commercial Code as enacted by that state. However, inasmuch as the enactments are substantially identical (at least as regards the topic at hand), I have chosen to treat the 2010 version of the 'official text' of the Universal Commercial Code as the governing state law. This text, which has not been enacted anywhere word for word, was promulgated jointly by The American Law Institute, which is a private, membership organisation, and the Uniform Law Commission, which is a quasi-governmental organisation.

The Universal Commercial Code contains special provisions applicable to transactions in consumer goods: defined as goods that are used or bought for use primarily for personal, family, or household purposes.[3] This discussion does not consider these special provisions.

1. General remarks about retention of title

1.1 Transfer of ownership

Under Section 2-401(1) of the Universal Commercial Code, title to goods passes from the seller to the buyer in any manner and on any conditions explicitly agreed on by the parties. However, title cannot pass under a contract of sale prior to the time the goods are identified to the contract.[4]

1 The District of Columbia also has its own law, as do the Commonwealth of Puerto Rico and the US Virgin Islands. My observations about states apply equally to those jurisdictions. For simplicity, I use 'state law' to include the law of those jurisdictions.

2 The Bankruptcy Code is Title 11 of the US Code. Citations herein to sections of the Bankruptcy Code are to the equivalent numbered sections in Title 11. Liquidation proceedings are brought under Chapter 7 of the Bankruptcy Code; reorganisation proceedings are brought under Chapter 11 of the Code.

3 Universal Commercial Code § 9-102(a)(23) (defining consumer goods).

4 Universal Commercial Code § 2-401(1).

In the absence of explicit agreement otherwise, title passes to the buyer at the time and place at which the seller completes his performance with respect to the physical delivery of the goods.[5] In particular, if the contract requires or authorises the seller to send the goods to the buyer but does not require delivery at a destination, title passes to the buyer at the time and place of shipment.[6] If the contract requires delivery at a destination, title passes on tender there.[7]

Special rules apply where delivery is to be made without moving the goods and the parties have not otherwise explicitly agreed. If the seller is to deliver a bill of lading or other document of title, title passes at the time when and the place where the seller delivers the document.[8] If the goods are already identified at the time of contracting and no documents are to be delivered, title passes at the time and place of contracting.[9]

1.2 Retention of title

The parties may agree that the seller retains title to goods until the seller has been paid for them. An agreement of this kind typically is called a 'conditional sale' or a 'title-retention contract'. However, title to goods is largely irrelevant to the rights and obligations of the parties to sale transactions under the Universal Commercial Code:

> *Each provision of [Article 2 of the Universal Commercial Code, governing sales of goods] with regard to the rights, obligations and remedies of the seller, the buyer, purchasers or other third parties applies irrespective of title to the goods except where the provision refers to such title.*[10]

Moreover, "[a]ny retention or reservation by the seller of the title (property) in goods shipped or delivered to the buyer is limited in effect to a reservation of a security interest."[11] Put otherwise, a transaction in which the seller purports to retain title until the price is paid is for all purposes – including priority and remedies – identical to a transaction in which the seller retains a security interest to secure the unpaid price.

Security interests created by contract are governed by Article 9 of the Universal Commercial Code. Generally speaking, Article 9 applies to: "a transaction, regardless of its form, that creates a security interest in personal property or fixtures by contract."[12] As defined in the Universal Commercial Code, "'[s]ecurity interest' means an interest in personal property . . . which secures payment or performance of an obligation."[13] Like Article 2 of the Universal Commercial Code (sales), Article 9 makes clear that, "the provisions of [Article 9] with regard to rights and obligations

---

5 Universal Commercial Code § 2-401(1).

6 Universal Commercial Code § 2-401(2)(a).

7 Universal Commercial Code § 2-401(2)(b).

8 Universal Commercial Code § 2-401(3)(a).

9 Universal Commercial Code § 2-401(3)(b).

10 Universal Commercial Code § 2-401.

11 Universal Commercial Code § 2-401(1).

12 Universal Commercial Code § 9-109(a)(1) (emphasis added). An earlier version of Article 9 gave examples of security interests created by contract. The examples included: "conditional sale . . . or other title retention contract." (Universal Commercial Code § 9-102(2) (1962)). When Article 9 was revised in the 1990s, the examples were deleted as serving no practical purpose.

13 Universal Commercial Code § 1-201(b)(35). The definition goes on to provide that: "[t]he retention or reservation of title by a seller of goods notwithstanding shipment or delivery to the buyer under Section 2-401 is limited in effect to a reservation of a 'security interest.'"

apply whether title is in the secured party [here, the conditional seller] or the debtor [the conditional buyer]."[14]

In short, under US law, a title-retention transaction or conditional sale is a secured transaction, pure and simple. The conditional buyer is an Article 9 'debtor', the conditional seller is an Article 9 'secured party', and the goods are Article 9 'collateral'.[15]

1.3 Foreign and international law

Generally speaking, the Universal Commercial Code permits the parties to choose the law governing their rights and duties in a title-retention transaction. Where the transaction bears a 'reasonable relationship' to the forum state and to another state or nation, the court will give effect to an agreement that the law of the forum state governs or that the law of the other state or nation governs.[16] In the absence of agreement, the forum state's law (ie, the Universal Commercial Code) will apply if the transaction bears an 'appropriate relationship' to the forum state.[17] When a federal court decides issues of state law, it applies the same substantive law as would a court of the state in which the federal court sits.[18] For example, the US District Court for the Northern District of Illinois would apply Illinois' choice-of-law rules.

Although the Universal Commercial Code affords the parties considerable autonomy in choosing the law governing their rights between themselves, the jurisdiction whose law governs the relative rights of the conditional seller (the secured party) and third parties is determined by statute and may not be varied by agreement.[19] More specifically, the priority of the seller's security interest is governed by the local law (ie, the substantive law, without giving effect to the choice-of-law rules) of the jurisdiction in which the goods are located.[20]

1.4 Retention of title in insolvency

The US Supreme Court has held that:

> *Property interests are created and defined by state law. Unless some federal interest requires a different result, there is no reason why such interests should be analyzed differently simply because an interested party is involved in a bankruptcy proceeding.*[21]

Accordingly, a US bankruptcy court will treat a title-retention transaction as a security interest, even if the conditional buyer or conditional seller is the subject of a case under the Bankruptcy Code.[22]

---

14 Universal Commercial Code § 9-202. This rule is subject to certain exceptions that are not relevant here.

15 See Universal Commercial Code § 9-102(a)(28) (defining 'debtor'), § 9-102(a)(73) (defining 'secured party') and § 9-102(a)(12) (defining 'collateral').

16 See Universal Commercial Code § 1-301(a).

17 Universal Commercial Code § 1-301(a).

18 See, eg, *Klaxton Co v Stentor Electric Manufacturing Co.*, 313 US 487 (1941). US district courts have original jurisdiction over all civil actions where the matter in controversy exceeds the sum or value of $75,000, exclusive of interest and costs, and is between citizens of different states, even if there is no question of federal law: Title 28 of the US Code § 1332(a)(1) (2012).

19 See Universal Commercial Code § 1-301(c)(8).

20 See Universal Commercial Code § 9-301(2), (3)(C).

21 *Butner v United States*, 440 US 48, 55 (1979).

22 As to the way title-retention transactions are treated in bankruptcy, see below under heading 2.3(d) (Effect in case of insolvency).

2. Retention of title

2.1 Validity and formal requirements

A security interest, including a seller's retention of title, does not become enforceable against the debtor (the conditional buyer) or third parties unless three conditions have been satisfied.[23] These conditions may be satisfied in any order, but unless all three are satisfied, the seller will not retain an interest in the goods after they are delivered to the buyer.

- The first condition is that the debtor (the conditional buyer) must authenticate a security agreement containing a description of the goods.[24] A security agreement is "an agreement that creates or provides for a security interest."[25] No particular wording is required, and the security agreement need not be contained in a separate document identified as such. An authenticated agreement stating that the seller retains title to the described goods is sufficient, inasmuch as a seller's retention of title after delivery of the goods to the buyer is, as a matter of law, a security interest.[26] However, to avoid disputes, it may be useful to state expressly that the buyer grants a security interest in the goods to secure their price (and, if applicable, other obligations).[27]

  The security agreement must be a written or electronic record that is authenticated by the debtor.[28] The authentication requirement means that a written security agreement must be signed, as broadly defined.[29] It must also contain a description of the collateral.[30] For these purposes, a description is sufficient, "whether or not it is specific, if it reasonably identifies what is described".[31] Description by any method reasonably identifies the collateral "if the identity of the collateral is objectively determinative".[32]

  A security agreement may create or provide for a security interest in "after-acquired collateral", that is to say, property that the debtor acquires in the future.[33] If a seller plans to engage in a series of title-retention (secured) transactions with a buyer, the buyer may agree that the seller retains title to (ie, a security interest in) all goods sold by the seller to the buyer now or in

---

23 Universal Commercial Code § 9-203(b).

24 Universal Commercial Code § 9-203(b)(3)(A). The security agreement requirement may be satisfied in other ways, but they cannot be used in a typical title-retention transaction.

25 Universal Commercial Code § 9-102(a)(74).

26 Universal Commercial Code § 2-401(1); § 1-201(b)(35) (defining 'security interest').

27 As to the obligations that may be secured under a title-retention agreement, see below under heading 2.2 (Scope of retention of title).

28 Universal Commercial Code § 9-203(b)(3)(A); § 9-102(a)(70) ('record' means information that is inscribed on a tangible medium or which is stored in an electronic or other medium and is retrievable in perceivable form.); § 9-102(a)(7) ('authenticate').

29 Universal Commercial Code § 9-102(a)(7) ("'Authenticate' means ... to sign..."); § 1-201(b)(37) ("'Signed' includes using any symbol executed or adopted with present intention to adopt or accept a writing."); § 1-201(b)(43) (writing includes any "intentional reduction to tangible form"). An electronic record is authenticated when a person, "with present intent to adopt or accept [the] record ... attach[es] to or logically associate[s] with the record an electronic sound, symbol, or process" (Universal Commercial Code § 9-102(a)(7)(B)).

30 Universal Commercial Code § 9-203(b)(3)(A).

31 Universal Commercial Code § 9-108(a).

32 Universal Commercial Code § 9-108(b)(6).

33 Universal Commercial Code § 9-204(a).

the future. If such an agreement is signed by the buyer, it will satisfy the requirement for a security agreement that contains a sufficient description of the collateral. In this case, there would be no need for additional title-retention (security) agreements as future sales are made.

- Secondly, value must be given.[34] In the case of a title-retention contract, the value typically is the credit extended by the seller. A pre-existing debt also constitutes value for these purposes.[35]
- Finally, the debtor (buyer) must have rights in the collateral.[36] This condition will be satisfied with respect to goods sold to the buyer because title (ownership) will pass no later than the time of delivery.[37] If the security agreement covers future sales, this condition will be satisfied, and the security interest in the after-acquired goods will become enforceable in the future, when the buyer acquires rights in the those goods.

When a security interest becomes enforceable against the debtor, it attaches to the collateral.[38]

2.2 Scope of retention of title

(a) Sale of goods delivered under retention of title

Whether the conditional buyer of goods delivered under a title-retention contract (ie, subject to a security interest) is permitted to sell the goods to a third party (B-2) before the conditional buyer has paid the price to the seller is determined by agreement between the parties. A security interest ordinarily continues in collateral notwithstanding its sale or other disposition.[39] This rule is subject to three major exceptions:

- If the conditional seller authorises resale, in the security agreement or otherwise, then B-2 will take the goods free of the conditional seller's security interest.[40]
- If B-2 is a buyer in ordinary course of business, then B-2 will take the goods free of the conditional seller's security interest.[41] A 'buyer in the ordinary course of business' is a person who buys goods:
  - in good faith;
  - without knowledge that the sale violates the rights of another person in the goods; and

---

34 Universal Commercial Code § 9-203(b)(1).

35 Universal Commercial Code § 1-204(2): "[A] person gives value for rights if the person acquires them … as security for … a pre-existing claim …"

36 Universal Commercial Code § 9-203(b)(2).

37 Universal Commercial Code § 2-401(1); § 1-201(b)(35) (defining 'security interest').

38 See Universal Commercial Code § 9-203(a). The parties may by express agreement postpone the time of attachment; however, there is almost never a reason to do so.

39 Universal Commercial Code § 9-315(a)(1).

40 Universal Commercial Code § 9-315(a)(1).

41 See Universal Commercial Code § 9-320(a). This rule does not apply with respect to farm products sold by a person engaged in farming operations. However, applicable federal law protects certain buyers; see, eg, US Code Title 7 § 1631 (2012).

- in the ordinary course of business, from a person in the business of selling goods of that kind.[42]

This rule protects ordinary-course buyers of inventory.

- If B-2 gives value and receives delivery of the goods without knowledge of the conditional seller's security interest and before it is perfected, then B-2 will take the goods free of the conditional seller's security interest.[43]

A secured party, including a conditional seller, acquires a security interest in any identifiable proceeds of a resale of the goods.[44] This security interest in the proceeds attaches automatically, regardless of whether the resale is authorised, regardless of whether a sub-buyer takes the goods free of the security interest,[45] and regardless of whether the resale is for cash (in which case the seller would acquire a security interest in the payment) or on credit (in which case the conditional seller would acquire a security interest in the conditional buyer's right to receive payment in the future). The proceeds of proceeds are themselves proceeds.[46] Suppose, for example, that the conditional buyer resells the goods on credit and the B-2 pays for them 30 days after delivery. The conditional buyer then deposits B-2's cheque into a bank account. The conditional seller's security interest will continue in the bank account to the extent that the seller can trace the funds credited to the bank account back to the payment for the goods.[47]

(b) Combining/mixing/mingling goods delivered under retention of title

If goods in respect of which the seller has retained title (ie, holds a security interest) are physically united with other goods in such a manner that the identity of the original goods is not lost, then the security interest continues in, and may be enforced against, the original goods.[48] Suppose, for example, that a tractor engine that is subject to a security interest held by seller A is installed in a tractor that is subject to a security interest held by seller B.[49] Seller A's security interest would continue in the engine, and seller B's security interest would continue in the tractor. As a general matter, after the buyer defaults, each seller would have the right to remove its own collateral (each item of collateral having become an 'accession') from the other goods, but must promptly reimburse the other seller for the cost of repair of any physical injury to the other goods.[50]

---

42 Universal Commercial Code § 1-201(b)(9) (defining 'buyer in ordinary course of business').

43 Universal Commercial Code § 9-317(b). The distinction between perfected and unperfected security interests is discussed below under heading 2.3(a) (Effect towards third parties).

44 Universal Commercial Code § 9-315(a)(2).

45 If B-2 takes the goods subject to the security interest, then the seller will hold a security interest in both the goods and their proceeds. Of course, the seller is entitled to only one satisfaction.

46 See Universal Commercial Code § 9-102(a)(64) (defining 'proceeds').

47 See Universal Commercial Code § 9-315(b)(2) (providing for identification of proceeds by the use of equitable principles). The right to payment is a right to the proceeds of the goods; the cheque is the proceeds of the right to payment and second-generation proceeds of the goods; the appropriate portion of the deposit account is the proceeds of the cheque and third-generation proceeds of the goods. Article 9 contains special rules governing the perfection and priority of a security interest in proceeds.

48 Universal Commercial Code § 9-335(a); § 2-401(1); § 1-201(b)(35) (defining 'security interest').

49 This example is drawn from Official Comment 3 to Universal Commercial Code § 9-335. As in that example, the discussion in the text assumes that the tractor is not subject to a certificate-of-title statute.

50 Universal Commercial Code § 9-335(f); § 9-102(a)(1) (defining 'accession').

Whether the holder of a security interest in one of the accessions (here, the tractor or the engine) acquires a security interest in the whole (here, the tractor plus the engine) ordinarily depends on the description of the collateral in the security agreement.[51] The priority of a security interest in an accession, including the relative priority of a security interest in an accession and a competing security interest in the whole, is determined by the general priority rules of Article 9.[52]

Commingled goods, that is to say goods that are physically united with other goods such that their identity is lost in a product or mass, are treated differently from accessions, which do not lose their identity.[53] Commingled goods include, for example, flour that is combined with other ingredients and baked into a cake, or ball bearings that are put into a container that contains other identical ball bearings.[54] No security interest exists in commingled goods as such.[55] However, if collateral (eg, the flour or the ball bearings) becomes commingled goods, a security interest attaches to the product (the cake) or mass (all the ball bearings in the container).[56]

The priority of conflicting security interest in the product or mass is ordinarily governed by the general priority rules of Article 9.[57] For example, the general priority rules would determine the relative priority of a security interest held by a conditional seller of flour as against a security interest in the conditional buyer's (debtor's) baked goods. However, if more than one security interest attaches to the product or mass as a result of the commingling, as would be the case if the eggs used in the cake were subject to a security interest held by a third party, then the security interests rank equally in proportion to the value of the collateral at the time it became commingled goods.[58]

(c) ***Processing of goods delivered under retention of title***

A conditional buyer may process the goods in such a manner that they are physically transformed but are not physically united with other goods.[59] For example, wheat may be ground into flour, olive oil may be extracted from olives, or a large diamond may be cut into smaller diamonds. In these situations, the security interest of the conditional seller will continue in the resulting goods.

---

51 Universal Commercial Code § 9-335 Official Comment 5.

52 Universal Commercial Code § 9-335(c). These priority rules are discussed below under heading 2.3 (Legal effect of retention of title). A special priority rule may apply if a certificate-of-title statute is implicated; see Universal Commercial Code § 9-335(d).

53 Compare Universal Commercial Code § 9-335 (governing accessions, which are defined in § 9-102(a)(1)) with Universal Commercial Code § 9-336 (governing commingled goods, which are defined in § 9-336(1)).

54 These examples appear in Official Comment 2 to Universal Commercial Code § 9-336.

55 Universal Commercial Code § 9-336(b).

56 Universal Commercial Code § 9-336(c).

57 Universal Commercial Code § 9-336(e). These priority rules are discussed below under heading 2.3.

58 Universal Commercial Code § 9-336(f). The discussion assumes that all security interests are perfected. As to perfection, see below under heading 2.3(a) (Effect towards third parties).

59 Goods that are physically united with other goods are accessions (if their identity is not lost) or commingled goods (if their identity is lost in a product or mass). Accessions and commingled goods are discussed above under heading 2.2(b) (Combining/mixing/mingling goods delivered under retention of title).

(d) Extension of retention of title

A security agreement may provide that the collateral secures future advances or other value, including advances that are discretionary.[60] Thus, a retention-of-title agreement (which is a security agreement) may provide that title does not pass to the conditional buyer until all of the buyer's obligations to the conditional seller, including obligations that may arise in the future and may bear no relationship to the goods sold, have been satisfied.

However, one must distinguish a conditional buyer's obligation for the price from the other obligations secured by the goods. The buyer's obligation for the price is a purchase-money obligation.[61] To the extent that the conditional seller's security interest in the goods secures this purchase-money obligation, the security interest is a purchase-money security interest.[62] To the extent that the conditional seller's security interest in the goods secures obligations other than the buyer's obligation to pay the price, the security interest is not a purchase-money security interest.[63]

As explained below, Article 9 treats purchase-money security interests more favourably than non-purchase-money security interests.[64] Where a seller holds both a purchase-money security interest and a non-purchase-money security interest in the same goods, the seller must prove the extent to which the security interest is a purchase-money security interest in order to avail itself of these benefits.[65] To make this proof, a seller (the secured party) who receives partial payment must determine which obligation (purchase-money or non-purchase-money) has been reduced by the payment. Article 9 provides rules that facilitate this proof.[66] It also dispenses with the need to allocate payments where a seller retains a purchase-money security interest in more than one item of goods that the buyer holds in its inventory and the buyer agrees that each item secures not only its own price but also the price of the other items. In those cases, the security interest in each item is a purchase-money security interest not only with respect to the price of that item but also with respect to the price of the other item(s).[67]

2.3 Legal effect of retention of title

(a) Effect towards third parties

Article 9 distinguishes between two types of enforceable security interest: perfected security interests, as to which a required public-notice step has been taken, and unperfected security interests, as to which a required public-notice step has not been taken.[68] The most common public-notice (perfection) step is the filing of a financing

---

60 Universal Commercial Code § 9-204(c).
61 Universal Commercial Code § 9-103(a)(2) (defining 'purchase-money obligation').
62 Universal Commercial Code § 9-103(b)(1) (defining 'purchase-money security interest').
63 A purchase-money security interest ordinarily does not lose its status as such, even if the purchase-money collateral (here, the goods sold to the conditional buyer) also secures an obligation that is not a purchase-money obligation (Universal Commercial Code § 9-103(f)(1)).
64 See below under heading 2.3(a) (Effect towards third parties).
65 Universal Commercial Code § 9-103(g).
66 Universal Commercial Code § 9-103(e).
67 See Universal Commercial Code § 9-103(b)(2).
68 See Universal Commercial Code § 9-308(a).

statement in the designated public filing office.[69] The cost of filing is relatively low (typically, less than $50), and many filing offices accept electronic filings.

As a general matter, the office in which to file is the filing office maintained by the state (or other jurisdiction) that Section 9-307 of the Universal Commercial Code specifies as the jurisdiction where the debtor is located.[70] Generally speaking, a domestic corporation (organised solely under the law of a single state or of the United States) is located in its jurisdiction of organisation.[71] A foreign corporation having only one place of business (broadly defined) is located at that place of business, and a foreign corporation having more than one place of business is located at its chief executive office (headquarters),[72] but only if the law of that jurisdiction:

> *generally requires information concerning the existence of a non-possessory security interest to be made generally available in a filing, recording, or registration system as a condition or result of the security interest's obtaining priority over the rights of a lien creditor with respect to the collateral.*[73]

In other cases, a foreign corporation is located, for purposes of Article 9 of the Universal Commercial Code, in the District of Columbia.[74] There is no authoritative list of jurisdictions outside the United States whose personal-property security law is described by the sentence quoted above. In case of any doubt, a filing in the District of Columbia is advised. Moreover, even when it is clear that the Universal Commercial Code contemplates a filing in the District of Columbia, if there is a risk that the question of perfection will be determined by law other than the Universal Commercial Code, one is advised not only to file but also to comply with that other law.[75]

To be sufficient and accepted by a designated public filing office, a financing statement must:

- provide the name and mailing address of the debtor (here, the conditional buyer);
- indicate whether the name provided is the name of an individual or an organisation;
- provide the name and mailing address of the secured party (here, the conditional seller) or a representative of the secured party; and
- indicate the collateral.[76]

An indication that the financing statement covers all assets or all personal property is sufficient, if the debtor so authorises.[77] A financing statement need not be

69 Universal Commercial Code § 9-310(a) (providing that, with certain exceptions, a financing statement must be filed to perfect all security interests); § 9-102(a)(39) (defining 'financing statement').
70 See Universal Commercial Code § 9-301(1).
71 See Universal Commercial Code § 9-307(e).
72 See Universal Commercial Code § 9-307(b)(2); § 9-307(a) (defining 'place of business'); § 9-307(b)(3).
73 Universal Commercial Code § 9-307(c). A non-possessory security interest is one where the secured party (here, the conditional seller) is not in possession of the collateral.
74 Universal Commercial Code § 9-307(c).
75 Recall, in this regard, that the priority of a security interest is governed by the substantive law of the jurisdiction in which the goods are located (Universal Commercial Code § 9-301(2) and (3)(C)).
76 Universal Commercial Code § 9-502(a); § 9-516(b)(4) and (5).
77 Universal Commercial Code § 9-504(2).

signed; however, a filed financing statement is not effective unless the debtor authorises the filing in an authenticated record.[78]

As a general matter, an unperfected security interest is subordinate to:

- a buyer of the goods, other than a buyer in ordinary course of business, who gives value and receives delivery of the goods without actual knowledge of the security interest and before it is perfected;[79] and
- a judicial lien (ie, an execution lien or other lien acquired through the judicial process) that arises before the security interest is perfected.[80]

Purchase-money security interests benefit from special priority rules. In particular, a purchase-money security interest as to which a financing statement is filed before, or within 20 days after, the debtor (conditional buyer) takes delivery of the goods, takes priority over the rights of a buyer, lessee or judicial lien creditor that arise between the time the security interest attaches and the time of filing.[81] Therefore, a conditional seller who perfects its security interest after the conditional buyer has resold the goods will prevail over the sub-buyer as long as the security interest is perfected by the filing of a financing statement within 20 days after the conditional buyer takes delivery.

(b) Effect in case of seizure of goods delivered under retention of title

Creditors of a conditional buyer who have obtained a judgment can acquire a judicial lien on the buyer's interest in goods in which the seller has retained title (ie, a security interest).[82] If the conditional seller's security interest is unperfected, the judicial lien will ordinarily have priority.[83] In this case, the sheriff or other public officer will sell the goods and apply the net proceeds to satisfaction of the judgment. The conditional seller will enjoy a claim to any remaining proceeds to the extent necessary to pay the buyer's obligation for the price (and any other obligations secured by the goods). If the seller's security interest is perfected before the judicial lien arises, then the security interest will have priority, and the secured obligations owed to the seller will be paid in priority to the judgment debt.

---

78 See Universal Commercial Code § 9-510(a); § 9-509(a)(1).

79 Universal Commercial Code § 9-317(b). Buyers in the ordinary course of business ordinarily take ownership free of perfected as well as unperfected security interests; see Universal Commercial Code § 9-320(a), discussed above under heading 2.2(a) (Sale of goods delivered under retention of title). An analogous pair of rules applies to lessees. Compare Universal Commercial Code § 9-320(c) (providing that a lessee acting in the ordinary course of business ordinarily takes free of a security interest, even if it is perfected) with Universal Commercial Code § 9-317(c) (providing that a lessee acting outside the ordinary course of business takes free of a security interest only if it gives value and receives delivery of the collateral without knowledge of the security interest and before it is perfected).

80 Universal Commercial Code § 9-317(a)(2).

81 Universal Commercial Code § 9-317(e). In contrast, buyers, lessees, and lien creditors ordinarily enjoy priority if they acquire their rights when a non-purchase-money security interest is unperfected; see Universal Commercial Code § 9-317(b)(2) (buyers); § 9-317(b)(3) (lessees); § 9-317(a)(2) (lien creditors). Attachment is discussed above under heading 2.1.

82 See Universal Commercial Code § 9-401(b) (providing that whether a debtor's rights in collateral may be voluntarily or involuntarily transferred is determined by law other than Article 9 of the Universal Commercial Code). Each state defines the property that is subject to creditor process and the procedures for acquiring and enforcing judicial liens. Provisional (pre-judgment) remedies are very limited.

83 Universal Commercial Code § 9-317(a)(2); but see Universal Commercial Code § 9-317(e) (concerning purchase-money security interests). These sections are discussed above under heading 2.3(a) (Effect towards third parties).

Creditors of a conditional seller can reach the goods that have been sold only indirectly. They would first need to acquire a lien on the seller's right to payment from the conditional buyer, which carries with it the seller's security interest in the goods. Typically, the secured right to payment would be sold, with the proceeds being used to pay the lien creditor's claim.

(c) Effect in case of a security right established over goods delivered under retention of title

A conditional buyer (an Article 9 debtor) may create an effective security interest in goods that are covered by a title-retention agreement (a security agreement), even if the agreement prohibits the buyer from creating a security interest.[84] An agreement to the effect that the creation of a security interest is an event of default will be given effect; however, any security interest created in violation of the buyer's promise not to encumber the goods will attach.[85]

The relative priority of the security interest of a conditional seller and a security interest held by a competing secured party is governed by the general priority rules of Article 9. There are two basic priority rules. One is easy to understand: a perfected security interest has priority over a conflicting unperfected security interest.[86]

The other rule, known as the 'first-to-file-or-perfect' rule, is less intuitive: "conflicting perfected security interests . . . rank according to priority in time of filing or perfection."[87] As explained above, the filing of a financing statement gives public notice that there may be a security interest in the collateral indicated.[88] Whether there is in fact a security interest depends on whether the conditions for attachment of the security interest have been satisfied.[89] A secured party may file a financing statement before a security interest attaches, or even before a security agreement is made.[90] Where a financing statement has been pre-filed, before the security interest attaches, the security interest is perfected at the same time it attaches.[91] However, the priority of the security interest dates from the time that the financing statement was filed and not from the (later) time that the security interest attached.[92]

As mentioned above, a security agreement may cover property that the debtor may acquire in the future.[93] A security interest in this after-acquired collateral does not attach (is not enforceable) until the debtor actually acquires rights in that collateral. However, if a financing statement covering the after-acquired collateral is

---

84 Universal Commercial Code § 9-401(b).

85 Universal Commercial Code § 9-401(b). For a case that imposes liability for tortious interference with contractual relations on a secured party who took a security interest with knowledge that the transaction caused the debtor to violate a covenant in an agreement between the debtor and another creditor, see *First Wyoming Bank v Mudge*, 748 P 2d 713 (Wyo 1988).

86 Universal Commercial Code § 9-322(a)(2).

87 Universal Commercial Code § 9-322(a)(1).

88 See above under heading 2.3(a) (Effect towards third parties).

89 Universal Commercial Code § 9-203(b), discussed above under heading 2.1 (Validity and formal requirements).

90 Universal Commercial Code § 9-502(d).

91 Universal Commercial Code § 9-308(a).

92 Universal Commercial Code § 9-322(a)(1).

93 Universal Commercial Code § 9-204(a), discussed above under heading 2.1 (Validity and formal requirements).

filed before the security interest attaches, the priority of the security interest dates from the time of filing.[94]

Standing alone, the first-to-file-or-perfect rule would enable a creditor to achieve first priority over all of the debtor's existing and after-acquired property. As a practical matter, once a creditor filed a financing statement covering all the debtor's assets, the debtor would be unable to obtain secured financing to acquire new property, as the new financier's security interest would be subordinate to that of the earlier, after-acquired property lender. (The after-acquired property lender's financing statement will have been filed before the new financier's financing statement was filed or its security interest perfected.)

Fortunately for debtors, and for those who finance the acquisition of new goods, Article 9 affords a super-priority to the holder of a purchase-money security interest. As explained above, a seller under a title-retention contract holds a purchase-money security interest.[95] To obtain priority over a conflicting security interest, a conditional seller (or other holder of a purchase-money security interest) must satisfy certain conditions:

- A purchase-money security interest in goods other than the debtor's inventory has priority over a conflicting security interest in the same goods if the purchase-money security interest is perfected when the debtor receives possession of the goods or within 20 days thereafter;[96] and
- A purchase-money security interest in inventory has priority over a conflicting security interest in the same inventory if the purchase-money security interest is perfected when the debtor receives possession of the inventory, and the holder of the conflicting security interest receives a notification of the purchase-money security interest before the debtor receives possession of the inventory.[97]

(d) Effect in case of insolvency

The filing of a petition under the Bankruptcy Code, whether a petition for liquidation under Chapter 7 or reorganisation under Chapter 11, creates an estate that includes "all legal or equitable interests of the debtor in property as of the commencement of the case", regardless of where the property is located and regardless of who holds it.[98] Therefore, if a conditional seller becomes the subject of

94 Universal Commercial Code § 9-322(a)(1).
95 See above under heading 2.2(d) (Extension of the retention of title).
96 Universal Commercial Code § 9-324(a). This priority extends to identifiable proceeds of the goods.
97 Universal Commercial Code § 9-324(b). One notification is effective for five years. The priority in identifiable proceeds of the inventory is quite limited.
98 Bankruptcy Code § 541(a)(1).
99 In a Chapter 7 liquidation, the conditional seller's trustee in bankruptcy will have the duty to enforce the seller's claims against the buyer; see Bankruptcy Code § 704(a)(1) (providing that the trustee shall collect and reduce to money the property of the estate). In Chapter 11 reorganisation, a trustee ordinarily is not appointed; see Bankruptcy Code § 1104(a). Rather, the seller, as debtor in possession, will enjoy this right; see Bankruptcy Code § 363(c) (providing that, if the business is authorised to be operated, the trustee may use property of the estate in the ordinary course of business); Bankruptcy Code § 1108 (providing that, so long as there is no court order to the contrary, the trustee may operate the business); Bankruptcy Code § 1107(a) (providing that, generally, a debtor in possession shall have the rights, and perform the functions, of the trustee).

a bankruptcy case, its right to payment of the price and its retained title (security interest) will become property of the estate and enforceable against the conditional buyer.[99]

If a conditional buyer becomes the subject of a bankruptcy case, its ownership interest in the goods will become property of the estate, subject to the conditional seller's security interest. The filing of a bankruptcy petition operates as a stay of any act to obtain property of the estate or property from the estate, any act to enforce a lien against property of the estate, and any act to collect any pre-petition claim against the debtor.[100] Therefore, if a conditional buyer becomes the subject of a bankruptcy case, the conditional seller is stayed from enforcing its security interest without first obtaining the permission of the court.[101]

During the case, the property of the estate, including goods subject to a security interest, may be used, sold, or leased in the ordinary course of business without a court order.[102]

Staying a conditional seller (the secured party) from enforcing its security interest and allowing the buyer (the debtor) to use or sell the goods during a bankruptcy case imposes on the seller the risk that the goods may decline in value during the proceedings. For example, the goods may be damaged or destroyed, or they may depreciate in value through use, the passage of time, or both. A secured party has the right to relief from the stay (including a lifting of the stay), nor may the estate use or sell them, if the estate does not provide adequate protection of the value of the collateral.[103] There is no required method for providing adequate protection.[104] Adequate protection against depreciation may be given, for example, by providing to the secured party periodic cash payments equal to the amount of the depreciation.[105] Adequate protection against damage or destruction may be provided by insurance.[106] In the event that the stay is lifted, the seller may take possession of goods from the estate and enforce its security interest under non-bankruptcy law.[107]

Property of the estate includes, in addition to the rights of the debtor, property

100 Bankruptcy Code § 362(a).

101 The estate can recover goods from a conditional seller who has repossessed them before the commencement of the bankruptcy case; see *United States v Whiting Pools, Inc*, 462 US 198 (1983) (affirming the issuance of a turnover order against the Internal Revenue Service, which had taken possession of property subject to a federal tax lien). Indeed, there is respectable authority that, even in the absence of a turnover order, a secured party violates the stay by retaining possession of repossessed collateral; See, eg, *Thompson v General Motors Acceptance Corp*, 566 F 3d 699 (7th Cir 2009).

102 Bankruptcy Code § 363(c). The statement in the text assumes that the business of the debtor is authorised to be operated, which, unless the court orders otherwise, will be the case in a Chapter 11 reorganisation but not in a Chapter 7 liquidation; see Bankruptcy Code §§ 1108 (Chapter 11) and 721 (Chapter 7).

103 Bankruptcy Code §§ 362(d) (relief from the stay) and 363(e) (use or sale). These sections provide that a secured party is entitled to adequate protection of its interest in the collateral. The Supreme Court has held that this interest refers to the value of the collateral, and does not include a secured party's right (which is suspended by the stay) to take immediate possession of the collateral, liquidate it, and apply the proceeds in payment of the debt; *United Savings. Association of Texas v Timbers of Inwood Forest Associates Ltd*, 484 US 365, 373–74 (1988).

104 See Bankruptcy Code § 361 (providing that adequate protection may be provided by taking certain specified acts or "granting such other relief . . . as will result in the realization by [the secured party] of the indubitable equivalent of such entity's interest in [the collateral]").

105 Bankruptcy Code § 361(1).

106 See Bankruptcy Code § 361(3).

107 Enforcement of a security interest is discussed below under heading 3 (Enforcement of retention of title).

that is brought into the estate through the use of the statutory powers to avoid pre-bankruptcy transfers, including the retention of title as a security interest, that satisfy certain criteria.[108] Of particular relevance is the Bankruptcy Code's 'strong-arm power', under which a trustee in bankruptcy enjoys the non-bankruptcy rights and powers of a hypothetical creditor who acquires a judicial lien as of the commencement of the bankruptcy case.[109] As explained above, an unperfected security interest is subordinate to a judicial lien.[110] Accordingly, if a security interest is unperfected at the commencement of a bankruptcy case, the trustee may ordinarily avoid the security interest and render the seller (the secured party) unsecured.[111]

In appropriate cases, a title retention (security interest) may be avoided as a fraudulent transfer or as a preferential transfer.[112] In this connection it is worth noting that, for purposes of the preference provisions of the Bankruptcy Code, the transfer of a security interest that is perfected more than 30 days after it attaches is deemed to occur at the time of perfection.[113] Therefore, if a conditional seller fails to file a financing statement before, or within 30 days after, its security interest attaches, its security interest will be deemed to have been transferred on account of an antecedent debt that was incurred when the seller gave value (extended credit) to the buyer. Deeming the transfer to occur upon perfection may bring the transfer within the reach-back period (normally, 90 days before the commencement of the bankruptcy case), even if the security interest became enforceable (attached) outside the period.

(e) *Effect in case of partial payment of the purchase price*

What has been said above applies regardless of whether the conditional buyer has paid a portion of the purchase price before entering bankruptcy. In any event, as explained immediately below, a conditional seller is entitled to receive from the estate the goods or their value, but only insofar as necessary to satisfy the obligations that the goods secure. The buyer is entitled to the value of the goods to the extent they exceed the secured obligations.

3. Enforcement of retention of title

After default, unless the conditional buyer has become the subject of an insolvency proceeding (a bankruptcy case), a conditional seller may enforce its title-retention

---

108 Bankruptcy Code § 541(a)(3); Bankruptcy Code § 101(54)(B) (defining 'transfer').

109 Bankruptcy Code § 544(a)(1). In Chapter 11, the debtor, as debtor in possession, ordinarily enjoys the rights of a trustee. Bankruptcy Code § 1107(a).

110 Universal Commercial Code § 9-317(a)(2), discusssed above under heading 2.3(a) (Effect towards third parties).

111 A trustee's rights as a hypothetical judicial lien creditor extend no farther than the rights of a real lien creditor under the Universal Commercial Code. Therefore, a purchase-money security interest that is perfected by filing a financing statement after the commencement of a bankruptcy case but within the 20-day period specified in Universal Commercial Code § 9-317(e) will not be avoidable; see Bankruptcy Code § 546(b)(1) (providing that a trustee's rights under Bankruptcy Code § 544 are subject to any generally applicable law that permits perfection of an interest in property to be effective against an entity that acquires rights in the property before the date of perfection).

112 See Bankruptcy Code § 548 (fraudulent transfers); Bankruptcy Code § 547 (preferences).

113 See Bankruptcy Code § 547(e)(2)(A).

contract (the security interest) by taking possession of the goods.[114] The seller may – but need not necessarily – proceed pursuant to judicial process.[115] The seller, or any person acting on the seller's behalf, may proceed without judicial process, provided it does so "without breach of the peace".[116] Article 9 neither defines nor explains the conduct that constitutes a breach of the peace, leaving that matter for continuing development by the courts.[117] Generally speaking, a repossessing secured party who does not retreat when told to do so would breach the peace. The seller need not notify the buyer or any other person before exercising its self-help right to repossess the goods.

After obtaining possession of the goods (whether through the judicial process or by exercising self-help), the seller may sell, lease, or otherwise dispose of them.[118] Alternatively, the seller may dispose of the goods without removing them from the buyer's premises, provided it does so without breaching the peace.[119]

The basic requirements for a disposition of collateral are very general:

- "Every aspect of a disposition of collateral, including the method, manner, time, place, and other terms, must be commercially reasonable."[120] If commercially reasonable, disposition may be by public sale (auction) or private sale.[121] However, a secured party may not buy the collateral at a private sale unless it is of a kind that is customarily sold on a recognised market or the subject of widely distributed price quotations.[122] Despite the statutory focus on "every aspect", the courts tend to consider all of the relevant factors together as part of a single transaction:[123] "[A] low price suggests that a court should scrutinize carefully all aspects of a disposition to ensure that each aspect was commercially reasonable."[124] But a low price is not in itself sufficient to establish that a disposition was not commercially reasonable.[125]
- "[A] secured party that disposes of collateral ... shall send to the persons specified [these persons include the debtor] a reasonable authenticated notification of disposition."[126] Ten days' advance notification is sufficient.[127] Article 9 provides that the contents of a notification are sufficient if the notification includes specified information;[128] however, a notification that

114 Universal Commercial Code § 9-609(a)(1). As explained above, if the buyer is subject to insolvency proceedings (ie, is a debtor under the federal Bankruptcy Code), the seller may not take any act to collect its claim or enforce its security interest in the goods without first obtaining leave of court; see above under heading 2.3(d) (Effect in case of insolvency).
115 Universal Commercial Code § 9-609(b)(1).
116 Universal Commercial Code § 9-609(b)(2).
117 Universal Commercial Code § 9-609 Official Comment 3.
118 Universal Commercial Code § 9-610(a).
119 Universal Commercial Code § 9-609(a)(2), (b)(2).
120 Universal Commercial Code § 9-610(b).
121 Universal Commercial Code § 9-610(b).
122 Universal Commercial Code § 9-610(c).
123 See, eg, *Westgate State Bank v Clark*, 642 P 2d 961, 969 (Kan 1982).
124 Universal Commercial Code § 9-610 Official Comment 10.
125 Universal Commercial Code § 9-610 Official Comment 10.
126 Universal Commercial Code § 9-611(b).
127 Universal Commercial Code § 9-612(b). Whether notice sent less than 10 days before disposition is reasonable is a question of fact (Universal Commercial Code § 9-612(a)).
128 Universal Commercial Code § 9-613(1).

> does not contain all the specified information may be commercially reasonable nevertheless.[129] The statute includes a form that, when completed, provides sufficient notification;[130] however, no particular phrasing of the notification is required.[131] The notification is in addition to any advertising and publicity that may be necessary to the conduct of a commercially reasonable disposition.

Although a debtor may not waive or vary these rules,[132] the parties may determine by agreement the standards by which the secured party's duties are to be measured, if the standards themselves are not manifestly unreasonable.[133] For example, the parties may agree that five days' advance notice is sufficient, if that period is not manifestly unreasonable.

The proceeds of a disposition are applied first to the reasonable expenses of retaking and disposing of the collateral and, to the extent provided for by agreement and not prohibited by other law, the reasonable attorney's fees and legal expenses incurred by the secured party (the conditional seller). Any remaining proceeds are applied to the obligations secured by the collateral.[134] The conditional buyer (the debtor) is entitled to any surplus and is liable for any deficiency.[135]

Ordinarily, the buyer's liability for deficiency is calculated by deducting from the proceeds of the sale the amounts specified in the preceding paragraph.[136] If, however, the conditional seller (the secured party) does not comply with its statutory obligations, the deficiency is further reduced by any additional amounts that a complying disposition would have yielded.[137] If the non-compliance does not affect the amount of the proceeds realised, then the buyer's liability for deficiency would not be reduced.

A disposition of collateral after a default transfers to a transferee for value all the debtor's (the conditional buyer's) rights in the collateral.[138] It also discharges the security interest of the enforcing conditional seller (the secured party) and any subordinate security interest or other lien.[139] A transferee acting in good faith takes

129 Universal Commercial Code § 9-613(2) (providing that whether the contents of a notification that lacks any of the specified information are nevertheless sufficient is a question of fact).

130 Universal Commercial Code § 9-613(4).

131 Universal Commercial Code § 9-613(5).

132 Universal Commercial Code § 9-602(7).

133 Universal Commercial Code § 9-603(a).

134 Universal Commercial Code § 9-615(a)(1) and (2).

135 Universal Commercial Code § 9-615(d). Before paying over any surplus, the secured party must apply the proceeds to the satisfaction of obligations secured by any subordinate security interest in (or other lien on) the collateral, if the holder of the conflicting encumbrance makes a timely demand (see Universal Commercial Code. § 9-615(a)(3)).

136 A special rule for calculating deficiency and surplus applies to certain low-price dispositions where the transferee is the secured party, a "person related to the secured party" (as defined in Universal Commercial Code § 9-102(a)(62) and (63)) or a secondary obligor (as defined in Universal Commercial Code § 9-102(a)(72)); see Universal Commercial Code § 9-615(f). See also Universal Commercial Code § 9-626(a)(5) (providing a supplementary rule for allocating the burden of proof with respect to a deficiency or surplus resulting from dispositions of this kind).

137 Universal Commercial Code § 9-626(a) contains rules that allocate the burden of proof and specify the method of calculating a deficiency in cases of non-compliance with Article 9. In rare cases, application of these rules may result in a surplus for which the secured party is liable.

138 Universal Commercial Code § 9-617(a)(1).

139 Universal Commercial Code § 9-617(a)(2) and (3).

the goods free of these rights and interests, even if the disposition does not comply with the requirements of Article 9.[140]

The author thanks his colleague, Professor Adrian J Walters, for reviewing this chapter.

140 Universal Commercial Code § 9-617(b).

About the authors

Sang Jin Ahn
Attorney, Kim & Chang
sjahn@kimchang.com

Sang Jin Ahn is an attorney in the firm's banking, mergers and acquisitions, foreign direct investment, real estate and Japanese practice groups.

He has extensive experience in a wide range of domestic and cross-border transactions and regulatory matters, including banking, corporate financing, ship financing, structured financing, acquisition financing, mergers and acquisitions of financial institutions and real estate acquisitions, representing top Korean, Japanese and international corporations.

N Can Artüz
Associate, Fırat-Izgi Attorney Partnership
can.artuz@firatizgi.com

N Can Artüz graduated from Bilkent University Law School and continues his studies as an LLM candidate at Bilgi University. During his internship, he worked in a leading business consultancy firm with a specific focus on anti-trust, consumer protection, energy regulation and litigation matters.

After joining Firat-Izgi Attorney Partnership as an associate, he mainly focused on energy law, labour law, execution and bankruptcy law, commercial law and commercial litigation. He gained considerable experience on complex commercial disputes and took an active role at every stage of their resolution.

N Can Artüz continues to represent clients before the Turkish civil, criminal and administrative courts and provide legal counselling services to multinational companies on behalf of Firat-Izgi Attorney Partnership in his areas of expertise.

Miguel de Avillez Pereira
Partner, Abreu Advogados
miguel.avillez.pereira@abreuadvogados.com

Miguel de Avillez Pereira graduated from the University of Lisbon law school in 1989. That same year he joined Albuquerque & Avillez law firm as an associate lawyer.

In 1992, he joined Maclay Murray & Spens law firm as a foreign lawyer. One year later, Miguel founded Avillez Pereira & Associados law firm, which was integrated by Abreu Advogados in 2002. Since then he has been a partner with Abreu Advogados.

Miguel has an LLM from the Europa Institute, University of Edinburgh.

As a lawyer Miguel has been involved over the years in some of the most significant transactions that Abreu has assisted on in Portugal, Angola and Mozambique, including the competitive bid for Portugal Telecom, the formation of the Angola LNG and the privatisation of ANA. He has consistently been noted by *Chambers Europe* and *Legal 500* as a top Portuguese mergers and acquisitions lawyer for the last 10 years.

Kelly Bai
Associate, R&P China Lawyers
baixuebing@rplawyers.com

Kelly Bai is an associate with R&P's Beijing office. Kelly is a Chinese qualified lawyer, who obtained her law degree from the East China University of Political Science and Law. She mainly assists foreign clients with commercial contracts and general corporate matters.

R&P China Lawyers is a boutique firm with about 25 Chinese qualified lawyers in Shanghai and Beijing. R&P focuses on assisting foreign companies who do business in or with China. As a Chinese firm, R&P is allowed to advise on Chinese law and represent clients in local courts. R&P's foreign management ensures that clients receive advice and service that is up to international standards.

Agustín Bou
Partner, Jausas Legal
abou@jausaslegal.com

Agustín Bou has been the head of Jausas' restructuring and insolvency department in Barcelona since 2003. He holds a degree in law and a masters in business science, and has specialised in restructuring and insolvency and other corporate projects for over 30 years while based in Madrid and Barcelona.

He is an outstanding specialist in insolvency proceedings, acting on behalf of debtors and creditors both national and international. Among his specialties, the purchase of productive units in the framework of insolvency proceedings should be highlighted. In addition, he has led several sale and purchase transactions and other restructuring operations for national and foreign clients. Due to his ability to negotiate in time-limited situations, he stands out in accelerated sale processes and other special situations (distressed mergers and acquisitions).

He is a member of the Spanish Private Equity and Venture Capital Association, with whom he collaborates in the organisation.

Moreover, he is a frequent collaborator in the area of insolvencies for *Expansión* and *La Vanguardia* newspapers, and an economic and law news writer for *La Vanguardia*'s legal blog.

Arno Brauneis
Partner, bkp Rechtsanwälte
a.brauneis@bkp.at

Arno Brauneis is the founding partner of bkp (Brauneis Klauser Prändl) Rechtsanwälte, based in Vienna, Austria. His areas of specialisation are corporate law and mergers and acquisitions.

Publishing regularly, he is the author of numerous books and articles in various fields of law, including corporate law issues, asset deals and share deals, to name but a few. He is also the author of an Austrian reference work on the leasing of enterprises.

Elisabetta Caccavella
Managing associate, Legance Avvocati Associati
ecaccavella@legance.it

Elisabetta Caccavella is a dual qualified lawyer (in both Italy and England and Wales), with more than 12 years of experience in practising contract and commercial law with internationally recognised law firms in Italy, as well as a visiting lawyer in the United Kingdom.

She holds a degree in law (*magna cum laude*) and in her current role as managing associate of Legance Avvocati Associati, one of Italy's leading law firms, she counsels international corporate clients on contracts and litigation cases. She has gained significant experience in out-of-court debt restructuring agreements as well as in judicial insolvency proceedings.

She is an active member of the insolvency section of the International Bar Association and is co-editor of the journal *Insolvency and Restructuring International*.

Kelby Carter
Associate, Gowling Lafleur Henderson LLP
kelby.carter@gowlings.com

Kelby Carter is an associate in the Financial Services Group at Gowling Lafleur Henderson LLP's Toronto office, practising in the areas of banking and insolvency law. Kelby acts for both lenders and borrowers in secured and unsecured lending transactions, including syndicated financing, subordinate debt financing and refinancing, as well as for receivers and secured creditors on insolvency matters.

Kelby also had the opportunity to gain valuable insight into the operation of financial institutions as in-house counsel while on a 12-month secondment with one of Gowlings' largest banking clients.

Carsten Ceutz
Partner, Bech-Bruun
cac@bechbruun.com

Carsten Ceutz represents financial creditors with exposures in finance and operational leases as well as loans to and charges over cooperative housing associations in distress. Carsten advises on the possession and administration of receivables charges and floating company charges, and on the commencement and administration of restructuring proceedings.

As restructuring administrator and trustee of many businesses subject to restructuring proceedings and estates in bankruptcy, Carsten employs his substantial professional expertise to safeguard the interests of estates in bankruptcy and creditors. He has vast experience in administering the bankruptcy estates of travel agencies and in the management of information technology, rights and employees in connection with corporate restructurings and insolvency.

Benedict F Christ
Partner, Vischer AG
bfchrist@vischer.com

Benedict F Christ is co-head of the corporate/mergers and acquisitions practice group of Vischer, a leading Swiss law firm. He specialises in mergers and acquisitions, banking, finance, contracts and corporate law. Ben has a wealth of transactional experience and advises regularly on real estate, private equity, structured finance and capital market matters, and regularly publishes in these areas. He is admitted in Switzerland and New York, and holds a licentiate in law (1996) and a doctorate in law (1999) from the University of Freiburg and an LLM (2001) from New York University.

Paulo Lopes da Silva
Partner, MOLITOR, avocats à la cour
paulo.dasilva@molitorlegal.lu

Paulo is a partner in MOLITOR's litigation and dispute resolution practice. He is regularly involved in commercial cross-border aspects of the law and is also very active in banking litigation, particularly matters involving the liability of banks and their directors. Paulo is ranked in *The Legal 500 EMEA* and *The Legal 500 US Special Edition*. He is seen as "well reputed" and an "excellent counsel", "extremely professional", "empathetic to clients" and has "an entrepreneurial spirit" (*Legal 500 EMEA*). *Chambers Europe* ranks him as a key individual, stating that he receives excellent feedback from all sides. One source describes him as "an excellent technician, a smart lawyer who goes straight to the point, identifying and understanding problems quickly". Paulo has a masters degree in commercial law from the University of Strasbourg (France). Paulo is a member of the International Bar Association.

Amélie Dorst
Associate, BMH Avocats
adorst@bmhavocats.com

Amélie Dorst is a member of the corporate/restructuring group of BMH Avocats in Paris.

She specialises in international transactions (cross-border mergers and acquisitions, distressed mergers and acquisitions, corporate finance) and in corporate restructurings and reorganisations.

Her experience includes advising banks, funds, insolvency practitioners and companies in relation to a wide range of transactions, including financial restructurings, cross-border acquisition finance and general bank lending.

Anja Droege Gagnier
Partner, BMH Avocats
adroege@bmhavocats.com

Anja Droege Gagnier is head of the corporate/restructuring group of BMH Avocats in Paris.

Anja has gained broad experience over 20 years in international transactions (cross-border mergers and acquisitions, joint ventures, distressed mergers and acquisitions, corporate finance) and in corporate restructurings and reorganisations in various industries, including steel, aeronautic, automotive, nuclear, petrol, co-generation energy, medical instruments, health, biotech, printing, banking, real estate and luxury goods. She advises mainly foreign investors, banks and trustees in transactions in France and in insolvency and pre-insolvency proceedings.

Anja is senior vice-chair of the insolvency section of the International Bar Association.

She publishes on a regular basis on subjects related to corporate and insolvency issues, in German and international magazines. Anja is co-author of the book *Gläubigerkommentar Anfechtungsrecht* (avoidance actions) (second edition) published in Germany in 2015 by Finanz Colloquium Heidelberg.

Evgenia Evdokimova
Associate, Egorov Puginsky Afanasiev & Partners
evgenia_evdokimova@epam.ru

Evgenia Evdokimova is an associate at the St Petersburg law office of Egorov Puginsky Afanasiev & Partners, where she specialises in contract law issues.

For the firm, Evgenia has worked on a large number of projects related to supply and construction contracts, insurance, security and investment agreements, and has represented both Russian and foreign clients in Russian courts and international commercial arbitrations.

Evgenia's education includes undergraduate (2006) and postgraduate (2008) degrees with honours at St Petersburg State University's school of law. She has also earned a master of laws degree with honours (LLM) at the University of Hamburg. Evgenia is now working on a dissertation regarding proprietary security interests, and is also teaching at the civil law department of St Petersburg State University's school of law.

Evgenia has been a member of the St Petersburg Bar Association since 2008. She speaks fluent English and German.

E Sevi Fırat
Partner, Fırat-Izgi Attorney Partnership
sevi.firat@firatizgi.com

E Sevi Fırat regularly supports multinational companies, including manufacturers of pharmaceuticals, biotechnology, medical devices, special food and feed, cosmetics and other consumer products, on important new legislative projects and policy developments in Turkey. She also provides consultancy on strategic planning of new investments in Turkey, regulatory compliance, anti-corruption and antitrust. She also has broad experience in litigation on life science matters, including product liability, advertising, customs controls and promotional activities. E Sevi Fırat is also experienced in complex deals, including technology transfer agreements, product portfolio transfers and distribution agreements.

She was deeply involved in the first ever court actions in Turkey initiated in order to protect patent rights, and has been involved in regulatory work with the Ministry of Health regarding enforcement of pharmaceutical patent rights, data protection and data exclusivity.

She regularly consults for multinational companies in relation to all kinds of legal matters relevant to direct selling systems and the regulatory environment.

Frank Flanagan
Senior associate, Mason Hayes & Curran
fflanagan@mhc.ie

Frank is a senior associate in the commercial litigation department of Mason Hayes & Curran.

Prior to joining Mason Hayes & Curran, Frank had a 20-year career in the communications and computer hardware industries, culminating as chief technology officer of a technology start-up where he was deeply involved in raising significant venture capital funding and in technology licensing and transfer to a Fortune 100 company.

Frank advises a wide range of clients in relation to commercial disputes, insolvency and restructuring and communications regulation.

Frank advises both insolvency practitioners and vendors, including a Fortune 100 vendor, in relation to the drafting and enforceability of retention of title provisions.

Frank co-authored the Irish chapter in Globe Law and Business's *Cash Pooling and Insolvency: A Practical Global Handbook*.

Ernst Giese
Partner, Giese & Partner, sro
giese@giese.cz

Ernst Giese is the managing partner of Giese & Partner. He has specific expertise in the field of corporate, banking and industry law. In the last 15 years he has been acting as legal counsel for Deutsche Pfandbriefbank (formerly Hypo Real Estate), UniCredit, Eurohypo and Commerzbank, and has been involved in major mergers and acquisitions transactions. He also has a very strong background and excellent references within the field of insolvency law. He has been involved in numerous restructuring and insolvency cases, especially in the automotive and construction industry. German, Austrian, British and practitioners from other countries regularly seek his advice in cases with reference to the Czech Republic and Slovakia.

Steven L Harris
Professor, IIT Chicago-Kent College of Law
sharris@kentlaw.edu

Steven L Harris is a professor at IIT Chicago-Kent College of Law, where he teaches courses in commercial law, bankruptcy and reorganisations, contracts and remedies. He also consults regularly on commercial law and bankruptcy and insolvency matters and has testified as an expert in state, federal and international courts and tribunals.

Steven has published widely. He is co-author (with Charles Mooney) of a popular casebook on secured transactions, and his articles have appeared in the Cornell, Virginia, Minnesota, UCLA and Vanderbilt law reviews, among others.

An active participant in law reform, he served as a reporter for the committee that drafted the revised Uniform Commercial Code Article 9 (secured transactions) and for the committee that drafted the 2010 amendments to the revised Article 9. He also served as a US delegate at the diplomatic conferences for the Cape Town Convention's rail and space protocols.

Yuval Horn
Partner, Horn & Co, Law Offices
yhorn@hornlaw.co.il

Yuval Horn is the founder of Horn & Co, Law Offices, an Israeli firm specialising in representation of technology-focused and multinational companies, investors, founders and board members.

He regularly advises his clients on cross-border transactions, including mergers and acquisitions, public offerings in the United States and Israel, intellectual property acquisitions and licences, international corporate reorganisations and all legal aspects of operations of technology-based companies.

Yuval serves as vice-chair (and incoming co-chair) of the Technology Law Committee of the International Bar Association. He was identified by *The International Who's Who of Life Science Lawyers* in 2013 and in 2015 as one of the five leading individuals worldwide in life sciences transactions. In addition, he was recommended as a leading Israeli practitioner by *Chambers Global* (in mergers and acquisitions: high tech); by International Asset Management (in intellectual property transactions) and by The European Legal experts (in corporate and mergers and acquisitions; information technology and telecoms).

Pekka Jaatinen
Senior partner, Castrén & Snellman
pekka.jaatinen@castren.fi

Pekka Jaatinen has throughout his long career specialised in mergers and acquisitions, insolvency and corporate law. He has advised large financial institutions and other clients acting as a leading legal counsel in relation to both domestic and international transactions, restructurings and insolvency proceedings. He is well recognised for acting as a trustee and administrator of the majority of the largest Finnish bankruptcy estates and restructuring proceedings. Pekka is also a board member of several domestic and international companies.

Chambers Europe, Chambers Global, Best Lawyers and *PLC Which Lawyer* rank Pekka Jaatinen among Finland's leading legal experts.

Attila Jákói
Junior lawyer, Szecskay Attorneys at Law
attila.jakoi@szecskay.com

Dr Attila Jákói joined Szecskay Attorneys at Law in 2014 and currently specialises in dispute resolution, contract and consumer protection law. He received his JD (*cum laude*) from the Eötvös Loránd University in 2014. In 2012 he studied at the law school of Tilburg University in the Netherlands on an Erasmus scholarship, where he studied European law, international private law, civil law and competition law. He is fluent in English.

David Jenny
Partner, Vischer AG
djenny@vischer.com

David Jenny is a partner of Vischer AG, a leading Swiss law firm. He has been advising and representing corporations since 1991 in transactions and corporate and commercial matters. In the insolvency field, he acts as a liquidator and advises governing bodies of corporations and creditors. David is one of the authors of the leading commentary on the Swiss Bankruptcy Code, and also acts as an arbitrator. He is a member of various boards of directors and foundation councils. David was president of the Basel Bar Association and co-chair of the insolvency, restructuring and creditors' rights section, now the insolvency section, of the International Bar Association. He holds a licentiate in law (1984) and a doctorate in law (1988) from the University of Basel and an LLM (1989) from the University of Michigan law school.

Jan Kieszczyński
Senior associate, Kocur & Partners
jan.kieszczynski@kocurpartners.com

Jan Kieszczyński is a senior associate in Kocur & Partners. He advises clients in contentious matters, including commercial, construction and labour law disputes. Jan has particular skills and experience in the field of arbitration and international litigation. Jan has been involved in many arbitral and post-arbitral proceedings, both domestically and internationally.

Constantinos N Klissouras
Partner, KP Law Firm
cklissouras@kp-lf.com

Constantinos Klissouras heads the firm's disputes and restructuring team, specialising in complex civil and commercial litigation and arbitration, finance, and domestic and cross-border restructuring and insolvency.

He has extensive experience with cross-border disputes and proceedings, and acts for domestic and foreign financial institutions and industrial undertakings from a variety of sectors in cross-border and domestic litigation and arbitration, contentious and non-contentious matters involving distressed, leveraged and structured finance, insolvency and restructuring, creditor takeovers, procurement and construction, fraud, and general commercial disputes. He has advised financial and strategic investors in respect of Greek privatisation assets and businesses.

He has authored and co-authored in English on finance, restructuring and insolvency, including most recently on financing domestic and cross-border group restructurings (OUP, 2015), and is a vice-chair of the International Bar Association's insolvency section, a fellow of the Center for International Legal Studies, a Gerson Lehrman educator, and a member of the Hellenic Procedural Law Association and the Hellenic Commercial Lawyers Association.

Hans Klopper
Managing director, Independent Advisory (Pty) Limited
hansk@corprecover.co.za

Hans Klopper is a registered attorney in South Africa specialising in restructuring and insolvency law. He is a director of the South African Restructuring and Insolvency Practitioners Association and, until March 2015, served on the Board of Directors of INSOL International, a worldwide federation of national associations for accountants and lawyers who specialise in turnaround and insolvency.

A major milestone in his career in recent years was his appointment as joint liquidator to Consolidated News Agencies, one of the largest and most controversial liquidations in recent times, in 2002. He is presently the business rescue practitioner of Shaftsinkers and Blue Chip Mining and Drilling, two prominent South African undertakings in the mining industry.

Hans chaired the Northern Provinces Law Society's committee for insolvencies and liquidations for five years. He has served on the insolvency standing committee of the Law Society of South Africa.

Michał Kocur
Partner, Kocur & Partners
michal.kocur@kocurpartners.com

Michał Kocur is the founding partner of Kocur & Partners, a Polish litigation boutique recognised by *Chambers Global*, *Chambers Europe* and *Legal 500*. Michał Kocur has represented clients in corporate and commercial disputes, and has advised clients in real property and construction litigation and arbitration matters. He has also been active in intellectual property disputes. He has served as counsel in numerous arbitration proceedings.

Michał regularly sits as an arbitrator at the Court of Arbitration at the Polish Chamber of Commerce and at the Lewiatan Court of Arbitration, Poland's leading arbitration institutions. He was entered on the list of most in-demand arbitrators in Poland by *Chambers Global*.

He has published various articles on arbitration, civil procedure and commercial law. He also writes the legal blog "Litigation and arbitration".

Yves Lenders
Partner, Lydian
yves.lenders@lydian.be

Yves Lenders graduated in 1998 as a licentiate in law from the University of Antwerp. He took specialisms at the universities of Louvain-la-Neuve (Université Catholique de Louvain) and Paris (Paris I Panthéon-Sorbonne), obtaining a DESS degree in economic law and a DEA degree in business law in 1999.

In 1999, he started as an attorney at Loeff Claeys Verbeke (now Allen & Overy Belgium), where he joined the commercial and litigation department. On January 1 2002 he joined Lydian, where he specialises in commercial law, litigation, port projects and logistics.

He handles complex construction litigation matters and also has experience in post-acquisition litigation work. Yves' work also includes shareholders' disputes. He regularly acts as trusted adviser to his clients on commercial matters, including advising, drafting and implementing legal documentation for his clients' businesses. Furthermore, he advises clients faced with insolvent or near-insolvent counterparties. He is a trained mediator.

Tiago Castanheira Marques
Associate lawyer, Abreu Advogados
tiago.c.marques@abreuadvogados.com

Tiago Castanheira Marques has been an associate lawyer with Abreu Advogados since 2008. He graduated from the University of Lisbon's law school in 2002, and obtained an LLM in international business law from the Portuguese Catholic University's law school in 2013.

Between 2002 and 2007, Tiago was an associate lawyer and former trainee lawyer with PACSA – Henriques da Silva, Pais de Almeida, Corrêa de Sampaio & Associados, Sociedade de Advogados RL.

As a lawyer, has been involved primarily in matters related to litigation (civil and commercial) and employment law.

Tomohiro Murakami
Counsel, Nishimura & Asahi
t_murakami@jurists.co.jp

Tomohiro Murakami is a counsel in the finance group of Nishimura & Asahi in Tokyo. He holds an LLM, and an MSc (in law and accounting), and has been involved in various types of finance transactions including public finance initiative/ public-private partnership projects, solar power projects and other project-financed transactions, and leveraged/management buyout finance transactions. He also has experience as a bankruptcy sub-trustee in bankruptcy cases. He has previously published articles including "Parallel-debt clause in secured syndicated loans".

Sándor Németh
Partner, Szecskay Attorneys at Law
sandor.nemeth@szecskay.com

Dr Sándor Németh specialises in mergers and acquisitions, corporate, public procurement law, biotech and property law.

He received his JD (*cum laude*) from the University of Miskolc in 2001. Before joining Szecskay Attorneys at Law, he worked as an associate at Arday Law Firm and at Jones Day.

He is president of the legal committee of the Hungarian Biotechnology Association and is a guest lecturer at Pázmány Péter University.

He is fluent in English and German.

Thomas Nicht
Associate, GÖRG Partnerschaft von Rechtsanwälten mbB
tnicht@goerg.de

Thomas Nicht is an associate in the insolvency and restructuring department of GÖRG Partnerschaft von Rechtsanwälten mbB in Berlin. Before joining GÖRG in 2013, Thomas worked in the corporate/real estate department of a highly reputed German law firm.

Christina K Papachristopoulou
Partner, KP Law Firm
cpapachristopoulou@kp-lf.com

Christina Papachristopoulou is a finance, corporate and commercial and capital markets partner, specialising in the entire spectrum of finance transactions, structures and methodologies and complex corporate transactions.

She has extensive experience in advising on a wide spectrum of corporate law matters (in particular in the fields of healthcare and life science, natural resources, manufacture and retail), trade agreements, group and corporate structuring and restructuring, including cross-border mergers, spin-offs, stakeholder agreements, debt and equity financing and export financing. She has advised Greek corporations in their listing on the London Stock Exchange's AIM and qualified investors in their participation in alternative investment funds.

She has co-authored in English on cash-pooling (Globe Law and Business, 2012) and the Greek privatisation programme (*Law and Financial Markets Review*, 2012).

She holds a JD from the University of Athens school of law (1994), an LLM from the University of Pennsylvania's law school (1995) and an MBA (hons) from the ALBA Graduate Business School (2011).

She is a Centre for Effective Dispute Resolution accredited mediator, and a member of the International Bar Association, the Hellenic Association for Financial Law and the Penn Alumni Association.

Elina Pesonen
Senior associate, Castrén & Snellman
elina.pesonen@castren.fi

Elina Pesonen advises clients on all aspects of insolvency law. Her main areas of practice also include general corporate law and contract law.

Elina has participated in various large bankruptcy and restructuring proceedings, both assisting the administrator of the estate and representing the creditors. She also assists clients in the event of imminent insolvency proceedings and in asset recovery matters. In addition, she has been involved in various pledge enforcement cases.

Elina handles a variety of corporate law assignments, in particular directors' liability matters. She also has experience in drafting and negotiating contracts and in other issues related to contract law. Elina has particular expertise in consumer law.

In addition to her law degree from the University of Helsinki, Elina has studied business law at the ESADE private university in Spain.

Chan Park
Partner, MOLITOR, avocats à la cour
chan.park@molitorlegal.lu

Chan Park is a partner in MOLITOR's corporate and mergers and acquisitions practice. He specialises in corporate and corporate finance transactions, mergers and acquisitions, cross-border restructuring centred in Luxembourg, and the implementation of complex corporate structures involving multiple jurisdictions. Chan regularly represents large groups of companies in the United States, Europe, Asia and international banks. He also has particular expertise in the coordination of multi-jurisdiction transactions involving local counsel and other advisors. Chan received his law degree from the University of Louvain (Belgium) and holds an LLM from the University of Pennsylvania Law School (United States).

Hai Jin Park
Attorney, Kim & Chang
haijin.park@kimchang.com

Hai Jin Park is an attorney in the firm's restructuring and insolvency, environment, arbitration and litigation practice groups.

She has a wealth of experience in a wide range of domestic and cross-border insolvency and restructuring matters, as well as in litigation involving finance, product liability, mass torts and environmental issues.

Before joining the firm, she served as a judge for five years at Seoul Central District Court, Seoul Eastern District Court and the Chungju branch of Cheongju District Court, hearing numerous civil and criminal cases involving financial institutions and corporations.

Tom Reingraber
Associate, Lydian
tom.reingraber@lydian.be

Tom Reingraber is an associate in the commercial and litigation department of Lydian in Belgium. He holds a masters degree in law and has also obtained a specialised masters degree in intellectual property law.

He often handles complex and international cases on distribution, insurance and intellectual property law. His work also includes corporate litigation and drafting commercial contracts.

He is also a teaching assistant at the institute for civil procedural law of the Catholic University of Leuven and has published several articles on (international) civil procedural law.

Kirsten Schümann-Kleber
Partner, GÖRG Partnerschaft von Rechtsanwälten mbB
kschuemann-kleber@goerg.de

Kirsten Schümann-Kleber is an insolvency and restructuring partner with GÖRG Partnerschaft von Rechtsanwälten mbB, one of Germany's largest business law firms with a leading reputation in insolvency law and restructuring projects. Kirsten is based in GÖRG's Berlin office. Before joining GÖRG in 2005, Kirsten worked in the corporate finance/financial restructuring department of an international firm.

Kirsten has particular expertise in the restructuring of German renewable energy and property projects. She has worked on numerous restructurings of German property portfolios, and frequently advises foreign clients on restructurings and insolvency proceedings affecting their German subsidiaries.

Kirsten is a member of the American Bar Association, an officer of the International Bar Association (insolvency and restructuring section), and belongs to the Committee for Restructuring and Insolvency of the German Lawyers' Association and the Berlin/Brandenburg Working Committee for Insolvency Law.

Steve Sunghwa Song
Attorney, Kim & Chang
steve.song@kimchang.com

Steve Sunghwa Song is a foreign attorney in the firm's banking practice group. He has worked with financial institutions and public companies on cross-border transactions including debt financing, acquisitions and renewable energy development projects.

Before entering the legal profession, he worked at the Korea Development Bank where he focused on corporate banking, project finance and infrastructure development.

Jennifer Stam
Partner, Gowling Lafleur Henderson LLP
jennifer.stam@gowlings.com

Jennifer Stam is a partner in Gowlings' Toronto office, practising in the area of corporate restructuring. For the past number of years, Jennifer has acted as one of the lead partners on a number of complex multi-jurisdictional matters, including company counsel to Nortel Networks and monitor counsel in Sino-Forest. She also has acted on a variety of other matters in a wide range of sectors, both domestic and international.

Jennifer regularly publishes and speaks in this area of law. She is a member of the board of directors of the Toronto chapter of the

Turnaround Management Association and an active member of other insolvency-related organisations.

Jennifer is recognised in *Chambers Global: The World's Leading Lawyers for Business 2015* for restructuring/insolvency.

Veronika Strizova
Junior lawyer, Giese & Partner
strizova@giese.cz

Veronika Strizova is a junior lawyer based in the firm's Prague office. She received her law degree at the University of West Bohemia in Pilsen and also holds a master's degree in international business economics and management from the Hogeschool Universiteit Brussel. Her practice area consists of litigation, insolvency law and procedure and corporate law. She is registered with the Czech Bar Association.

Sergey Strembelev
Senior associate, Egorov Puginsky Afanasiev & Partners
sergey_strembelev@epam.ru

Sergey Strembelev is a head of real estate practice at the St Petersburg office of the firm. He has managed and worked on a large number of real estate and investment projects, including client representation and state registration for Russian and multinational property acquisitions and drafting loan security agreements.

He is recommended by Chambers' guides *The Legal 500 EMEA* and *Best Lawyers* for real estate and construction in Russia.

Sergey graduated from St Petersburg State University school of law (2003) and completed his PhD there (2009). He also studied at the Academy of American and International Law (Dallas, USA) in 2008.

Sergey has been a member of St Petersburg Bar Association since 2006. He has written a number of books on the legal aspects of real estate. Sergey lectures on real estate at St Petersburg State University's school of law and at the law faculty of St Petersburg State Economic University.

Christer Svartström
Associate, Castrén & Snellman
christer.svartstrom@castren.fi

Christer Svartström advises clients in assignments concerning insolvency proceedings. His main practice areas also include various aspects of dispute resolution and corporate law. Christer has participated in various bankruptcy and restructuring proceedings, both assisting the administrator of the estate and representing the creditors.

In addition, Christer has experience in contractual and non-contractual damages and in corporate law.

Ken Titchen
Partner, Gateley Plc
ken.titchen@gateleyplc.com

Ken Titchen is a partner in the restructuring and corporate recovery department of Gateley Plc in London. He has a degree in law, is a licensed insolvency practitioner and has worked in the restructuring and recovery industry for over 23 years.

He principally advises lenders, insolvency practitioners, restructuring professionals and boards, and has been involved in a number of substantial restructuring projects across a wide variety of sectors. Examples include retail assignments for Aquascutum, Jaeger, La Senza and Peter Werth. Ken was the solicitor for the administrators in the reported retention of title case *Sandhu t/a Isher Fashions v Jet Star Retail Limited (in administration) t/a Mark One.*

Ken is a member of R3, the Insolvency Lawyers Association and INSOL Europe, and a regular speaker on insolvency-related topics. He is also joint author of a well-known text on buying and selling insolvent businesses.

Assaf Unger
Associate, Horn & Co, Law Offices
aunger@hornlaw.co.il

Assaf Unger is an associate at Horn & Co, Law Offices.

Assaf advises technology-focused companies and their founders and board members. He advises the firm's clients on corporate finance agreements, cross-border transactions, including mergers and acquisitions, and ongoing issues related to corporate law and labour law.

He received his LLB from Bar-Ilan University in 2012 (*cum laude)* and his LLM in 2013 from the same institution.

Filipe Portela do Valle
Associate lawyer, Abreu Advogados
filipe.p.valle@abreuadvogados.com

Filipe Portela do Valle graduated from the Lisbon University law school in 2006.

That same year he joined Lusojurist Advogados as a trainee lawyer. In 2008 he became a trainee lawyer with Abreu Advogados as a result of Lusojurist's integration, becoming an associate lawyer one year later.

As a lawyer, Filipe has been assisting his clients primarily on matters related to litigation (debt recovery and civil litigation)

Rogier van Bijnen
Director, R&P China Lawyers
vanbijnen@rplawyers.com

Rogier van Bijnen heads the Beijing office of R&P China Lawyers. Rogier has lived in China since 2009 and advises multinationals on mergers and acquisitions, joint ventures, general corporate and commercial matters and dispute resolution. He regularly assists foreign clients in negotiations with Chinese business partners. Prior to joining R&P, Rogier worked for a magic circle firm in Beijing.

Maria Vertesich
Associate, bkp Rechtsanwälte
m.vertesich@bkp.at

Maria Vertesich joined bkp (Brauneis Klauser Prändl) Rechtsanwälte, based in Vienna, Austria in November 2012 after working for two years for the Austrian Ombudsman Board in Vienna.

She passed the Austrian Bar exam in 2015 with distinction, and is specialised in the fields of real estate, litigation and public law.

Ian Walker
Partner, Minter Ellison
ian.walker@minterellison.com

Ian Walker has been a partner at Minter Ellison working in insolvency and reconstruction and dispute resolution for 27 years.

His insolvency practice includes advising insolvency practitioners generally in liquidations, receiverships and administrations, and advising third parties affected by insolvency such as creditors and particularly directors, who can face pressure when their company is approaching insolvency.

Ian has significant expertise in security enforcement for all types of creditors, banking litigation and insolvency, reconstruction and work out issues. Ian has also participated in a number of mediations of litigious matters.

Ian acts for government, statutory corporations and corporate clients on a range of litigious and non-litigious matters, particularly in the area of contractual disputes.

His litigation practice involves acting in the superior courts, either federal or state, in contested litigation, and Ian is experienced in the mediation, negotiation and resolution of complex commercial disputes.

Marcel Willems
Partner, Kennedy Van der Laan NV
marcel.willems@kvdl.com

Marcel Willems studied law at the universities of Nijmegen, Leiden, Berlin and Osnabrück (Germany).

He started his professional career in 1988. In 1992 he co-founded Kennedy Van der Laan, now one of the leading firms in the Netherlands. Marcel has broad experience in insolvency, banking and finance and dispute resolution, mostly in a cross-border setting. He acts for several banks, particularly in the areas of security rights and insolvency. He also regularly advises on complex financings. Marcel publishes regularly. He has been active in the insolvency section of the International Bar Association for a large number of years, and is currently senior vice-chair.

Marcel heads the German desk of Kennedy Van der Laan, which caters for the needs of the firm's German-speaking clients.

As a deputy judge in the Court of Appeal of Arnhem-Leeuwarden, Marcel himself also regularly renders judicial decisions.